VANISHED WALES

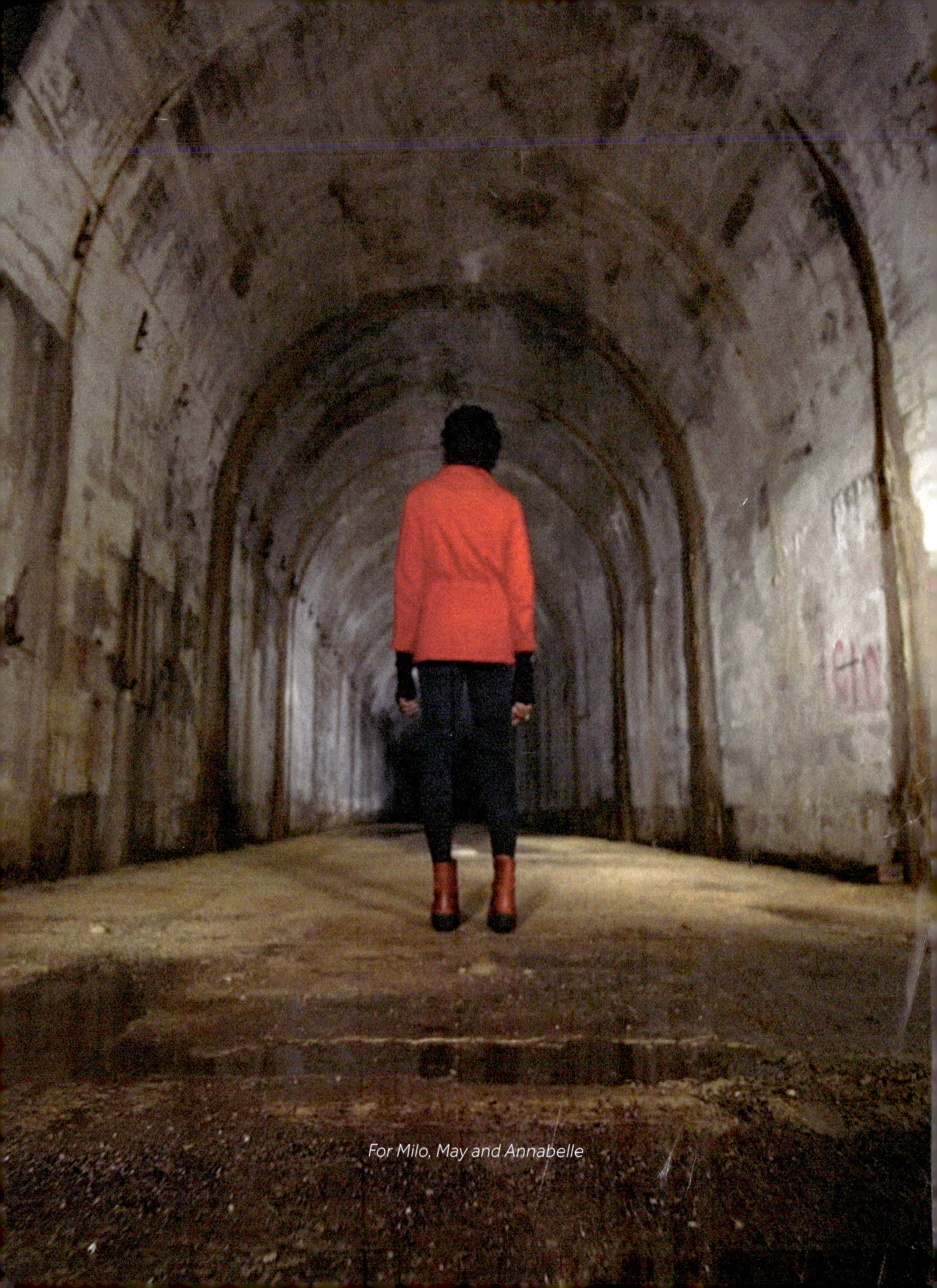

For Milo, May and Annabelle

VANISHED WALES

PLACES LOST IN LIVING MEMORY

CARWYN **JONES**

FOREWORD BY **JONATHAN HILL**
AFTERWORD BY **ADEOLA DEWIS**

SEREN

Seren Books is the book imprint of
Poetry Wales Press Ltd
Derwen Road, Bridgend, Wales

www.serenbooks.com
Find us on social media @SerenBooks

ISBN 978-1-78172-786-7

A CIP record for this title is available from the British Library

The publisher works with the financial assistance
of the Books Council of Wales.
EU GPSR Authorised Representative
Logos Europe, 9 rue Nicolas Poussin, 17000,
La Rochelle, France
E-mail: Contact@logoseurope.eu

Printed by 4Edge Ltd, Hockley.

CYMRU WALES

CONTENTS

FOREWORD by Jonathan Hill i
INTRODUCTION iii

METTOY FACTORY 7
WALES EMPIRE POOL 16
RHYL PAVILION THEATRE 23
GROES 28
VALLEY WORKS 37
SEVERN FERRY SERVICE 45
LOVELL'S CHOCOLATE FACTORY 50
TROEDRHIWFUWCH 56
MUMBLES RAILWAY 65
LAURA ASHLEY FACTORY 73
FLYING BOATS OF PEMBROKE DOCK 82
CAPITOL THEATRE 91
BRYMBO STEELWORKS 99
GILBERN CARS 106
DUNRAVEN CASTLE 117
THE TRIANGLE 124
TONFANAU ARMY CAMP 131
KING'S HALL 138
RHYL'S HOVERCOACH 144
BWLCH-Y-GWYNT & MACHYNYS 153
VICTORIA PIER 161
CRUMLIN VIADUCT 169

AFTERWORD by Adeola Dewis 176
ACKNOWLEDGEMENTS 178
PHOTOGRAPHY ACKNOWLEDGEMENTS 179

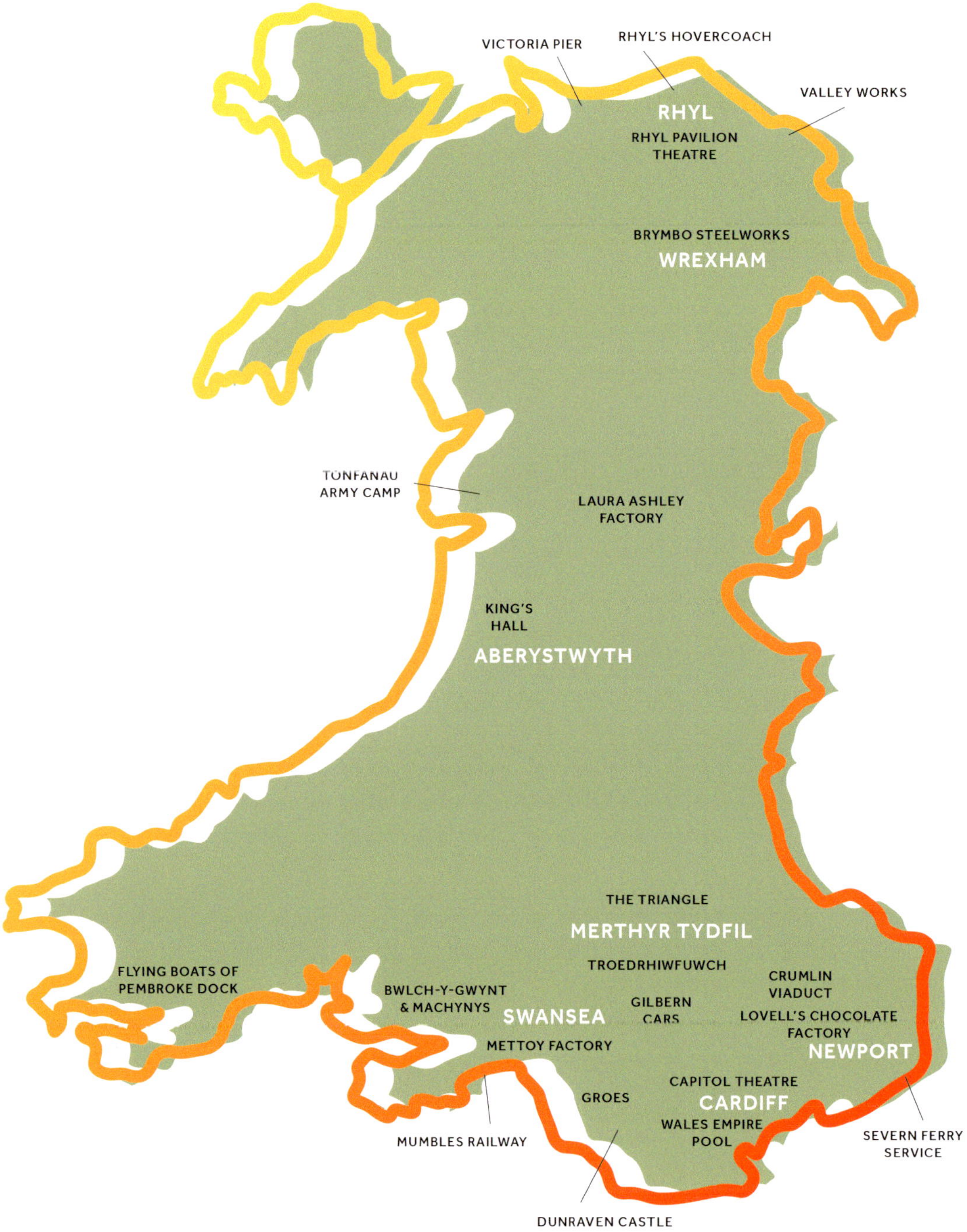
VICTORIA PIER
RHYL'S HOVERCOACH
VALLEY WORKS
RHYL
RHYL PAVILION THEATRE
BRYMBO STEELWORKS
WREXHAM
TONFANAU ARMY CAMP
LAURA ASHLEY FACTORY
KING'S HALL
ABERYSTWYTH
THE TRIANGLE
MERTHYR TYDFIL
TROEDRHIWFUWCH
FLYING BOATS OF PEMBROKE DOCK
BWLCH-Y-GWYNT & MACHYNYS
SWANSEA
GILBERN CARS
CRUMLIN VIADUCT
LOVELL'S CHOCOLATE FACTORY
METTOY FACTORY
NEWPORT
CAPITOL THEATRE
GROES
CARDIFF
WALES EMPIRE POOL
MUMBLES RAILWAY
SEVERN FERRY SERVICE
DUNRAVEN CASTLE

FOREWORD

by Jonathan Hill

It has been the privilege of my life to have spent the last 30 years with ITV News in Wales reporting on the story of our nation during a time of enormous change. Pictures speak a thousand words, and in the digital world it's heartening that TV journalism continues to make an impact through the many different ways viewers now access and watch it. From devolution and the establishment of a Welsh parliament to the loss of traditional industries, our story is always evolving, ever changing. I will forever remember presenting the six o'clock news from Tower Colliery in the Cynon Valley as the final shift clocked off and walked away from hundreds of years of mining history. Looking back into the pit head baths I recall that many of the miners had just left clothes hanging on their open locker doors, like they were intending to return in the morning. It was a seismic moment. Deep mine coaling had come to an end in Wales before my eyes, without so much as a whimper, a whole way of life gone within living memory. Reporting on those momentous events has taken me the length and breadth of Wales and I have met many extraordinary people with remarkable stories to tell.

I firmly believe that we in Wales are natural storytellers and that's what makes the job of a journalist here so rewarding. It's so important that we capture those personal stories and memories about our history that would otherwise be lost to time. Fortunately, ITV Cymru Wales' rich archive is now curated and preserved for future generations at the National Library of Wales in Aberystwyth. It is a treasure trove of eye-witness accounts and accompanying moving pictures from the last six decades and it's very easy to lose yourself once you begin to search the reels of film and video. I like to think that I know Wales pretty well but the greatest thrill comes when I discover something new, and I say to myself, "I didn't know that!" Change always happens faster than expected and slower than predicted and its significance is scarcely noted at the time.

For this reason, the *Vanished Wales* series is a gem in ITV Cymru Wales' schedule, and is a must for anyone interested in the story of our nation. It delves into the forgotten histories and lost communities of Wales, masterfully weaving together archive footage, expert interviews, and on-location explorations to paint a vivid picture of a Wales that once was.

One of the strongest aspects of *Vanished Wales* is its ability to connect with viewers on an emotional level. The stories of lost villages and industries are not just historical facts; they are tales of real people whose lives were deeply intertwined with their surroundings. Under the direction of accomplished producer Carwyn Jones, the series humanises these stories, making them relatable and poignant. The use of archive footage provides a real link to the past, while the present-day footage shows how events continue to shape the landscape and our communities. The cinematography is beautiful, capturing the rugged beauty of the Welsh landscape and the subtle nuances of the stories being told. With meticulous research, heartwarming first-hand accounts and unseen footage, it is a people's history of an ever-changing land. Its stories are as diverse as the landscapes they are hewn from, and constantly surprise and intrigue. In this fast-changing world, *Vanished Wales* is a chance for viewers to pause for half an hour and reflect on the people and places that are now just a memory, erased often in the name of progress.

The series has been a huge success on the channel and this book is a wonderful opportunity to celebrate some of the many highlights from the last four series.

Vanished Wales is an important and valuable contribution to Welsh television. Like all the best ideas it's a simple one. Never cynical, always warm, the series has taken us into the corners of Welsh life we never knew existed. Presenter Adeola Dewis is a perfect companion, gently holding our hand through the journey into the past, asking just the right questions. Beautifully crafted, *Vanished Wales* is a fresh take on social history that entertains and informs us about places that we thought we knew.

Life seemed simpler back then and perhaps it was.

Photograph: Adeola Dewis & Carwyn Jones

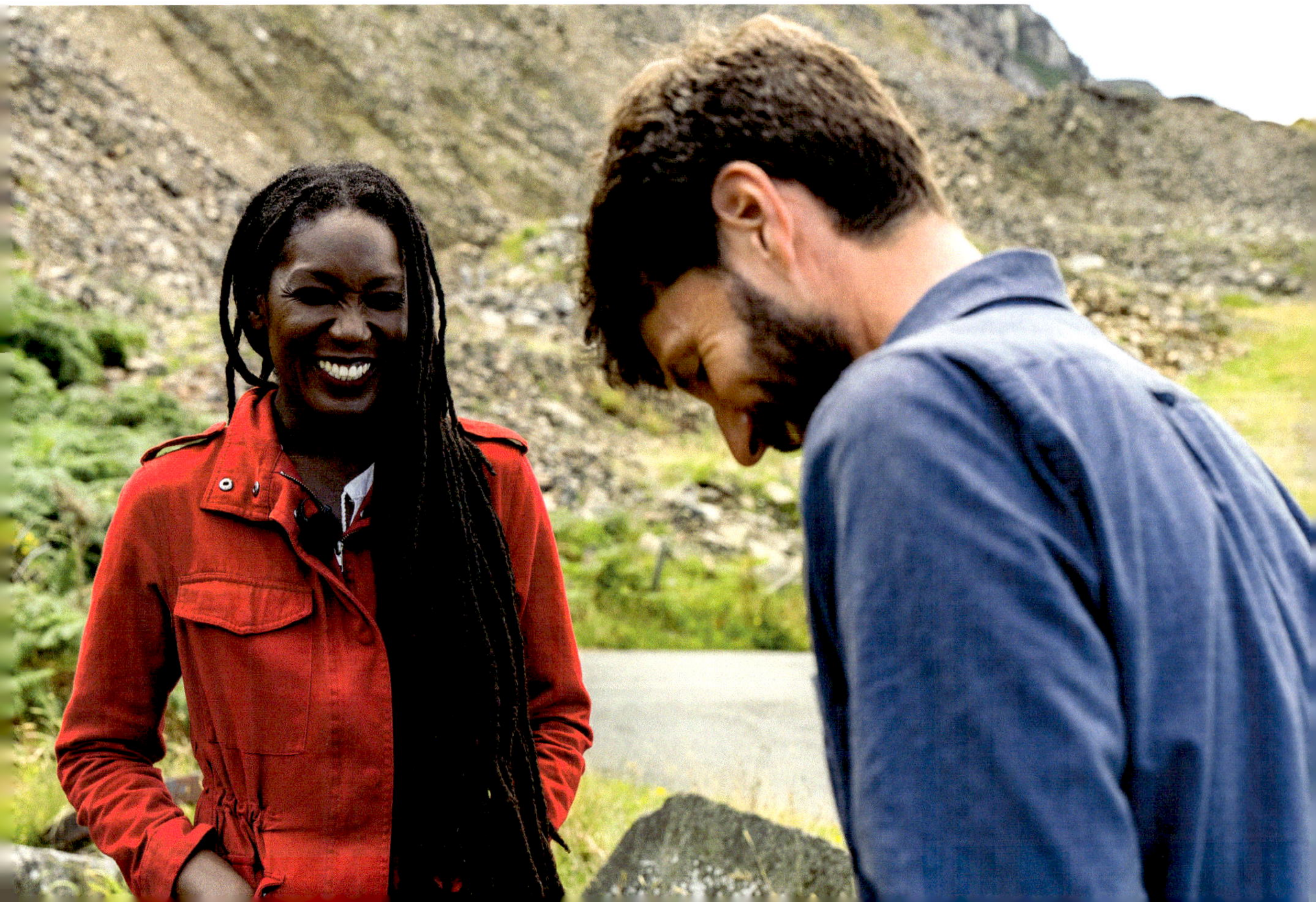

INTRODUCTION

15 years ago I found myself on a bare stretch of coastline on the Machynys Peninsula, just south of Llanelli. The weather was refusing to commit to a course of action, offering a pallet of hazy greys and a biting breeze. I had wound my way to the banks of the Loughor Estuary to film a story for that evening's television news. It centred on a pair of neighbouring villages that had once stood in this wide-open corner of Carmarthenshire but had since been demolished without trace. Where I was standing would have been a tight cluster of factories and family homes. The streets would have pulsated to the sing-song rhythms of community life. Now there was just silence.

I had arranged to meet Sandra Jenkins, who had been born and bred in those coastal villages. Along with hundreds of fellow residents she had been forced to move away from the area as demolition loomed. Nothing now remained of her childhood home or the way of life she once knew. Sandra had kindly agreed to share her memories on camera, and her emotions were close to the surface. She spoke proudly of having grown up on those cheek-by-jowl terraced streets. But there was anger too. Had it really been necessary to flatten those settlements, to fracture the community, to redevelop the land so exhaustively? Her sense of loss was absolute.

An hour or so later, with the camera equipment packed away, Sandra and I gave each other a hug and parted company. The sun had finally resolved to cut through the gunmetal cloud. As I drove off, I glanced back at the landscape slowly fading in my rear-view mirror. How had two industrial districts simply disappeared? If I hadn't just been told about those twin neighbourhoods, once home to countless families, would I ever have known they'd existed at all? The villages had been torn down in the 1970s, just a year or two before I was born. These weren't early medieval sites lost in the mists of time, awaiting teams of archaeologists to unearth their footprint centuries later. This felt a much more modern form of extinction; vibrant spaces that had been unwillingly abandoned and purposely swept away in the second half of the 20th century.

Over the passing years, I found myself drawn time and again to this oblique sense of absence. I wondered how many more echoes of the past still whistle through our communities; significant structures that have been replaced in our lifetime by car parks, high-rise buildings or merely empty patches of ground. The unrelenting pace of progress can make it difficult to track these changes. We sometimes lose sight of what used to stand on the spot of our present-day supermarkets, industrial estates and office blocks. Were they residential streets? Was it a cinema? Is that where the old factory used to be?

In 2021, I took a leap of faith and pitched a programme idea to my colleagues at ITV Cymru Wales. I suggested a social history series that would reveal the stories behind our lost landmarks: the history and heritage that had disappeared from our towns, cities and villages within living memory. It would be an exploration of what's missing from modern Wales – a celebration of some extraordinary places whose time had unexpectedly run out. I put forward some possible examples, ranging from lost communities to bygone sites of industry, via cultural venues, wartime installations and imposing structures of architectural renown. To my relief and excitement, the project received the green light. *Vanished Wales* was born.

That summer I found myself back on the Machynys Peninsula, filming once more with Sandra Jenkins. There was no need for hats and scarves this time: the weather was wall-to-wall sunshine. Although we hadn't seen each other for 15 years, Sandra and I immediately picked up where we had left off. Her passion for those former villages along the coast, and her outrage at the fate that befell them, burned as brightly as ever. I realised that what mattered most to her, and the erstwhile villagers with whom we also filmed that day, was to know that there was a mechanism to keep those memories alive, something that might allow their eyewitness accounts of the past to percolate through the generations, long after their days.

Vanished Wales became that mechanism. Within the pages of this book you can read about the chain of events that led to the destruction of Sandra's community. You'll also find a further 21 remarkable tales of lost landmarks from right across the country. They represent just some of the 70 long lost sights that we've covered in *Vanished Wales* to date, (all current and previous episodes are available to watch on ITVX). This publication includes bonus material and expanded first-hand commentaries that you won't have seen in the television programmes. The story selection is wide-ranging, indicative of the scale and scope of our missing heritage: there are communities and industries, superstructures and stately homes, piers and pavilions, even modes of transport. The one thing they all share in common is that they were demolished, dismantled or discontinued in our lifetime or that of our parents' and grandparents'. None of this, sadly, is ancient history.

Vanished Wales has always been a collaborative effort, and at the back of this book you'll find a list of the many people who have worked tirelessly, at different points in time, to bring these precious stories to life for the screen. I have been lucky enough to work alongside three key collaborators from day one, and each deserves a special mention here: Adeola Dewis, an intelligent, incisive and compassionate presenter; James Harries, one of the finest (and friendliest) camera operators in the country; and Owain Meredith, the Indiana Jones of the ITV Cymru Wales archives and a sublime social historian, whose input has been invaluable from the very beginning.

Someone once asked me whether my commitments on *Vanished Wales* mean I have one foot forever stuck in the past. The short answer is: yes. But it's about the present, too. There's a through-line between the destruction of a treasured landmark, one that provided a cohesive sense of identity, and how we find a way to move forward in the slipstream of that loss. These buildings were once the bricks and mortar of our lives. They provided employment, entertainment, a home for our parents, partners and children. They enshrouded a lifetime of memories. Society will invariably embrace renewal and regeneration; it's the way of things. But the course of modern history has a sobering lesson to teach us: there will always be a human price for progress.

Photograph (Left to Right):
James Harries, Adeola Dewis and Carwyn Jones.

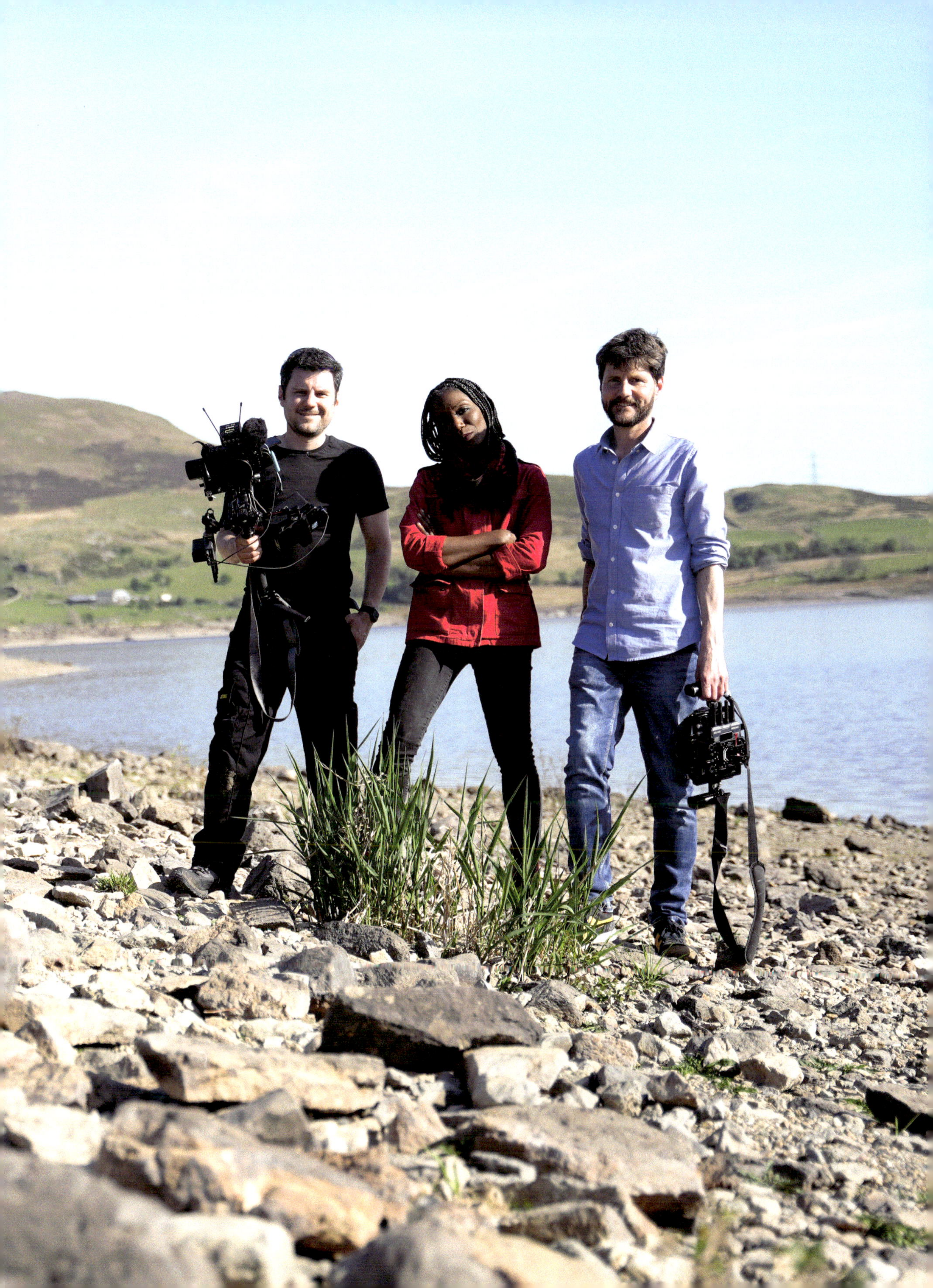

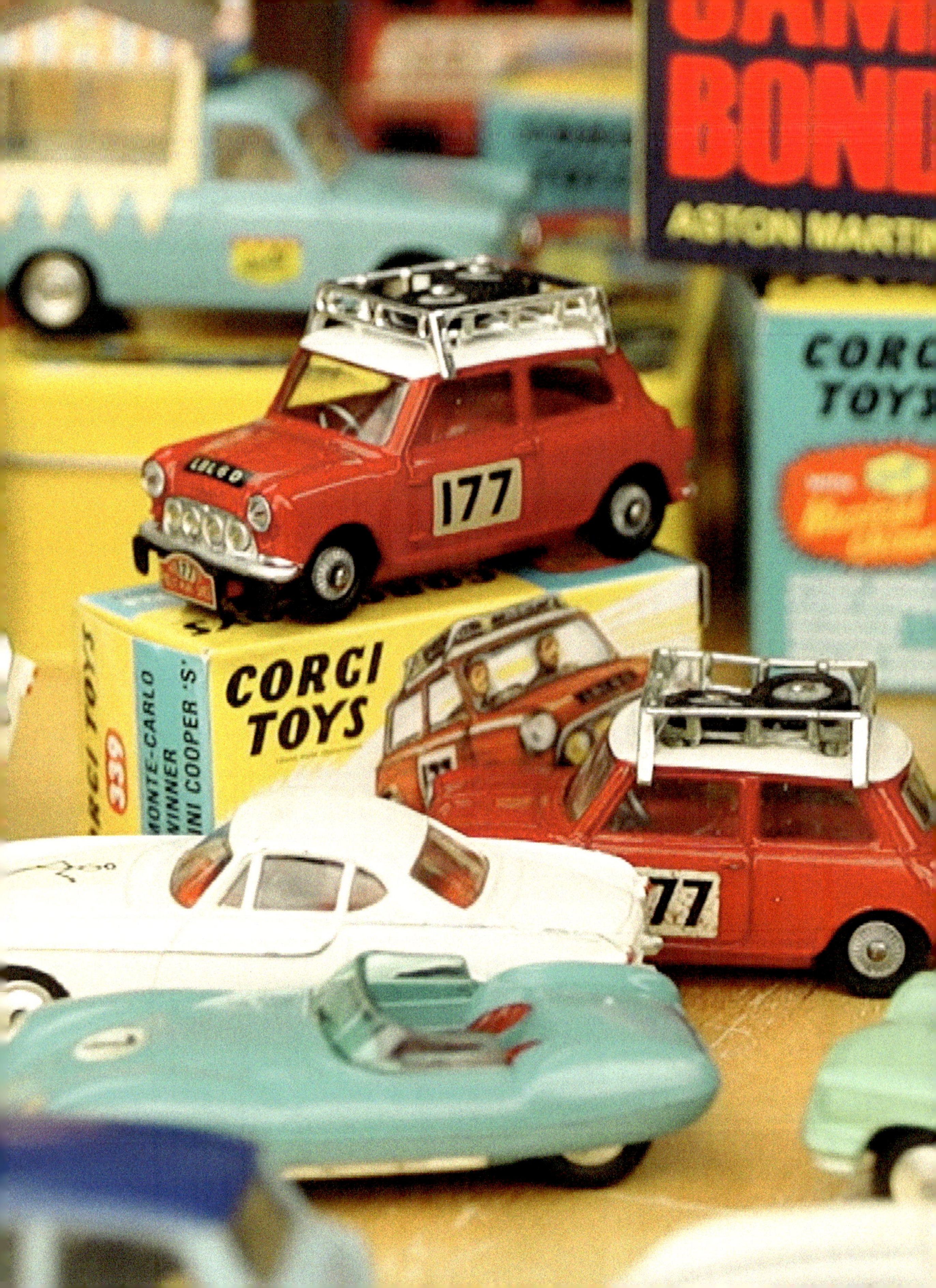
CORGI
TOYS
177
CORGI
TOYS
339
MONTE-CARLO
WINNER

METTOY FACTORY

The home of Corgi cars

Toys are time machines; they beam you straight back to childhood. Playthings from the past have a unique psychological power. They belong to a specific stepping stone in life that's impossible to recapture: the pre-school years of dependency are a memory; the helter-skelter of adolescence is just around the corner. Between those two worlds is a precious pocket of time, when a simple toy is all that is needed to nourish boundless scenarios of infinite invention.

From the 1950s to the early 1990s, millions of British children took to their hearts one particular range of small, lovingly detailed metallic vehicles. In bedrooms and playgrounds across the country, little hands clasped little cars, whizzing them along carpets and concrete in vividly imagined races and chases. The four-wheeled objects of their affection were Corgi Toys, a staggeringly successful brand that was cherished by children for generations. On the chassis of each car was stamped: 'MADE IN GT. BRITAIN'. It was a detail largely lost on juvenile consumers, but it was to prove hugely significant for communities across South Wales. Corgi Toys were indeed manufactured in Great Britain…specifically, in Swansea.

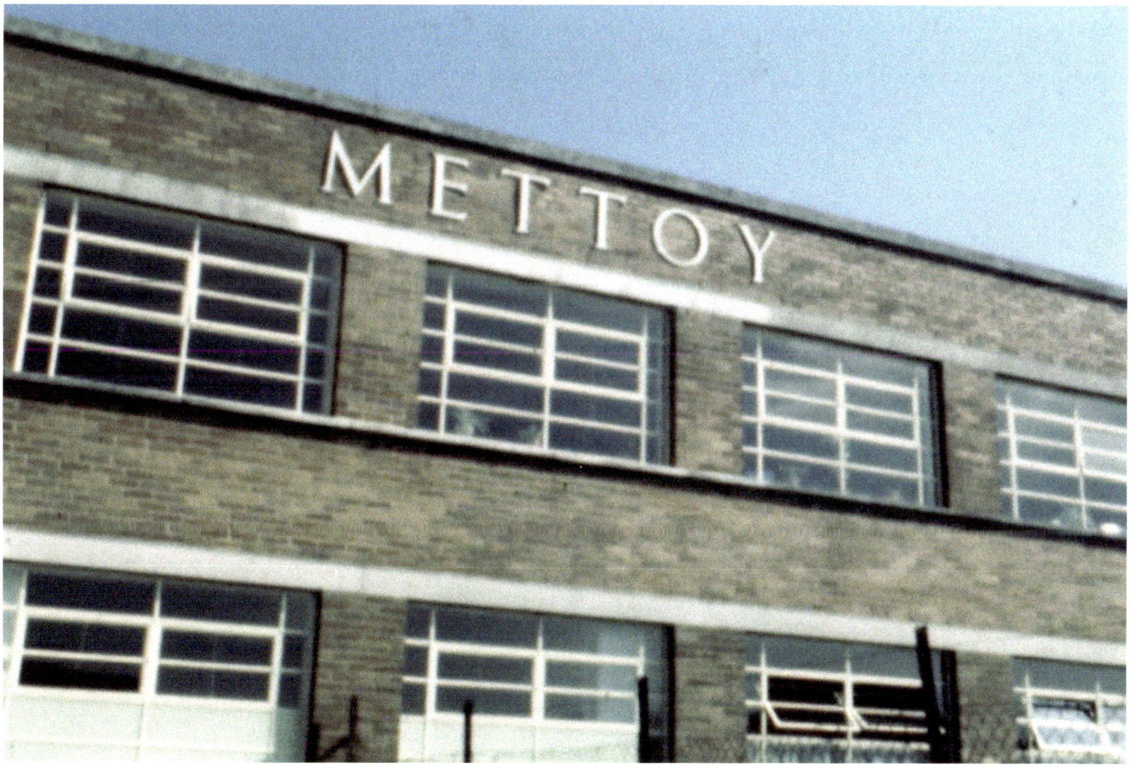

Where tiny toys were big business: the Swansea factory in 1978.

If you're unfamiliar with the miniature cars in question, and the impact of their Welsh connection, it's worth stressing just how famous these vintage vehicles were during their own lifetime. The company produced a giddying assortment of die-cast products, from trucks and tractors to aeroplanes and ambulances, bikes and buses, speedboats and submarines – even milk floats and ice cream vans. But Corgi's cultural cachet stemmed from its film and TV tie-ins. It held the licenses to develop ranges of toys based on seminal small screen shows like *Batman*, *The Saint*, *The Man From U.N.C.L.E.*, *Starsky & Hutch*, *Spiderman*, *The Professionals*, *Charlie's Angels* and *The Muppet Show*.

Most memorable was its long association with the James Bond movie franchise. During Roger Moore's tenure as 007, many a child marvelled at Corgi's rendering of the Lotus Esprit from *The Spy Who Loved Me* (boasting exciting features like rear window missiles and retractable fins) and the space shuttle from *Moonraker* (open the cargo bay doors and – ta-da! – you'd find a secret satellite). Yet the biggest seller, by far, belonged to the Sean Connery era. First released in October 1965, sandwiched between the *Goldfinger* and *Thunderball* films, Corgi's diminutive model of Bond's Aston Martin DB5 was a runaway success. There were gadgets galore: a working ejector seat, front-mounted machine guns and a rear bulletproof screen. When it was re-issued a few years later, it sported added extras like revolving front and rear number plates and a telescopic tyre-bursting device. The attention to detail was eye-popping. Millions of these little cars were sold throughout the 1960s and 70s, and the DB5 remains one of the world's most celebrated and covetable playthings.

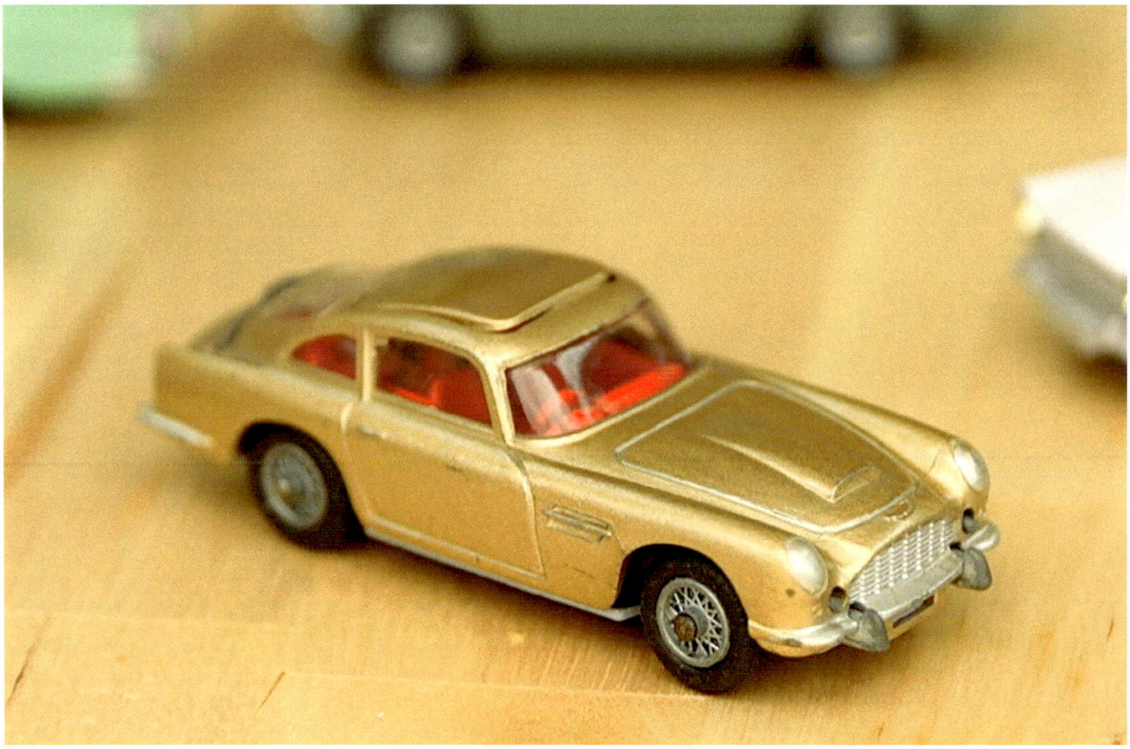

Corgi's all-conquering Aston Martin DB5 in its original gold finish. Later versions were painted silver.

The bedrock of Corgi's sustained success was its supersized factory in Swansea. The sprawling complex, sited in the Fforestfach suburb of the city, spanned more than 250,000 square feet. At the height of Corgi mania, workers were assembling one million products per week. Lyndon Davies lived near the factory and joined the workforce in the 1970s:

> "It all started when I was 11 years old, when kids in my school used to bring in little toys that had been made in the factory. I used to bunk off school and sneak through the wire fence by the factory's foundry, where there would be scrap toys. We'd help ourselves to the cars and try to sell them. They were always a bit scrappy, and they didn't always work, but I managed to make a bit of money from them. It was better than a paper round!
>
> "I eventually started in the factory at 16 as an apprentice. I began on the production lines and there were 3,500 employees there, so it was a massive site. We had foundries with 50 die-casting machines; we had plastic-injection moulding machines there, hundreds of them. It was an incredible space to actually be in.
>
> "Such a lot of energy would go into producing a toy vehicle. To actually get a product from concept to production took over a year. You'd have to research it, design it, and get the engineering right. A great tool maker would take six to eight months to produce a mould. In fact, the toolmakers would keep all of the old moulds out of respect for the craftsmanship of their original makers. It would be heartbreaking to even consider throwing them away."

During the 1950s and 60s, the British toy industry was on a roll. Competing with Corgi as large-scale manufacturers of mini machines were Dinky (owned by Meccano Ltd) and Matchbox (created by Lesney Products). Corgi had a parent company too: Mettoy. Founded in the early 1930s by two German Jewish refugees, Philip Ullman and Arthur Katz, Mettoy initially manufactured tinplate models and wind-up toys in Northampton. In the 1940s, it eagerly expanded its operations when a more modern factory site became available in Swansea. In time, the company would select the city for its headquarters, and that gargantuan facility in Fforestfach churned out carefree amusements like space hoppers, dolls' houses and *Dan Dare* ray guns. Mettoy's decision to launch its Corgi brand in 1956 was a complete game-changer. The vehicles immediately had the edge over their rivals, thanks to novel features like rubber tyres, moulded seats and opening boots and bonnets. The promotional slogan said it all: 'The Ones With Windows.' Grace Beaman started at the Mettoy factory in 1966, aged just 17:

> "Corgi was quality, there's no question. The weight of the car for a start. They weren't flimsy or light, this was a real solid product. My children played with them and my children's children played with them. The *Chitty Chitty Bang Bang* car wasn't a favourite, though. The factory had a lot of trouble with that one. There were lots of bits on it. Often, the wings wouldn't work and the plastic used to clog up the machinery!
>
> "It was good money at Mettoy and there were loads of women on the assembly lines. My sister worked there, as did my aunt and mother-in-law. There was a family feel about it. But it was also very noisy with all the machines. They'd sometimes break down and you'd be calling for the guys to fix them. Eventually, we started fixing them ourselves, even though that was frowned upon! The job was fun, it was interesting, and it was a big part of my life."

In 1966, the same year that Corgi unveiled its Adam West-era Batmobile (which sold like gangbusters), Mettoy was presented with the Queen's Award to Industry. It was regal recognition of the company's success in the export market, as Corgi toys gained traction in Australia, North America and South East Asia. By 1968, nearly 10 million products were being boxed up for sale overseas. Back in Swansea, shifts on the factory floor were unremitting, as the company pulled out all the stops to meet global demand. Ann Harrison worked there at the time:

> "I was mainly in the plastics department, where we'd do the chassis, interiors and wheels. They'd come off the machine and you had to trim the rough edges: what they'd call 'fettling'. You'd put plasters around all your fingers and by the end of the day the tops of them would be raw. But your fingers just adapted. All those tiny, fiddly pieces and you had to work really fast to assemble them. My first job when I started was to sit on a long table, where I had the dashboards and steering wheels of cars. All day, for eight hours, I'd have to flip the steering wheels into their notches. I don't know how I stayed!
>
> "Some of the workers would steal the toys. It was risky because there were random checks when you left the factory. They'd hide them in all kinds of places, even in their underwear!
>
> "I remember putting the ejector seat into the James Bond car. At the time it was just a job. It's only years later that you realise how iconic the toys are, how people value them, the prices they fetch. When I see them today, I think to myself: that could be one of the cars I made."

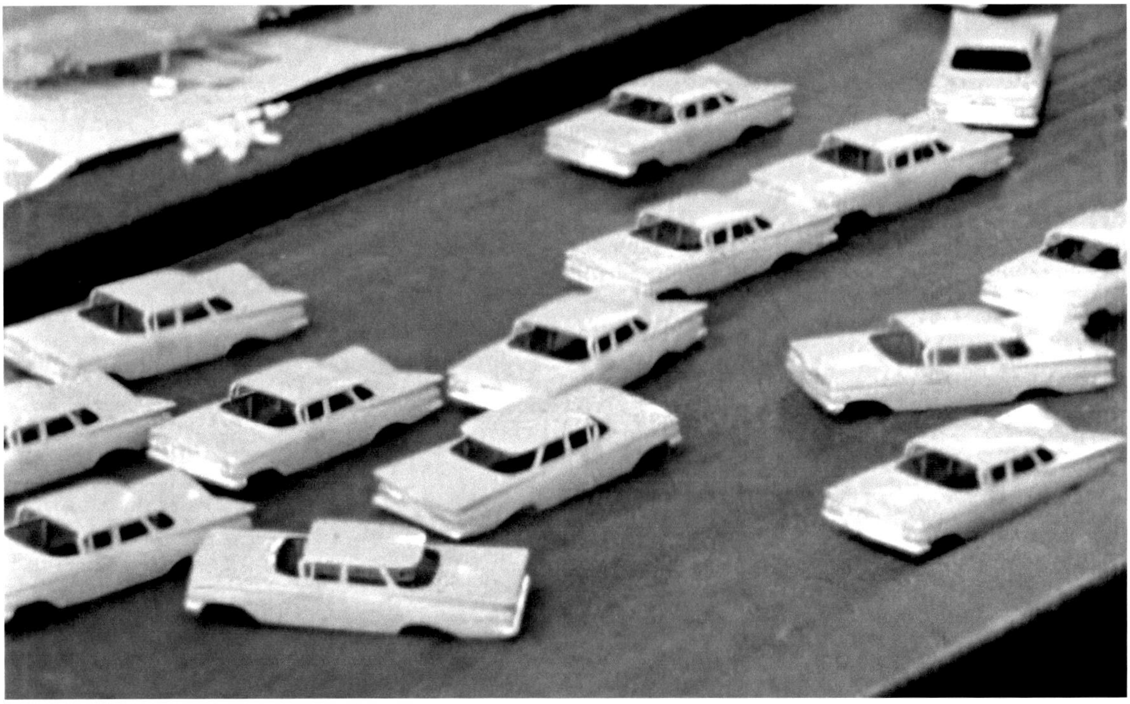

Above: cars trundle along the conveyor belt, destined for the US market.

Right: women did the hard graft on the factory floor.

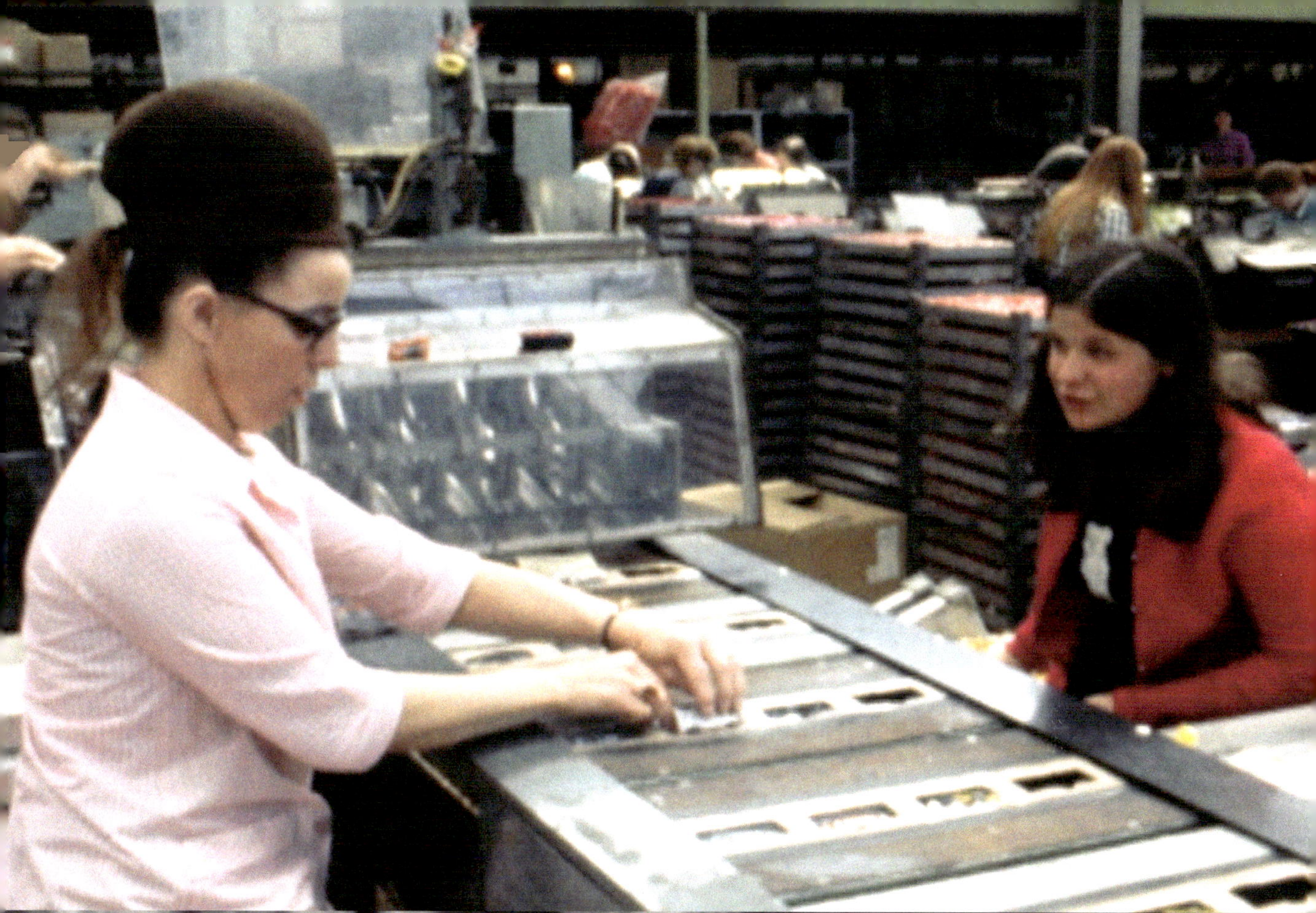

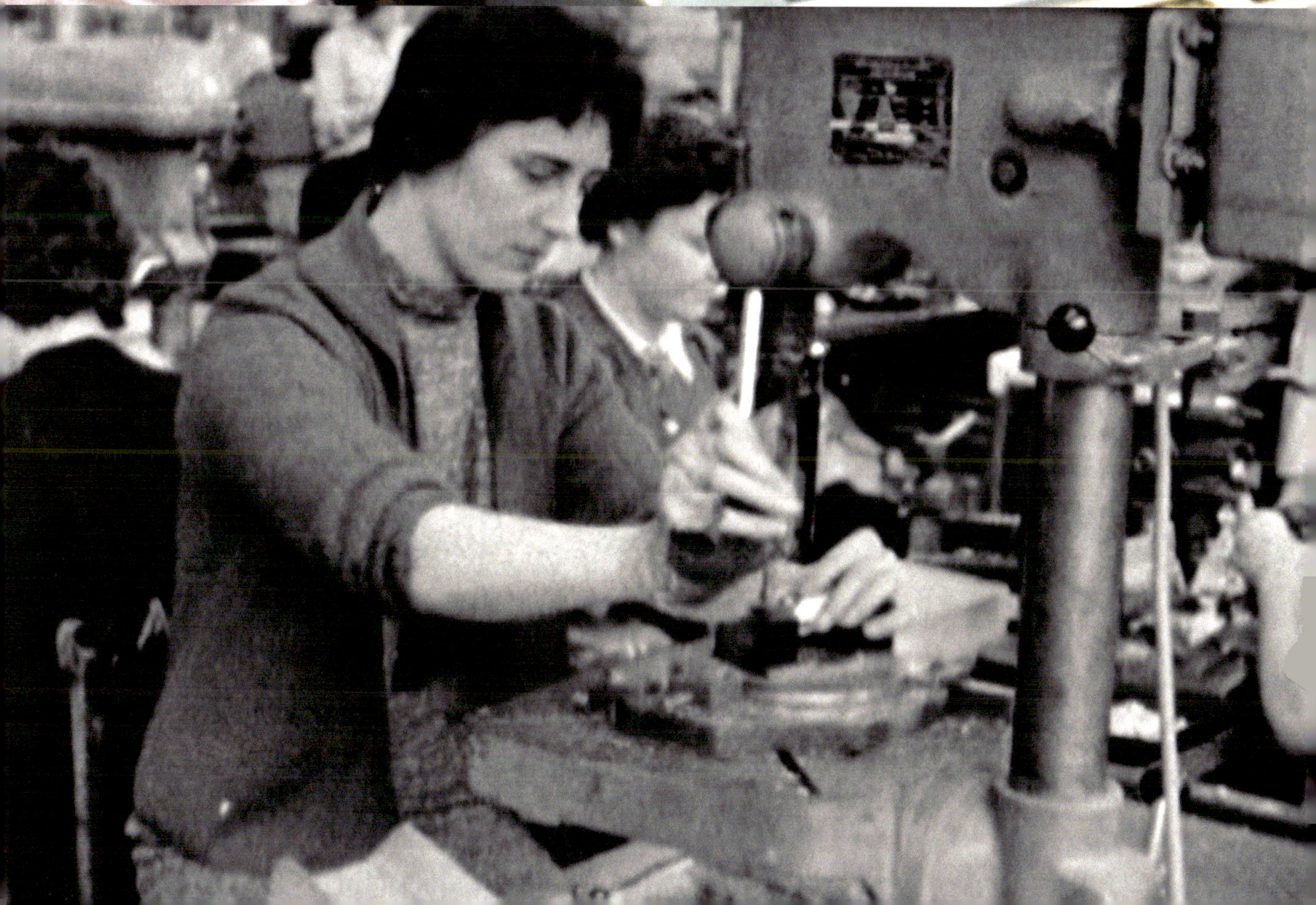

As a leading purveyor of playthings, Mettoy appeared impregnable. But by the early 1980s, despite its recent range of comic book merchandise (the Supermobile; the Spidercopter; Captain America's Porsche), the company was steadily collapsing. In many ways, Corgi cars suffered the same fate as Britain's actual motor industry. Increasing UK production costs, combined with a sluggish domestic economy, opened the floodgates to cheaper imports from international competitors. The toy industry was changing too. Children demanded more stimulation from their models and figurines – malleable objects that could light up or make sounds. Plastic took prominence over metal, as die-cast vehicles suddenly went head-to-head with slick *Star Wars* spacecraft and endlessly transformable Lego sets.

The most fundamental realignment came with the emergence of computer games and the growing popularity of hand-held electronic devices. The genie was out of the bottle. One by one, the bastions of British toy production went to the wall. Dinky closed its factory in 1979. Lesney stopped producing its Matchbox cars in 1982. Mettoy, the last of the 'Big Three' metal toy manufacturers, staved off the receivers for as long as it could, but the war was already lost. The company went bust in October 1983.

There were immediate fears for the Fforestfach complex and its loyal workforce. Within a few months, a management buyout was able to secure the Corgi brand, and die-cast production continued, albeit in reduced quantities. In 1989, the marque was taken over by US toy giant Mattel (famous for Barbie and Hot Wheels, the latter a direct challenger to Corgi cars) who promptly moved all production overseas. Two years later, the entire Swansea factory was shut down and its workers were made redundant. It signalled the end of four decades of toy production on the site. No more Batmobiles, no more *Moonraker* shuttles.

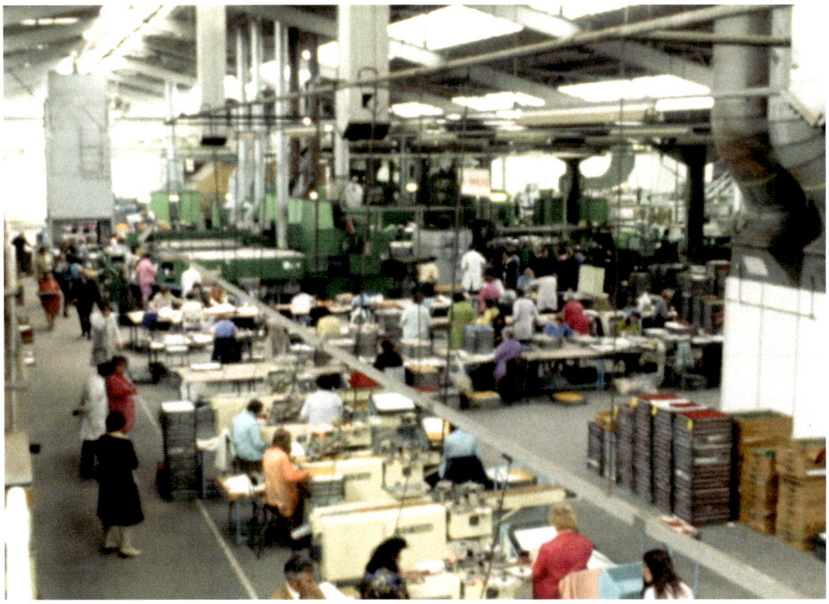

These days, what remains of the old Mettoy factory has been incorporated into the Swansea West Business Park. A fire in 2011 destroyed several significant buildings; the surviving structures are used by local firms for light industry and as office space. As for Corgi, it's still going. The brand, original designs and intellectual property rights are now in the hands of Hornby Hobbies, who also own perennial favourites Scalextric and Airfix. The company has affectionately reanimated many of the classic Corgi vehicles from the 1960s and 70s, which continue to command a faithful following, especially with adult collectors. In a sign of the times, the cars no longer bear the stamp: MADE IN GT. BRITAIN. They're now, inevitably, manufactured in China.

Opposite: the factory site spanned 250,000 square feet.

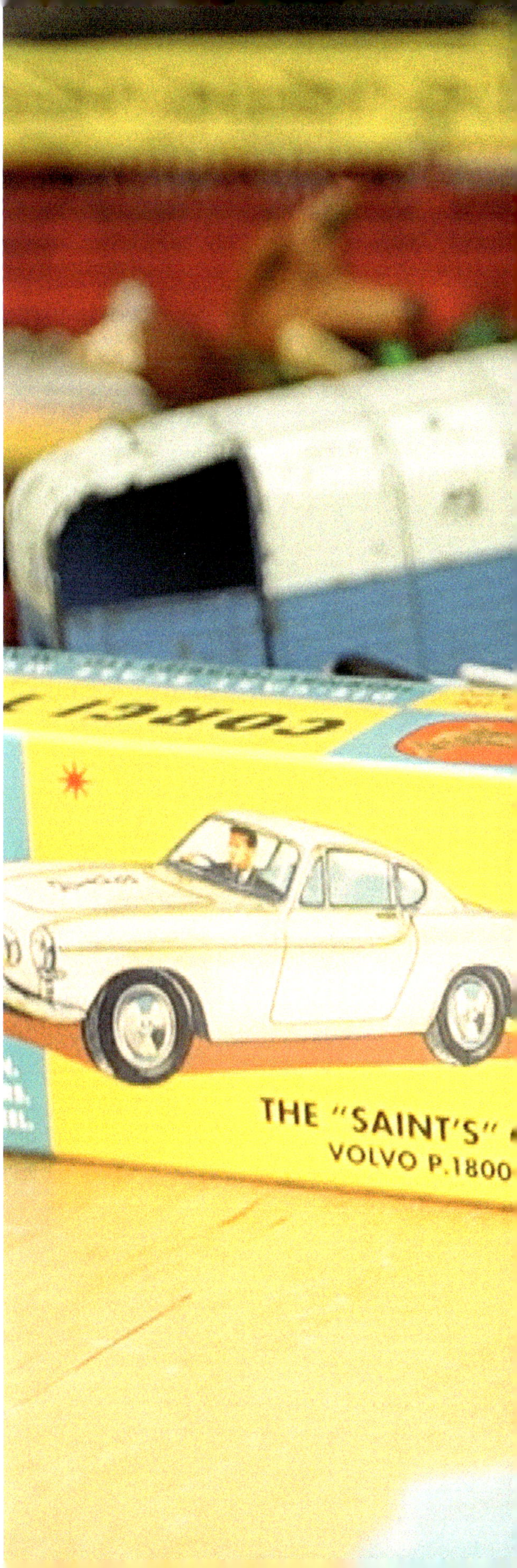

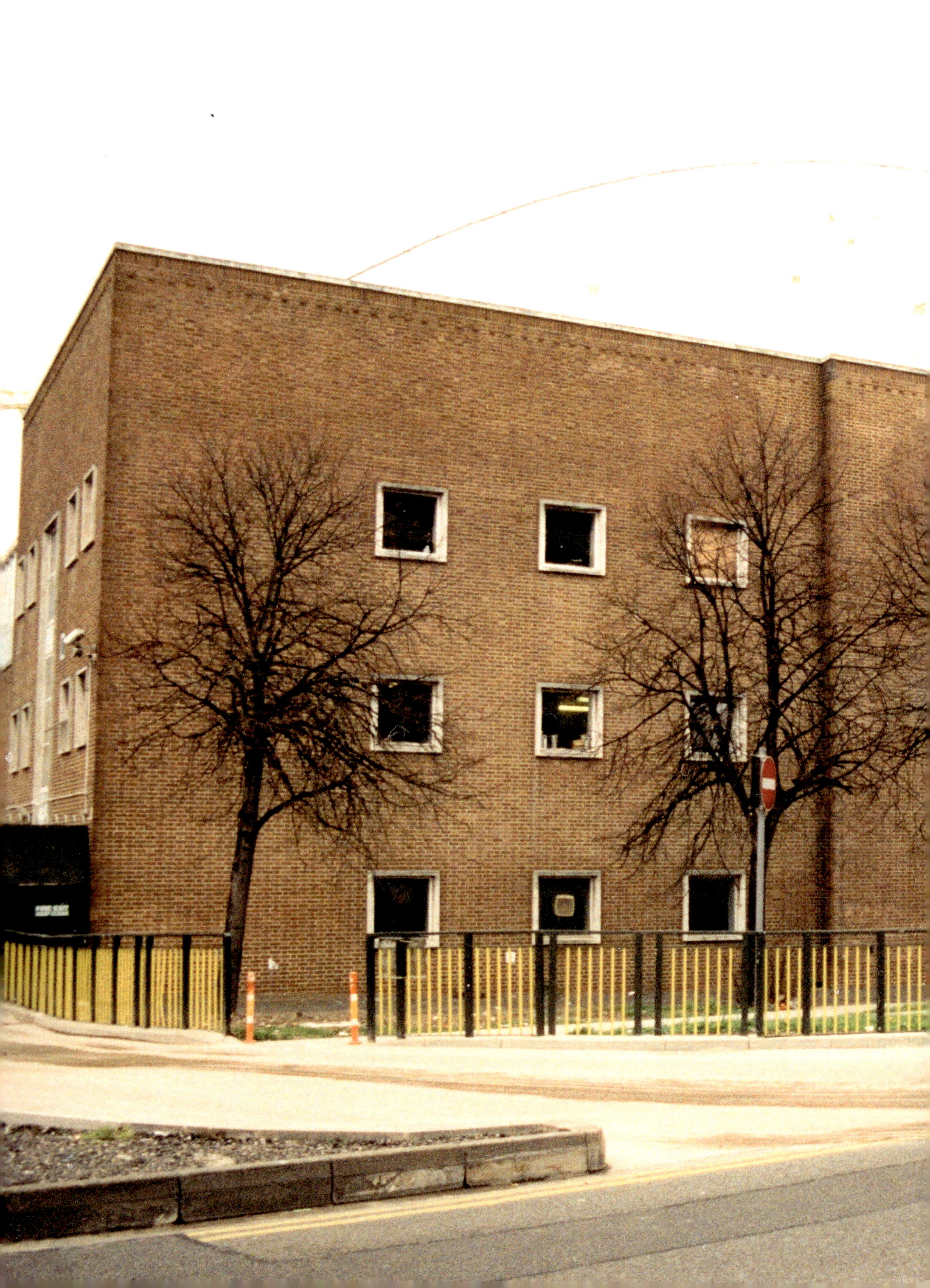

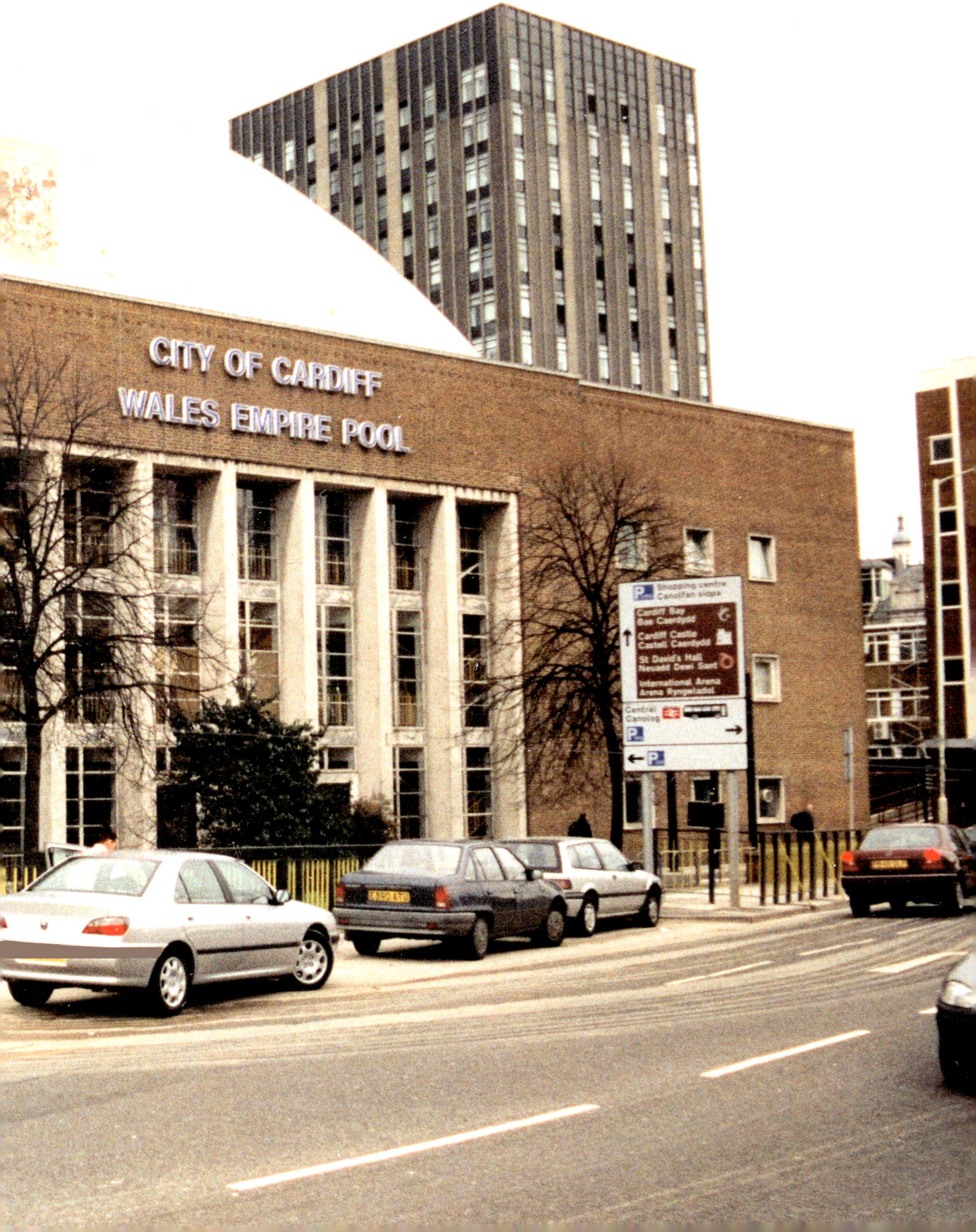
CITY OF CARDIFF
WALES EMPIRE POOL

Overleaf: big, bold and beloved. The Wales Empire Pool dominated Cardiff's skyline for 40 years.

WALES EMPIRE POOL

Cardiff's barrel-roofed leviathan

The 1950s was a momentous decade for the city of Cardiff. It had fended off competition from Aberystwyth and Caernarfon to be confirmed as the capital of Wales in 1955. Just three years later it saw its streets and suburbs invaded by the world's media. Tales of Cardiff were transmitted to television sets and transistor radios, from Singapore to South Africa, Nigeria to New Zealand. In the summer of 1958 the fledgling capital found itself staging a real bobby-dazzler: the British Empire and Commonwealth Games.

Across nine sweltering days, Cardiff became a crucible of sport. 1,122 athletes from 35 territories descended on Wales, the smallest nation to host the event up to that point. Between the mass release of carrier pigeons marking the start of the Games, and the RAF flypast that signalled its close, competitors faced-off in nine sports – athletics, cycling, fencing, lawn bowls, boxing (in which Wales won its only gold, courtesy of Merthyr's Howard Winstone), rowing, wrestling, weightlifting and swimming & diving. These last two events had initially put Cardiff in a tight spot. The city didn't have a swimming pool large enough to host aquatic showdowns to an international standard. No pool meant no Games. In the end, Cardiff Corporation doubled down and commissioned a brand-new building.

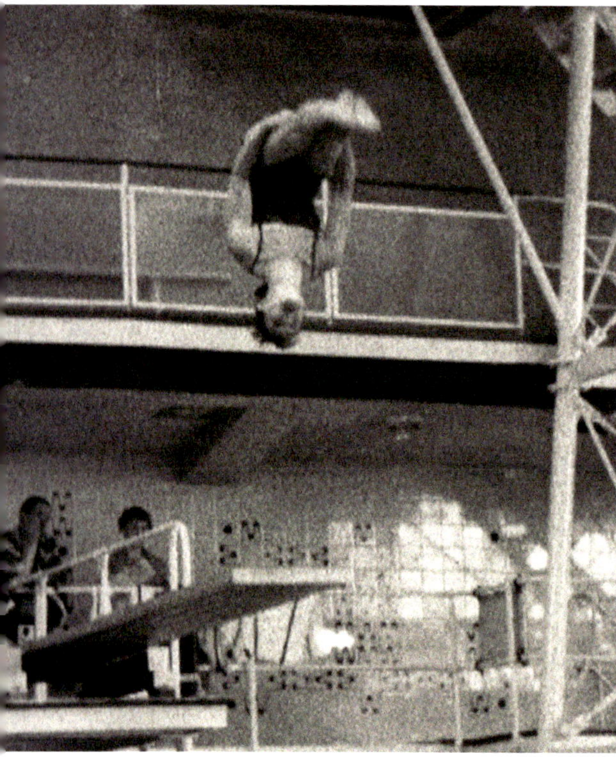

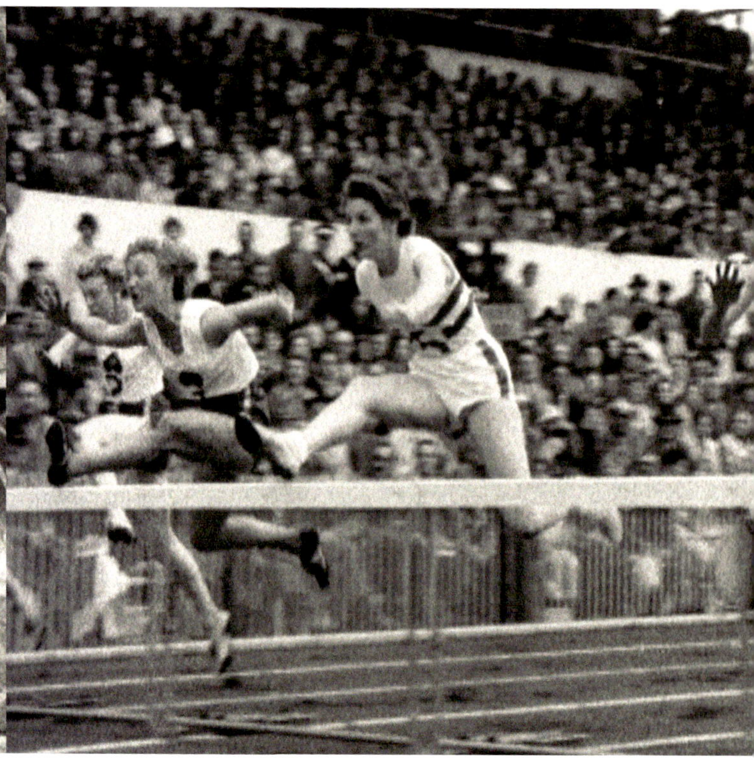

The design brief was purposeful: the venue must be capacious, confident and state-of-the-art. The world was watching. It had to be a showstopper.

The result was the Wales Empire Pool. It opened on 18th April 1958 and was unlike any other building on the city skyline. It was a full-on head-turner: an imposing concrete structure, brick-clad, modernist in style, with a flat facade and elegantly curved roof patterned with pastel blue and white tiles. What took your breath away was the sheer size and scale of the place. Cardiff's new swimming pool was colossal. It could accommodate nearly 2,000 spectators across four floors. The main pool was more than 50 metres long, 16 feet deep. At one end was an assortment of dizzyingly high diving boards, the loftiest rising 10 metres above the chlorinated water. It was like swimming inside a giant aircraft hangar.

Left: athletes compete in the 1958 Games.

Below: the daunting diving boards.

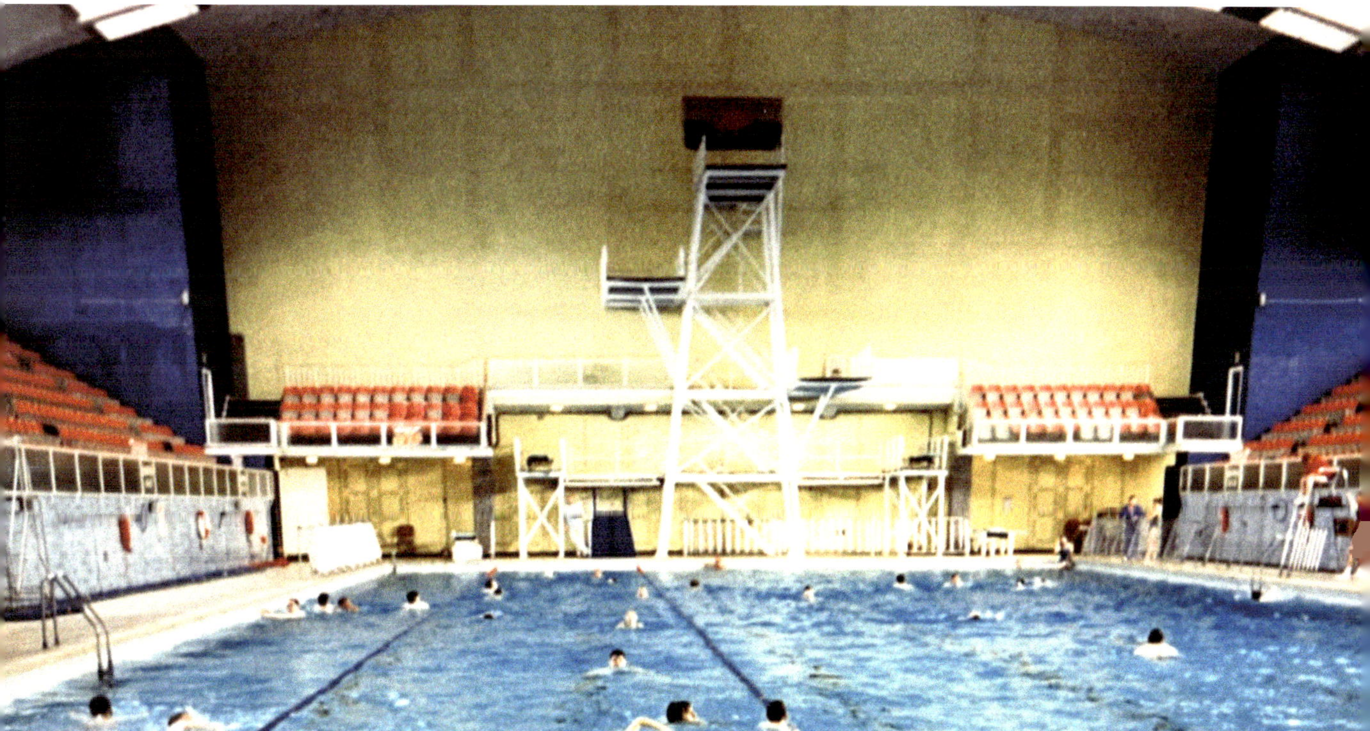

Crowds were suitably wowed. The new building, hot off the press, showcased Wales to the world, serving as the centrepiece of that year's Empire and Commonwealth Games (the stats: Australia reigned supreme in the swimming, England dominated the diving). At the end of that summer of '58, once the athletes and officials had packed up and moved on, the Wales Empire Pool entered its new phase as a popular public amenity; a king-sized facility enjoyed by families across Cardiff and beyond. An entire generation of Welsh children learned to swim there. Joe Llewellyn was one of them:

> "I first went there when I was really young with my parents because it was just around the corner from my house. I remember seeing the diving boards and all the rows of seats and thinking, wow, this is a spectacular space. It had an impact on you as a young person, you almost got a sense of importance from it. It was like a swimming amphitheatre. You definitely don't see pools like that anymore.
>
> "That was my first experience of swimming and it influenced how I thought about sport. I did my five-metre badge, my ten-metre badge, doing lengths, doing all the different strokes. Later I became a lifeguard and even now I still swim in oceans and rivers. So my passion for swimming really started at the Empire Pool, all those years ago."

The gigantic baths were a bona fide landmark in Cardiff. If you were making arrangements for a rendezvous in town, you'd use it as a milestone: 'I'll meet you by the Empire Pool.' The structure was sandwiched between Cardiff Arms Park and the city's bus station, on an area of land once known as Temperance Town – an inner-city suburb of terraced streets demolished wholesale in the 1930s. (Cardiff's urban planners swept away a number of traditional districts like Temperance Town during the 20th century. Hundreds of homes in Lower Splott, Newtown, Gabalfa and Tiger Bay were also bulldozed into oblivion…but that's a story for another time.)

The Empire Pool stood on the same corner site overlooking the River Taff for 40 years. Once you'd entered the cathedral-sized building your senses took over. That serious expanse of water beneath the soaring roof could be fairly intimidating, especially for younger swimmers. Even so, the venue was well-regarded and extremely well-used. If you remember any of these experiences then you know you've spent a chunk of your past at the Empire Pool:

* Plucking up the courage to jump off the higher diving boards.

* Bracing yourself for the freezing cold water in the main pool.

* Silently congratulating yourself at managing to swim an entire length.

* Being treated by your parents to hot Bovril, Oxo crisps and Iced Gems from the cafeteria.

* Saturday afternoon discos in the pool.

* Returning to the changing rooms with eyes stinging from the chlorine.

* Adjusting to the ringing sound in your ears when you realised that the Empire Pool was effectively one big echo chamber.

One man who knew the venue inside and out is Paul Budd. He worked at the Empire Pool for two decades, joining in 1975 as a 21-year-old straight from a job on the railways. His first role was to arrange the crates for the customers' clothes. He gradually rose through the ranks and ended up managing the venue:

"It was the only pool of its size and everyone in Wales seemed to know about it. Lots of people would come down from the Valleys to make use of it. We'd have hundreds in there every day, with six lifeguards on duty. There was a teaching pool round the back, for private lessons. You had the Turkish baths – saunas, steam rooms and jacuzzis. There was a laundry too – when I started, we had six people working there, washing and drying the towels. There were two boiler men, two filter men. The place was huge.

"A lot of the Welsh rugby team used to come there back in the day, players like Barry John. And when there were big boxing events in town, and the boxers needed to get their weight down, they used to come to the Empire Pool. We used to see them in the steam room and they'd be there with a skipping rope trying to shed a couple of pounds before the weigh-in.

"Rugby international days were busy. Everybody would have come from the pubs, on their way to the Arms Park, and they'd come in and say, 'Can I use your toilet?' So to keep the profits up we used to charge them 20p spectators' fee so they could go in!

"Whenever we held a swimming gala we'd have the eight lanes out. At that time schoolchildren would often join us for work experience. So what we used to do was get two buckets and tell them there wasn't enough water in lane seven, could they go and get the water from lane two to level it out. And they were quite happy to do it!"

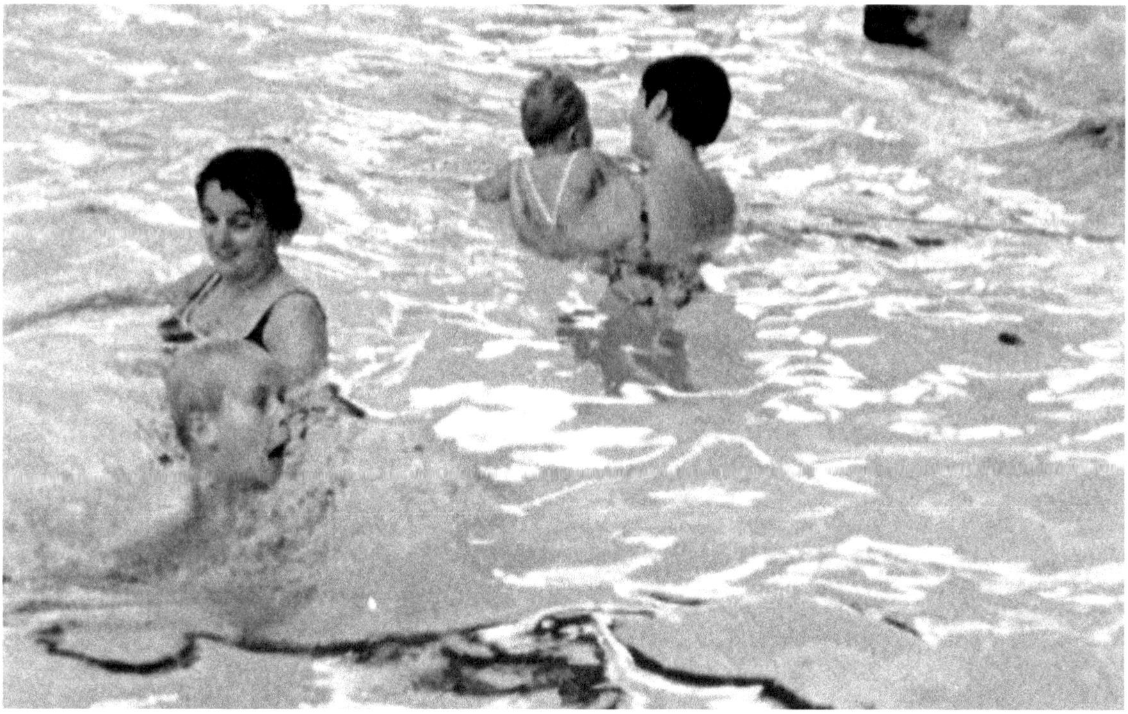

Taking the plunge: family fun at the Empire Pool.

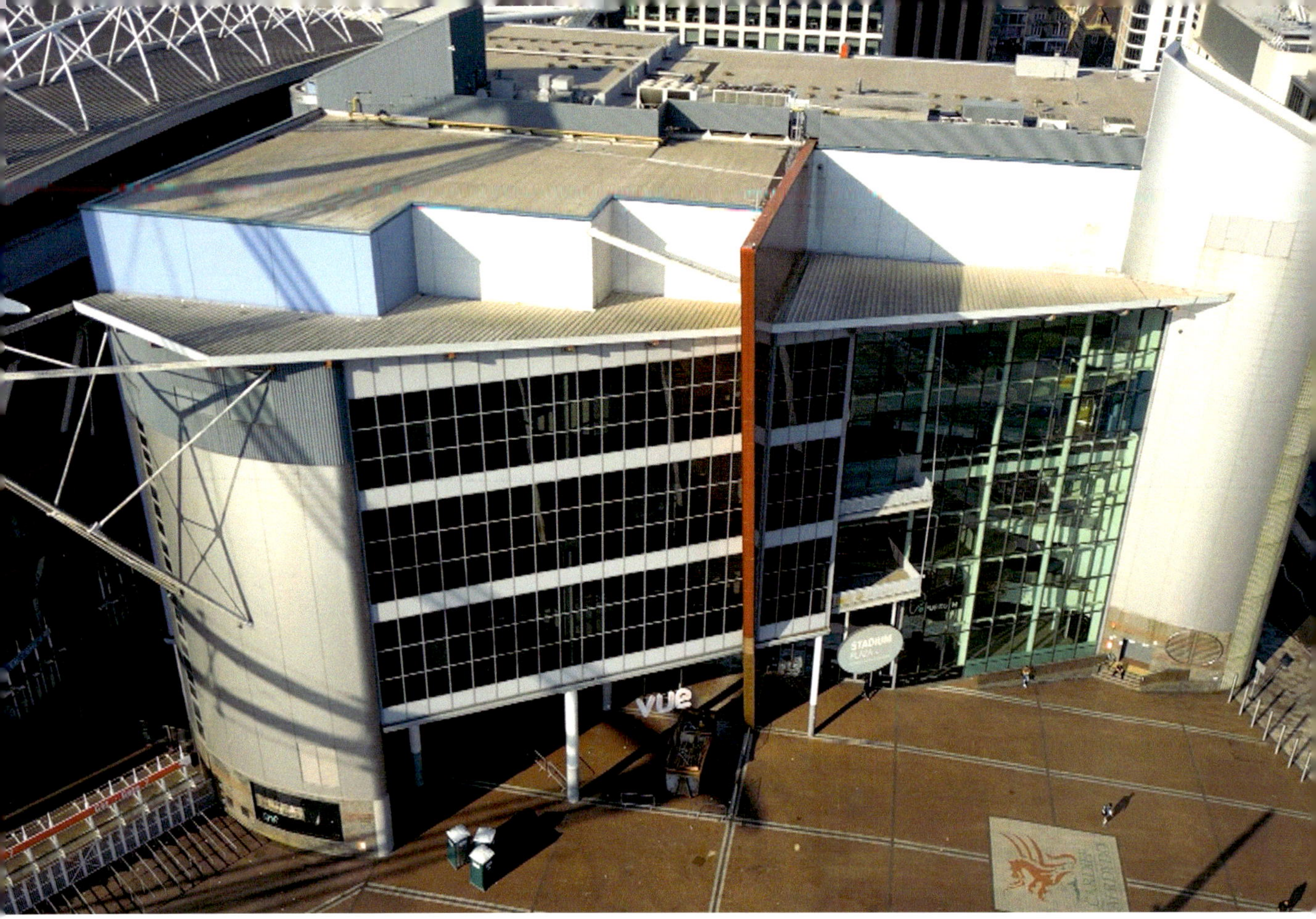

Back in the Fifties, an international tournament had precipitated the building of the Wales Empire Pool. In the 1990s, another sporting spectacle, again staged in Cardiff to great fanfare, was to trigger its destruction. It had been announced that the city was to host the 1999 Rugby World Cup. A new national stadium was in the offing, to be situated along the riverfront. It would cost £121 million, with a seating capacity of more than 70,000, and would be known as the Millennium Stadium. There was just one problem…the Wales Empire Pool was standing in the way.

As one landmark rose, another fell. In 1998 the seminal swimming baths were torn down. While there was genuine enthusiasm at the sight of a swanky new stadium taking shape, there were plenty of Cardiff residents, like Janice Macartney Herbert, who mourned the monument it replaced:

"I was sad for my children mostly. We lived so close to the pool and it was so good for them to go there, to learn to swim. My fondest memory is seeing my children happy in that pool. They were very upset. And they were angry.

"I never understood why it had to be demolished in the first place. I mean, it was built for the Empire Games so surely that meant it held enough history in itself. I couldn't understand it. I wish there could have been an alternative."

Out with the old, in with the new: the leisure complex that replaced the Empire Pool.

Today, the footprint of the old Empire Pool has been subsumed into the southern section of the Principality Stadium (as it became known) and the multiform leisure complex next door, comprising a cinema, gym and bowling alley. After the elimination of the Empire Pool it took a further 10 years for the people of Cardiff to have another international standard swimming pool on their doorstep. Its replacement is a glass wraparound edifice located on the western edge of Cardiff Bay. As you make your way round to the front door, you'll spot a long, rectangular slab of stone encased in glass. It's the original plaque commemorating the opening of the Wales Empire Pool in 1958.

Back in the late '90s, Paul Budd was given a bittersweet task. On the final day of business, once all the customers and staff had left for the day, he had to lock the front doors of the Empire Pool knowing they'd never reopen to the public:

> "It was sad, turning that key for the last time. All of a sudden it was gone.
>
> "The people who were children when I was working there would probably have still been bringing their children there today, and they'd be saying to their children: this is where I learned to swim, this is where your grandfather learned to swim. Yes, it's very sad. Cardiff's lost a lot of history."

The end of an era: staff mark the closing of the pool.

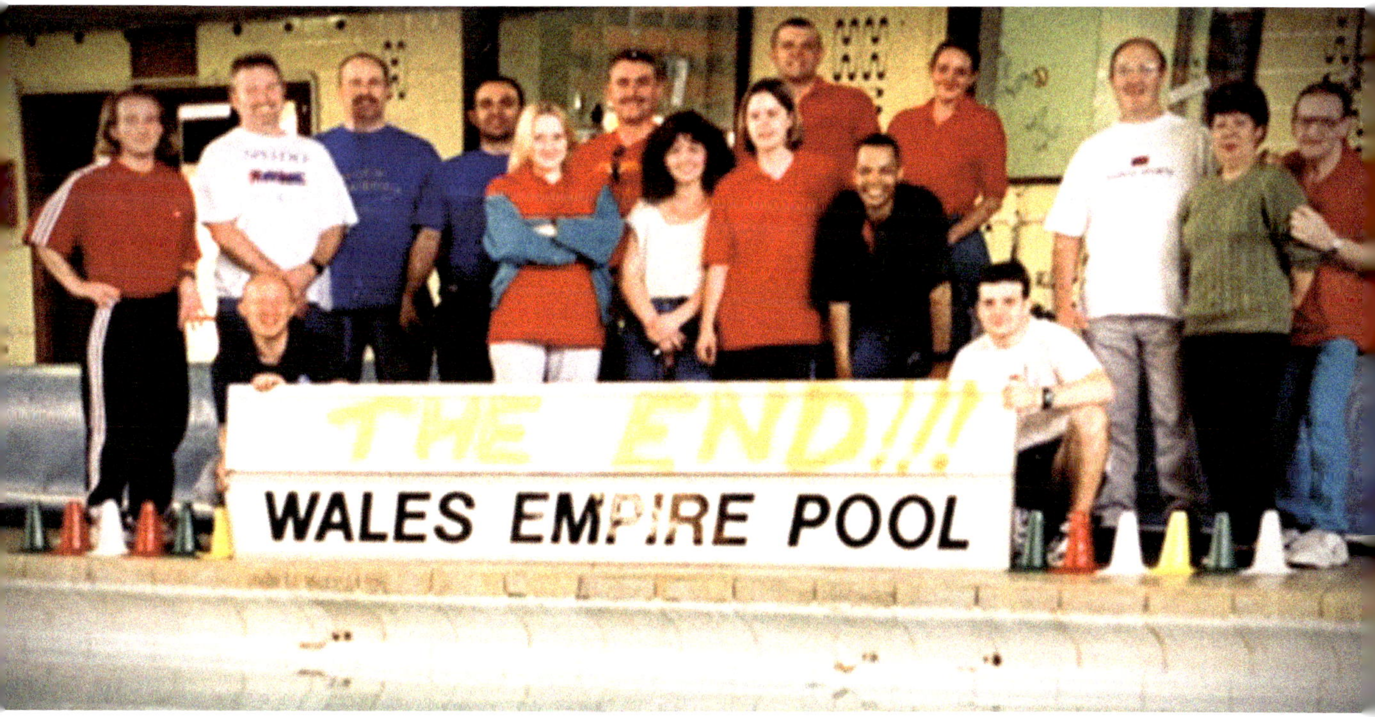

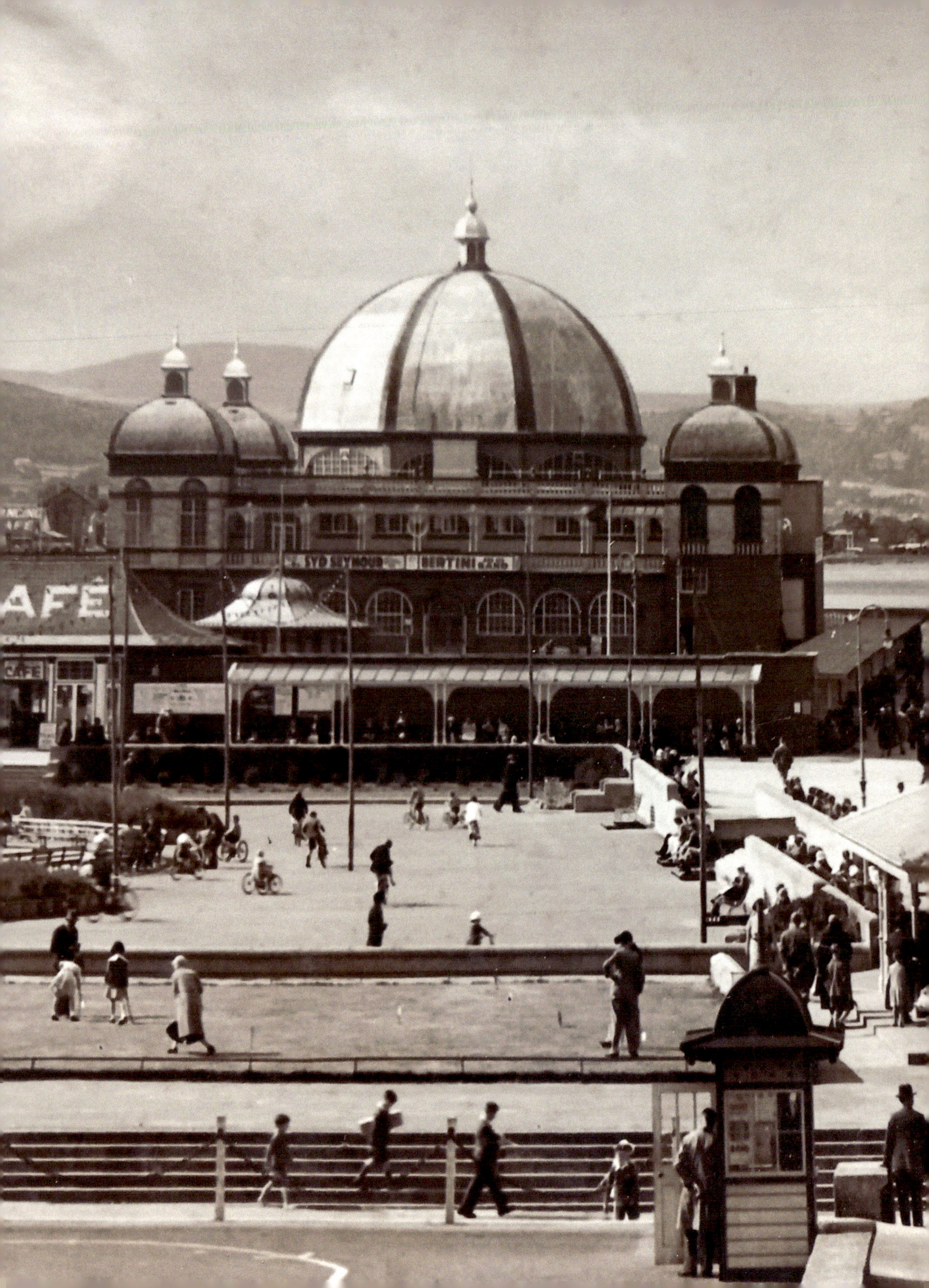
SYD SEYMOUR
CAFE

RHYL PAVILION THEATRE

The multi-domed culture palace by the sea

During its golden years as a holiday resort, the coastal town of Rhyl really knew how to put on a show. From the Victorian era, visitors were treated to amusements, attractions and distractions across the full sweep of its endless promenade. In 1908 a brand-new building appeared on the seafront that took razzle-dazzle to a whole new level. It dominated the skyline and stood as a symbol of popular entertainment for almost 70 years.

The Rhyl Pavilion Theatre was impossible to miss. Situated at the very centre of the promenade it was designed as a whopping, no-expense-spared statement of intent: 'Let us show you a good time.' The venue could seat well over 1,000 people and became instantly iconic thanks to its five inimitable rooftop domes. Audiences sometimes complained that the huge central dome affected the acoustics of the auditorium, allowing the sound to rise up into the heavens. These concerns were largely outweighed by the spectacle of seeing the domes lit up at night, vibrant, glowing and constantly changing colour. It was an illuminated landmark that could be seen from miles away, Rhyl's very own Blackpool Tower.

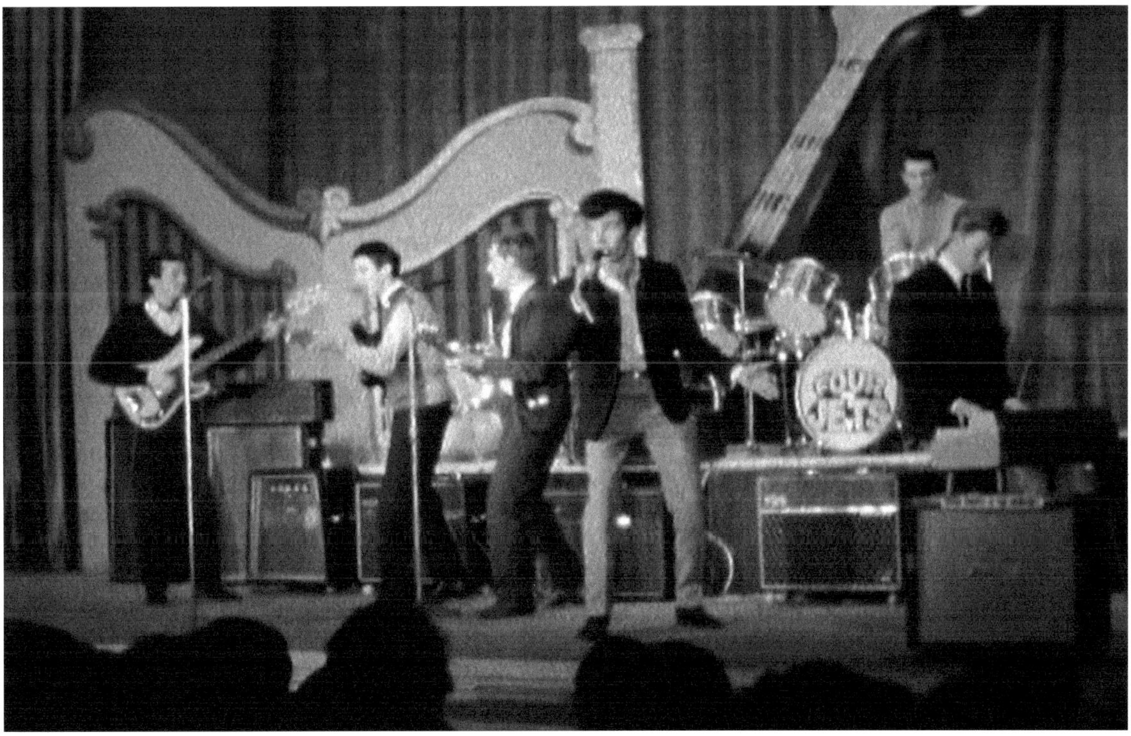

Opposite: the Pavilion in its prime.

Above: rocking Rhyl in the 1960s.

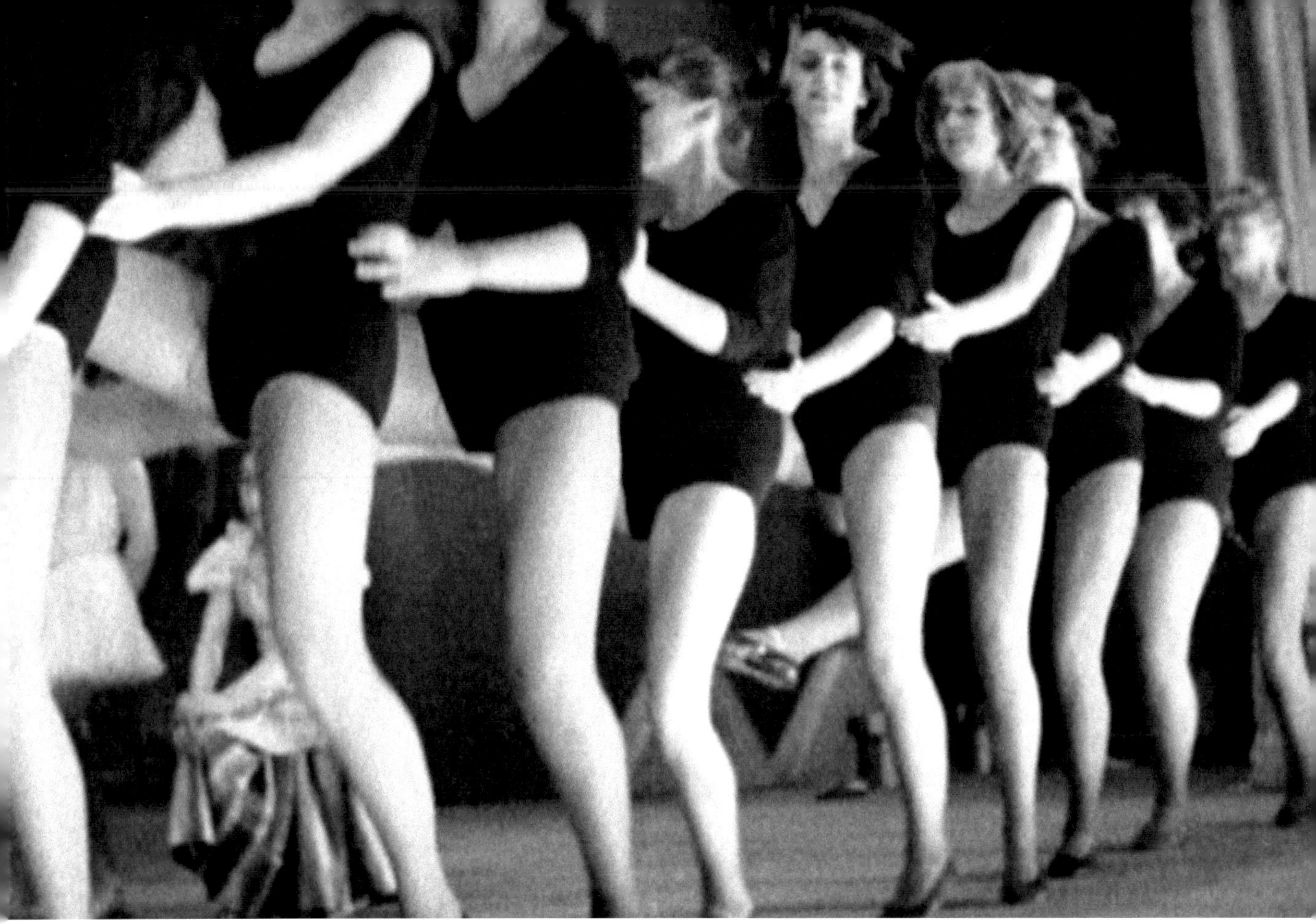

Over the years, the Pavilion staged a terrific potpourri of concerts and events. The seasonal schedules included: circuses, pantomimes, drama productions, revues, choral recitals, fashion shows, variety performances, orchestral evenings, rock 'n' roll gigs and opera. The circuses proved especially popular and residents delighted at watching elephants being led into the sea to cool down before and after a show. Rhyl historian Colin Jones remembers the Pavilion, and the civic pride it engendered:

> "It looked important and impressive, like a little Taj Mahal sitting on the prom. It was the town's principal theatre and it bound the community together. Its likeness appeared all over the town, on letterheads, picture postcards, and photographs in restaurants and pubs.
>
> "The original idea was to create a large assembly space for any kind of event that required a lot of seating. It wasn't strictly theatrical. For instance, in the early years they would have talks there on specialist subjects, sometimes illustrated by lantern slides. In fact, a young Winston Churchill delivered a talk there.
>
> "In the 1930s the Pavilion was adapted to accommodate a ballroom and a cabaret space. During World War Two they stopped lighting up the white domes and camouflaged them. The Manchester Repertory Company was based there during the war years. They'd been evacuated to Rhyl and it was handy to have them because there were lots of military personnel billeted locally and they all needed entertaining!"

In its heyday, the venue hosted a revolving door of household names. Paul Robeson, Shirley Bassey, Vera Lynn, Arthur Askey and Morecambe & Wise all performed at the Pavilion, which at one time boasted the largest stage in North Wales. The annual programme of events also made room for productions that celebrated local talent. The final concert in the Pavilion's history was the Children's Showtime charity performance in aid of Rhyl Lifeboat and Rhyl Scouts. The show was produced by Gay Harris – a dancer and soprano who moved from the West Midlands to establish a lasting legacy in Rhyl. The Gay Harris Dancers are the longest-running dance group in the town, and Gay herself remembers the halcyon days when the Pavilion was in its prime:

"Back then the whole town was about the holiday industry and performing and entertainment. It was a vibrant place, Rhyl. The seasons were 26 to 28 weeks long! Everybody went to the theatre then; it was just wonderful. It was a very exciting time, and I loved show business, so Rhyl to me was like heaven!

"The Pavilion itself was just a beautiful place and it brought the town and tourists together. Everyone was in an uproar when that building came down."

Opposite: dancers line up to entertain the town.

Below: the 'Taj Mahal of Rhyl.'

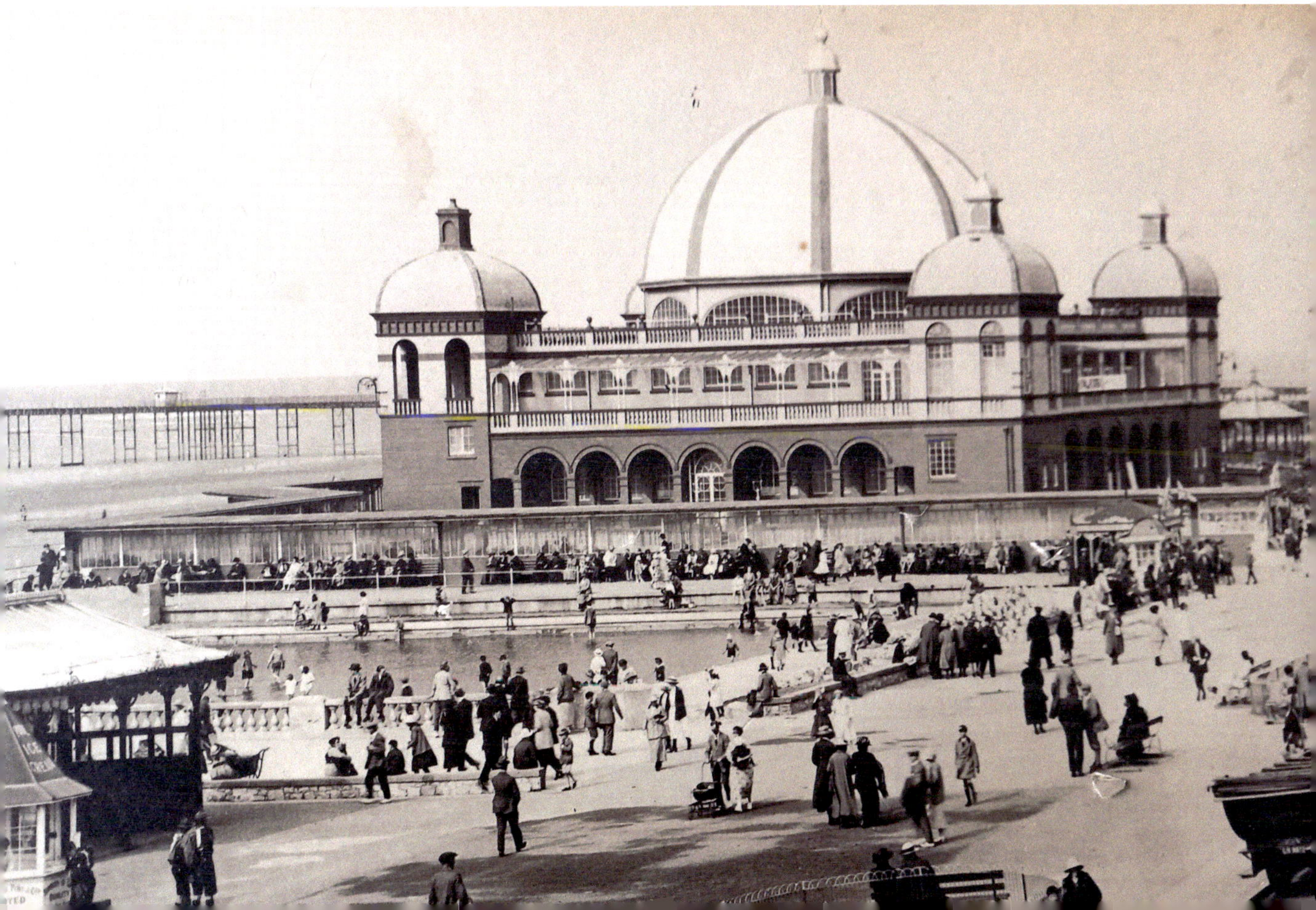

Like many traditional seaside resorts, Rhyl saw its economy slide during the 1960s and 70s. Cheap package deals abroad were drawing more and more tourists away from British beaches. The Pavilion faced its own threat: most households owned a television set. Why pay for live variety shows at a local theatre when you've got *Sunday Night at the London Palladium* in the corner of your sitting room? Meanwhile, the age of the venue was starting to show. An inspection report revealed that the Pavilion, which was owned by the county council, required extensive renovation. Of particular concern were the cracks in the central dome, a potential safety hazard. There was a stark choice to be made: commit to the repairs or radically rethink the building's future. The council eventually reached its decision: tear it down.

In 1974 the Pavilion Theatre was completely demolished. To the anger of onlookers, the apparently dangerous dome came down intact and in one piece. The town was heartbroken. Pat Jones, a lifelong Rhyl resident, still feels a sense of loss:

> "The Pavilion stays in your memory. In those days everybody thought 'something new should come.' But not always is the new as good as the old. Sometimes you think to yourself: why the heck didn't we save that?
>
> "It was very sad to see it go. When you're young you don't feel quite as much for those buildings as you do when you're getting older.

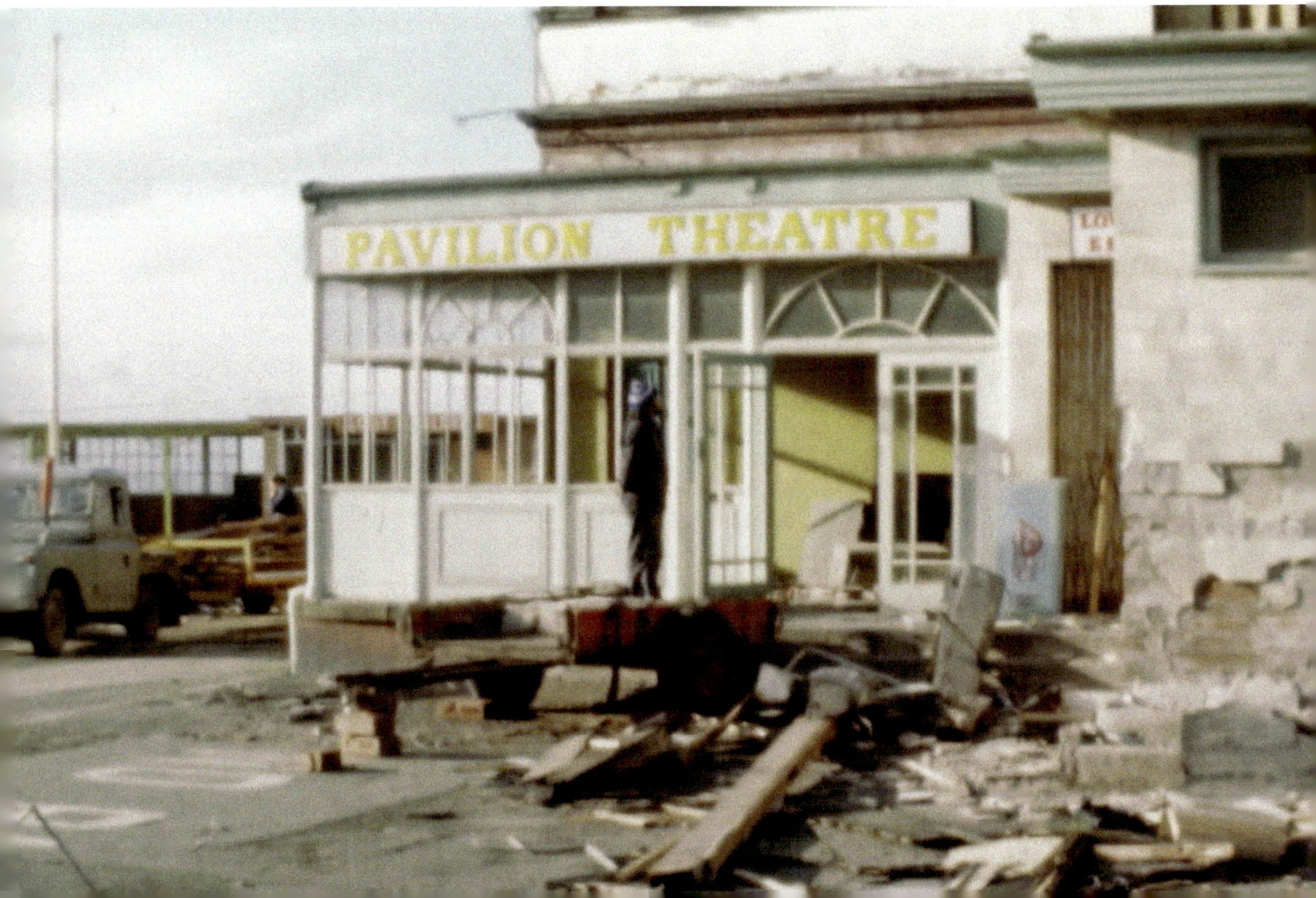

And then you think: we should have fought for that. So if you feel in your heart that something shouldn't come down and shouldn't be destroyed, please fight for it. Fight for it."

It took 17 years for a replacement venue of comparable size to be built in Rhyl. The new Pavilion Theatre stands just a few hundred yards from its Edwardian predecessor – an echo of the past along an ever-changing coastline. You can't always hold back the tide of change but memories of Rhyl's lost landmark still shine brightly.

Opposite: demolition begins.

Below: the replacement Pavilion Theatre (not a dome in sight).

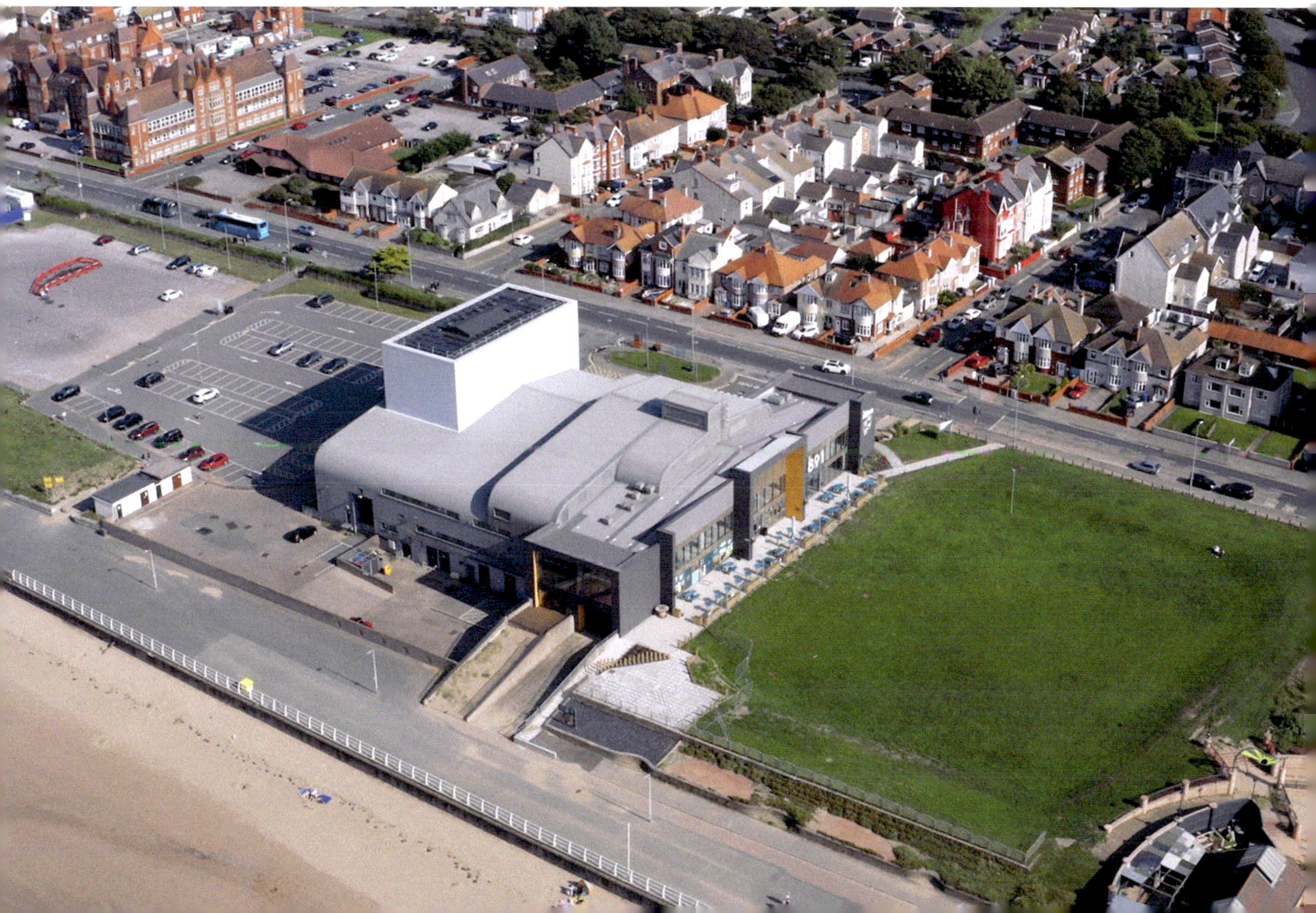

GROES

The picturesque village flattened to make way for the M4

Snaking through South Wales, the M4 motorway has become ingrained in our landscape. But one section has a special significance. Drivers thundering past Junction 39, between Margam and Port Talbot, may be unaware of the historic village that was sacrificed in the 1970s to fast-track the road's westward expansion.

That village was Groes and it was utterly unique. There were thatched cottages, a school and an elegant octagonal chapel in honey-coloured stone. Although it stood within sight and sound of Port Talbot's steelworks, Groes had a rustic charm all of its own. The village boasted a bucolic style of architecture that wouldn't have seemed out of place in the Cotswolds.

The community evolved during the 1830s. The wealthy industrialist and politician C.R.M. Talbot (after whom Port Talbot is named) was constructing a new home for himself two miles to the south: the Gothic swagger of Margam Castle. Eager to enlarge his private parkland, he instructed his architects to erect a brand-new village to house the tenants of the farms and cottages that peppered his vast estate. Groes was duly built and the residents were resettled. Over time, the villagers gained their own place of worship in Beulah Methodist Chapel (1838) and a substantial four-gabled school (1860).

Opposite: Groes in happier times. Note the octagonal chapel and pastoral cottages. Incredibly, the belching steelworks of Port Talbot were just a stone's throw away.

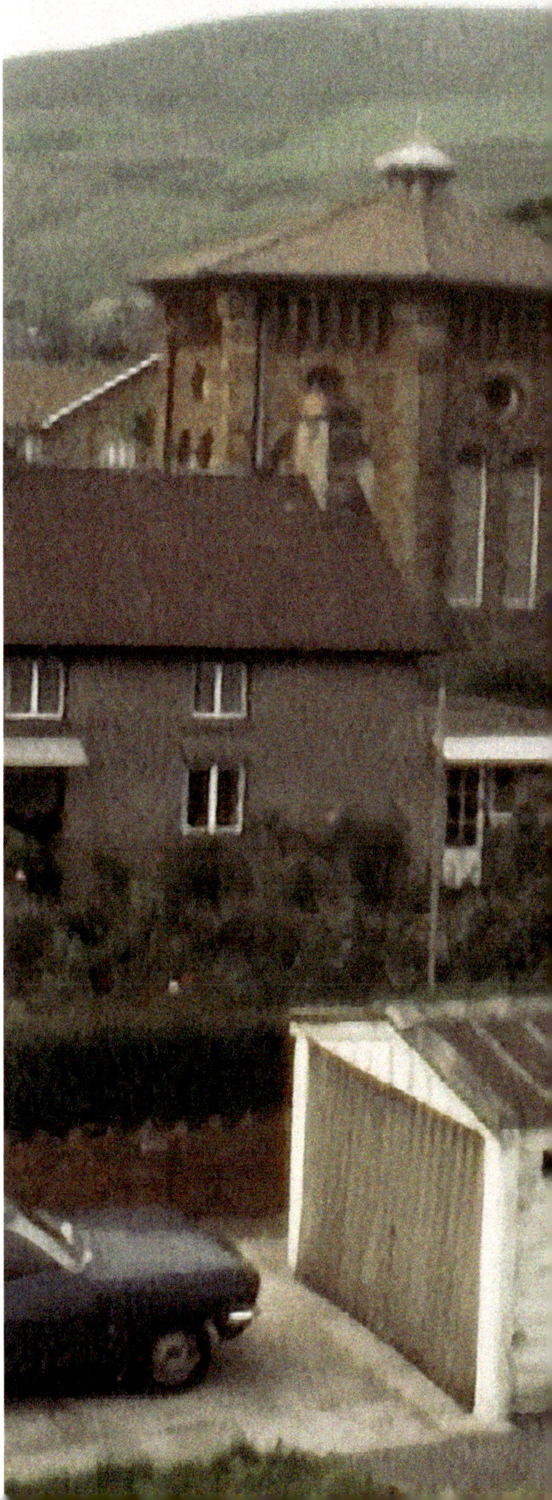

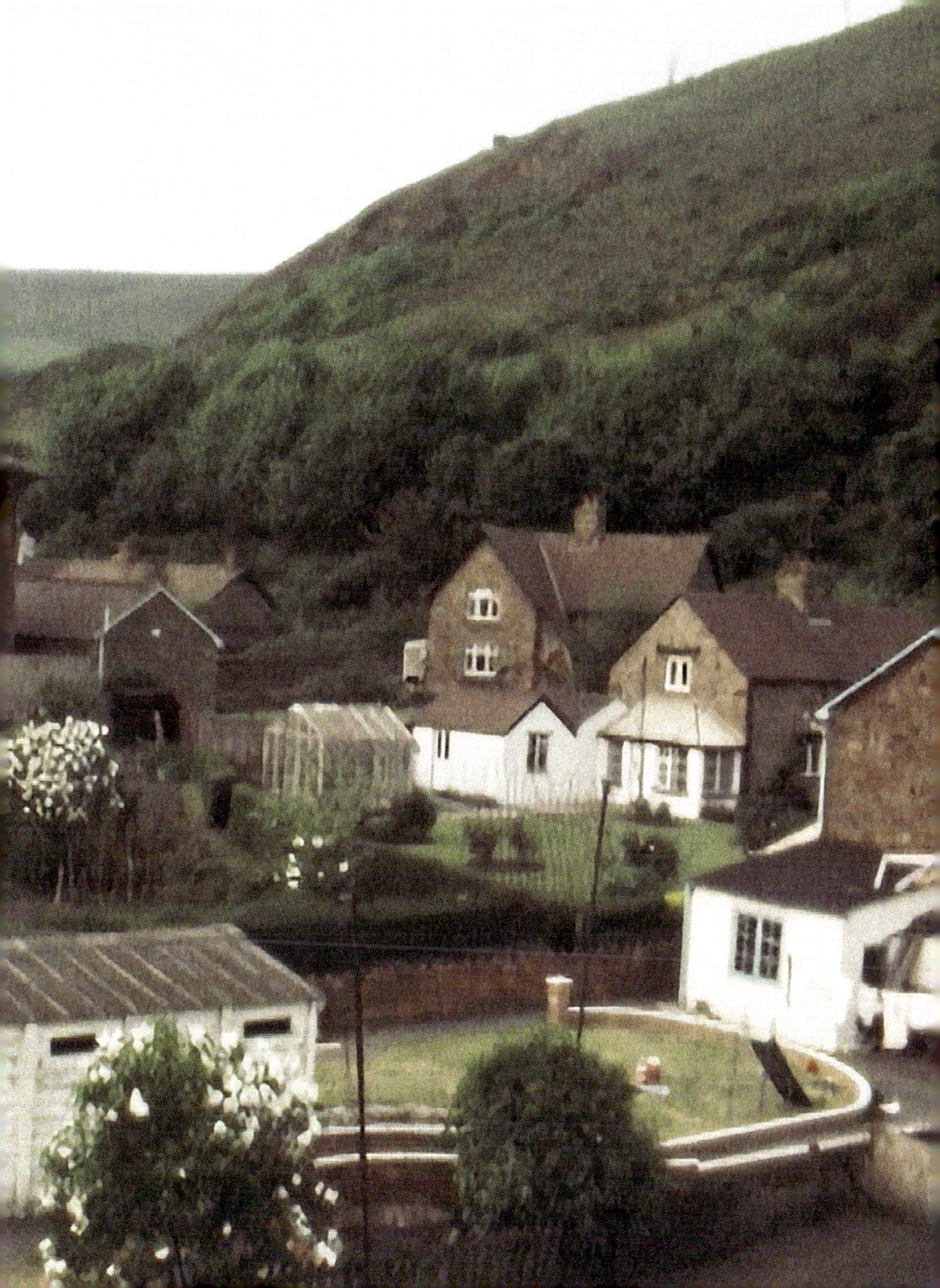

By the mid 20th century the surrounding landscape had become a vortex of rolling mills and blast furnaces. Yet Groes still stood, untouched by time. Ian Humphreys was born in the village in 1959. He lived at No.17, his grandmother at No.16 and his aunt at No.13.

"Growing up there was fantastic, I loved it. We had about a third of an acre of land around the house where we had apple trees. If there was ever an excess of apples, I used to give them to the local shop. I was only 12 years old at the time. The shopkeeper would sell them and whatever he made on them he'd split it half each with me. So I was a bit of an entrepreneur!

"You never had to worry about locking your front door. Everyone helped each other and it was just a great community. I sorely miss it. I've told my children that when I pass away my ashes are going to be spread on the hill right behind where Groes was. Born there and died there."

Below: demolition crews begin tearing down the old homes.

Opposite: daily life before the motorway.

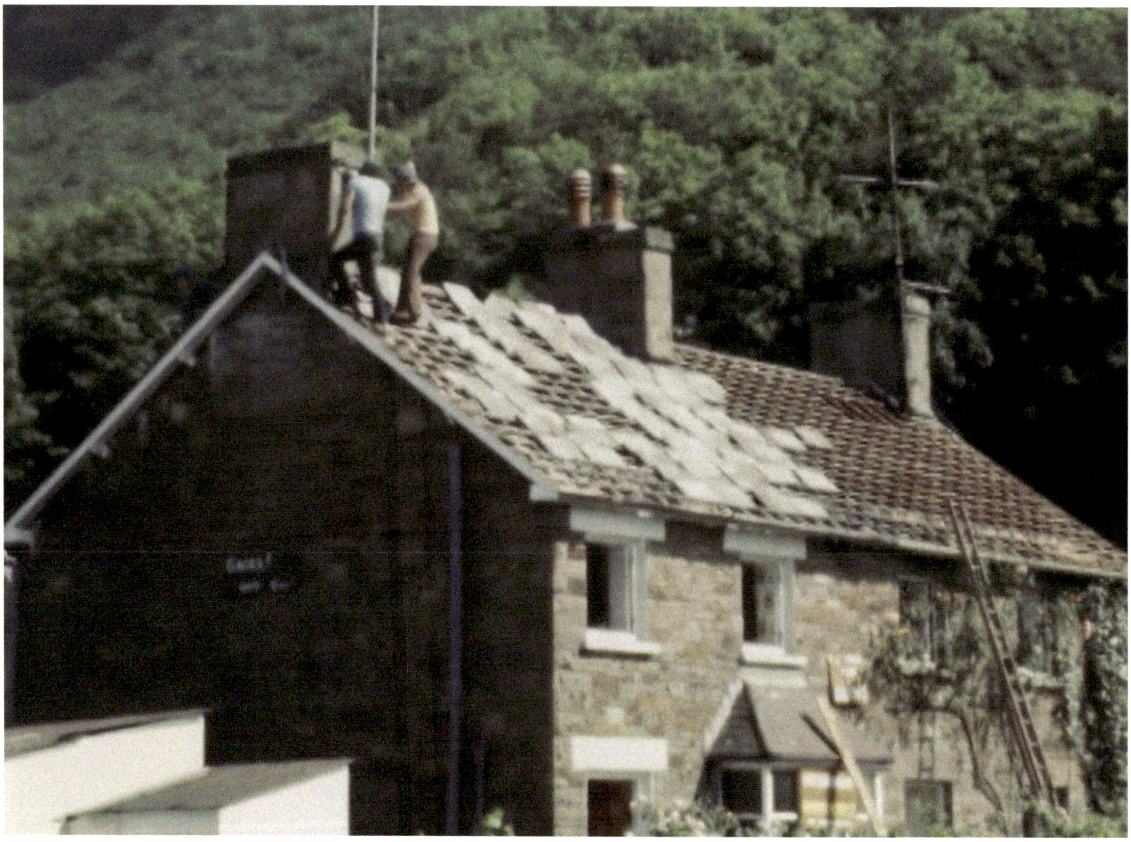

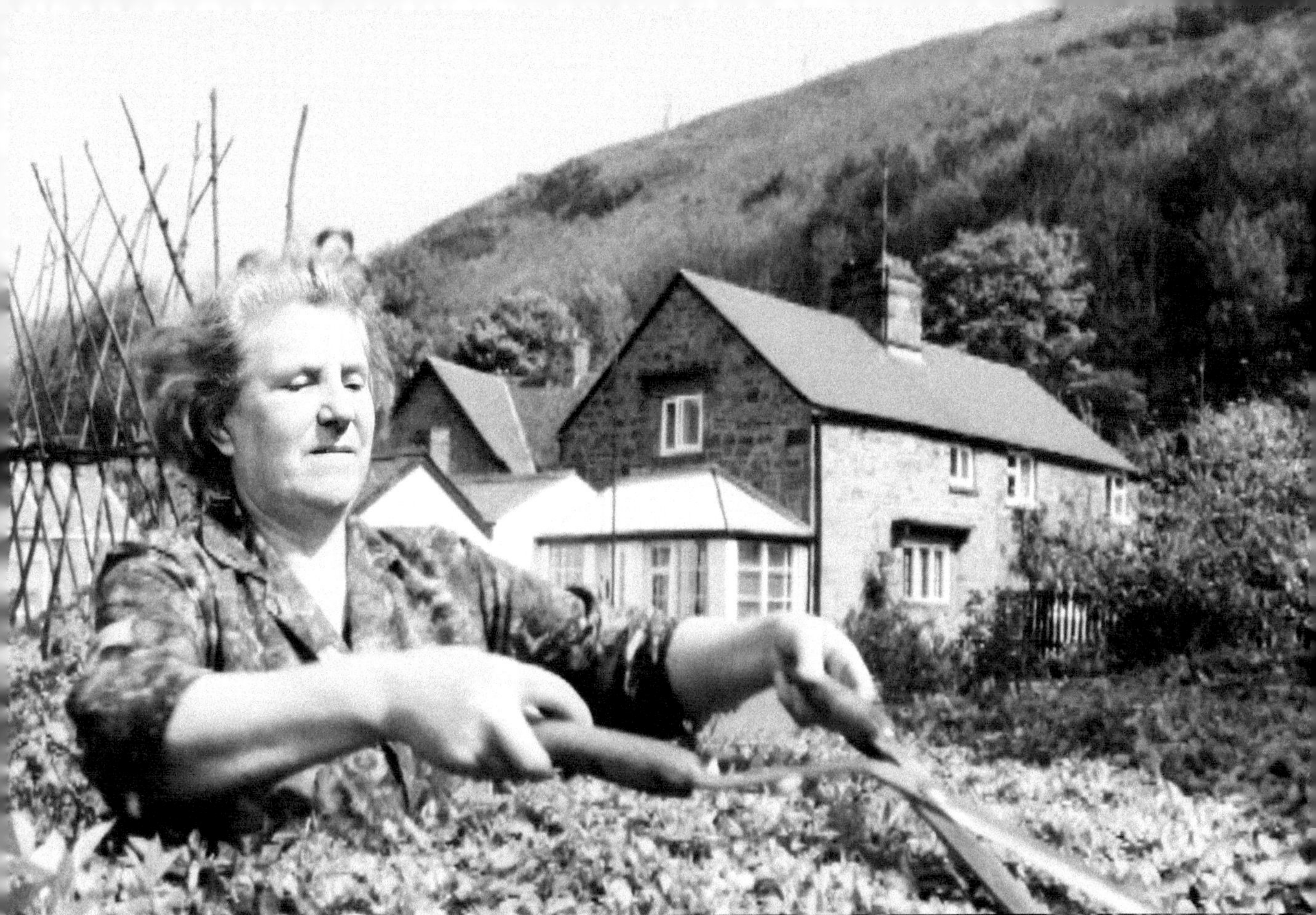

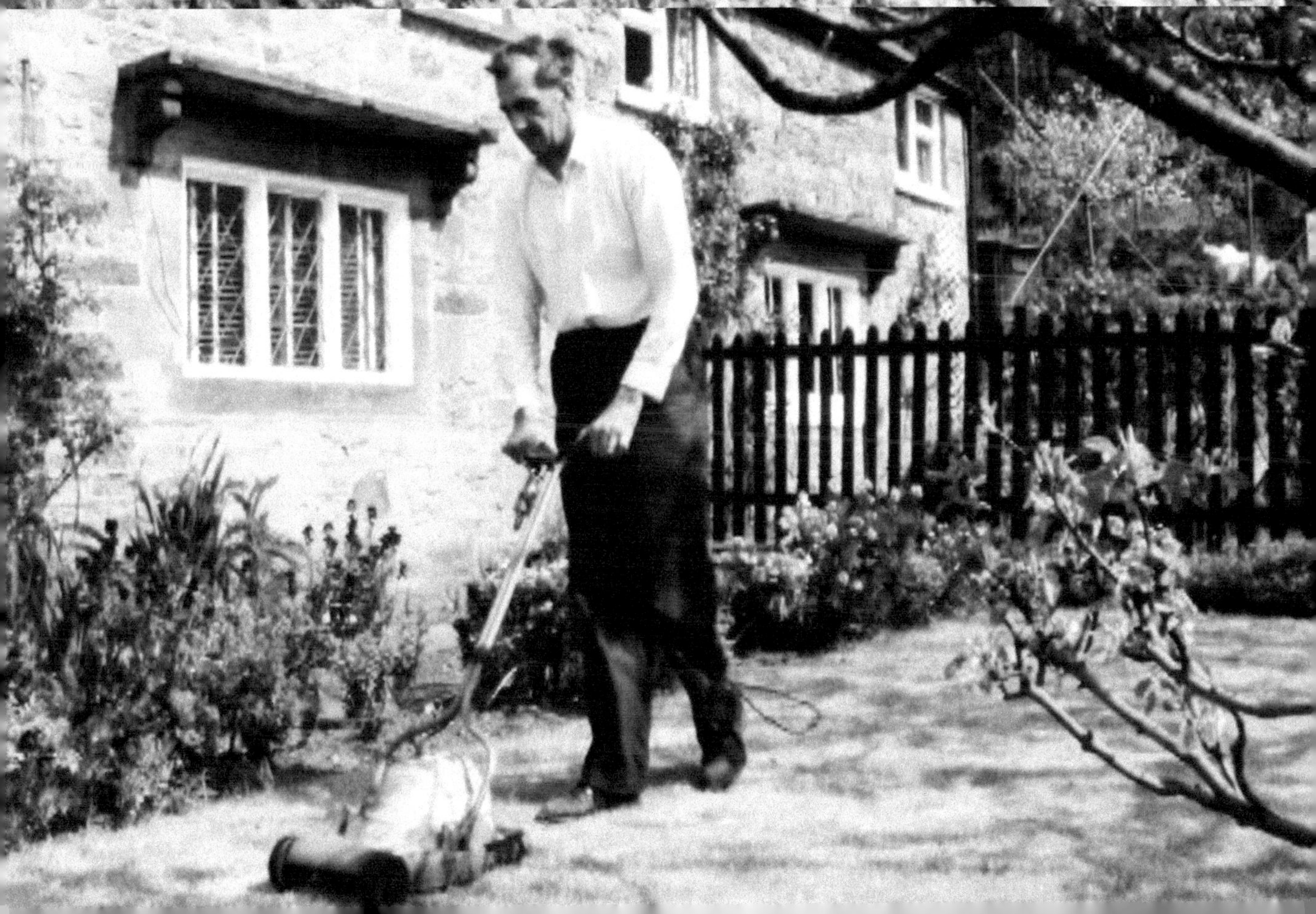

For almost 150 years, the village remained perfectly preserved. But it found itself on the wrong side of progress. All around Groes a huge motorway was taking shape. The M4 was being extended from the east to join up with the Port Talbot bypass, with the aim of creating a multi-lane link to Swansea. Groes was directly in the path of the proposed route.

A spirited campaign was launched in the early 1970s to try to save the village. There were protests, petitions and myriad public meetings. One resident of Groes made headlines across the UK thanks to his creative campaign of opposition. Romeo Meli took his bed, armchair and television set and protested, day after day, on the side of the A48 dual carriageway. His daughter Francesca remembers her late father's fight:

"I recall sitting with him in the rain with a duffle coat on. There were TV cameras and newspapers. It was a battle I think he knew he couldn't win but that didn't stop him. Nothing was going to stop him.

"Groes was a precious place, it was unique. And he wanted to save it. He was a panel beater in Port Talbot and he'd lost his business when the town was redeveloped. Not long afterwards, Groes happened. It must have been tough. He lost his job then he lost his home. Our home."

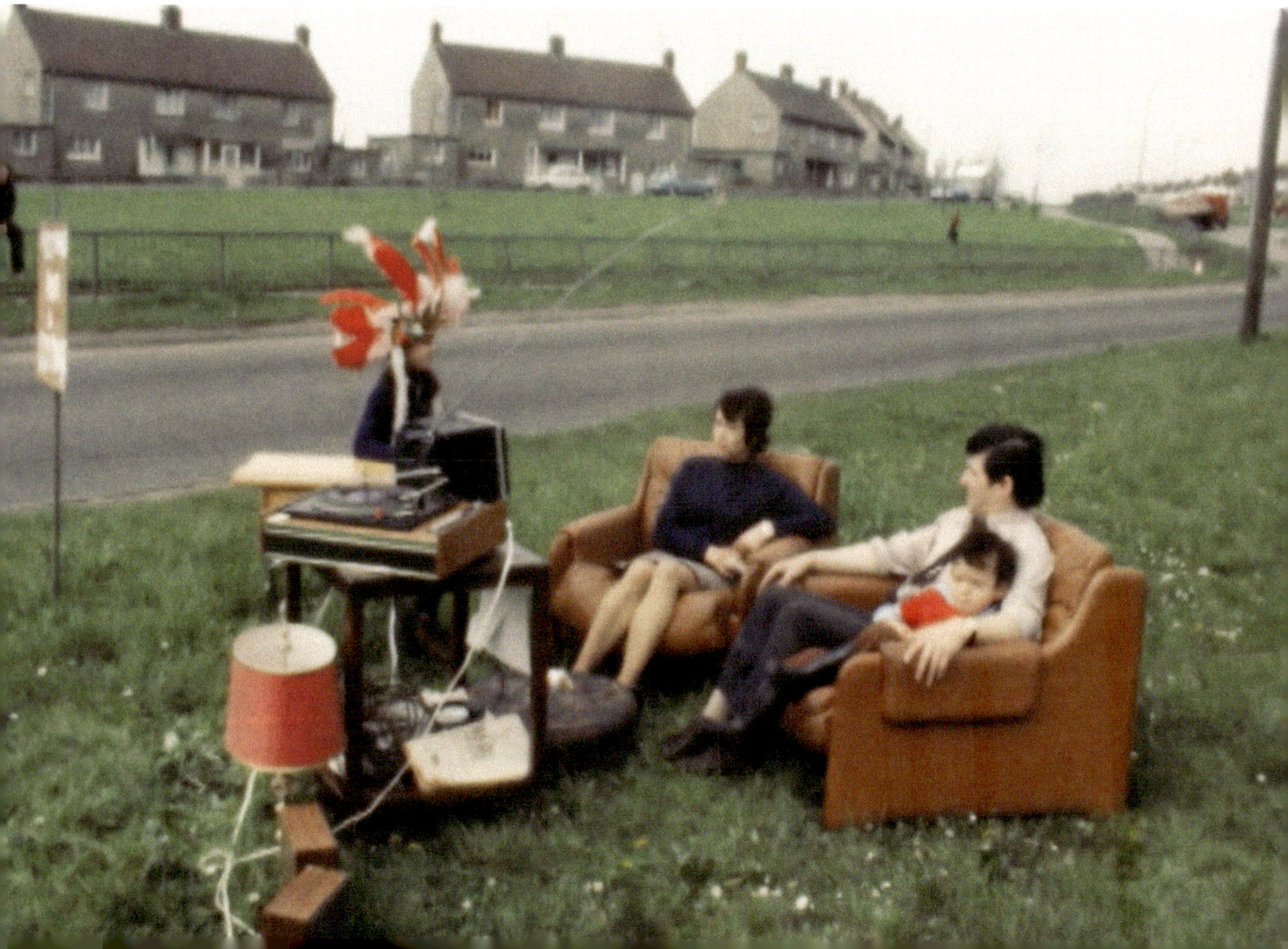

Although the odds were stacked against the residents, a faint glimmer of hope emerged. The County Council suggested an alternative route for the motorway, moving it further south and extending its construction by a mere 51 metres. In this new configuration the road would have circumvented Groes entirely and the village would have been spared. The final decision rested in the hands of the Welsh Office and in 1974 that decision came through: Groes was to be flattened.

Campaigners were slack-jawed in horror. Amid the swirl of dismay, the planning process kicked into gear. The villagers' homes were subject to compulsory purchase orders. Around 100 people were forced to move out and relocate to other corners of the county. In the summer of 1975, as demolition crews stood on standby, Romeo Meli and his family finally packed up their belongings. They were the last residents to leave Groes.

All 20 houses came crashing down, as did the school. A beautiful and genuinely distinctive pocket of Victorian Wales was methodically and comprehensively pulverised. The sole survivor was Groes' eye-catching octagonal chapel. It was dismantled, brick by brick, and rebuilt half a mile away at Tollgate Park in Margam where it still stands today.

In many ways it's a lonely building, separated from the old stone cottages that once surrounded it. But its current congregation is loyal and the building has been given Grade II* listed status as the only octagonal chapel remaining in Wales. The Groes of old now forms part of the raised embankment at Junction 39 of the M4. For local author and poet Lynne Rees, the destruction of the village has left an invisible scar on the landscape:

"It's the loss of our history, it's the loss of people's stories, the loss of culture. And that's important. It wasn't just people's houses, it was their social life, it was their neighbours, how they lived and how they worshipped.

"All of that was broken up and the villagers were dispersed elsewhere. And that's the sadness of it. Communities are destroyed for the sake of progress. And when there was an alternative, an option not to do any of that, it makes the story of Groes particularly tragic."

Opposite: Romeo Meli and his family protest against the planned destruction of their home. His daughter Francesca is on the far left.

Overleaf: the stretch of the M4 motorway where Groes used to stand.

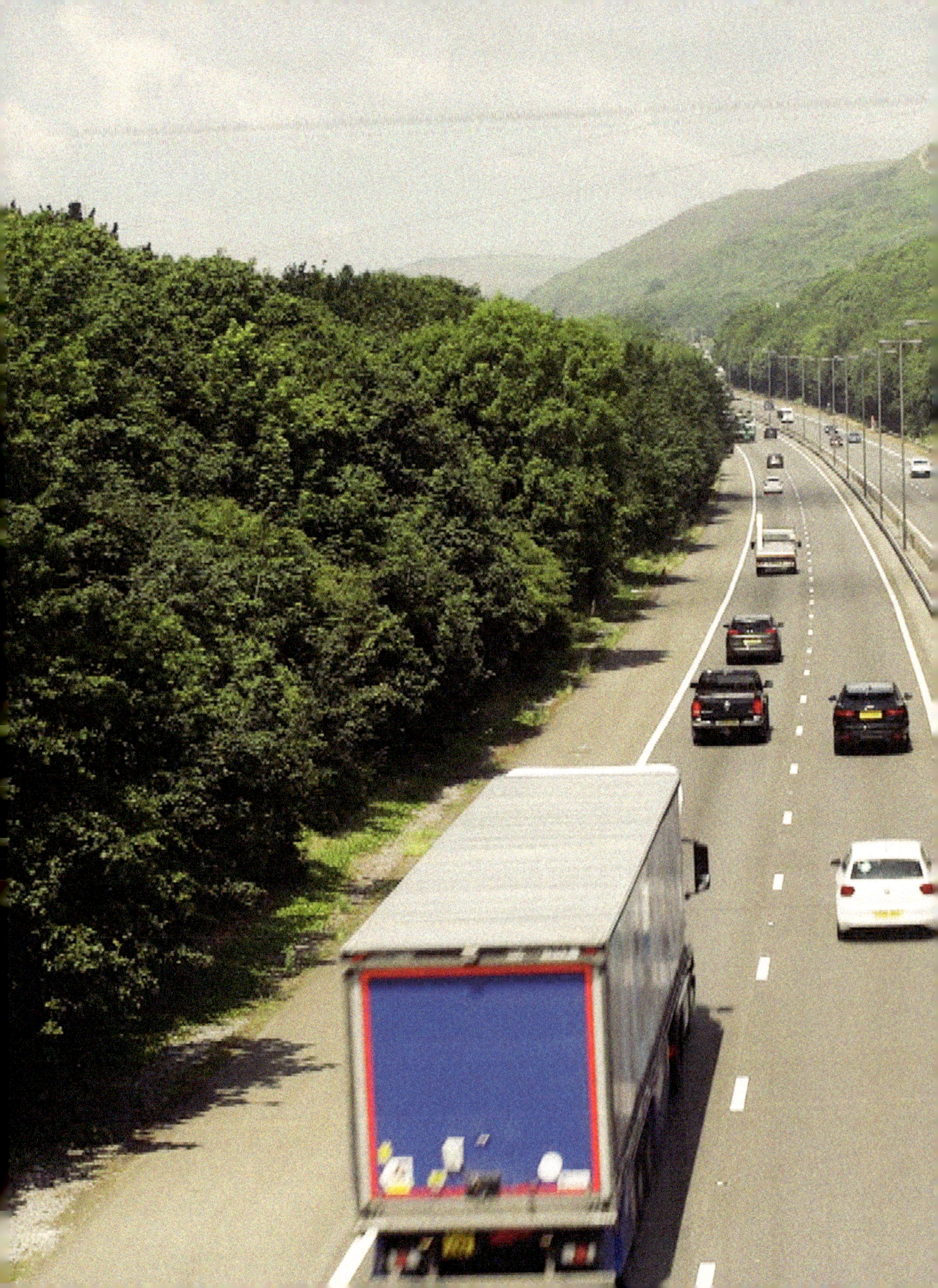

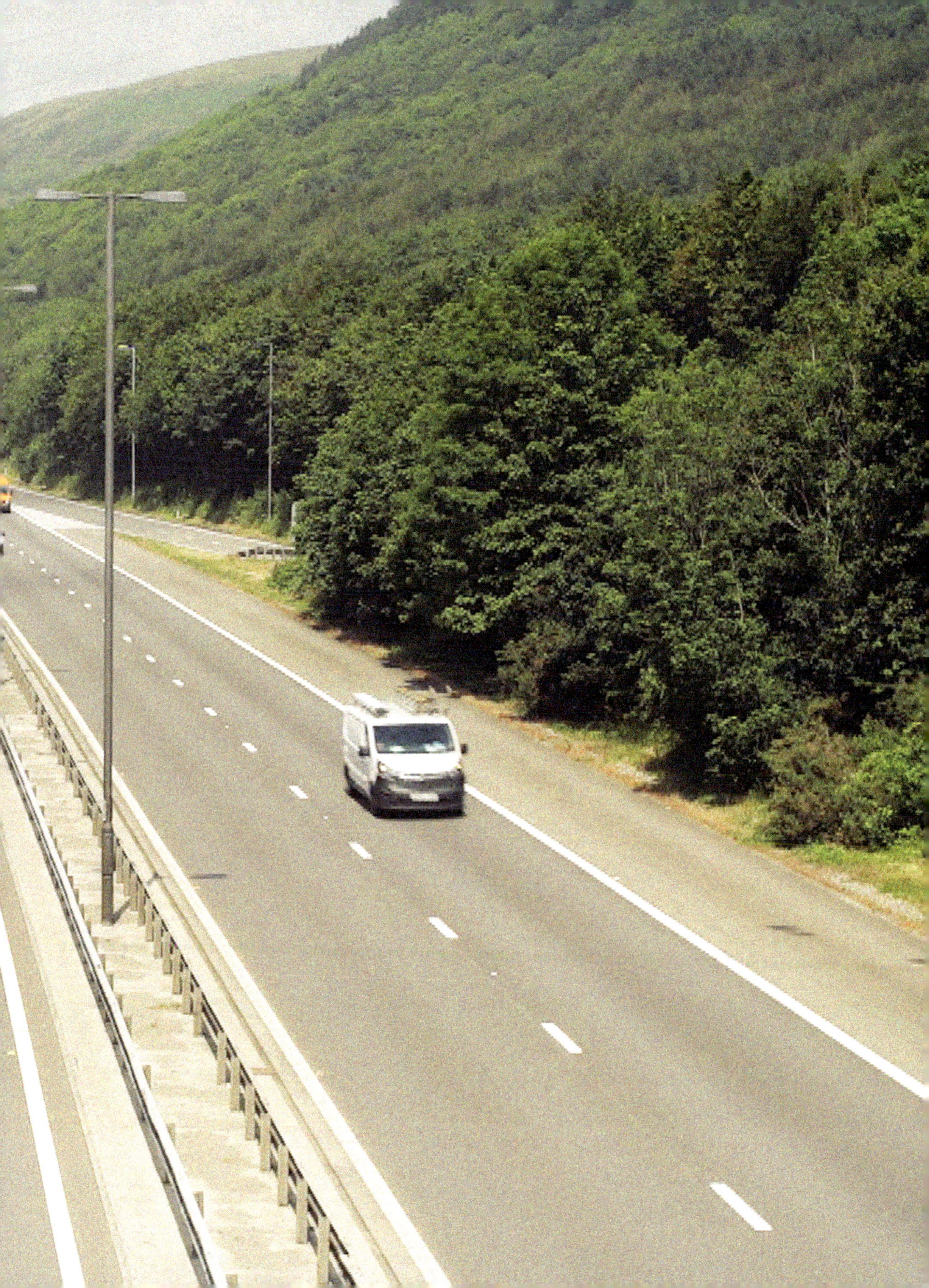

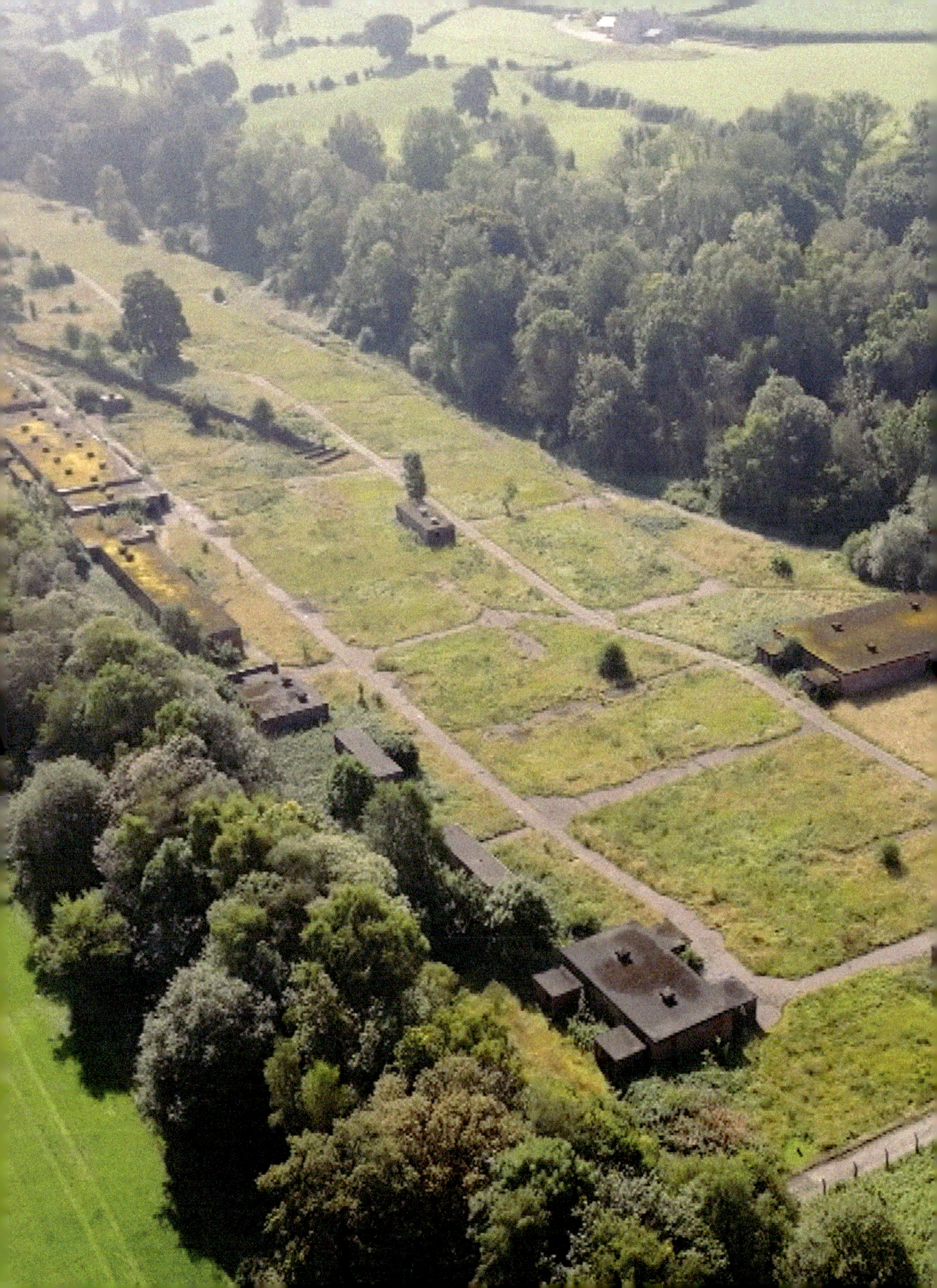

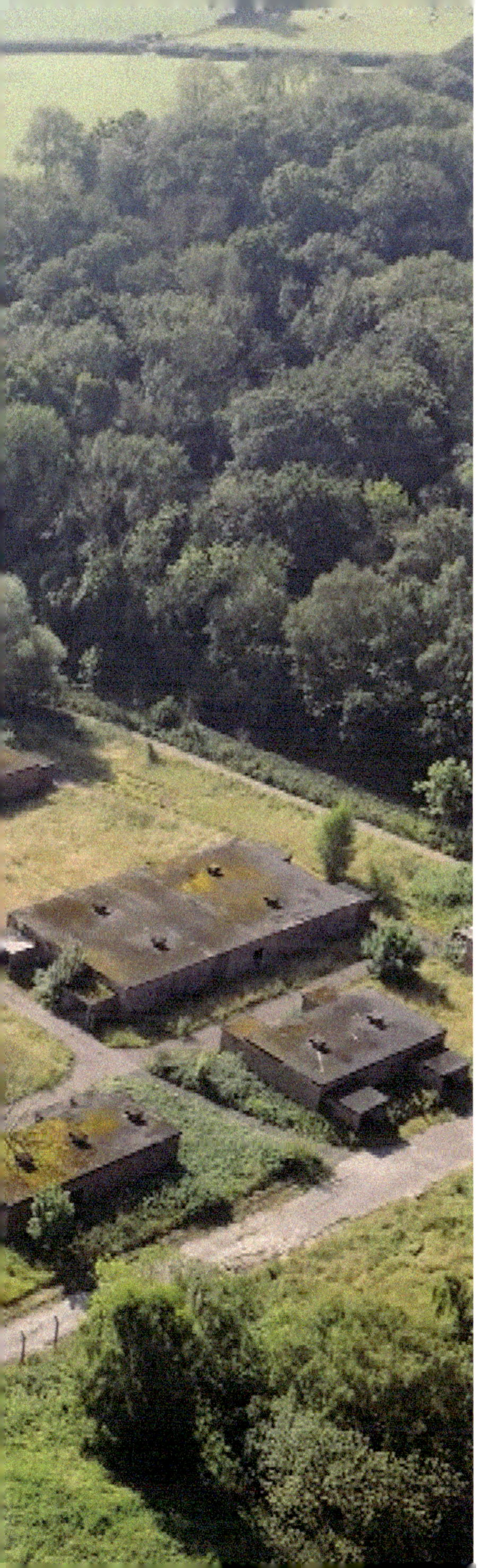

THE VALLEY WORKS

A top-secret site that sparked the atomic age

The quiet Flinshire village of Rhydymwyn, three miles north-west of Mold, boasts a charming Victorian church, a filling station that doubles as a convenience store and a public park with slides and swings for the children. It also has the remains of a vast chemical weapons factory that kindled the annihilation of Hiroshima and Nagasaki.

During World War Two, this secluded corner of the Upper Alyn Valley was selected by the British government for an extraordinary purpose. The remoteness of Rhydymwyn made it perfect for an off-grid, hush-hush project to manufacture and store huge quantities of mustard gas. Germany had deployed chemical warfare against the Allies during the First World War, to devastating effect; this time around, Britain was taking no chances. Astonishingly, and in one of history's mind-bending domino effects, the installation of this weapons factory in North East Wales would lead to the development of the atomic bomb.

That chain of events was initiated in 1939. The Ministry of Supply purchased 87 acres of land in Rhydymwyn and transformed the fields and woodlands into a sprawling factory site with an unassuming appellation: the Valley Works. Approximately one hundred brick and concrete buildings – some the size of football fields – sprung up in distinct zones, where sulphur mustard was produced and processed to fill shells, bombs and grenades. The armaments were then sent by train (the factory had its own railway line) to bases across Britain so they could be flown out of the country at a moment's notice for deployment on the battlefront.

The Valley Works: a site so secret, Nazi Germany was unaware of its existence.

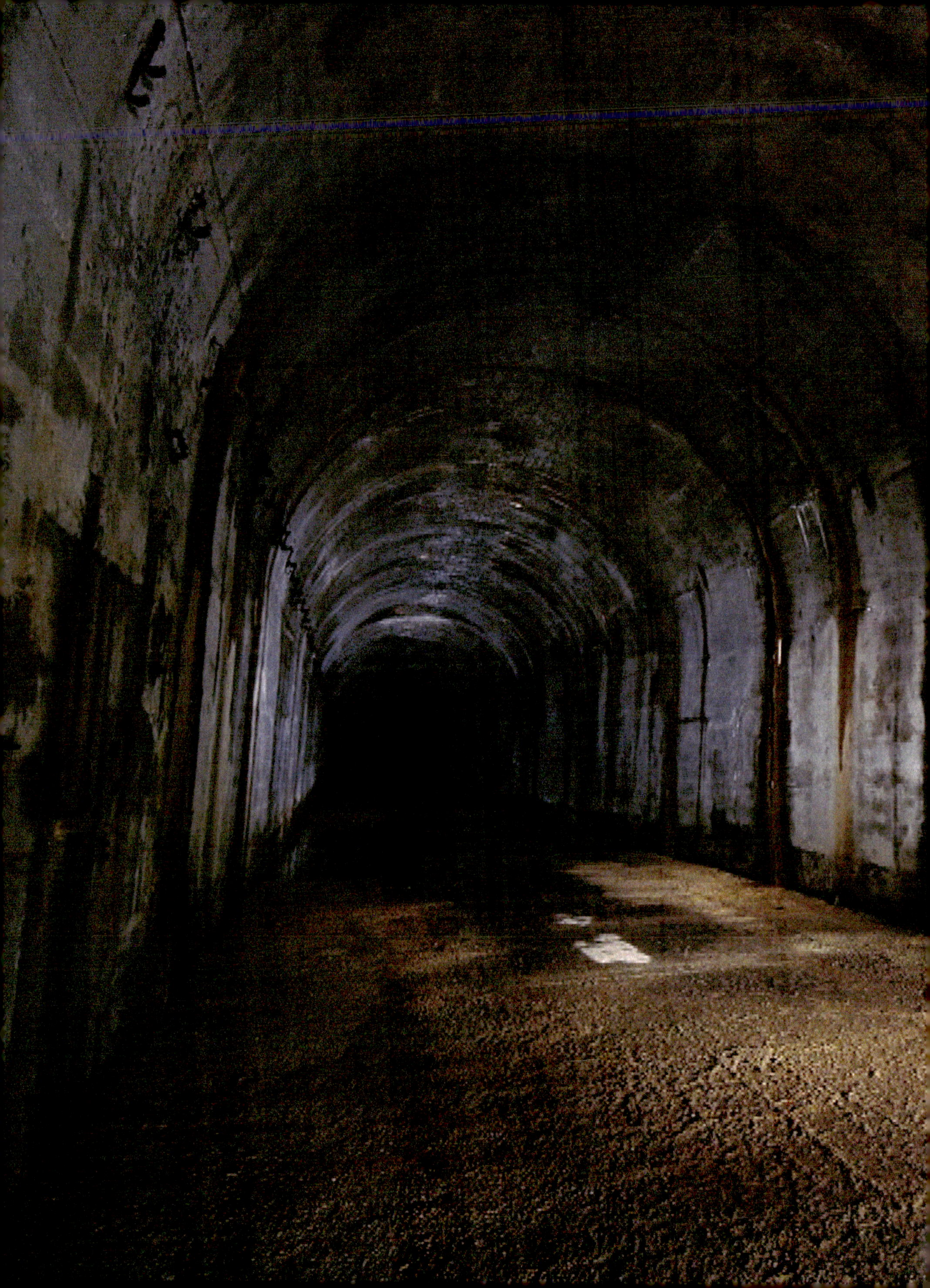

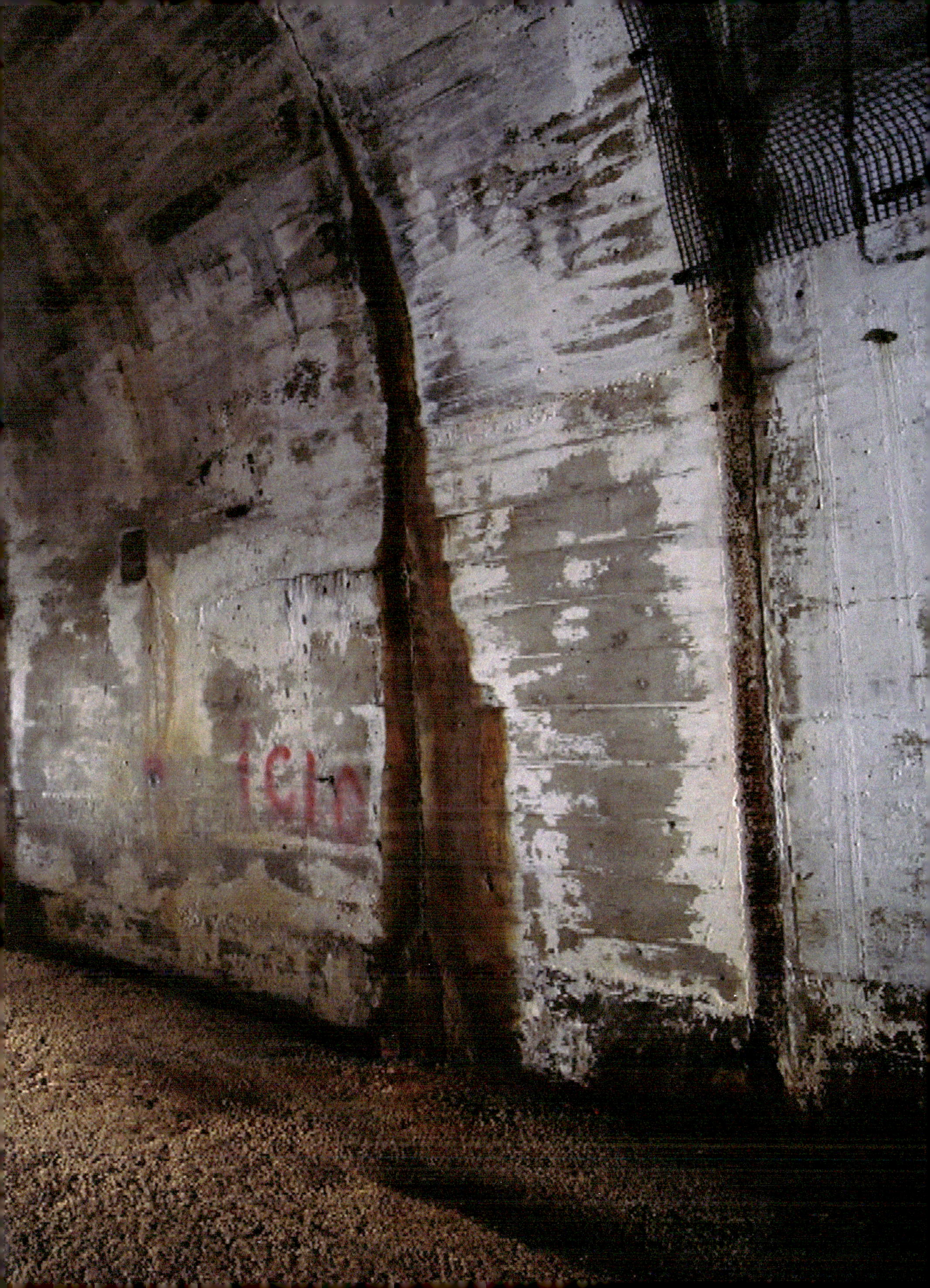

Overleaf: one of the vast tunnels used for the storage of deadly mustard gas.

One striking feature of the factory is undetectable at ground level, and for good reason. Cut deep into the rock of the valley's sloping sides, and possible only after 18 months of back-breaking labour, is a labyrinthine network of underground tunnels. This is where the mustard gas (which has the consistency of an oily liquid at room temperature) was securely stored in bombproof caverns. Three tunnels of 700ft join up with eight connecting passageways to form an immense subterranean grid. At one point in time, a staggering 5,000 tonnes of mustard gas were stored underground in 78 lead-lined tanks.

For the factory's employees, each shift was high-risk. This was dangerous, deadly work and everyone knew it. One slip-up, one moment's lapse in concentration, and it was game over. Mike Malyon, of the Rhydymwyn Valley History Society, has carried out research into the drastic safety measures that were enforced across the site:

"When mustard gas gets on your skin it keeps burning and it will go to the bone; you can't stop it. So when the workers arrived, they had to go into changing rooms, take off all their clothes and wear an all-in-one suit, like the police use today. And then big, thick rubber gloves. But before they put on their gloves, they used to cover both hands in very thick grease – between the fingers, under the nails, everywhere. So if there was a leak, and it got on the glove, it would burn a hole in the rubber; but the grease would give them long enough to quickly get the gloves off before getting burned.

"When the gas tanks and bombs were stored in the tunnels the temperature had to be 42 degrees to stop any condensation forming on the mustard gas shells. You couldn't pick up a metal shell if it was slippery with water. That's why there was a ledge around every one of the tunnels. Those ledges were made by installing 92,000 square metres of steel plates to create a false ceiling. The warm air would travel above it and could be directed down to the specific areas that needed it."

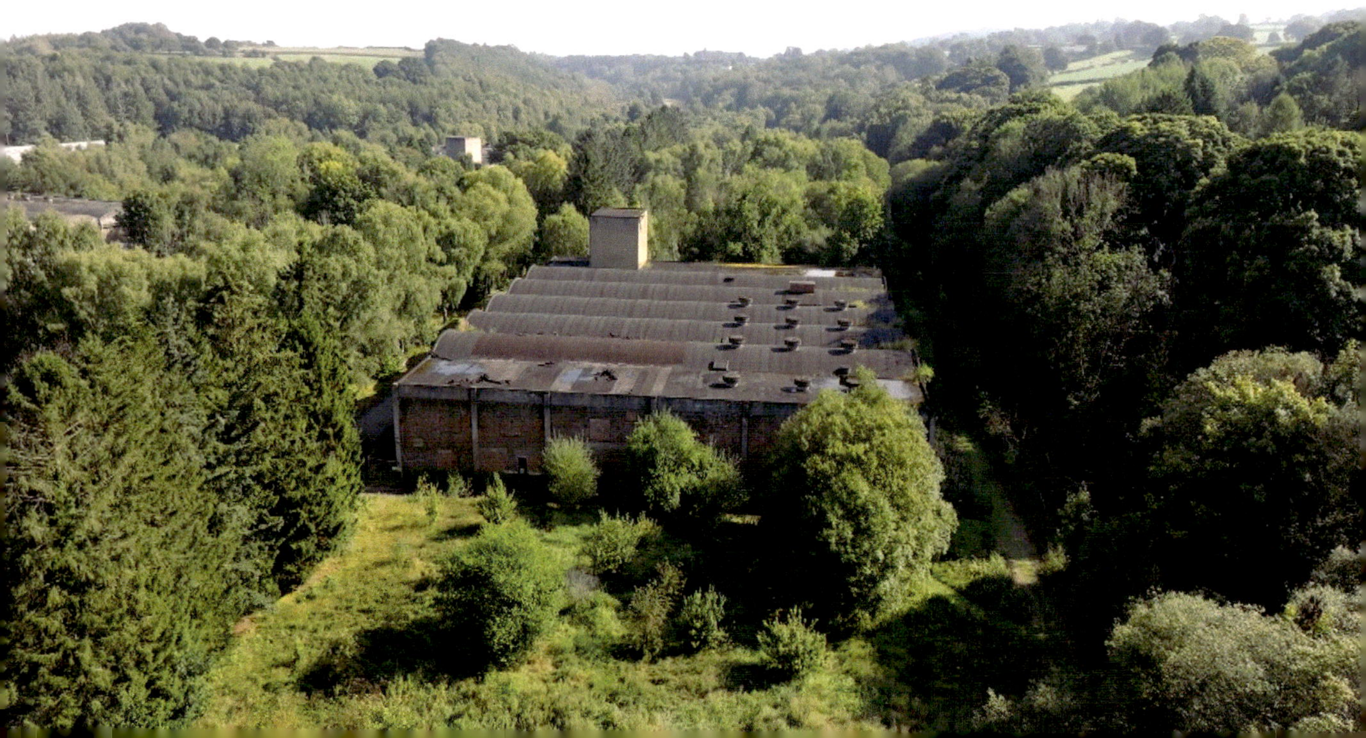

During the dark days of war, the Valley Works escaped unwelcome attention by the Luftwaffe. There were no bombing raids here. The site was so clandestine that Nazi intelligence didn't even know it existed. In peak production, more than 2,000 people worked at the factory and every single one of those employees was sworn to secrecy. Moria Owen's mother, Caroline, travelled to Rhydymwyn every night to fill mustard gas bombs and check the integrity of live ammunition. Incredibly, Moira only learned of her mum's wartime past a great many decades later:

> "She was well into her eighties when she started telling me that at night she used to come to the factory on a bus, like many local ladies used to do, and work a shift. Then, they'd all go back home and the following day they'd stand in the bread queue just like everyone else. It was an absolutely amazing thing to find out all those years later that that's what she did. I was shocked. When I was growing up my mum was a dinner lady! But like a lot of people they didn't talk about it; it was kept very secret. To mum it was a way of combating the threat from Hitler. She accepted it as her war work and felt it was her duty. I will always feel proud that mum made that contribution and was able to talk about it."

In 1941, the factory was chosen for a new assignment, which was to run alongside the daily manufacturing of munitions, using the services of a hand-picked team of specialists from across Britain. The project would be based in P6, a voluminous building at the Valley Works, that happened to be standing empty. Over many months P6's internal layout was modified to accommodate an upgraded power supply, an air conditioning system, a 24ft lift, laboratories, offices and workshops. When preparations were complete, Rhydymwyn received a batch of weighty experimental devices and a contingent of some 70 personnel.

Those devices were gaseous diffusion machines. The personnel were some of the world's greatest scientists, including 10 Nobel Prize laureates. The assignment had been given the code-name Tube Alloys. Its end goal: to develop a nuclear bomb.

During the early years of World War Two, Britain was on the defensive. Its European Allies were falling like ninepins; the US had yet to enter the war. The country's position was perilous. There had already been major breakthroughs in the field of nuclear fission by both British-based scientists (James Chadwick, Rudolf Peierls, Otto Frisch) and their counterparts in Germany (Otto Hahn, Fritz Strassmann).

The MAUD committee, a scientific working group reporting to the British government, was tasked with answering three key questions: is it theoretically possible to develop an atomic device?; would Britain have the necessary resources to actually achieve it?; and could it be accomplished in time to turn the tide of the war? The terrifying alternative would have seen the Allies finishing in second place to Germany's own nuclear weapons programme. The committee's findings hinged upon the radioactive element uranium and its conversion into a power source for a manoeuvrable, deployable weapon of mass destruction. The laws of physics pointed to a positive outcome. However, that working hypothesis required a practical, real-world stress test.

Opposite: Building P6. One of the world's most significant, and least known, military structures.

The authorities settled on Rhydymwyn as the point of convergence. As a covert military complex, the site already had in situ the requisite security, infrastructure and physical capacity for such an audacious venture. Between 1942 and 1943, Building P6 at the Valley Works was the nexus of a scientific trial that would change everything. Colin Barber, Chair of the Rhydymwyn Valley History Society, takes up the story:

> "P6 is one of the most important buildings, not only in this country, not only in Europe, but in the world. Within those walls scientists perfected the first ever attempt to produce, on an industrial scale, the isotope of uranium in sufficient quantities to cause a nuclear explosion. The proof of the achievability and effectiveness of an atomic weapon was established in Rhydymwyn.
>
> "In Britain, at the time, we had some of the most eminent scientists in history and they cooperated on a scale that was unique. This was literally a meeting of the minds. To succeed, they needed to separate an isotope which is a 188th part of an atom. It was the greatest ever feat of engineering – and it had never been done before."

Winston Churchill's wartime government had opened its cheque book to fund the Tube Alloys project. The tests were groundbreaking, a world-first, finally proving the mechanisms for the development of an atomic weapon. There was just one problem: Britain was broke. It simply didn't have the resources to advance the trials to the necessary next level.

In August 1943, Churchill and Franklin D. Roosevelt signed the Quebec Agreement – a pact of collaboration between the UK and the US on all nuclear matters. The innovations and expertise pioneered in Rhydymwyn, along with many of those same scientists, crossed the Atlantic to form the foundations of America's new wave of atomic research: the Manhattan Project.

The ensuing timeline reshaped the modern world. Under Robert Oppenheimer, scientists at Los Alamos Laboratory successfully designed and tested an atomic device. On 6th August 1945, the Enola Gay took to the skies and released the bomb, codenamed 'Little Boy', on the Japanese city of Hiroshima. Three days later, its sister device, 'Fat Man', was unleashed on Nagasaki. Tens of thousands of men, women and children were killed. Nothing would be the same again.

After the war, weapons production at Rhydymwyn was wound down. In the 1950s all the supplies of munitions and mustard gas were removed from the Valley Works and the area was decontaminated. For the next 40 years, the factory served as a general storage depot, still in government ownership. It was finally decommissioned in the 1990s. During the remediation work that followed, many of the original buildings were demolished.

These days, the former chemical weapons facility is a nature reserve. A landscape that was once stark and greyly industrialised now teems with wildlife, home to badgers, bats and birds of prey. You can still spy some abandoned reminders of the factory's past. Several warehouse-sized structures tower high above the treetops. Those labyrinthine tunnels remain intact too, disappearing deep into the hillsides.

A short walk from the entrance gate, standing silently on the edge of a path, you'll find Building P6. It's been granted Grade II listed status in recognition of the role it played during World War Two. Within those walls, all those decades ago, the course of world history was forever changed.

Opposite: silent reminders of Rhydymwyn's wartime past.

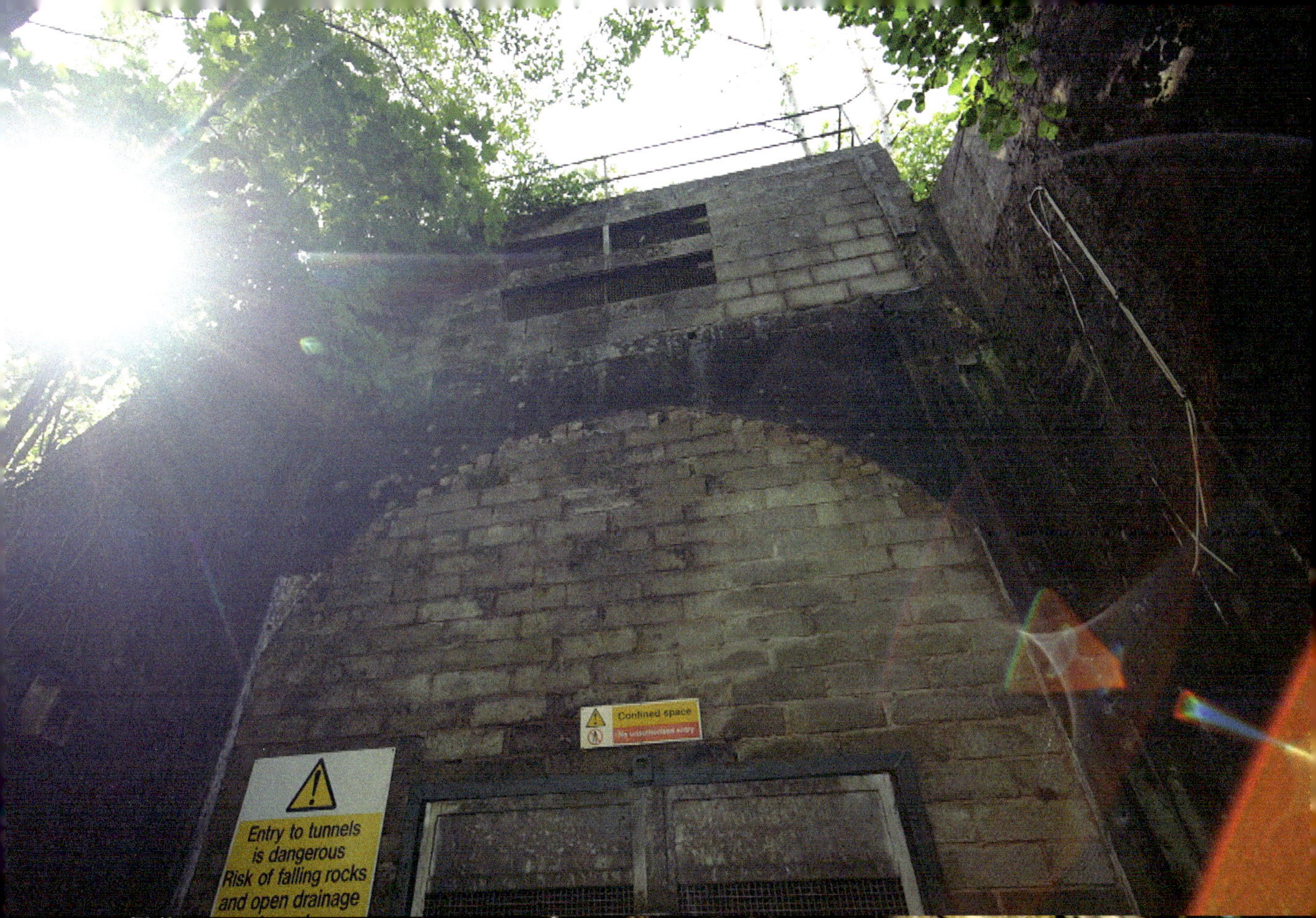
Confined space
Entry to tunnels is dangerous
Risk of falling rocks
and open drainage

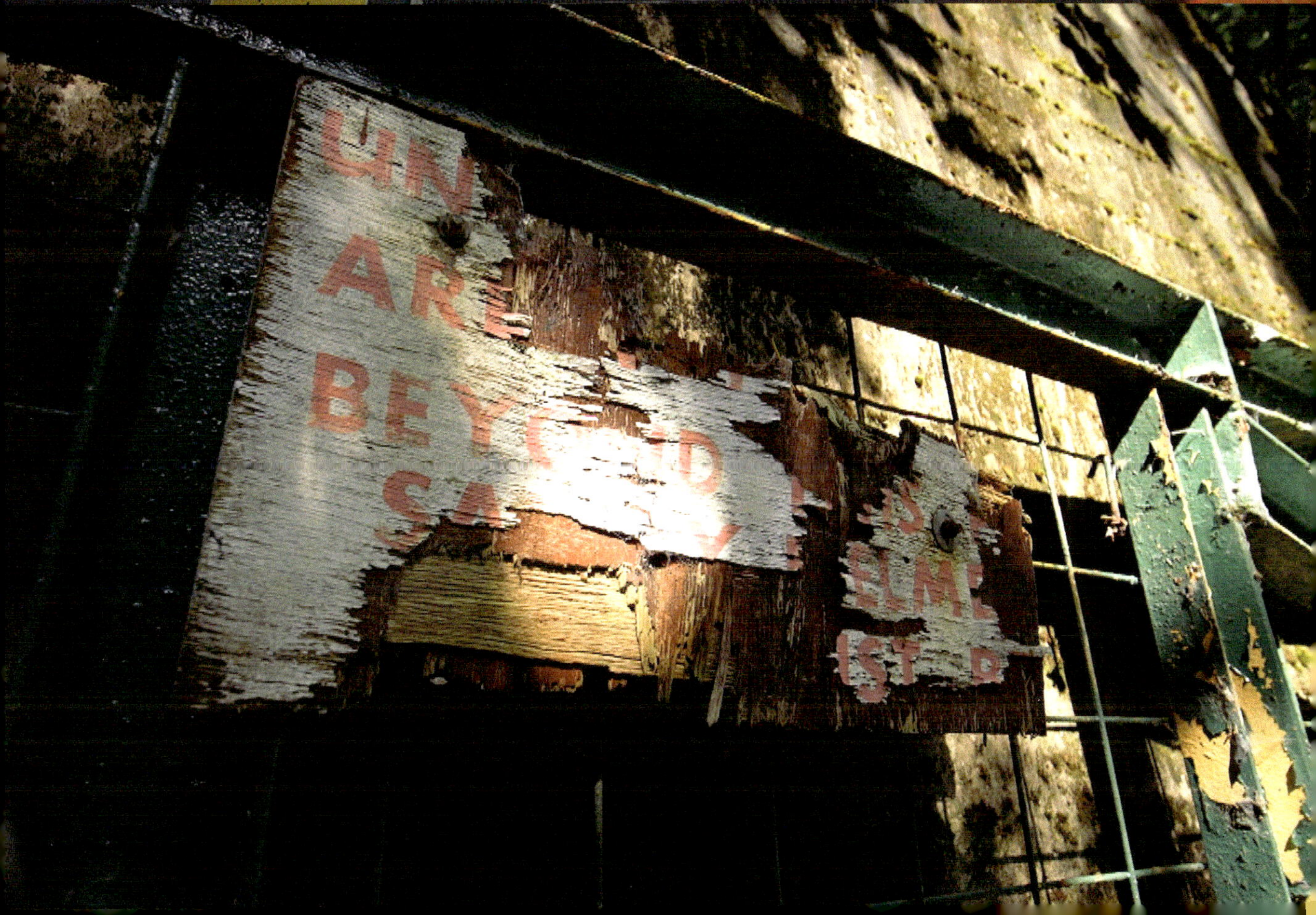

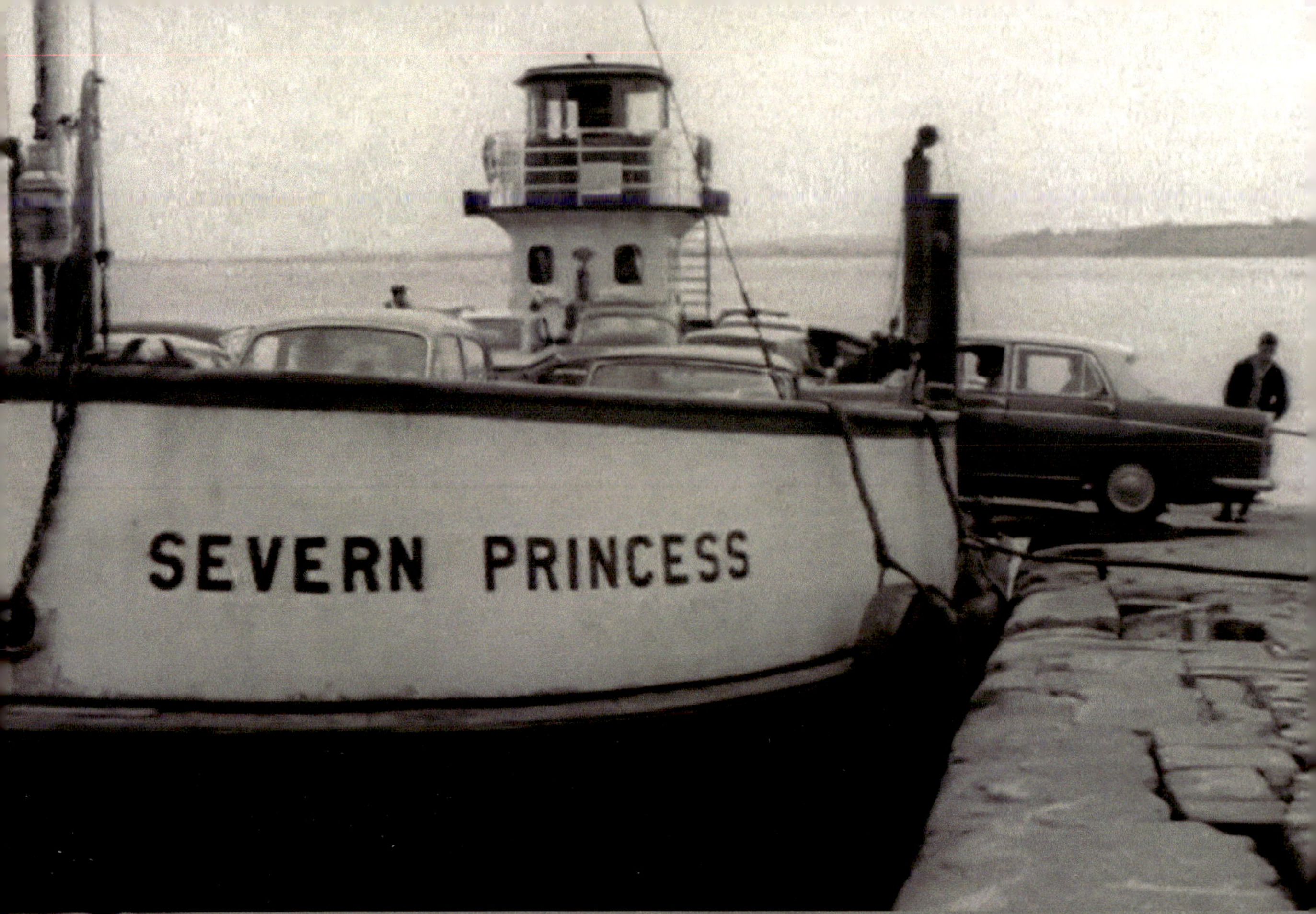
SEVERN PRINCESS
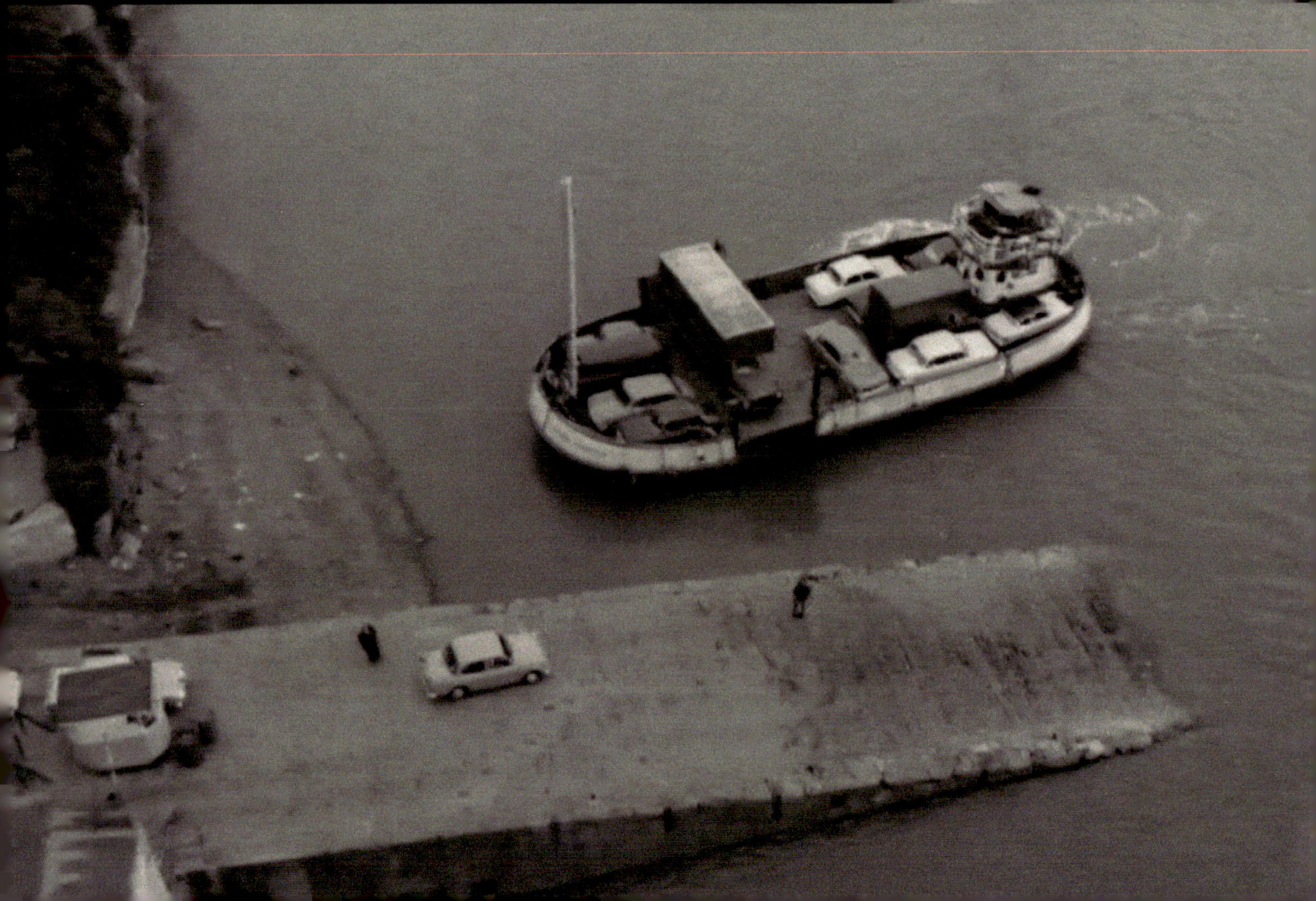

SEVERN FERRY SERVICE

Three regal vessels, one sole survivor

The towering twin bridges that span the river Severn carry tens of thousands of vehicles between Wales and England every day. When the first suspension bridge opened in September 1966, drivers were delighted at the direct, dedicated motorway route that instantly linked the two stretches of coastline. Before the bridge, taking your car across the Severn would have been a markedly different experience. It involved buying a ticket, driving your vehicle along a narrow stone slipway and carefully manoeuvring it – onto a ferry.

Launched in 1926, and running right up until the opening of the bridge, the Severn Ferry Service carried almost seven million passengers during its 40-year working life. The fleet included three vessels that travellers might still remember: the *Severn King*, *Queen* and *Princess*. Each boat had a distinctive turntable that spun the vehicles into position. When all three ferries were in action, the service would run every 20 minutes between Beachley, close to Chepstow and Aust, south Gloucestershire: a 10-minute crossing that spared motorists a lengthy 50-mile detour via Gloucester. The boats could each carry up to 17 cars at a time and they sailed the Severn every day of the year except Christmas Day.

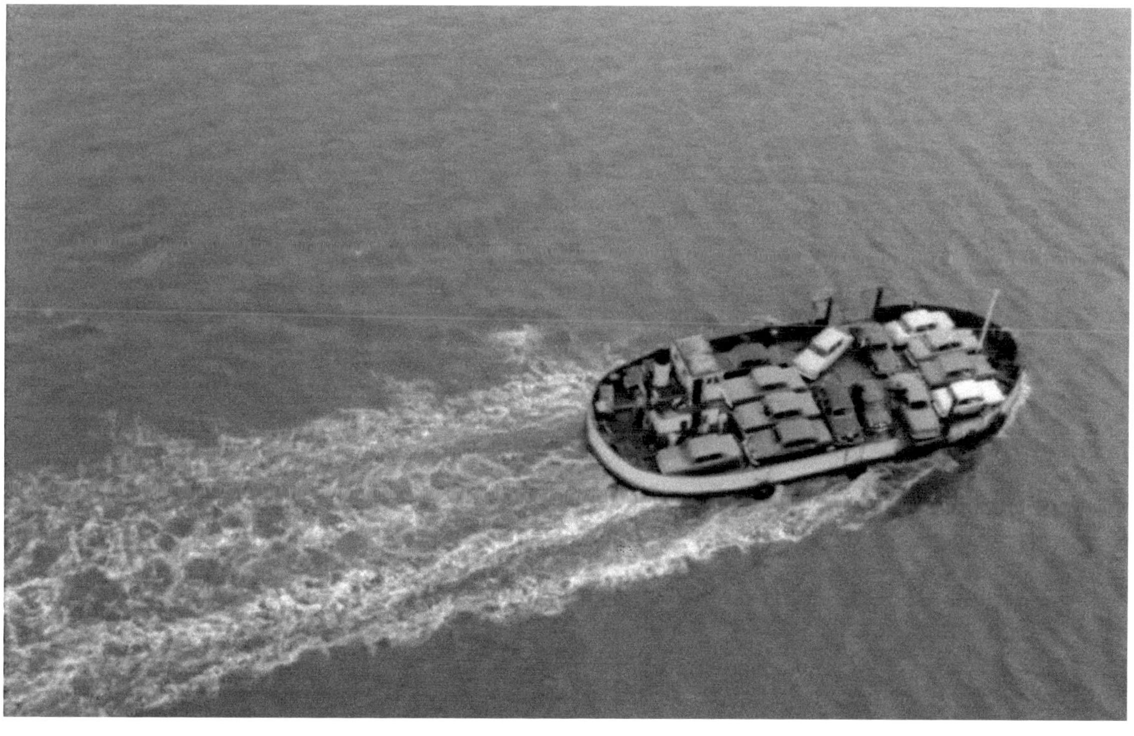

The Severn ferries in full flow during the 1960s.

The ferry service was a family-run business. It began as the brainchild of Enoch Williams from Swansea, a qualified architect who was working for Newport Borough Council at the time. There's a lovely story within the family suggesting that Enoch's desire to establish the service was influenced by difficulties in getting over to Somerset, where his sweetheart Ida lived. In the early days, the boats were limited to foot passengers and a few bicycles. Gradually, as the service became better known and car ownership increased, it became clear that the ferries needed to offer a vehicle transportation service. That meant redesigning the boats. The question was: how? Enoch's grandson, Richard Jones, knows the answer:

"They were trying to work out how they could get all these cars onto a relatively small boat of about 41 feet in length. What they were pondering over was how they could manoeuvre the cars into position. My grandparents made models, they made drawings, and they still couldn't work it out. And then my grandmother, Ida, had a dream. She was a native of the Bath area and she had been taken by her grandfather to the railway station in Bath and had seen engines being rotated on a turntable. And she woke my grandfather up in the middle of the night and said, 'I've got it! A turntable!' So from then on all of the boats had turntables, which allowed the cars to be rotated into position to get as many on as possible – which pleased my grandfather's monetary mind!"

Going for a spin: the ingenious turntable.

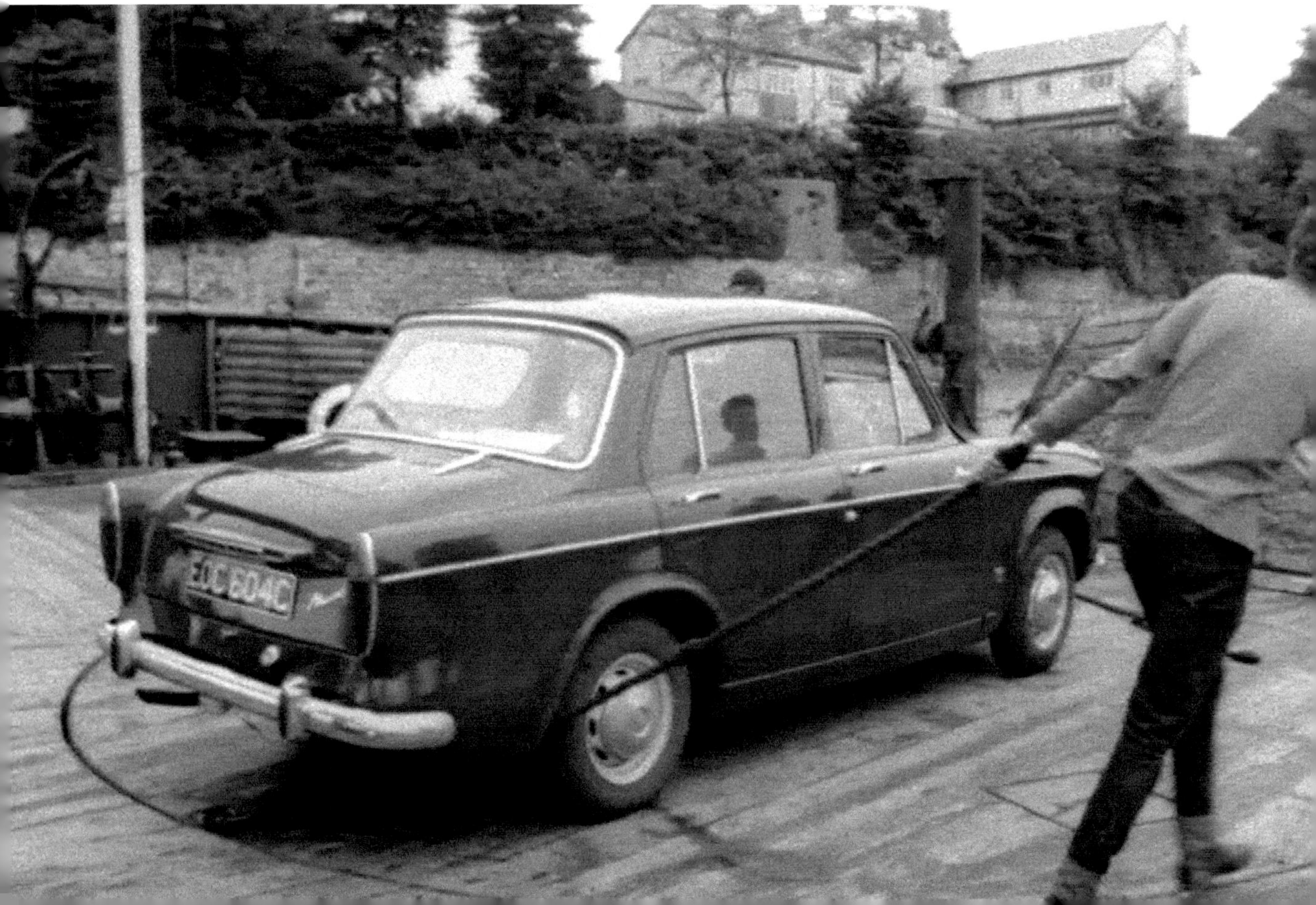

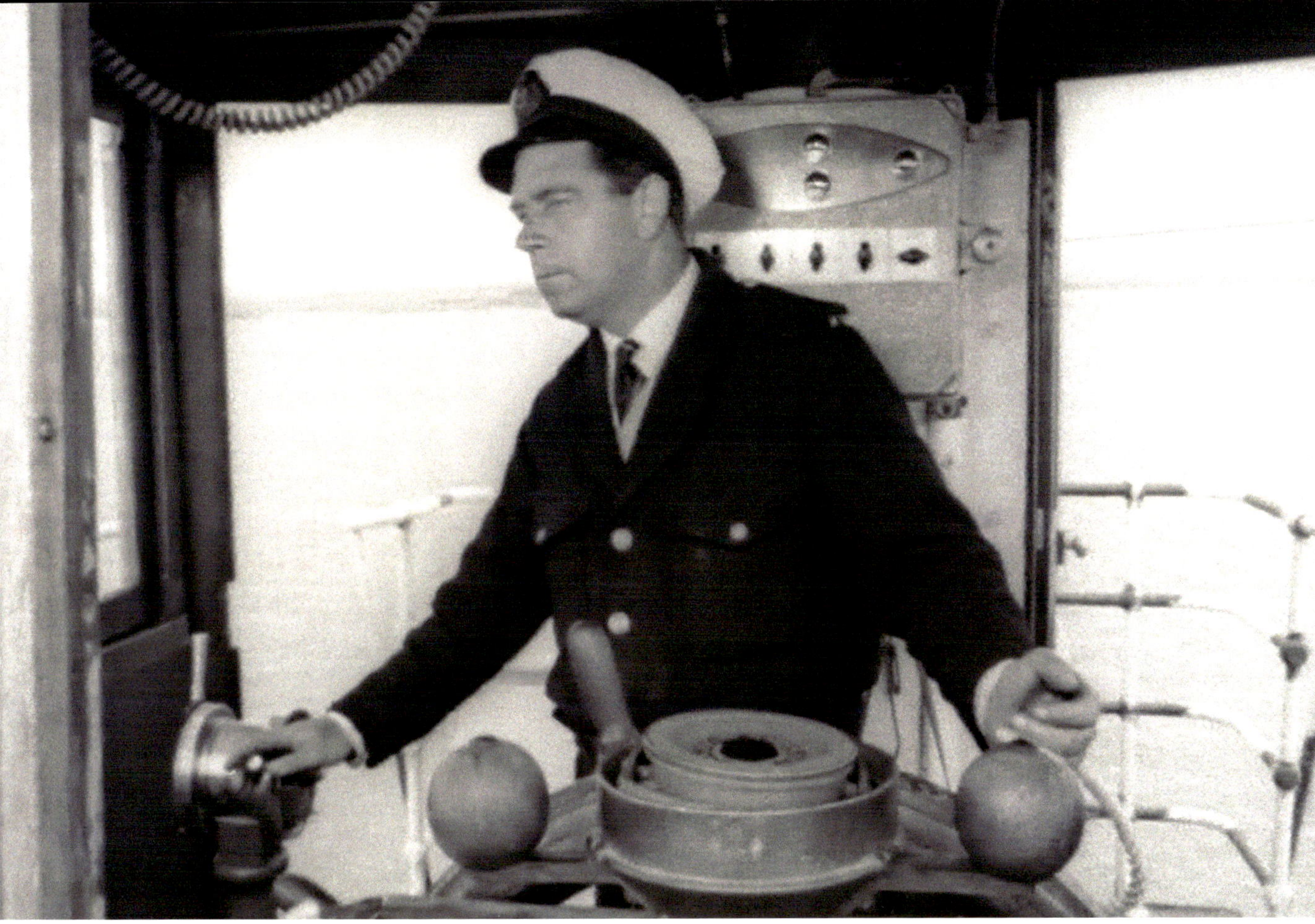

When Richard was a teenager, he inevitably got roped into helping out with the family business:

> "The most difficult part of being a pier boy was tying the boats in. Also, towards the end of the day, there would be a queue of cars all hoping to get across the river before the service ended for the day. And the pier boy – me – had to count the cars waiting to board the boat. When I got to the one that was going to board next, I would tell the driver how lucky he was. And the car behind that...I had to inform the driver that unfortunately he would have to go around Gloucester. And they weren't at all pleased on the many occasions I had to tell them that!
>
> "The ferry service itself was quite an undertaking. The very thought of piloting any craft on the river Severn, which has one of the highest tidal flows in the world, is extremely daunting. The way in which the crew, the skippers, the engineers and the deck hands had to brave all weathers, everything that was thrown at them by this difficult river, was a really remarkable feat. They're all to be admired for it. My grandfather had the idea but he wasn't the one who had to operate the service!"

Of course, Richard and his grandparents were keenly aware that the opening of the bridge in 1966 would signal the end of their family's maritime business. And so it was. The *Severn King*, *Queen* and *Princess* boarded their final passengers just a few hours before the superstructure was inaugurated. When those first cars crossed the bridge, the tradition of a ferry service traversing the Severn – a practice that had dated back centuries – was consigned to the history books.

Above: navigating the unpredictable waters of the Severn Estuary.

The ferry boats were sold on. The *Severn King* sunk; the *Queen* was scrapped. Their sister, the *Princess*, was bought by an Irish company, put to use and then disappeared. For decades, no-one really knew her fate. But take a trip to Chepstow, head towards the tubular Brunel-designed railway bridge and, incredibly, you will find her. She's now moored on dry land near the riverbank in the care of the Severn Princess Preservation Trust. The heritage group was formed by local volunteers with the aim of repairing, restoring and safeguarding the last vestige of the old Severn Ferry Service. How the boat ended up in Chepstow in the first place is a tale worth telling. The Trust's Tim Ryan was part of the rescue effort:

> "In 1999, a friend of ours was in Galway in Ireland and did the Connemara coast. He went to a little fishing village called Kilkieran for lunch, and in the harbour was this big, old, rusting boat. And he thought, 'That's the *Severn Princess*!'
>
> "She was wedged up on the harbour wall, she'd been hit by a massive Atlantic storm and had been abandoned by the owners. So we thought, let's get this thing home. Galway County Council had placed a demolition order on her. They were going to scrap her. Amazingly, we managed to get her out of Kilkieran the day before she was due to be scrapped by the council! So it was a real mad dash.
>
> "We towed her across the Irish sea and that's a story in itself. She got hit halfway across by a five-hour, Force 9 gale. And she was being towed by a tug. She took on heavy water and was sitting lower and lower into the sea. They managed to get her into Swansea Bay but she was sinking. Now, the guy we'd paid to bring her back, he jumped on board this sinking boat with a generator and a pump and pumped out just enough water for her to limp into Swansea. He spent the rest of the day pumping her out and then she made the last leg of the journey up to Chepstow. And as she came under the Severn Bridge, I'll never forget it. We stood on the bridge along with hundreds and hundreds of other people. It was absolutely magical and a huge cheer went up – wow!"

Restoring the *Severn Princess* has been a true labour of love. In recent years the Trust has reinstated the original turntable (which still turns) and tracked down its long-lost anchor. Most significantly, the boat has been included on the National Historic Ships Register, designating her as being of national interest (also on that register are the *Cutty Sark* and SS *Great Britain*). It's unlikely the Severn Princess will ever set sail again; instead, she'll serve as a living museum piece, a precious reminder of the past. For Tim, the boat is a time capsule:

> "What this vessel does is to remind people of a period in the 1950s and '60s when they were young, their families were young; maybe they had their first car, their first opportunity to go to Burnham-on-Sea or Weston-super-Mare. It brings back sweet, lovely memories for a whole generation. It's proper history, people's history."

The Severn Princess: restored and reunited with her original turntable.

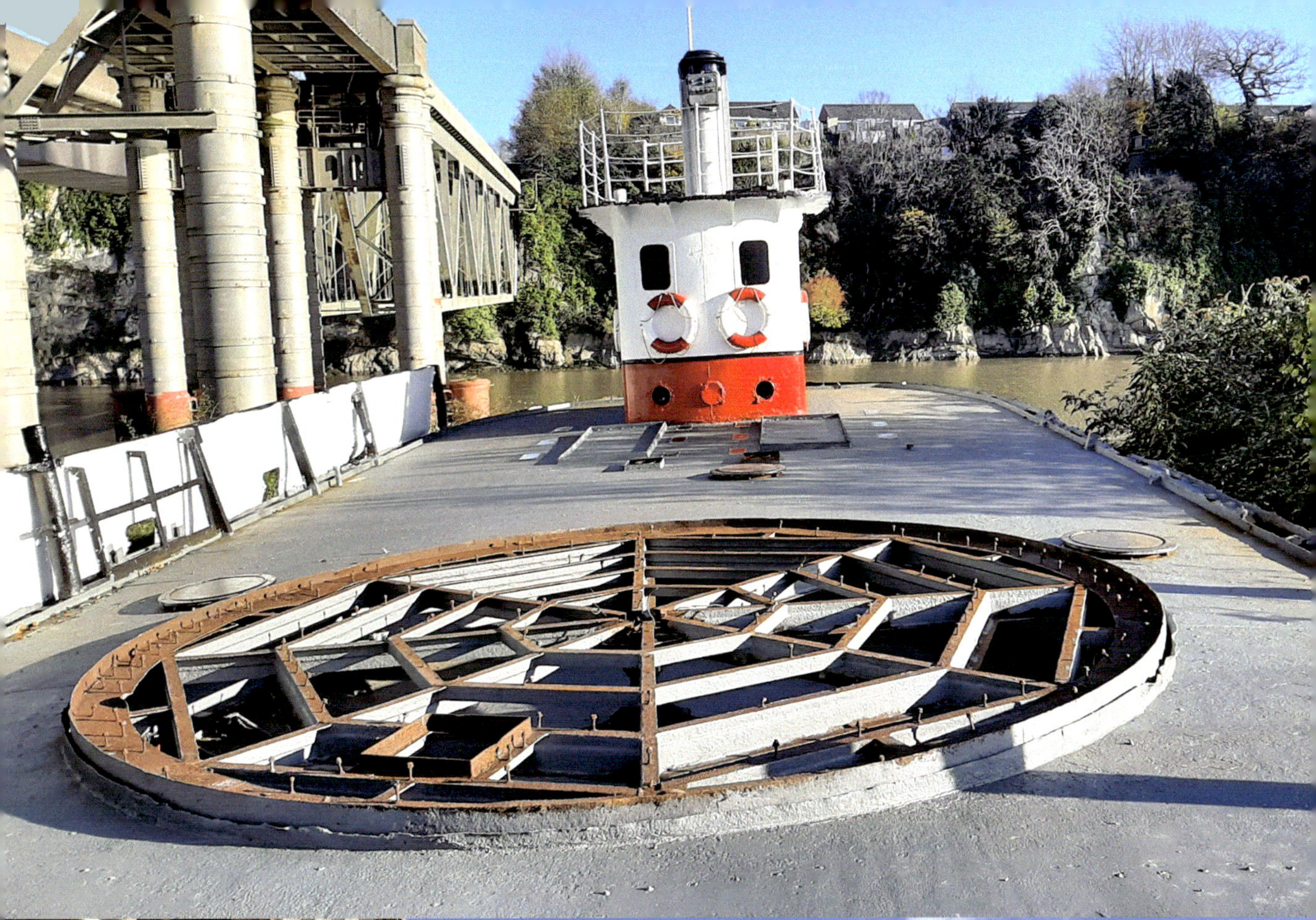

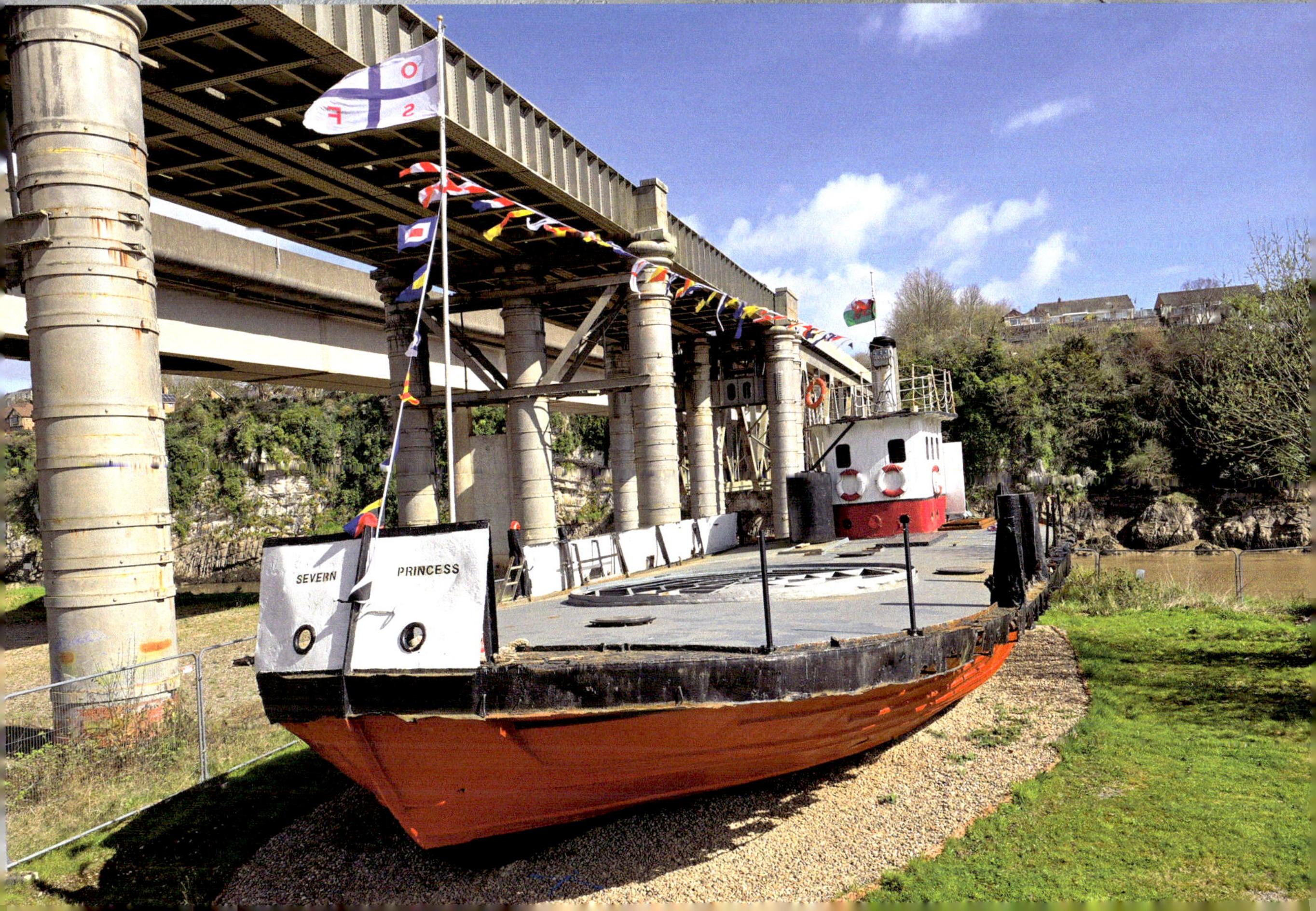
SEVERN
PRINCESS

LOVELL'S CHOCOLATE FACTORY

Newport's empire of sweet treats

On the banks of the river Usk, on a residential street at the northern end of Newport, stands a long, unassuming building. Some sections have been subdivided into business units. Others are empty, with boarded-up windows and stained brickwork overwhelmed by buddleia. There's just one clue that suggests this site had some former significance: a faded, painted sign, high up on one of the corner walls, reading Lovell's.

This building was one of the city's biggest employers for the best part of a century. The products developed within those walls became part and parcel of daily life, a source of delight for customers young and old. Lovell's wasn't involved in the industries you'd typically associate with Newport, like steel or shipping. Lovell's made treacle toffees, fruit jellies, Turkish delight, chocolate raisins, nougat, nut clusters, mints, macaroons, eclairs, creamy rolls, barley sugar, pear drops and fudge.

The family-run business became Wales and the West's biggest confectioner. Its sweets may have been bite-size but its ambitions were whopping! Joan Davis worked there for 20 years:

> "We had an export department and we sold sweets all over the world, to countries like Malta, Greece, Iceland, all over Europe actually. Also to the Middle East, to Oman and Jordan. I remember the Icelandic customers used to love the hard toffees! We had television adverts too, and even a jingle: 'Lovell's are lovely, lovely, lovely, Lovell's are lovely!'"

The sweet smell of success was down to one man: George Frederick Lovell, Wales' very own Willy Wonka. Born in 1862, the son of a sugar boiler, he started with a small shop in Newport selling homemade toffee. Business boomed and in the closing years of the 19th century he unveiled Rexville: his huge confectionery complex. As well as the factory, Lovell's eventually owned a string of sweet shops and cafes, a second production site in Manchester, and wholesale depots in London, Liverpool, Swansea, Pontypridd, and Wrexham.

G.F. Lovell earned the nickname 'The Toffee King' after creating his famous, long running line of super-chewy sweets, Toffee Rex. Another popular product was the Milky Lunch bar, a concoction of nougat and crispy rice smothered in chocolate. The company's adverts proclaimed: 'The sort of sweets people taste once and come back for again and again.' And they did, in their droves.

The original factory sign: faded but still visible.

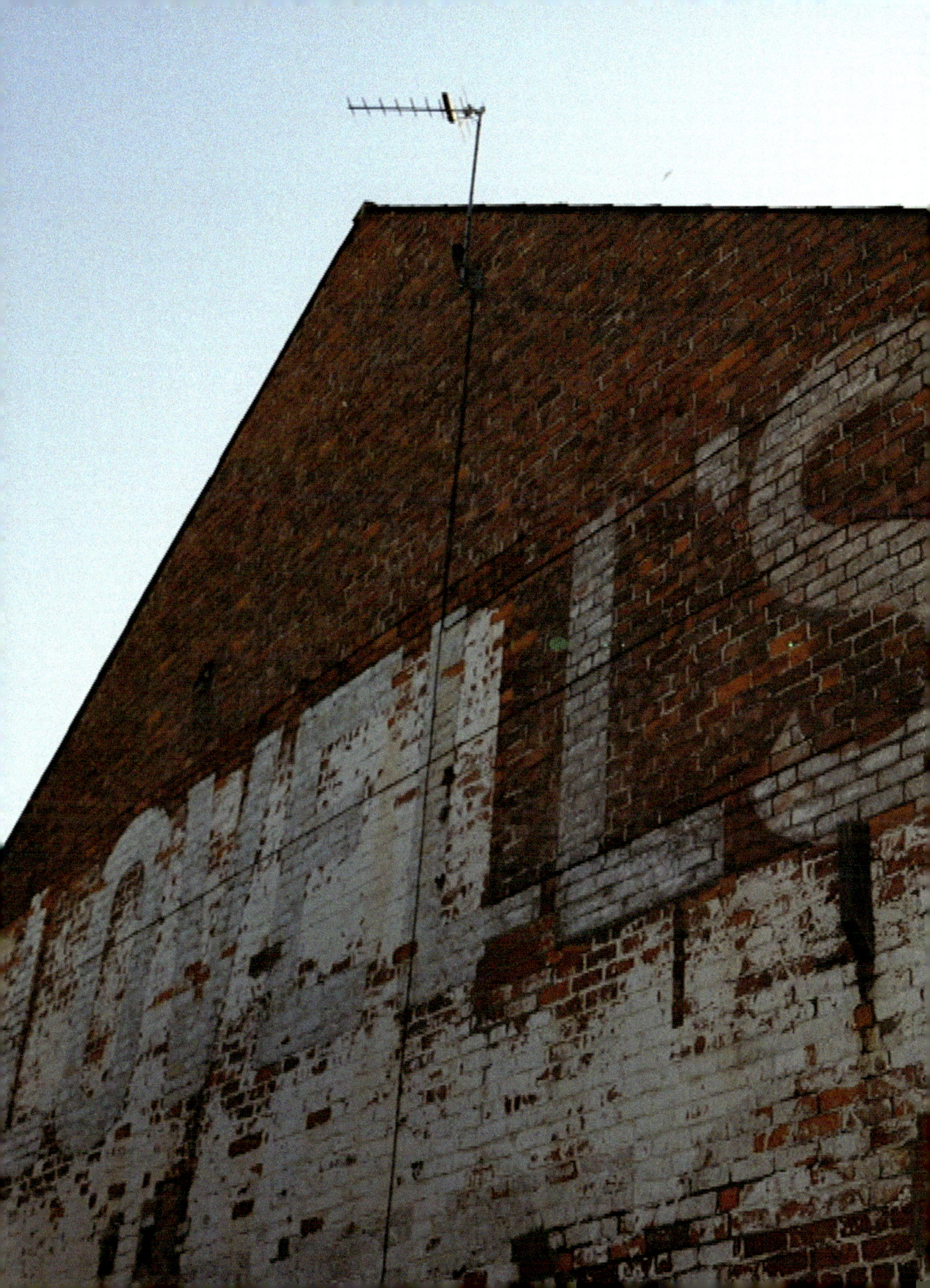

G.F. Lovell died in 1949 but his family kept the company moving forward. One of its longest serving employees is Gwyneth Owen, who worked at Lovell's for an incredible 55 years, starting when she was just 15 years old:

"On my first day at the factory I was waiting at the clocking-in area with the rest of the girls as they were heading into their department, the nougat room. I was at the clock when a young man appeared and one of the girls said, 'What are we doing today then Billy?' and he said 'We're doing French.' Immediately, I squirmed. I didn't learn French at school. But he meant French nougat!

"The chocolatiers were so clever. And the chocolate itself was good quality. All the confectionery was done by hand. When I was 16, I was allowed to go on a knife and cut the Milky Lunches. Then I moved to the packing department doing fruit jellies. Eventually I progressed to being a supervisor and I ran the factory shop as well.

"Lovell's was my life. I actually had my wedding reception in the Lovell's cafe on the high street. I pass the old factory building quite often and I look at it and reminisce. I've got some lovely memories."

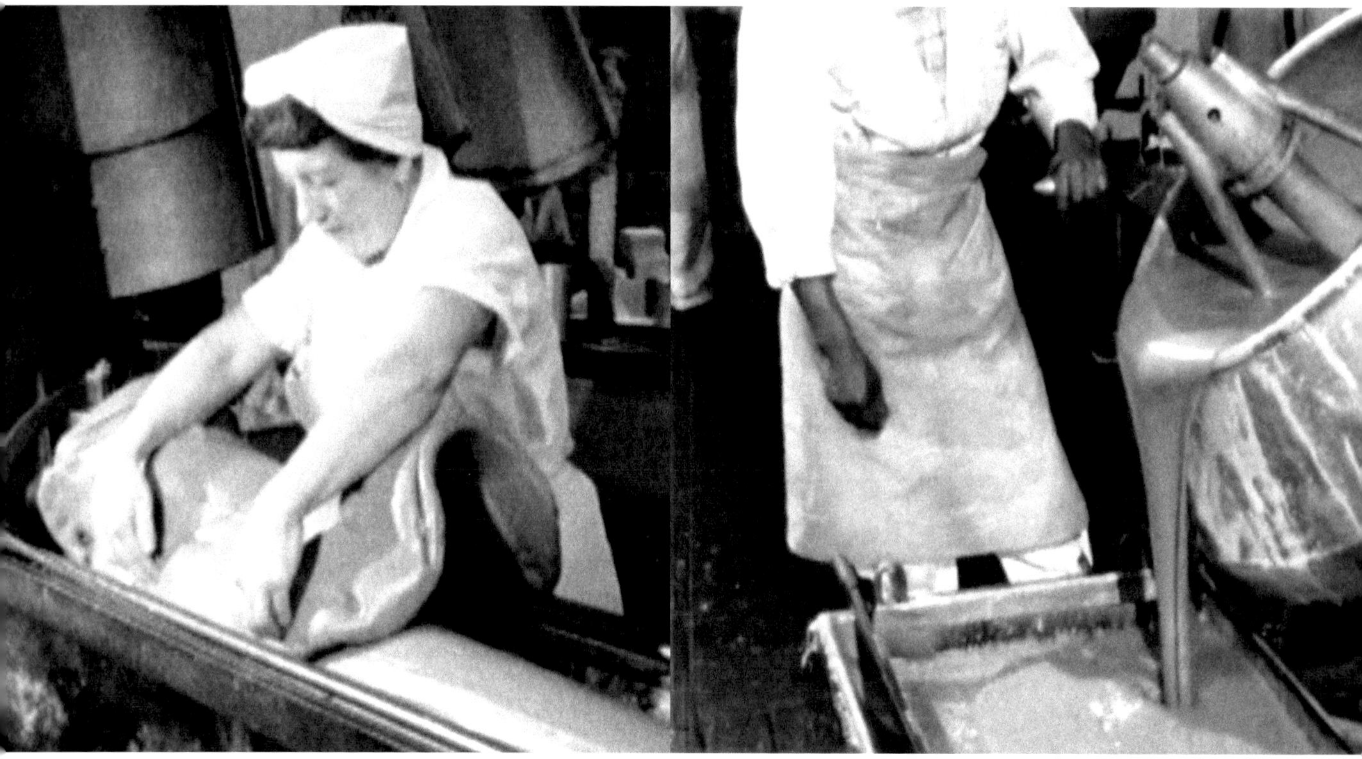

Sweet memories: creating confectionery in the Lovell's factory, 1964.

In its sugar rush days, Newport's chocolate dominion employed 700 people in the city (and just as many across its other sites). It wasn't uncommon for parents to work on the factory floor alongside their children. As a general rule you could get onto the payroll thanks to a good word from your aunt or uncle, sibling or cousin, who'd probably end up working next to you on your first day on the job. Brian Woolley has a very special connection with the confectionery company. His family home stood directly opposite the Lovell's factory, where his father was the foreman:

"My dad's office was literally 20 yards away from where we lived, so he could never be late for work! In the evenings he would come home from the factory and as kids we'd rush up to him and he'd pat his pockets and take out some sweets for us.

"I always remember they had these great big vats of chocolate, one milk, one plain. And when they'd cooled it down over the weekend there would be a tap and there'd be a great big stalactite of chocolate; one big spike coming down. So I'd immediately run up and snap that off and you'd have one milk chocolate treat and one plain chocolate."

Lovell's sweet tins were known for their eye-catching designs.

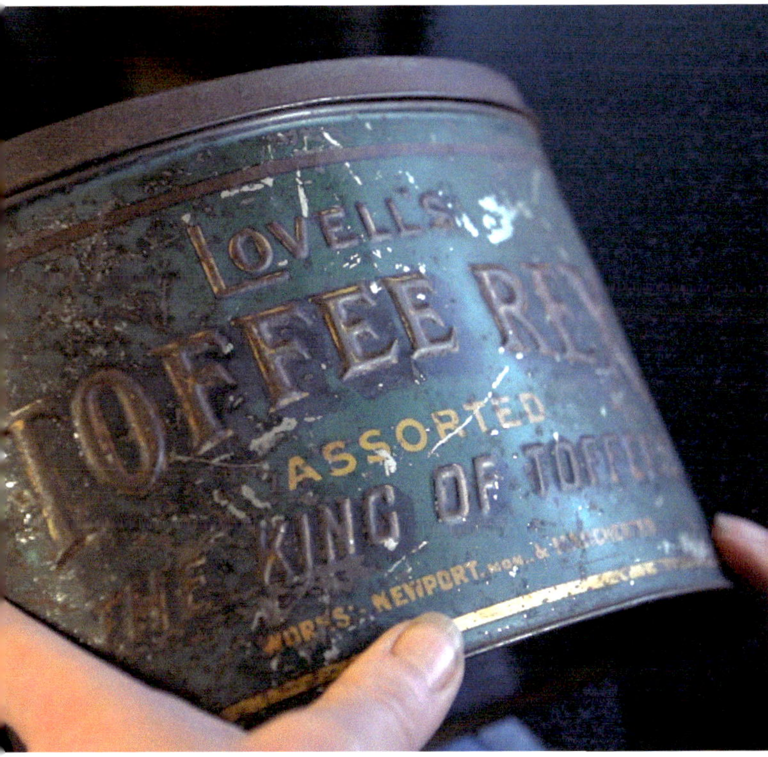

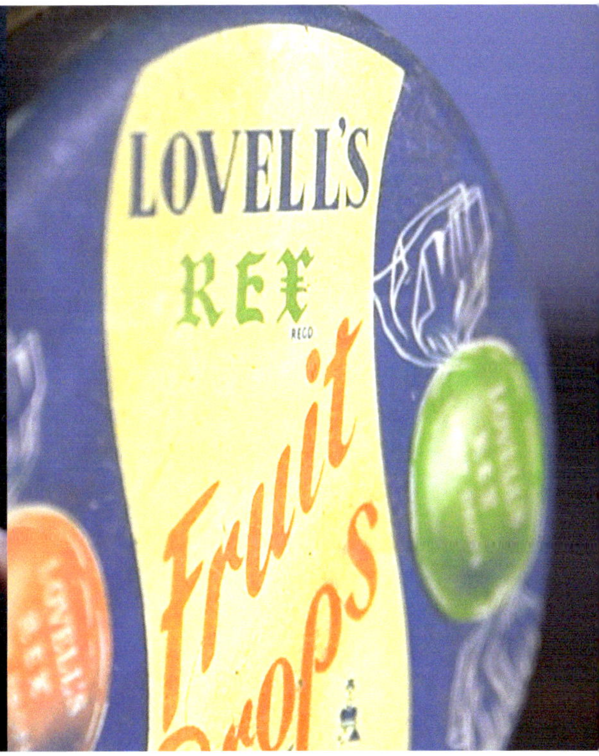

The Rexville factory had a lively social scene which was enthusiastically encouraged by Lovell's. There would be dances every Saturday at the social club and the company even constructed a sports complex for its staff, including tennis courts, bowling greens and a football pitch (the well-known works team, Lovell's Athletic F.C, played from 1918 to 1969 and became Welsh Cup winners).

If you didn't fancy getting fit outside working hours, the daily shifts on the factory floor kept you in shape. Karen Pardoe joined the company in the 1970s and still remembers those 40-hour weeks:

> "It was hard work. You were lifting a lot of heavy stuff like 40lb slabs of toffee and fudge. Or they'd send us down to the sugar rooms – you're talking about 60lb bags of sugar – and they'd say, 'Right, we need ten of them'. You didn't need a gym. All the weight training we needed was in the factory!
>
> "The men did the recipes, the cooking and the boiling. But the girls outnumbered the boys so we were in charge! There'd be flour fights and sometimes people would get chucked in the nougat for a joke.
>
> "When you first started working there you thought, great, I've got all these sweets to choose from – and you could eat as many as you liked. But after a while it did get sickly. And if you were coming into work after a night out on the town, you really didn't want to smell sweets, I can assure you!"

Lovell's had dominated the confectionery market for generations. But during the 1980s and 90s the chocolate empire began to crumble. A wave of buyouts, takeovers and restructuring led to the eventual closure of Newport's Rexville factory. The shops and cafes gradually ceased trading and the company's recreation ground was sold off for redevelopment (it later became a housing estate called The Turnstiles). Little by little, Lovell's products disappeared from the shelves of our sweetshops and supermarkets. A homegrown industry melted away.

No more Milky Lunch, no more Toffee Rex. Just a faded ghost sign on an old factory wall.

Lovell's famous Toffee Rex:
gone but not forgotten.

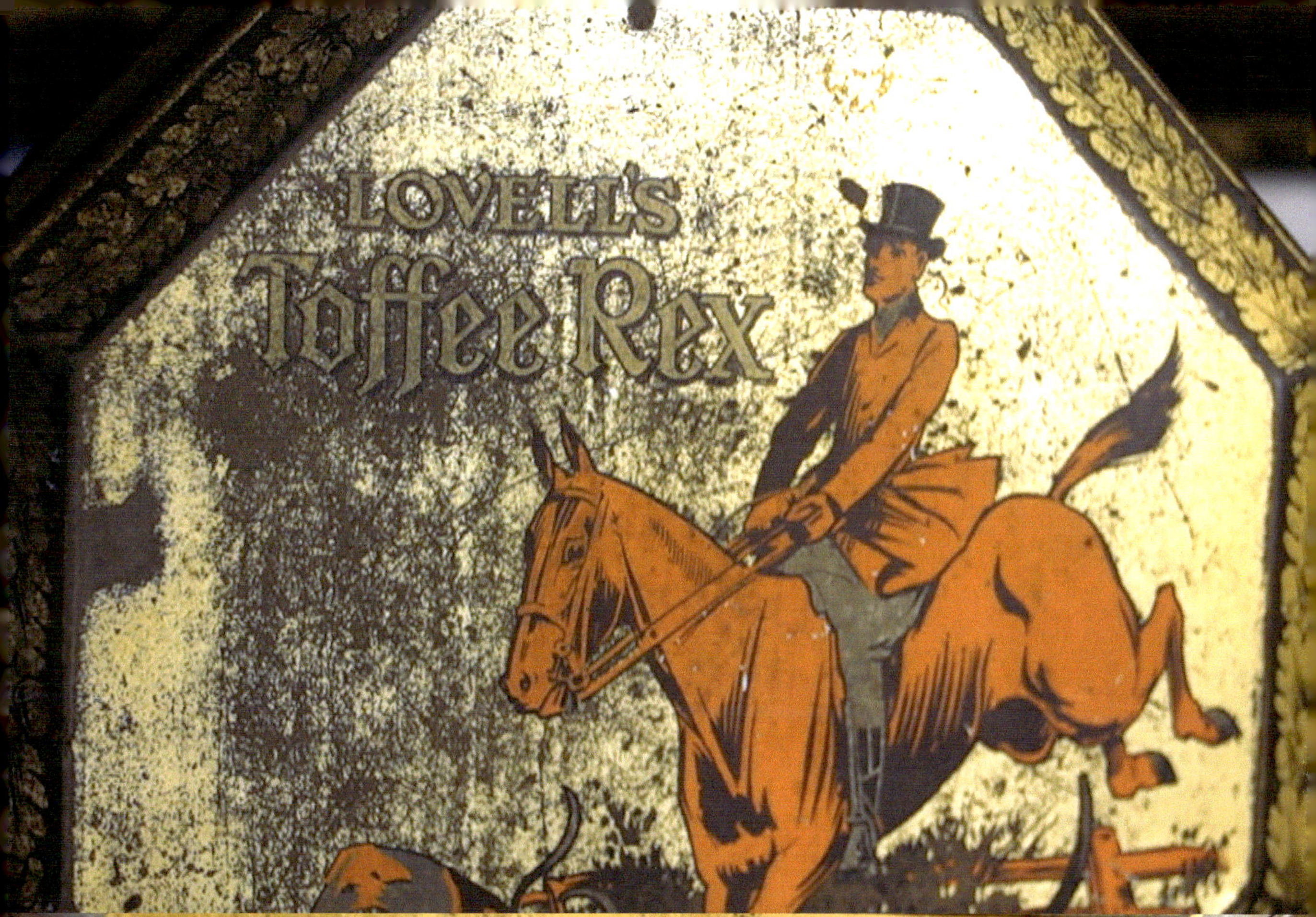
LOVELL'S
Toffee Rex

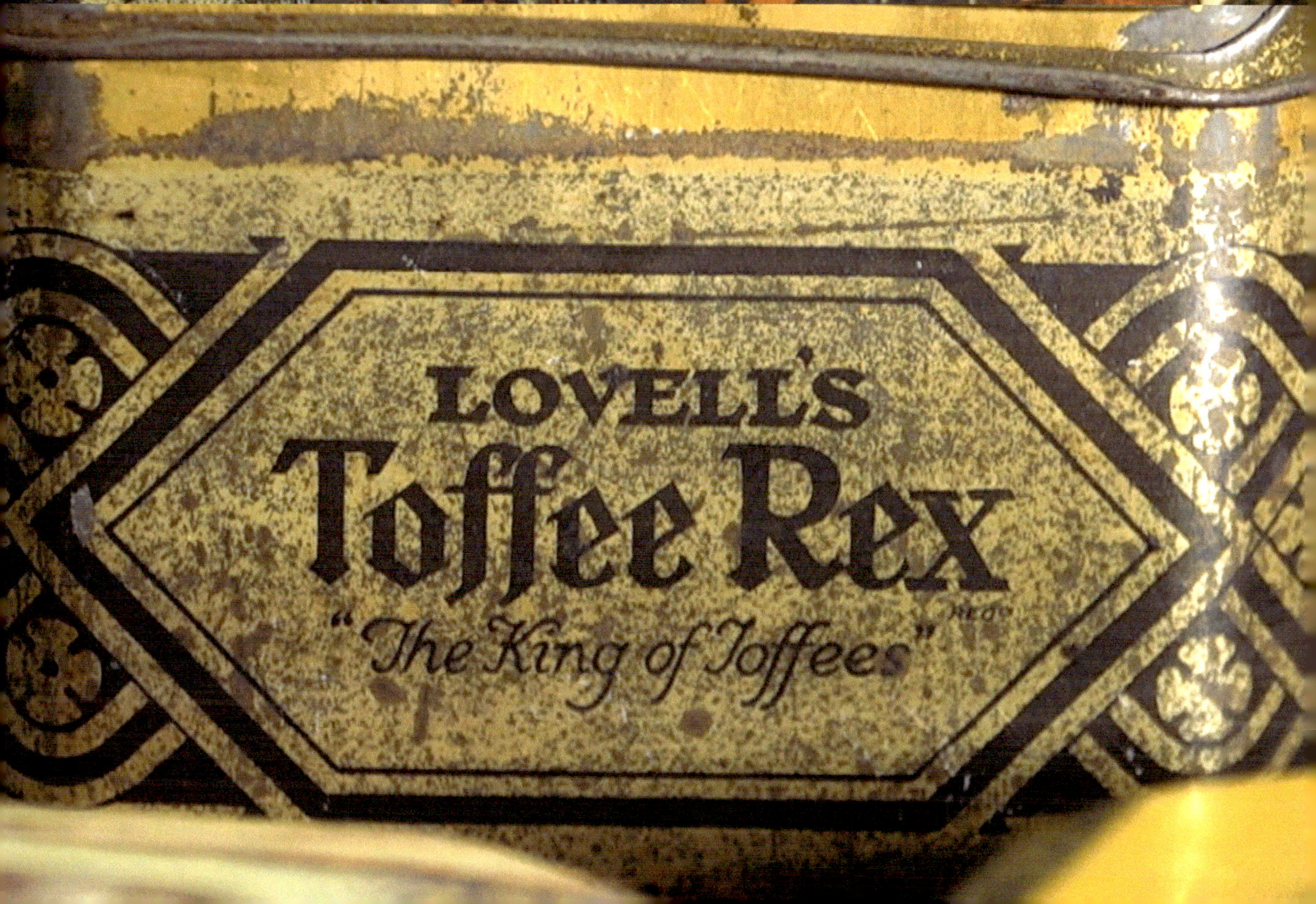
LOVELL'S
Toffee Rex
"The King of Toffees"

TROEDRHIWFUWCH

The mining village and its moving mountain

Drive along the A469 between New Tredegar and Pontlottyn in the Rhymney Valley and you'll pass vast tracts of open countryside. It feels like the landscape has forever been this way. But it hasn't.

From the road you'll barely notice the rusted iron railings and old stone walls standing silently in the fields. Up until the 1980s this corner of Caerphilly county was home to a vibrant village. 600 people once lived there. You'd find churches, pubs, and a large infant school. There was a shop and a post office, a farm and a library. On either side of the road, advancing onto the steep mountainsides, were row upon row of tightly packed terraced houses.

The village was called Troedrhiwfuwch. Its English translation evokes a rustic way of life when animals would graze at 'the foot of a cow's slope.' In truth, the settlement was born out of industry. During the 1850s, moneymen fixed their sights on the area for commercial development, for coal and quarrying. Houses were built to accommodate the workers and their families, and as local mining operations expanded so did the village. The following decades saw the opening of a Baptist chapel and St Teilo's Church for religious fulfilment, and the Troedrhiwfuwch Arms and the Rising Sun Inn for nourishment of a more fermented kind.

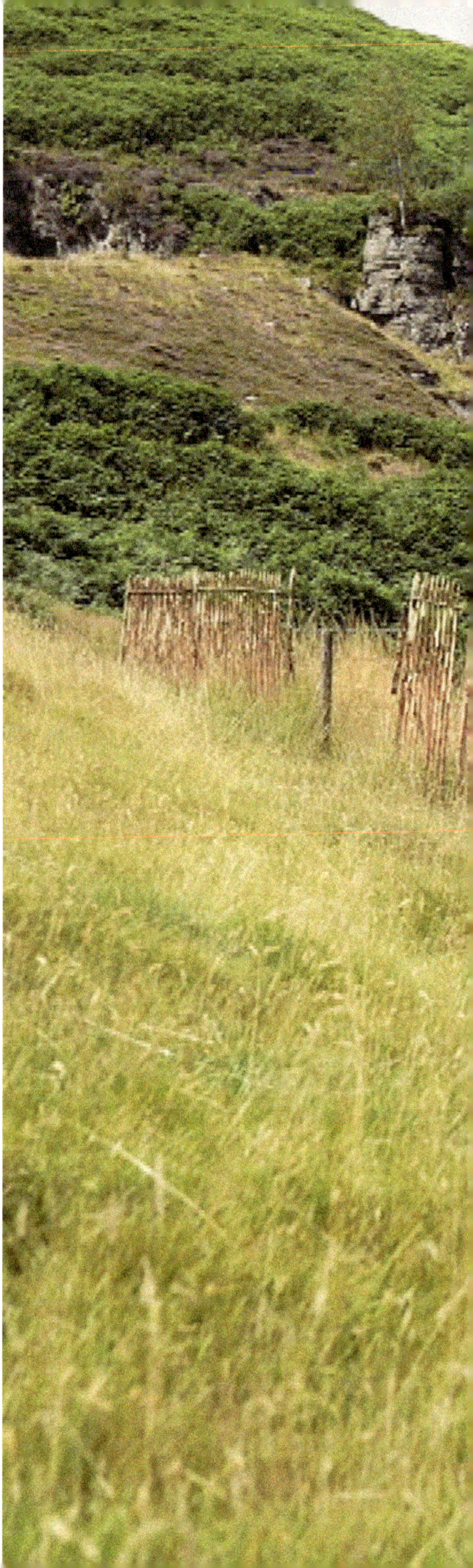

The vestiges of the lost village of Troedrhiwfuwch.

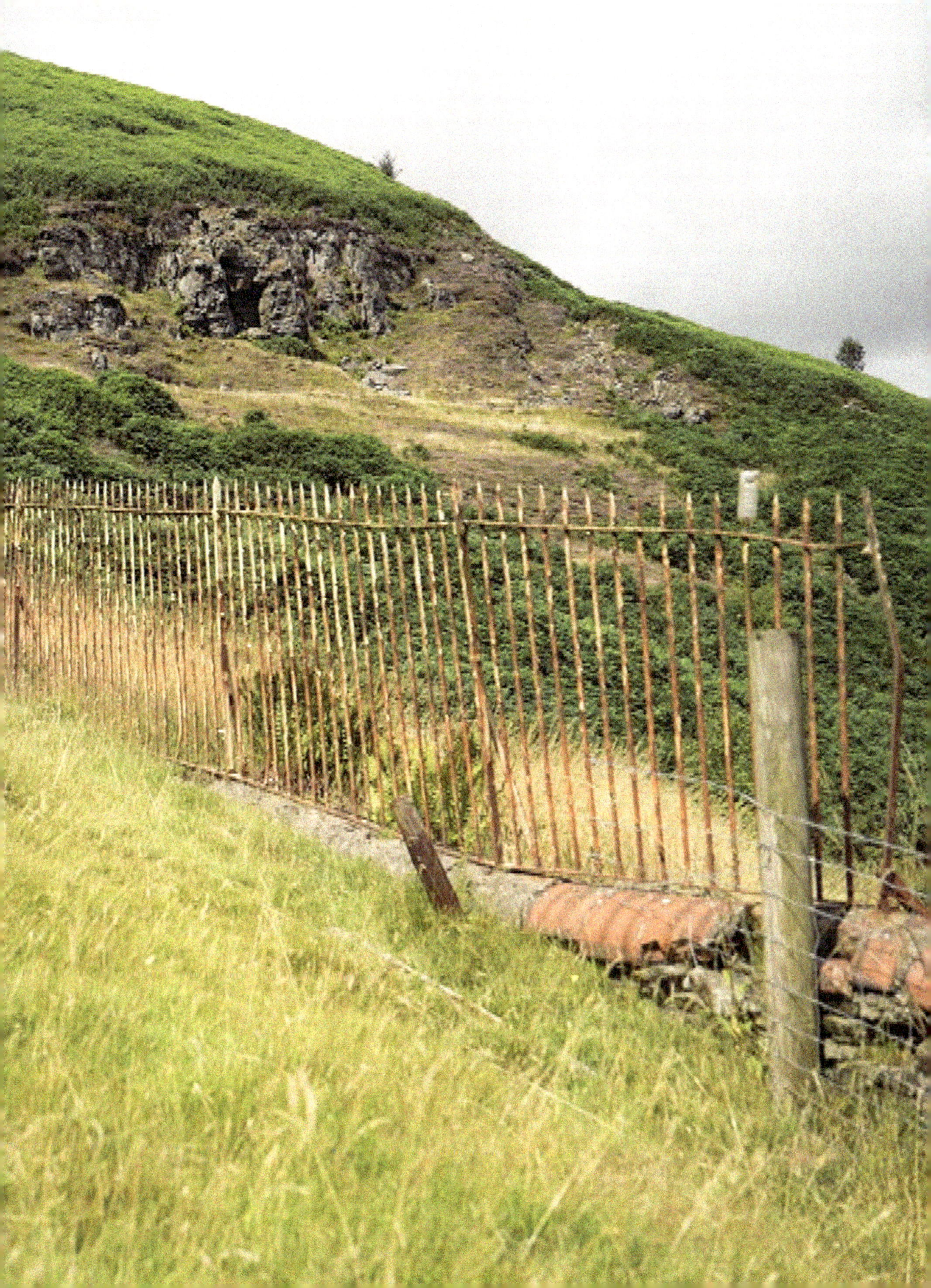

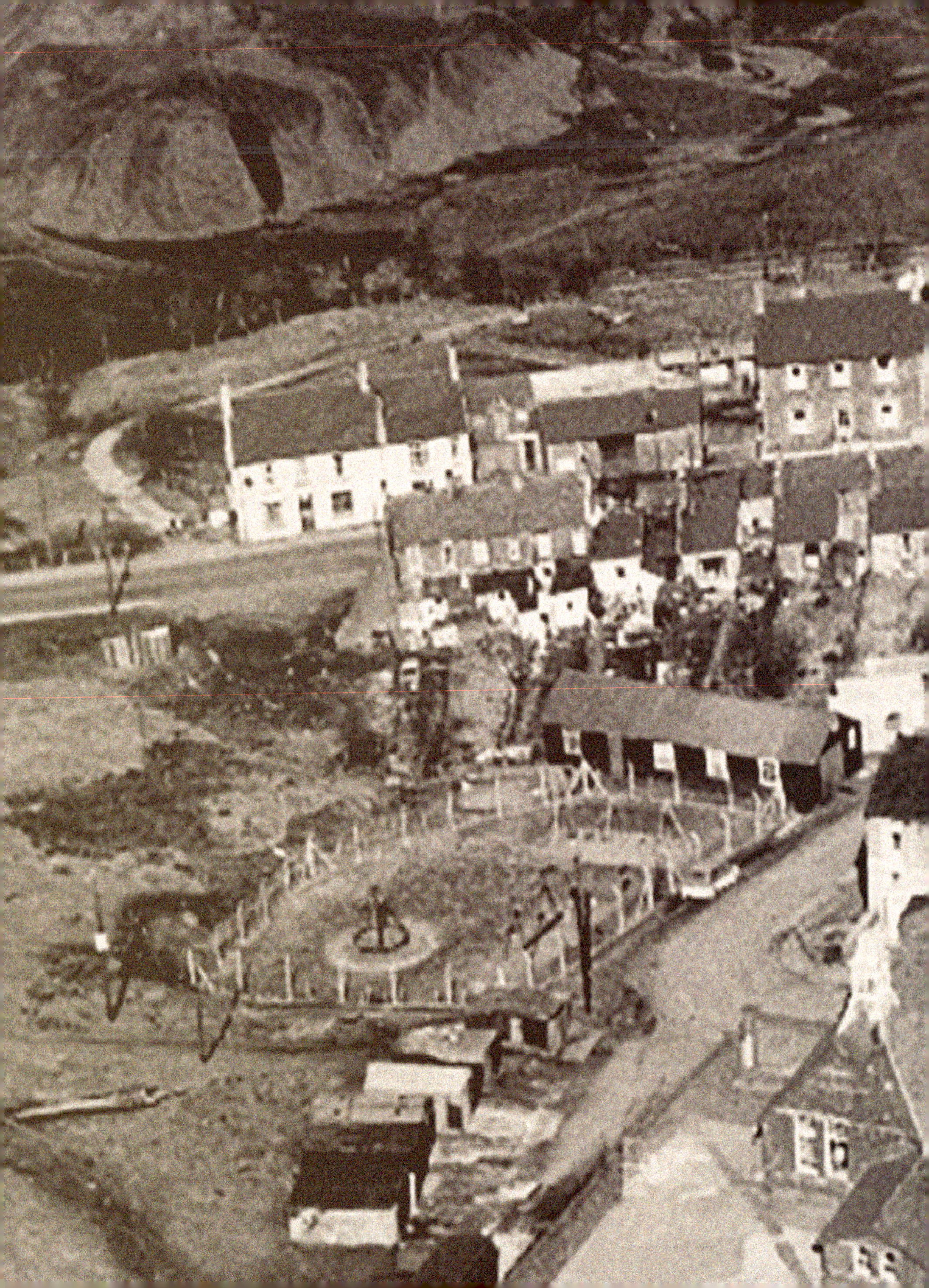

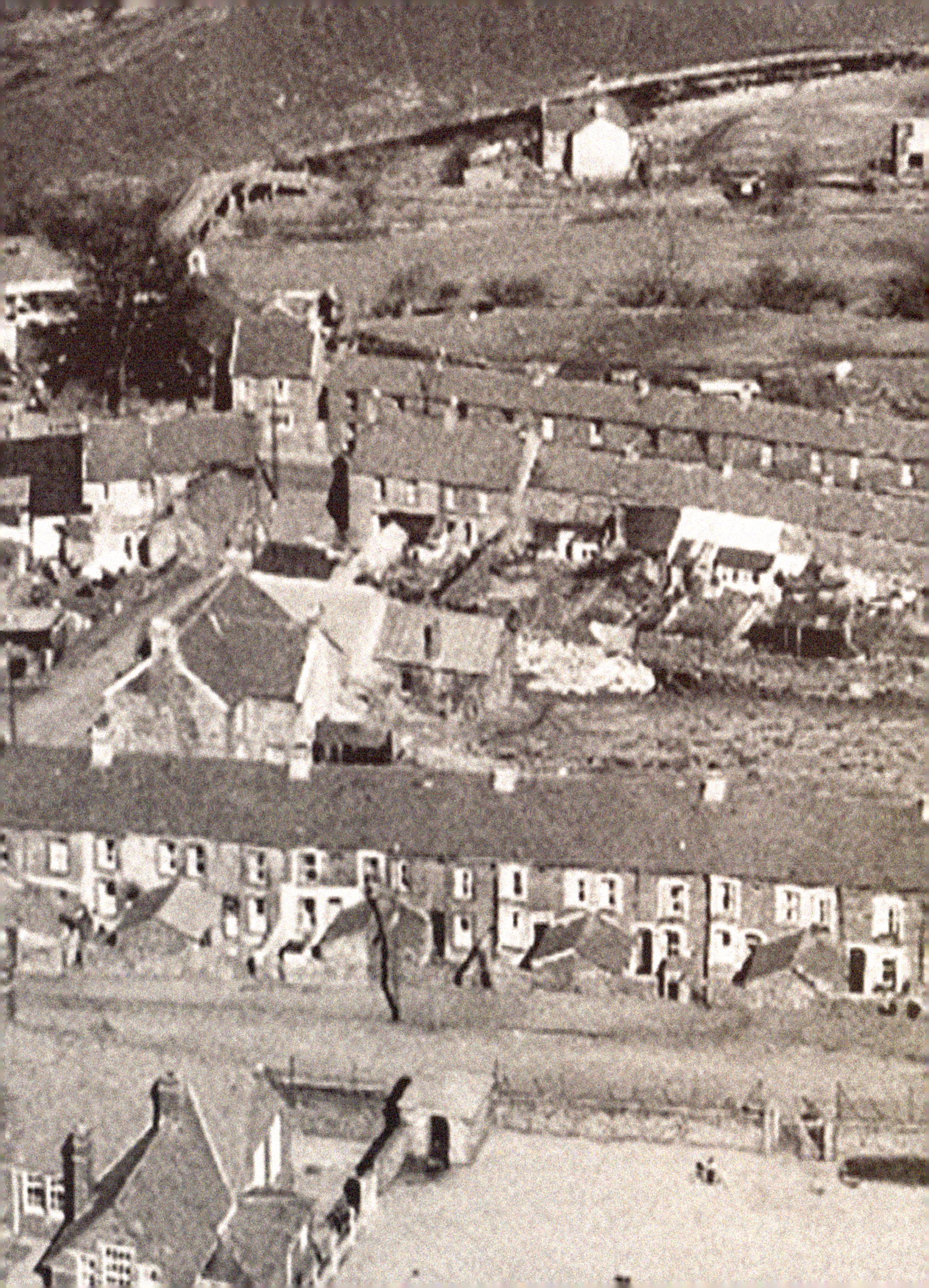

Overleaf: Troedrhiwfuwch as a flourishing community. The village school can be seen in the lower part of the photograph.

As the years rolled by, the villagers formed a community that was as tight as they come. Life in Troedy (as residents fondly called it) was like one big family. In fact, it pretty much was one big family as most people had blood ties to each other through only a few degrees of separation. Bernadette Cooper grew up in the village, just like her parents, grandparents and great-grandparents:

> "Most of the people in the village were related to each other. There were lots of cousins or second and third cousins. Everyone was an aunty or an uncle. I can remember my father saying, 'Oh, you know, it's so-and-so's brother's sister's daughter's husband' and you wouldn't have a clue who it was, but you just took it for granted! When people got married, they didn't think about leaving the village, they stayed within the community. So we all had a shared background and there was a real sense of belonging. It was a gorgeous place to grow up
>
> "All the children played together. The front doors were always open and you could go into anybody's house. So if your mother was out you could just pop into a neighbour because everyone knew each other and we were all really close. It was a safe place to grow up and so much fun. It's difficult to describe but it just enveloped you. I was blessed to live there."

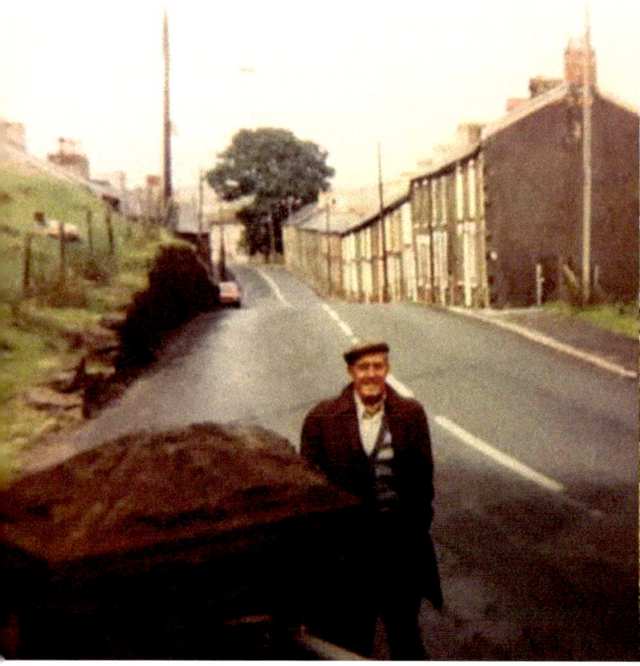
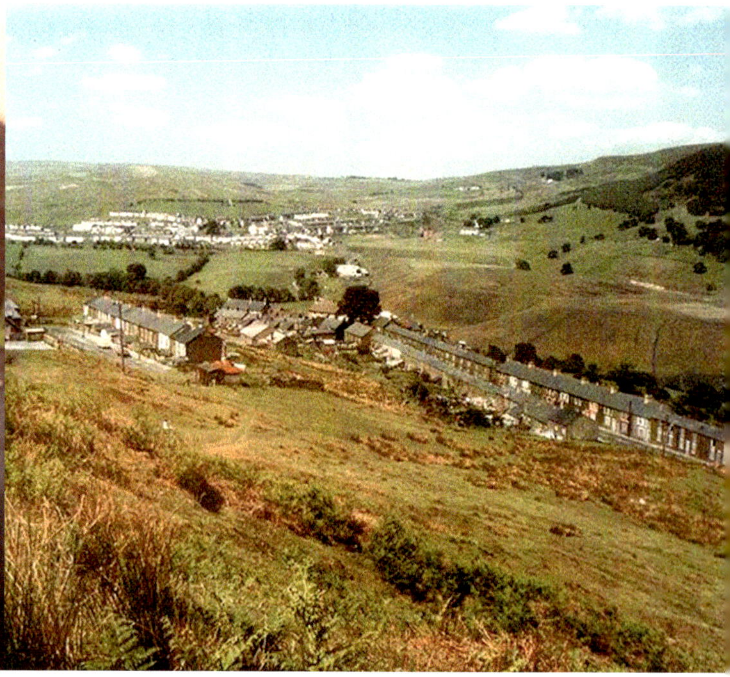

Village life in the years prior to demolition.

Life in Troedrhiwfuwch was filled with traditions and rituals. There was the annual carnival with costumes, floats and marching bands. Religious worship was all-encompassing on a Sunday and there would be church outings for the community throughout the year. On rainless days, children would climb the mountain on their doorstep to pick wimberries or slide down the slopes on leftover cardboard boxes from the local shop. The mountain itself had always loomed large over the village. It stood as a sentinel in the landscape, providing Troedrhiwfuwch with a strong sense of identity. It would also play a decisive role in the settlement's destruction.

For generations, the geology of the upper Rhymney Valley had been making headlines. Heavy rains in 1906 caused a landslip, leaving villagers without a water supply. An even bigger landslide blighted the area in the 1930s, causing the press to exclaim that 'Wales has a moving mountain at Troedrhiwfuwch.'

The community was largely unfazed. They knew that these slips and slides might occur from time to time. They didn't feel that they were in any immediate danger and there was certainly no suggestion of abandoning Troedrhiwfuwch. What changed all of that was the tragedy at Aberfan in 1966. The collapse of a colliery spoil tip, just 10 miles west of Troedrhiwfuwch, resulted in the loss of 144 lives, most of them children. It was a wake-up call for local authorities to re-appraise the safety of communities in the South Wales coalfields. Rhymney Valley District Council commissioned a geotechnical report on the state of Troedrhiwfuwch's mountain. That report was submitted to the council, who ruled on the village's fate:

> 'The area of Troedrhiwfuwch is inherently unstable. Under those circumstances no investment in extending the life of any property should be contemplated…the properties would be demolished and the site cleared…restoring the area to natural hillside."

And so it played out. The infant school was shut down and compulsory purchase orders were issued on the terraced houses. During the 1970s and 80s, with a heavy heart, residents began to move away from their beloved village. Wendy Williams left Troedrhiwfuwch in 1976:

> "We lost the care of our neighbours and of our families because we were all dispersed and we were out on our own. When we moved away, we didn't have a next-door neighbour to go and knock on the door if there was anything wrong, because we didn't know who our next-door neighbour was. So it was the community that was lost.
>
> "Troedy will always be my home. And if I had the chance to return – if someone said, 'come back, we'll build you a house,' – then I'd be there, like a shot. But we have our memories and no-one can take that away from us."

By 1986, the entire village had been demolished, even the places of worship. Today, all that remains of the rows of terraced streets are two solitary houses. But one very significant landmark managed to escape the wrecking ball: Troedrhiwfuwch's war memorial. It stands by the roadside in the consecrated grounds of what used to be St Teilo's church. Although the village around it has disappeared, the stone Celtic cross remains: alone but not forsaken. On Remembrance Sunday each year, the old community comes together to remember their fallen ancestors.

Overleaf: Troedrhiwfuwch is razed to the ground.

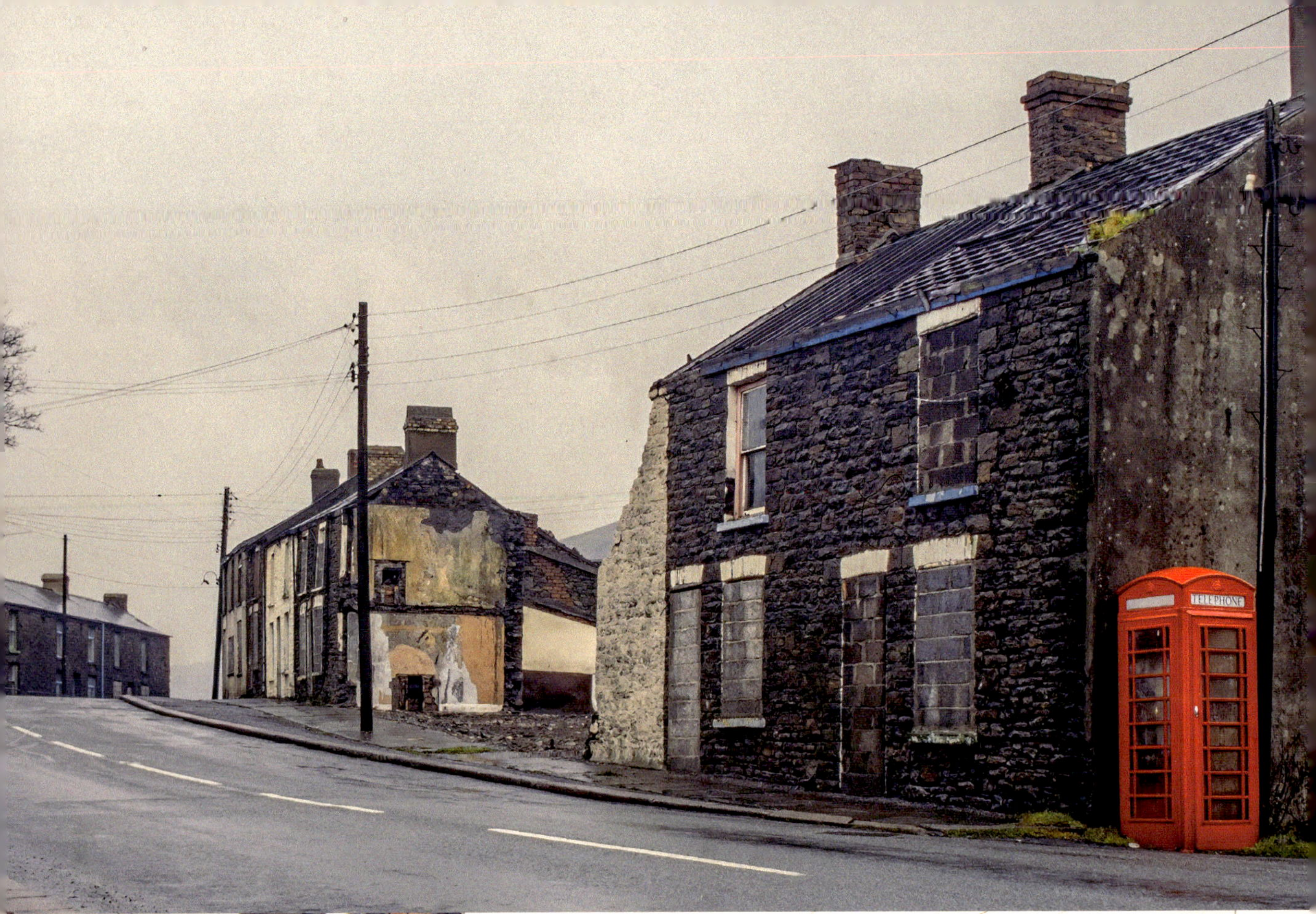
TELEPHONE

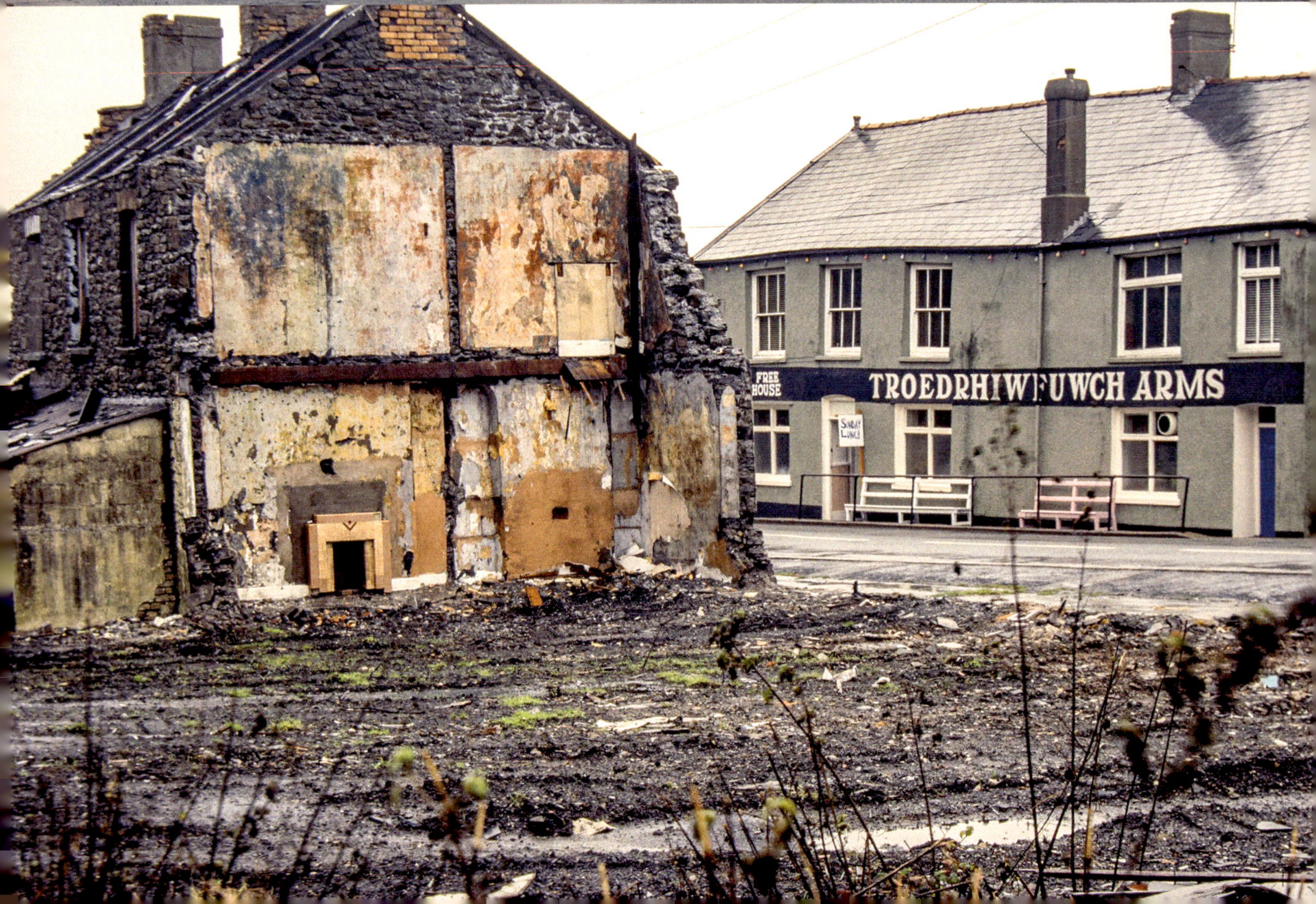
FREE HOUSE
TROEDRHIWFUWCH ARMS

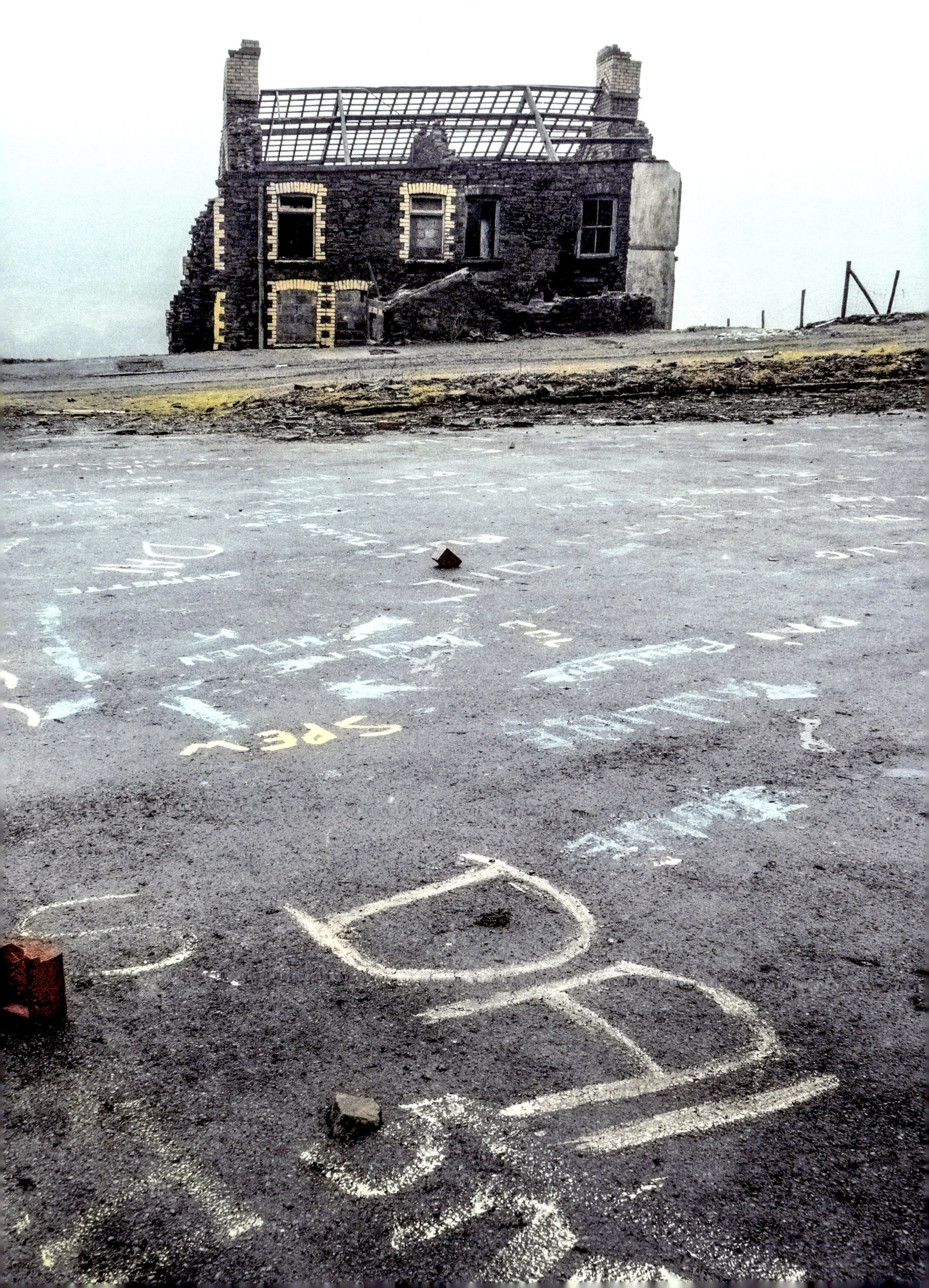

The sacrifice made by the young men of Troedrhiwfuwch during the First World War is deeply moving. At the time there were 94 households in the village; from them, 110 residents went to war: more than one per household. It was the second highest number of enlistees, per capita, in the whole of Great Britain. Inscribed on the memorial are the names of 16 local men who died between 1914 and 1918. One of those names is Private R.J. Williams who was killed at the age of 22 at Mametz Wood in the Battle of the Somme. To Elizabeth Jones, he was Great Uncle Johnny:

"When I was a little girl, everyone still spoke of him as if he were still here, like he'd never gone away. The war memorial was actually paid for from collections house-to-house by the whole village. Everyone contributed. And it took from 1918 until 1933 before they could actually afford to pay for one. Of the men on the memorial, there are only four with known graves. For the rest of the dead men's relatives there's nowhere else they can visit. So the war memorial isn't just a memorial for the village, it's actually a family grave too.

"Once a year it becomes a touchpoint for the community. We all take different roles; some people come and clean the memorial, other people put the crosses on. I make a wreath. It's one of the last remaining pieces of our past and it's very precious because of that. We've lost the village, the men have lost their lives, but the war memorial keeps the memory of Troedrhiwfuwch alive."

Remembrance Day service at the village war memorial.

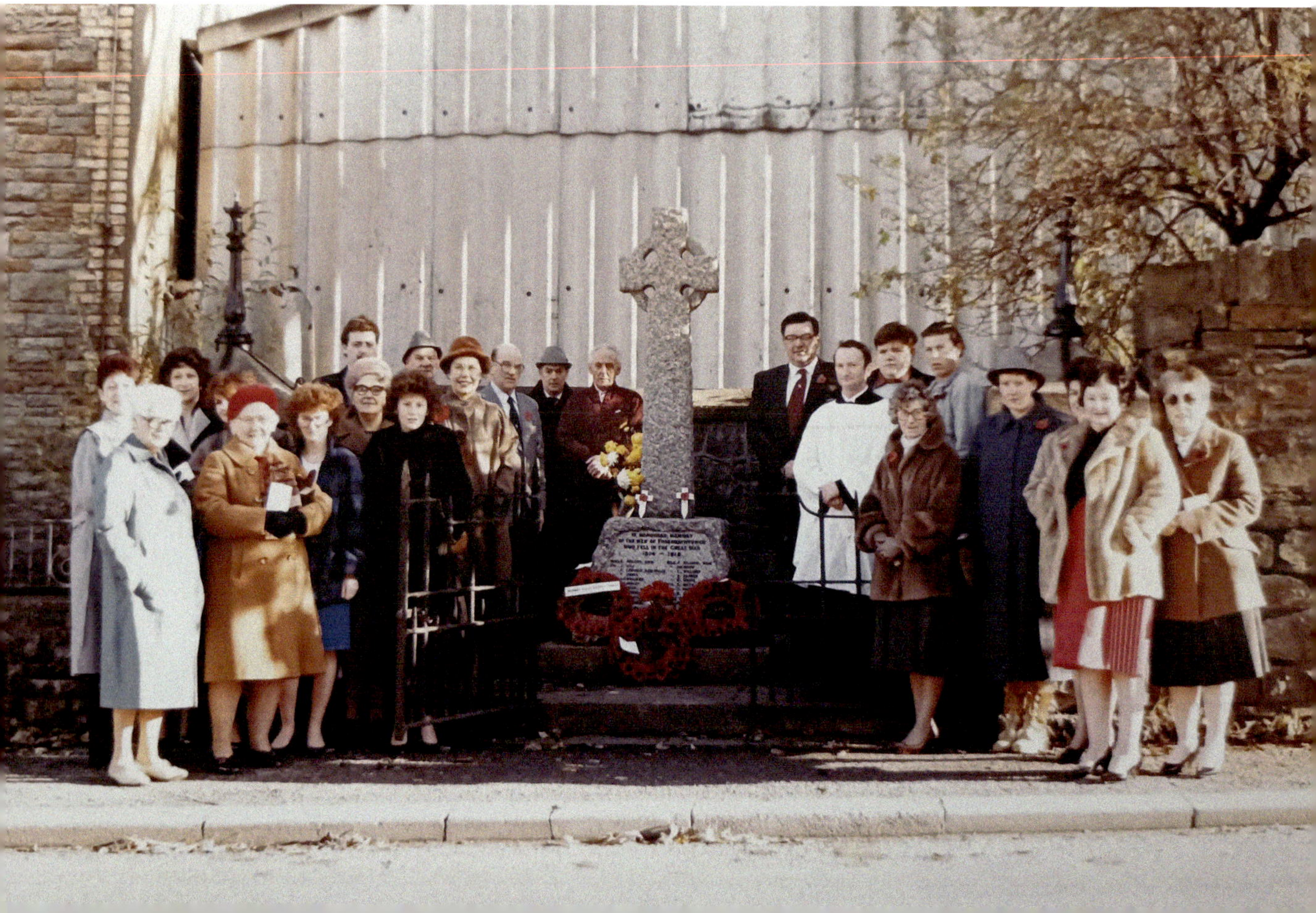

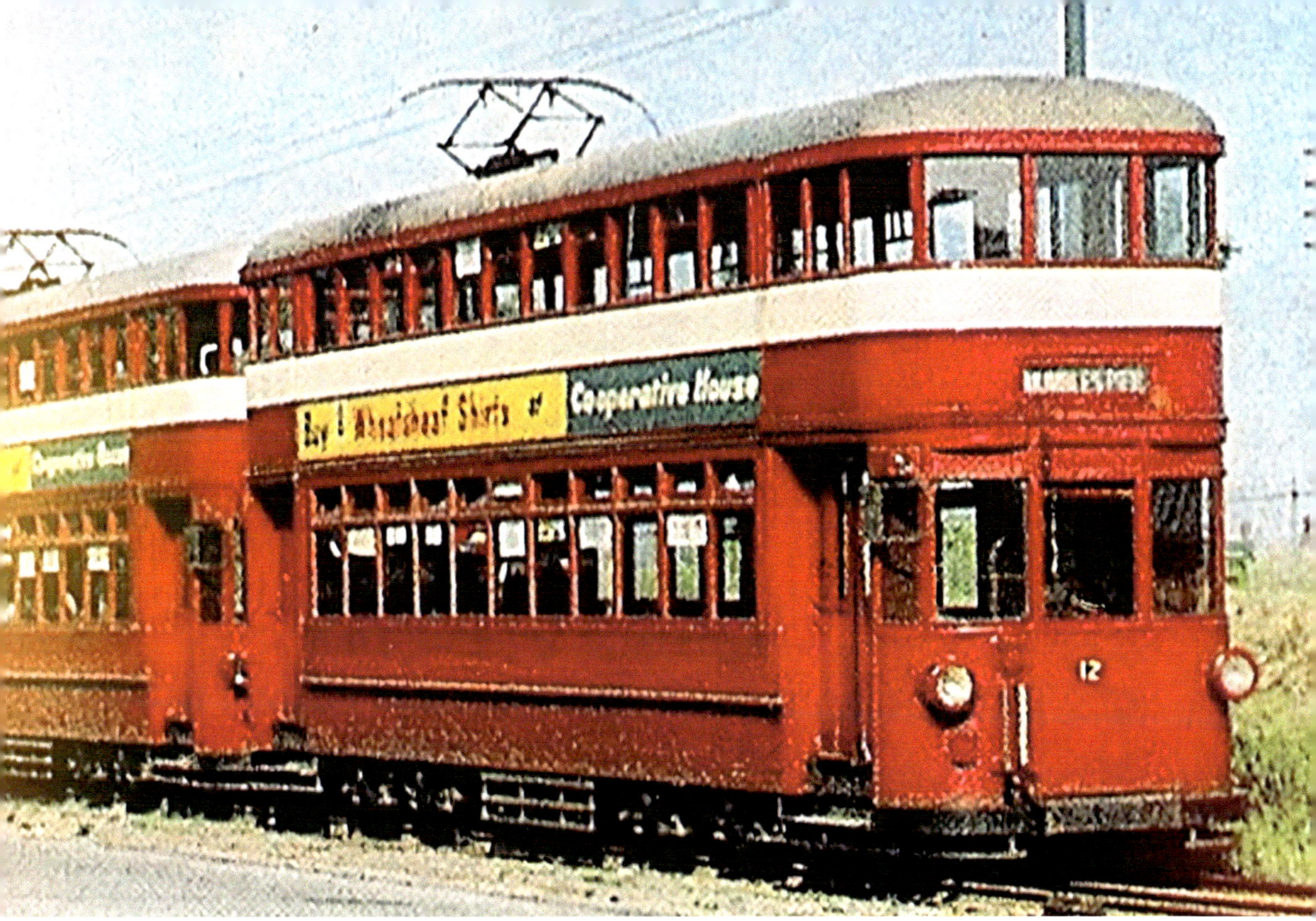

MUMBLES RAILWAY

A world beater in Swansea Bay

It's a fascinating quiz question: where in the world was the first ever passenger railway line? The answer: Swansea. It was the Mumbles Railway and it ran for more than 150 years. Six decades since the line was controversially closed, you'll still find plenty of people with fond memories of riding the bright red trains as they rattled their way from the city centre to Mumbles Pier.

The railway had been established by an Act of Parliament back in 1804 and was initially intended for carrying cargo. When it took its first fare-paying passengers, three years later, the carriages on the rails were drawn by horses.

Steam powered locomotives arrived in 1877 and the railway surged in popularity. Fast forward to the 1920s when the line was electrified and the distinctive red double-decker trains had become an intrinsic part of Swansea life.

Above and overleaf: the unmistakable red trains wind their way around Swansea Bay.

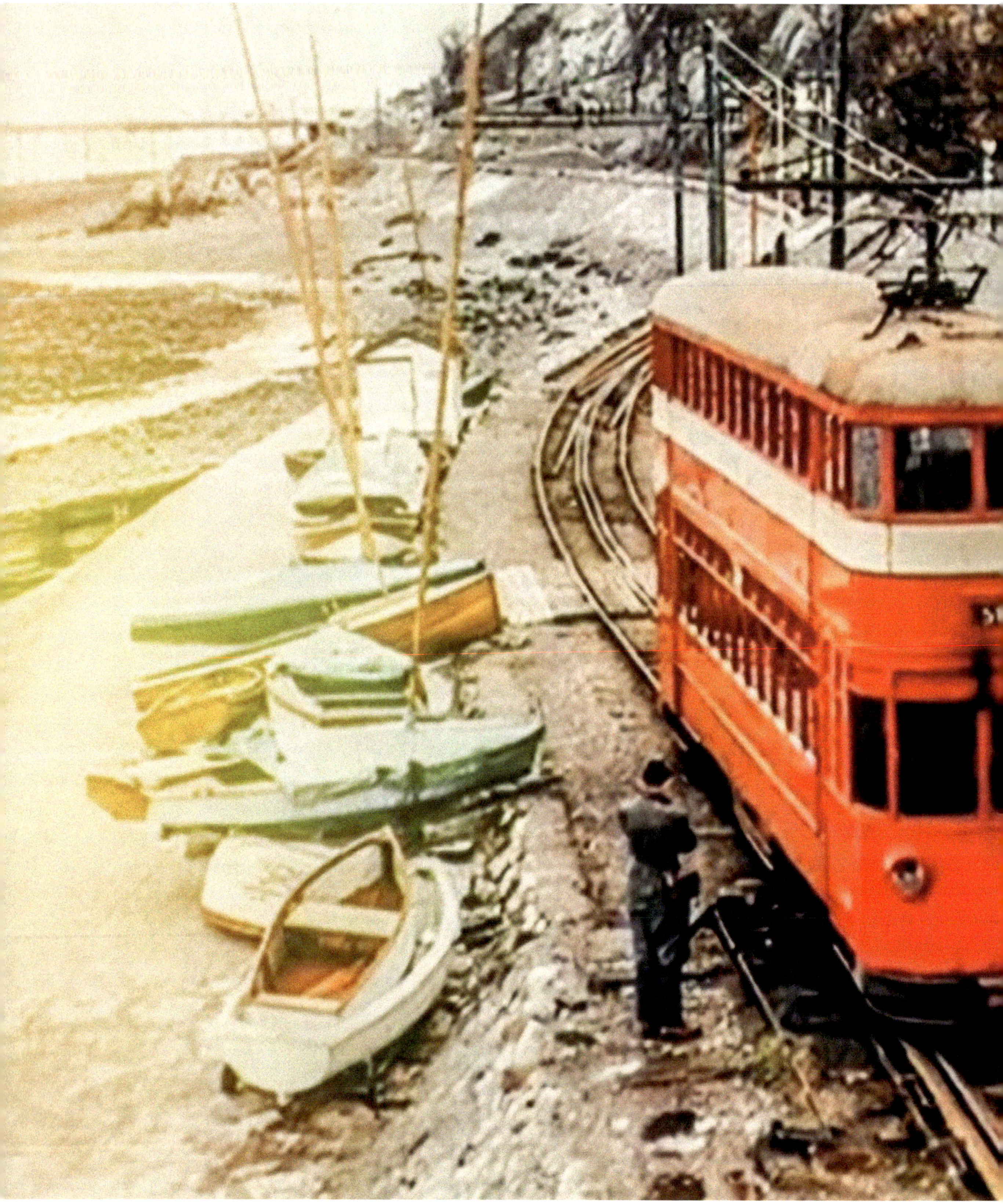

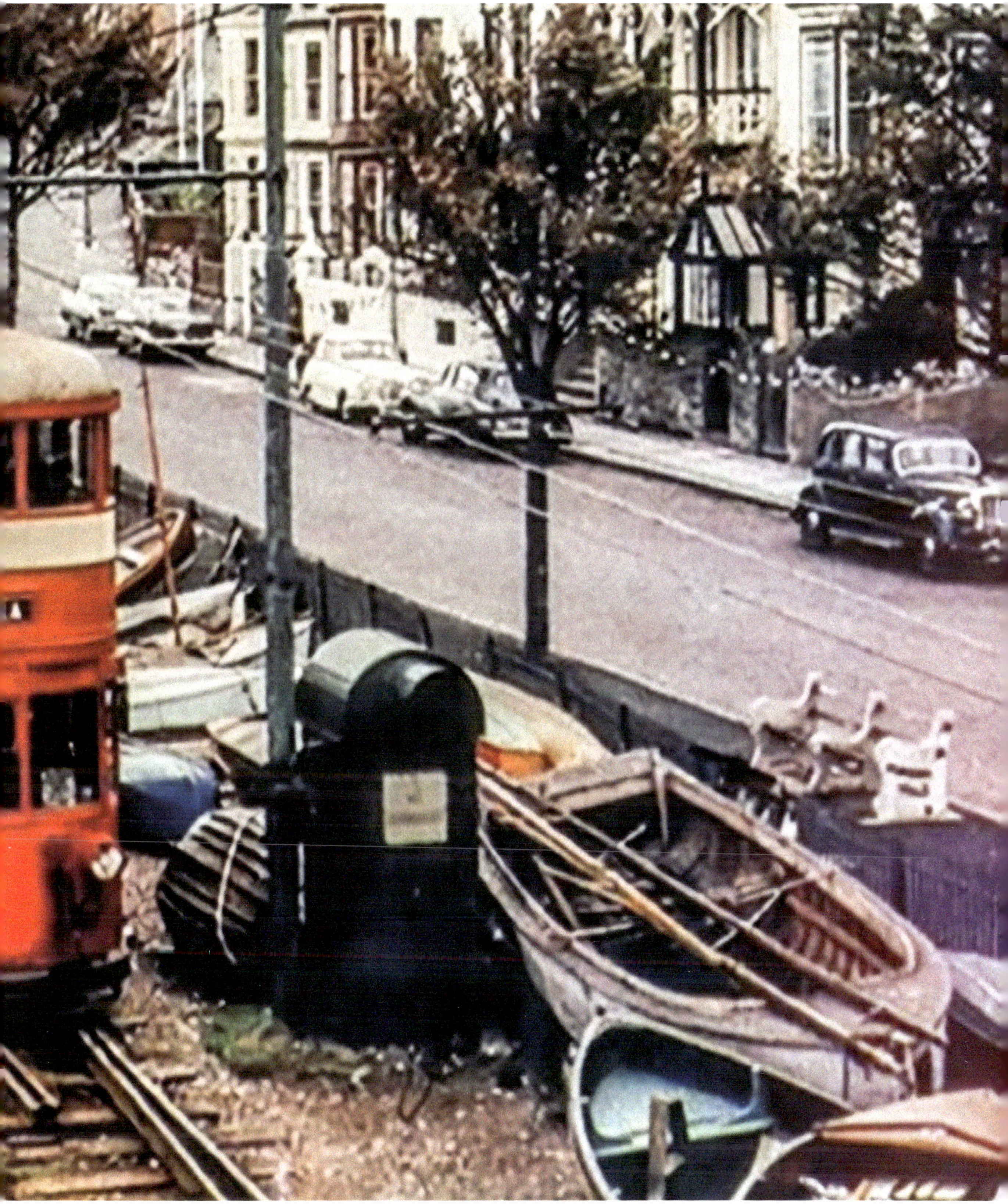

The service was reliable and resilient. During the Second World War, when Swansea was ravaged by Luftwaffe bombing raids, the trains continued to run. If there was an emergency out at sea, the drivers would make a special stop to pick up the lifeboat crews. In the summer months the carriages were crammed with holiday makers. In the dead of winter the trains could be just as busy, as locals jumped on for their daily commute to work, to do the shopping or to go to the hospital. In one year alone, 1945, a staggering five million passengers rode the Mumbles Railway. It could even boast royalty as previous passengers included Edward VII and George V.

One of the railway's biggest fans is Tony Cottle, who made full use of the service from a young age:

"I travelled to school on it and they were wonderful old trains. They used to rock and roll along the tracks – it was great fun. The trains would run seven days a week, in all weathers. If it snowed the drivers would come into work in the early morning and go back and forth clearing the line to ensure the service could keep going. Whenever the trains passed St Helen's cricket ground in the summer, they would slow down so that the passengers could see the result! It was an amazing railway, it really was. It was so much part of the community."

Each double decker train could seat 106 passengers, or 212 if two of the train cars were hooked together (as they often were at the height of summer). Inside the carriages there was a rather nifty design feature for the comfort of passengers: each seat could be both rear and forward facing. All you had to do was grab a handle, give it a pull, and your leather seat was instantly reversible. From as early as 5 am, the trains would trundle from Rutland Street station to the terminus at Mumbles Pier, and back again. It was a five mile, 20-minute journey encompassing the full sweep of Swansea Bay. Peter Tremewan, who grew up in Mumbles, knew the route well:

"I rode on the railway most days. My memory is of going to sit upstairs (and the stairs were rickety so you had to be very careful) but you had the view right around the Bay from the top deck. It was really quite exciting. The other thing I used to like to do, to the irritation of the driver, was stand right next to his cab looking out of the front window. He used to go nuts. He'd say, 'Sit down boy!' But I kept doing it!

"The last train from Mumbles at night used to leave from the old Pier Hotel, which had a dance hall. And when the last train was due to depart, the driver, in full uniform, would go onto the dancefloor and say, 'Right everybody – I'm going in five minutes so if you need the train then come on out!'

"When I was young, pocket money was not that plentiful. The train to go into town was six old pence, return. But that was expensive for me. So I used to bunk off at Argyle Street, which was the last station but one, and run into town – that way it was only four pence!

"It was the way that we all travelled, rattling, banging along on those trains. And to think that Swansea had the very first passenger railway and it was still running. Some parts of the world would have given their eyeteeth to have that, which made it so sad when it closed."

Opposite top: the Mumbles Railway in its steam-powered days.

Below: a packed carriage in the 1950s.

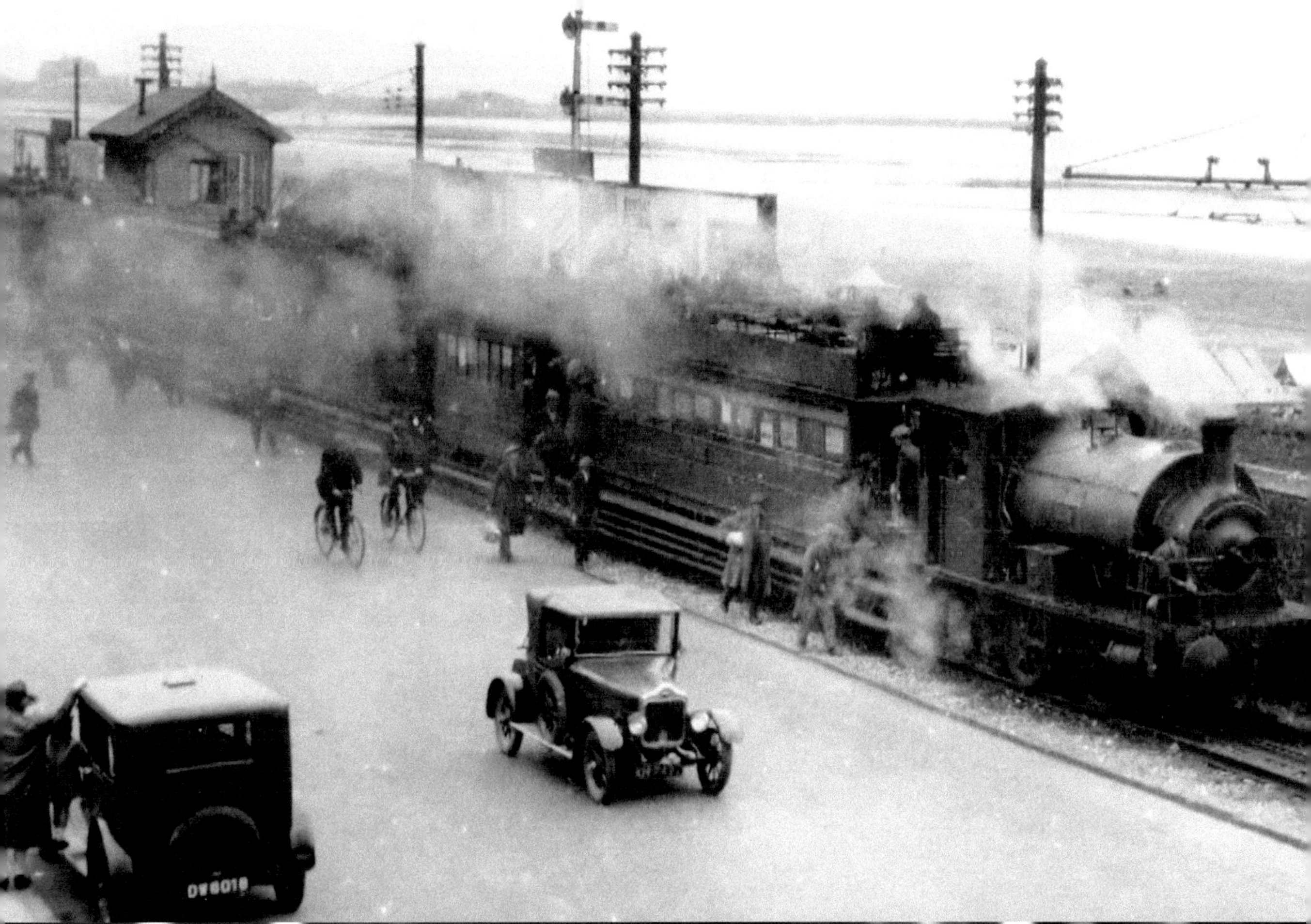

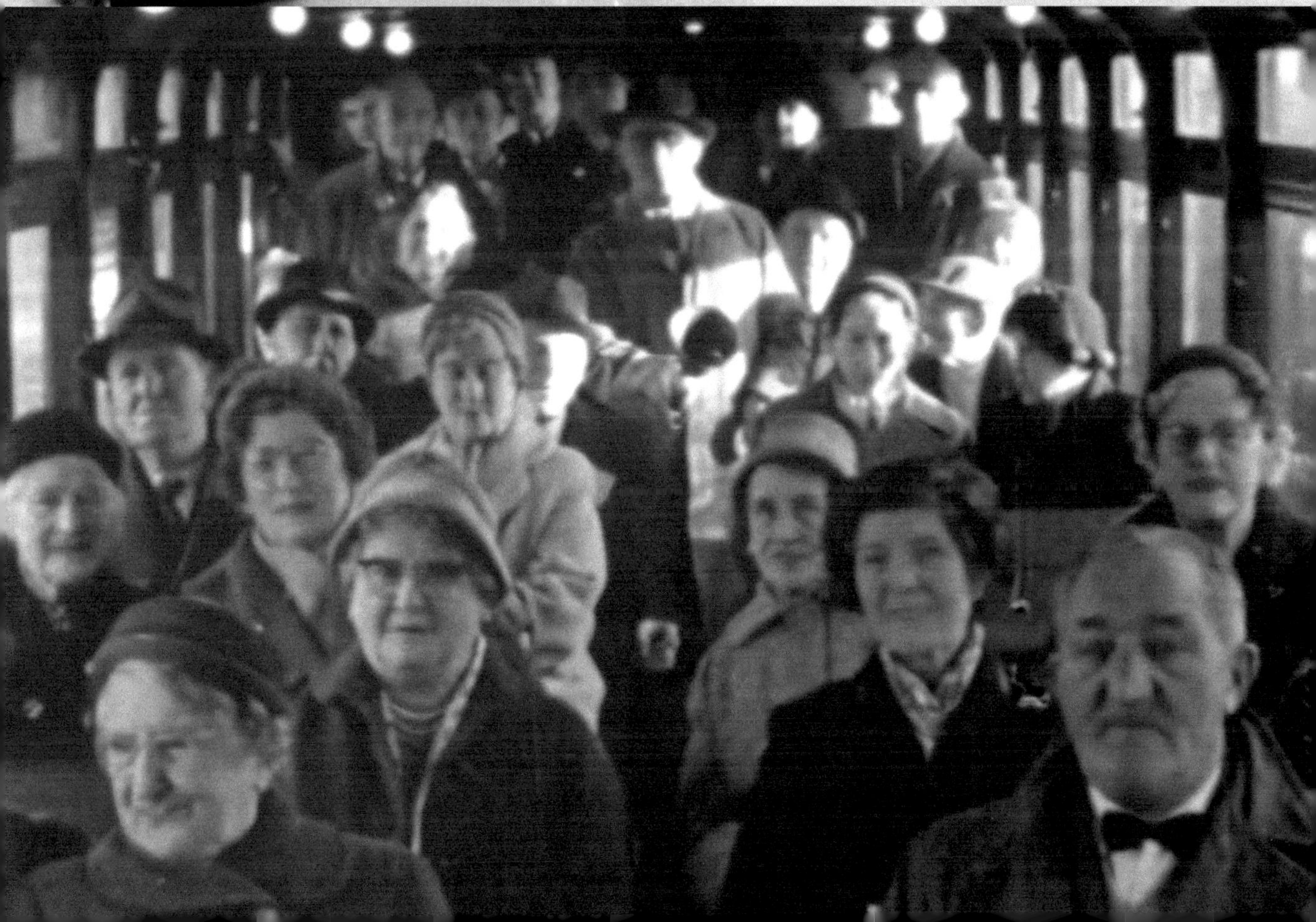

The loss of the Mumbles Railway is an excruciating tale to tell. All these years later there's still a wellspring of outrage, and no shortage of bewilderment, that it was even allowed to happen at all. In 1958, the South Wales Transport Company Ltd took over the running of the Mumbles Railway. It was a bus company at heart and its vision for Swansea's public transport system zeroed in on wheels, not rails. It believed that buses were more flexible, reliable and cheaper to run than an old railway. The company argued at council and Government level that the Mumbles Railway should be scrapped swiftly and completely. And that's exactly what happened.

The final day of operation was 5th January 1960. Devotees of the railway gathered in large numbers, dressed in mourning attire and carrying a mock coffin, to watch the last trains complete their route and return to the depot. Within hours, the rails and infrastructure were being ripped up. The beloved bright red trains were unceremoniously stripped, sliced apart and smashed up. After serving Swansea for 156 years, the Mumbles Railway was suddenly gone.

Today, there are a few affecting reminders of the old line scattered about the city. The former Black Pill station, which also served as an electrical sub-station for the railway, has been converted into a cafe. Some of the traction poles,

Destined for the scrapyard: the ignominious end of the Mumbles Railway, 1960.

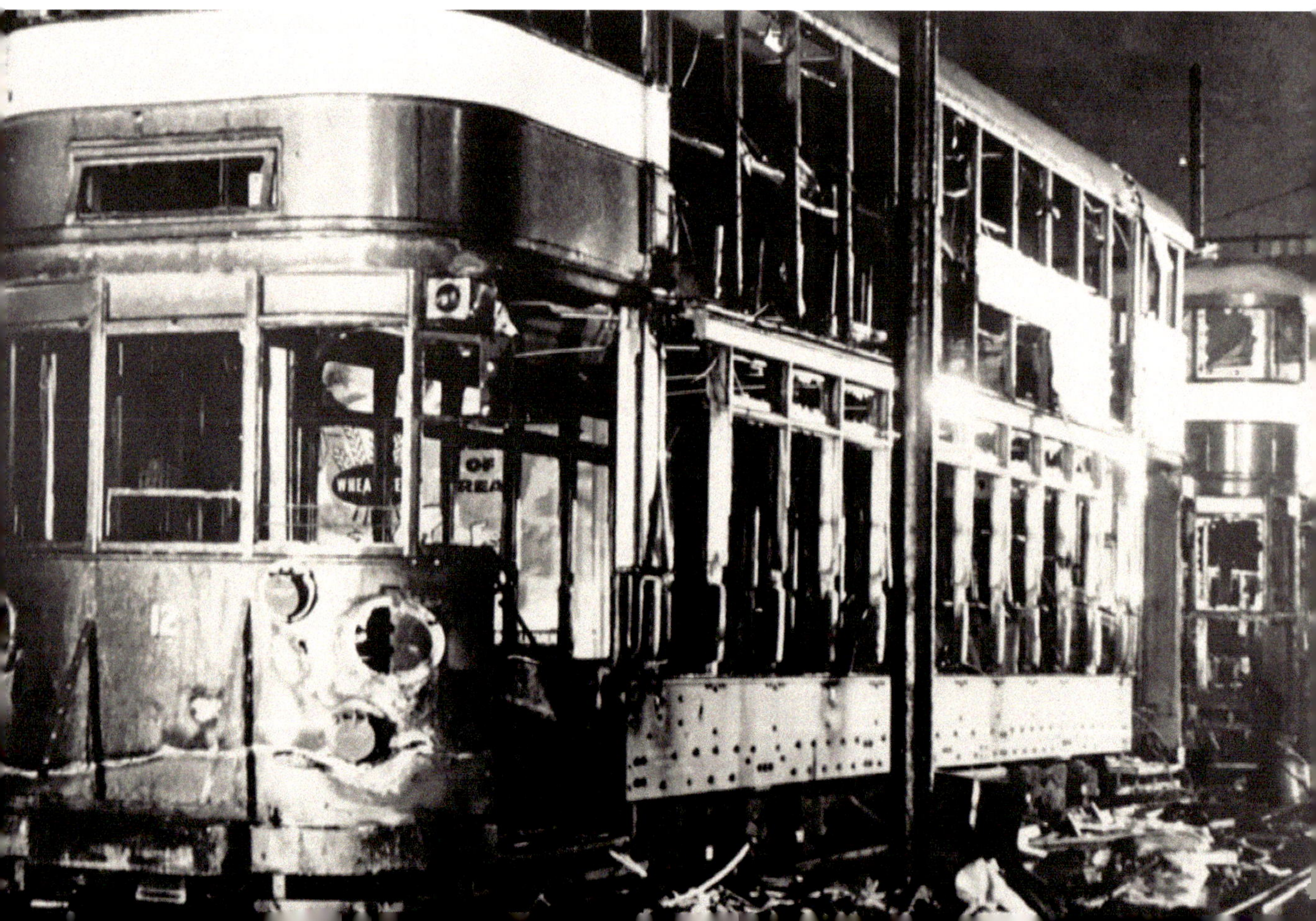

which used to support the overhead wires, can still be seen along the seafront. Most beautifully, the Mumbles Railway has been immortalised in stained glass at All Saints' Church in Oystermouth, forming part of a window dedicated to St Christopher, the patron saint of travellers.

If you're hoping to find a complete, fully preserved train you'll be sorely disappointed. The city didn't keep one. The closest you'll get is the front end of the No. 7 train which is being cared for by Swansea Museum at its Tramshed site in the Marina. The cab has been restored and mounted to a wall, and forms part of a permanent display celebrating the Mumbles Railway. Barry Hughes from the Museum is heartened by the depth of feeling that still exists for the long-lost line:

"Visitors come in here and sometimes they share stories. Stories of playing school rugby on the seafront, seeing the train go by and stopping to wave at the train, disrupting the game! A lot of people referred to it as the trên bach. The translation is 'small train' but of course in Welsh 'bach' has a lot more connotation with it. There's a lot of affection in that word.

"It's one of those things that's always remembered with fondness in the local psyche. It's about pride, a sense of place…knowing where we come from. And for the Mumbles Railway, it certainly is something to be proud of.

"It was a world first."

The last of its kind: the restored No.7 train.

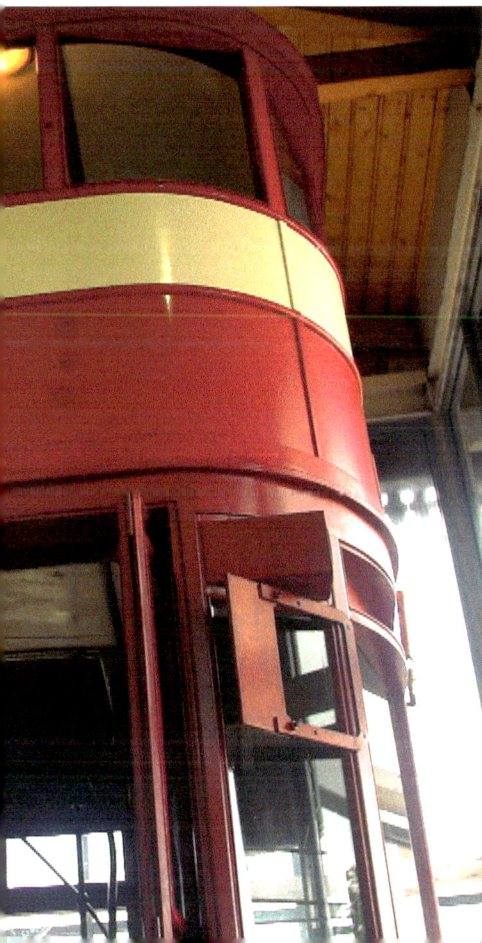

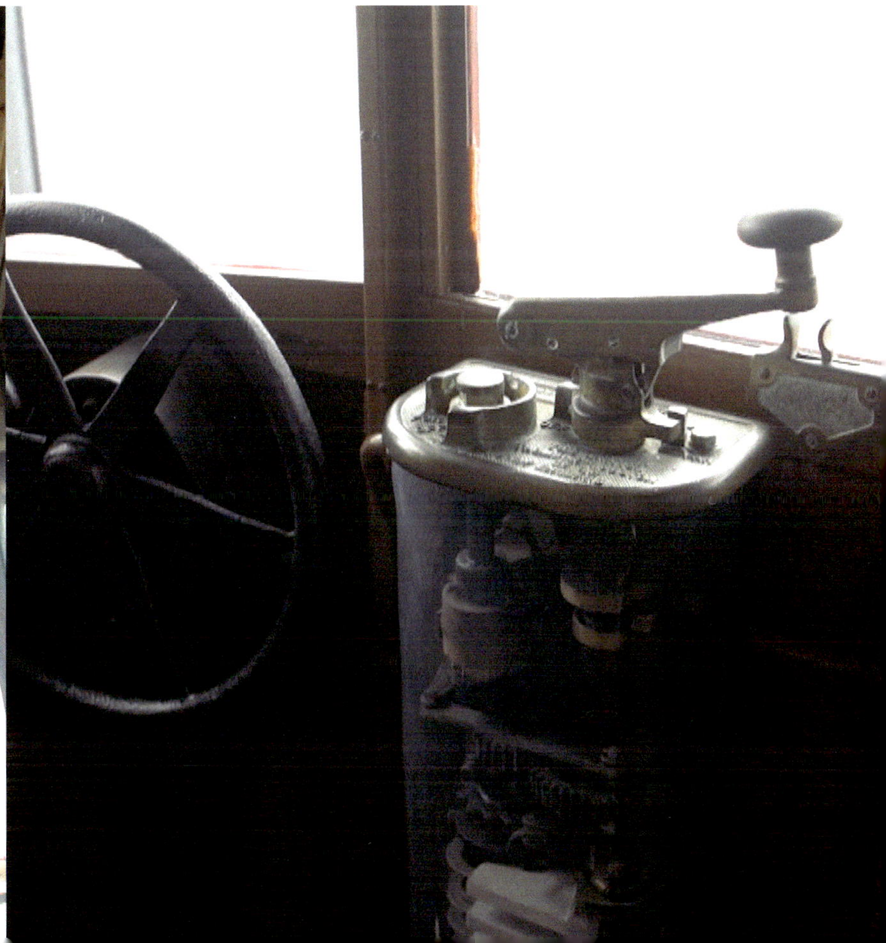

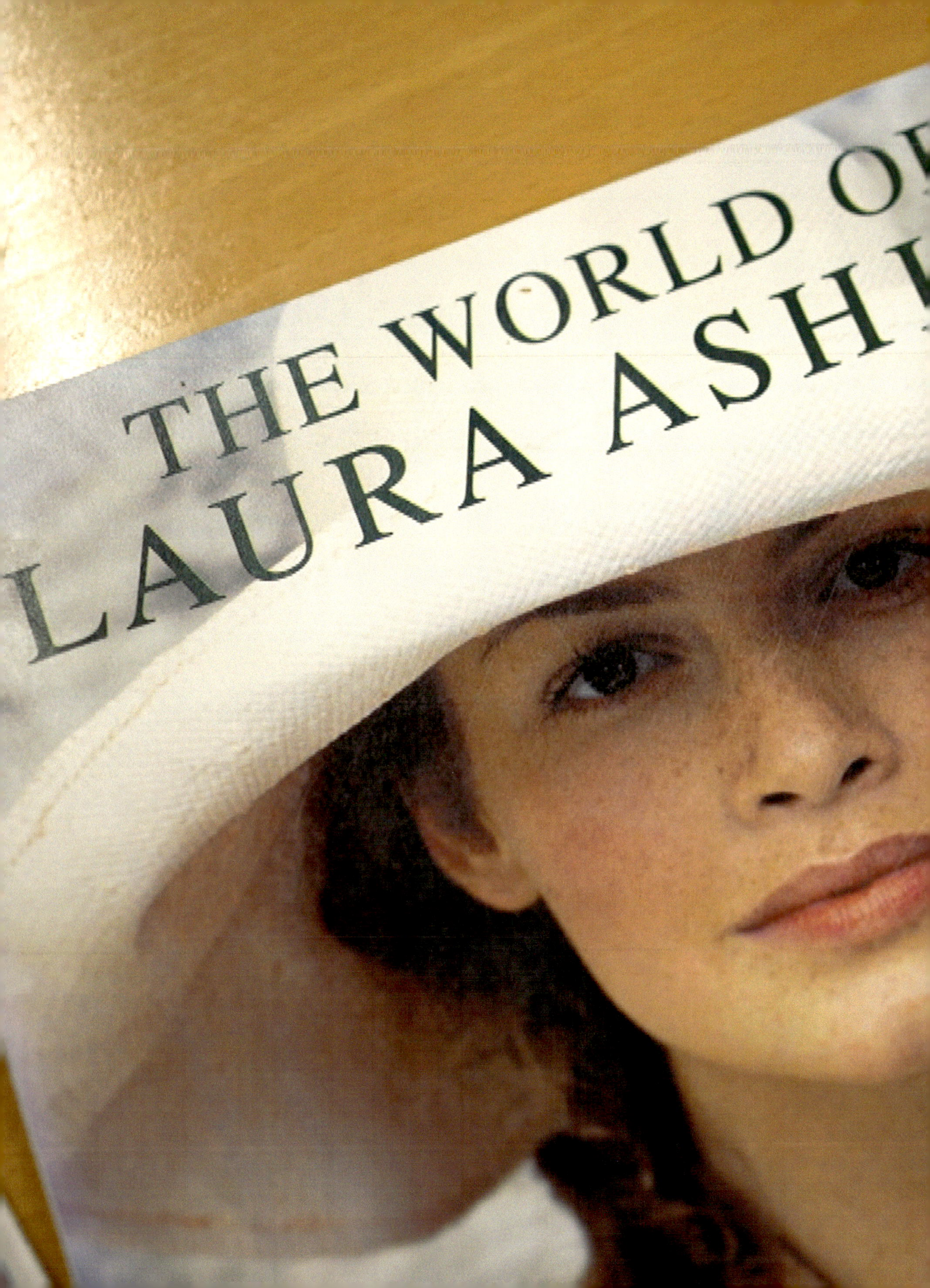
THE WORLD
LAURA

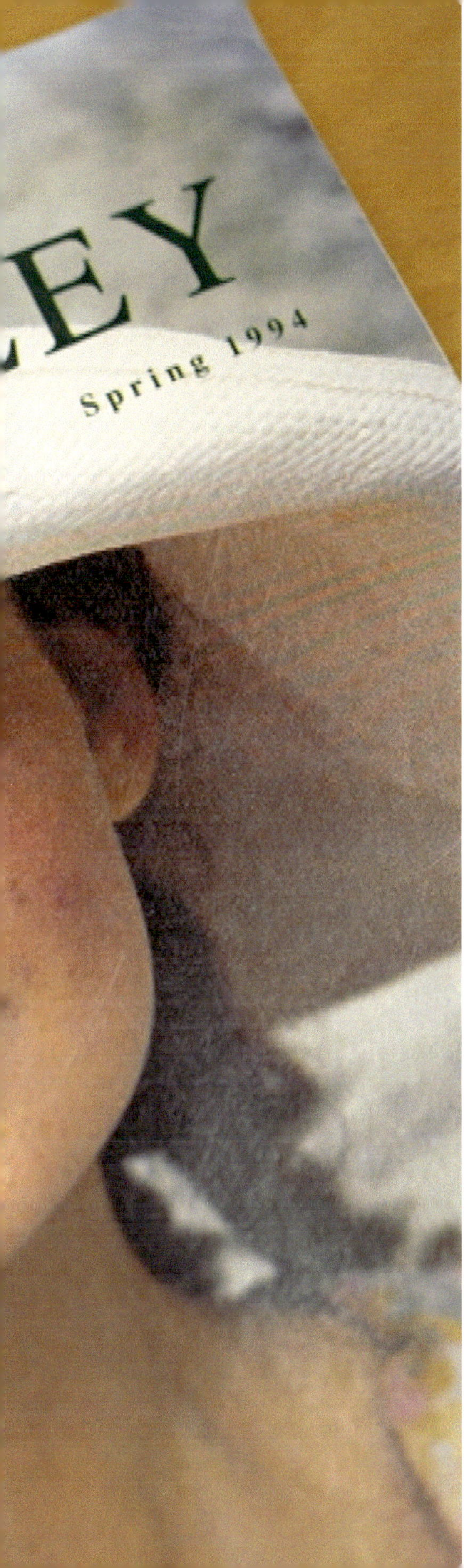

LAURA ASHLEY FACTORY

London, Paris, New York...and Carno

The quiet countryside of Mid Wales may not be the most obvious centre of operations for a multi-million-pound global fashion empire. But for half a century, the parishes of Powys were at the heart of one of Britain's most successful clothing, furnishings and textile companies. Its products were snapped up by customers as far afield as the US, Australia and Japan, while its Victorian-inspired designs became so instantly recognisable that the following two words will probably summon styles and patterns in your mind's eye: Laura Ashley.

Famous for its flowing dresses and floral fabrics, the business had concentrated its activities in Wales from the very early days, and one building, in one community, became synonymous with this uniquely Welsh world-wide enterprise.

Left: a global brand that was proudly Welsh.

Overleaf: the huge Laura Ashley factory in Carno.

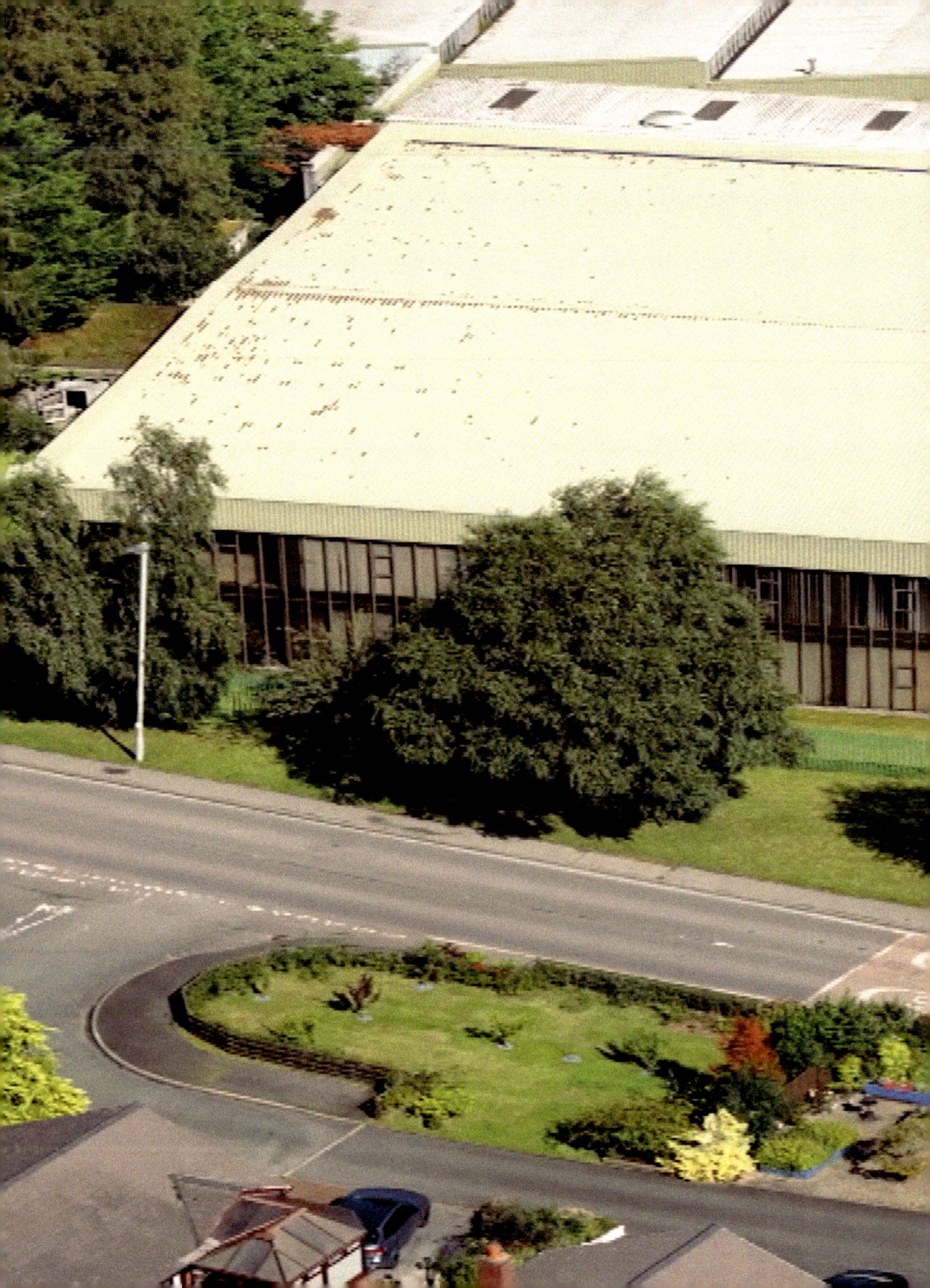

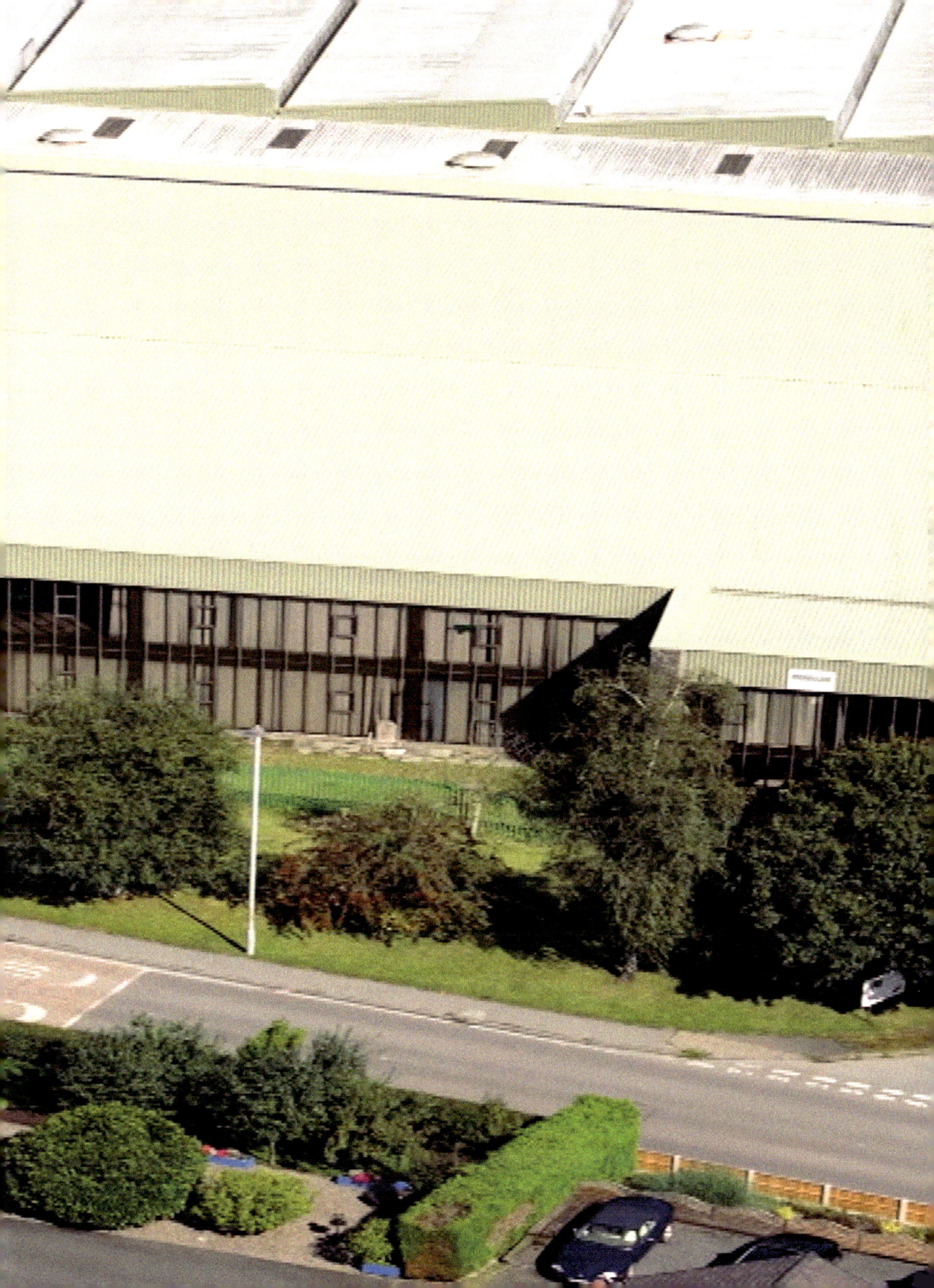

In the 1960s, the placid pace of village life in Carno, northwest of Newtown, ratcheted up several notches with the opening of a brand-new factory. It had originally been sited in a community hall, then a disused railway station, before a huge, specially constructed complex appeared in the landscape. The buildings can still be seen today on the main road through the village: glass fronted with side walls of stone and a faintly greenish hue. This was once the nerve centre for the burgeoning Laura Ashley company. Hefin Jones was one of hundreds of local people who found employment there:

> "It was a big change for me. I'd worked at home on the farm so it was new for me to work in a factory. I did lots of different jobs there, whatever was required on that particular day: inspecting and laying the cloth, cutting patterns out. Two or three times a week I went down to London to supply the Laura Ashley shops. I only had the family car at the time so the garments went on the back seat and the fabric went in the boot! But there was enormous demand in those days."

The incongruity of Carno as a cornerstone of chintz was the result of an unswerving vision by Laura Ashley to provide steady jobs for the local community. Laura herself was Welsh, raised in Dowlais, Merthyr Tydfil of a strict Baptist family. She launched her first venture in London in the 1950s, before relocating to Mid Wales with her young children and her husband Bernard, the company's co-founder. Her very first shop opened in Machynlleth in 1961. As demand grew for her quintessentially English (but actually designed in Wales) botanic motifs and flowing frocks, Laura and Bernard settled on the restful village of Carno as the base for their business.

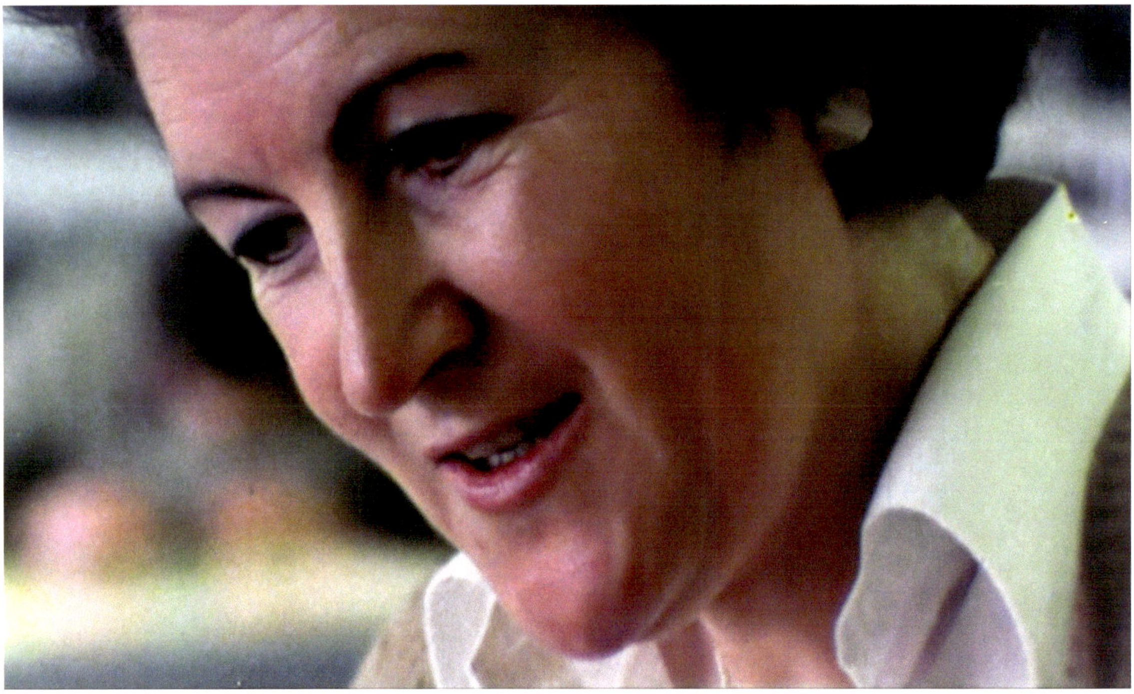

Above: Laura Ashley.

Opposite: workers weave their magic on the factory floor.

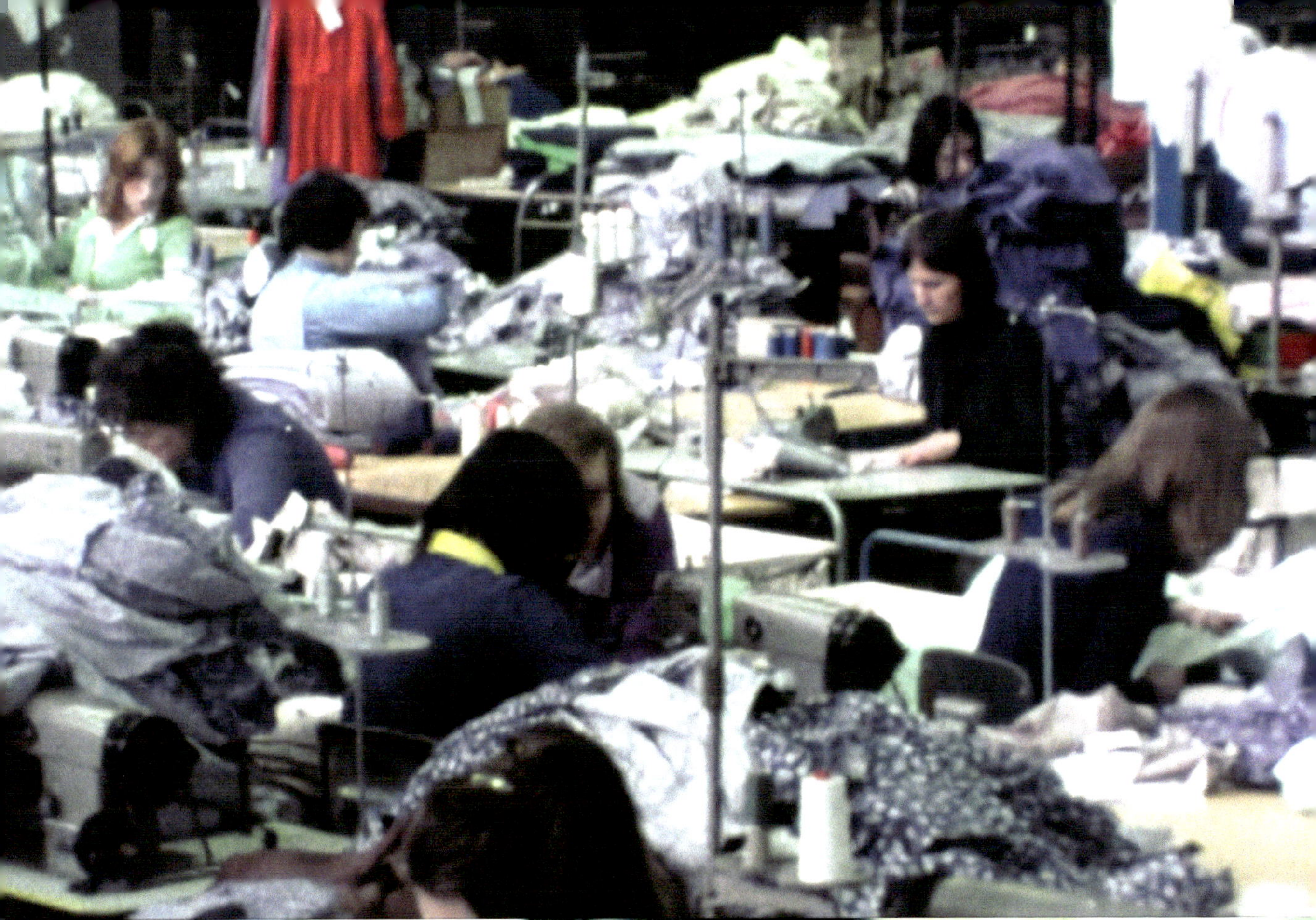

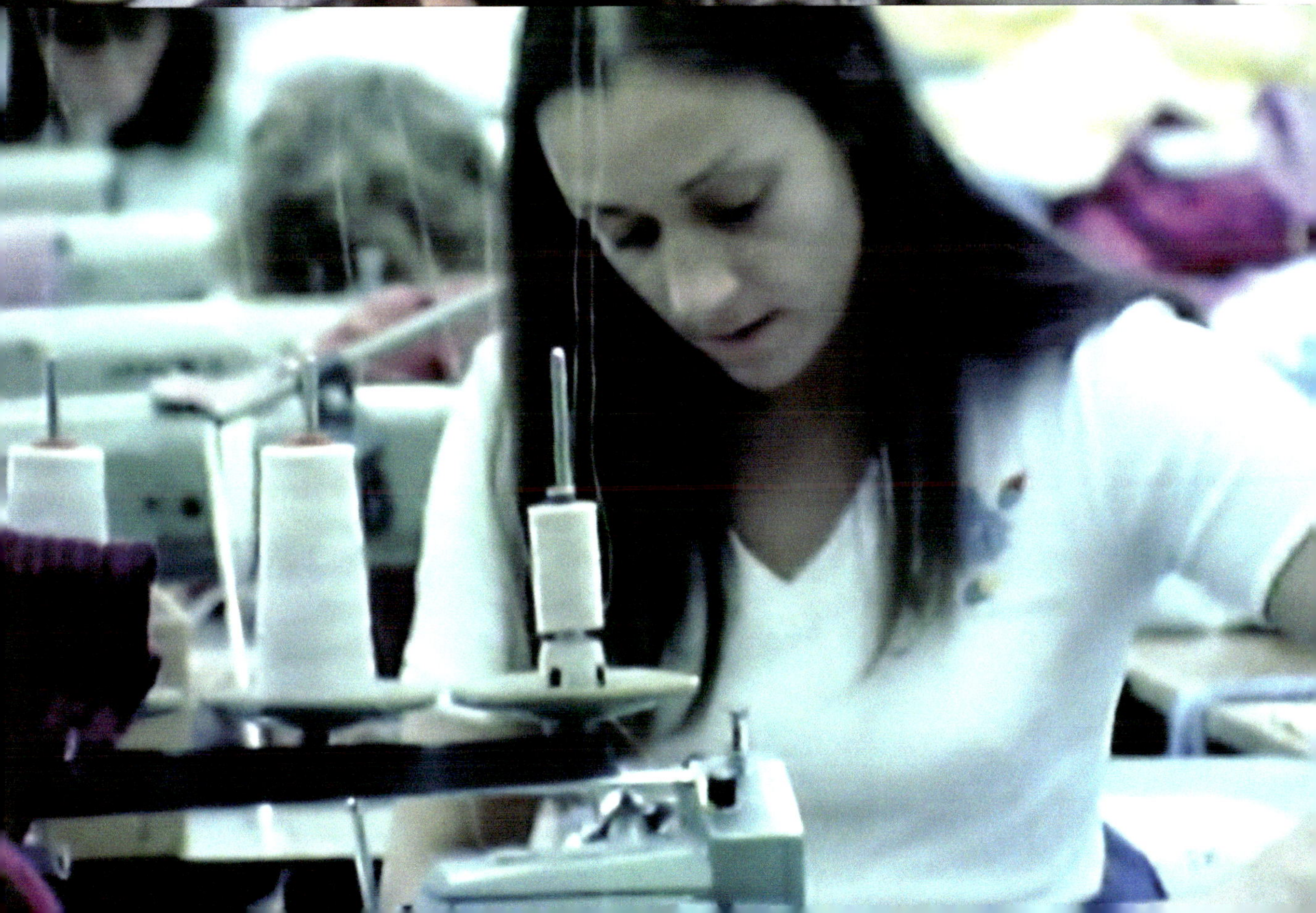

This rural community suddenly had a busy design studio and manufacturing hub at close range. Jobs in the area had been few and far between: not anymore. A loyal, local workforce helped to transform the flourishing fabric and fashion brand into a global player. Former employee Joy Jones from Carno remembers the company's flexible approach to working:

> "They were very good with us young mothers. I went on 'outwork' when my children were small. That meant they supplied you with a sewing machine, you did the work at home, and then they collected the fabrics when you'd finished them. If your children were sick you were allowed to look after them or take them to a clinic and there was never any question that you wouldn't be paid for doing that. There was a lot of trust. We felt like it was our company. They were helping us and we were helping them."

Even in her early days as a designer, Laura Ashley was known for taking inspiration from fragments and artefacts that caught her eye: an old postcard, a piece of china, a Victorian book cover. As business boomed, a young Brian Jones was brought in to work alongside Laura at the Carno factory, helping to turn her unbounded ideas into patterns for printing:

> "I was a young artist at the time. My parents had seen an advert in the local paper for the Laura Ashley design studio. My father said, 'Why don't you apply?' And I said 'No, I don't want to work in a factory.'
>
> "Behind my back they sent for an application and a letter came back asking me to bring my portfolio up to Carno for the interview. I thought: what's a portfolio? So I just took some work off the walls at home, drove up to Carno in my green Hillman Avenger, with my hair long, wearing a velvet tie – it was the '70s! – and I got into the waiting room and it was full of graduates with their diplomas. I'd just come with my little pictures. Anyway, I went in to be interviewed and Laura Ashley was sitting opposite me. She was very softly spoken, black hair, black eyeliner, very modern. As the interview was over, I left the room and somebody put their hand on my shoulder and said, 'You've got the job.' I started a week later and my life changed forever.
>
> "Every day we were meeting new people. You didn't know who was going to walk through the door next. It could be a pop star, a politician, they all came to Carno. One of my prints ended up on cushions in Kensington Palace for Diana, the Princess of Wales. So that was a real buzz. In 1988, the Princess of Wales was visiting and I was able to explain to her how thrilled we were to see our prints in her sitting room!"

By now, Laura Ashley had become a household name. Those rustic 19th century-style decorative designs were everywhere: wallpaper, bedspreads, cushions, curtains, rugs, teapots, toothbrush holders. At its height the company employed 13,000 people with 500 shops worldwide, from South Kensington to San Francisco. A commercial masterstroke came in the form of Laura Ashley By Post, a home delivery service that brought mail order fashion into the mainstream as early as 1976. Ann Evans joined the staff at Carno at the age of 19 and soon found herself working on this new and highly lucrative offshoot:

"Thousands of orders came through… sackfuls…envelopes containing little pieces of paper and a cheque. Of course, we didn't have computers then so everything had to go into a ledger. I think after the first newspaper advert we had about 3,000 orders. I remember Bernard Ashley came in one day and he said, 'Oh, I hear that this mail order operation is going really well, it's expanding.' We'd just fixed a paper clip to a cheque and he literally threw the money up in the air and said, 'We're rich!' He couldn't believe how big the operation had developed overnight.

"1981 was the first home furnishings catalogue. Later, there were the clothing catalogues too and we'd use models who are famous now, like Kate Moss. It was an amazing opportunity for so many people to be able to work on this new enterprise. I went on business trips overseas and you were allowed to travel on the Laura Ashley company plane – so I travelled in style! You'd go anywhere in the world and you'd meet someone who either knew of Laura Ashley, worked at Laura Ashley or loved Laura Ashley."

Cutting the cloth at Carno.

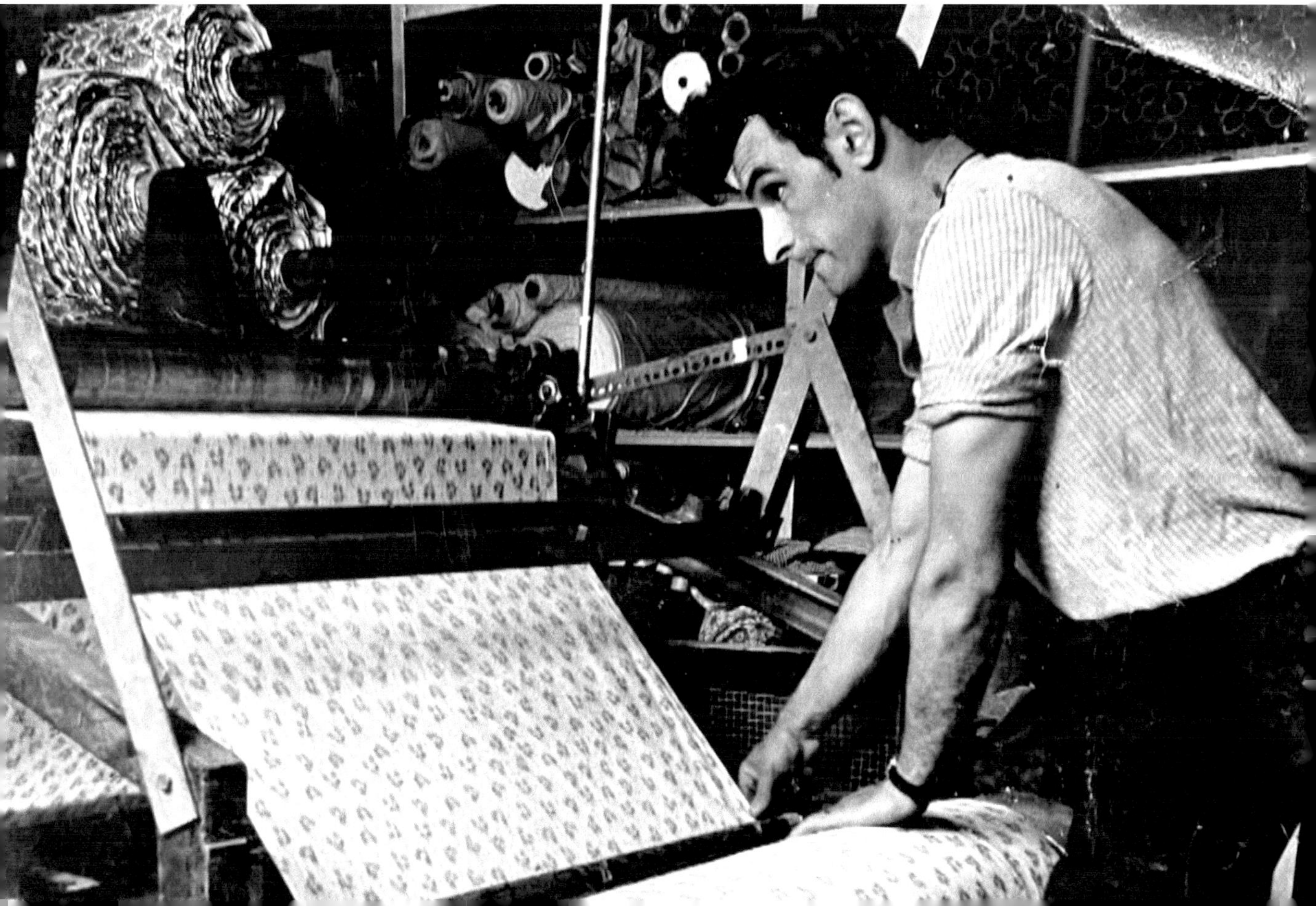

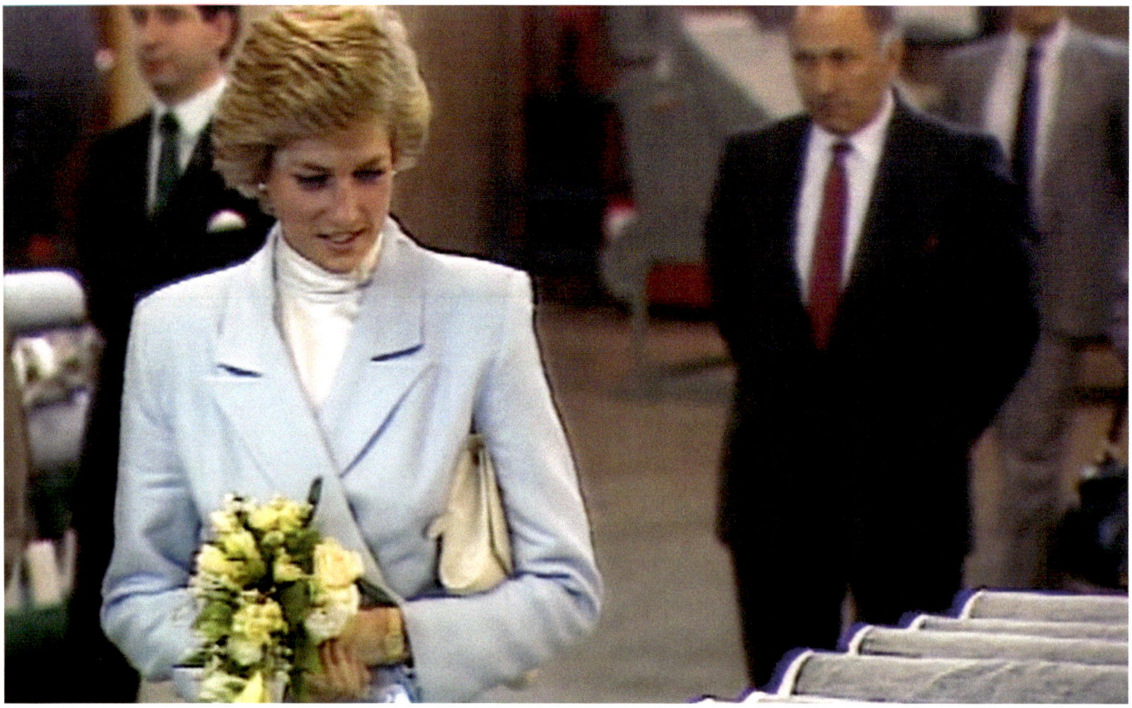

In 1985, at the height of the zeitgeist, came tragic news. Laura Ashley, who had given her name to one of the most beloved British brands, had died. She had fallen at her daughter's home shortly after celebrating her 60th birthday. The Ashley family resolved to honour Laura's vision and continue the business. The next few years saw further productivity and profits. But the fashion industry can be tough. Styles come and go, fortunes rise and fall.

In the 2000s the financial threads of the business began to unravel. The factory in Carno closed, high street shops and other manufacturing sites were shut down and the company's retail presence overseas was drastically scaled back. The coronavirus pandemic of 2020 was the final straw: Laura Ashley filed for administration and scrapped its remaining UK stores. The brand now exists as a licensed business model; the Laura Ashley name and intellectual property rights acquired by a holding company. You won't find any of those nostalgic fabrics and furnishings rolling out of Mid Wales anymore.

In Carno, the old Laura Ashley factory still stands. It's been put to other commercial use and some rear sections of the site have already been demolished. But the village will always be linked to this unlikely success story. In the grounds of St John the Baptist church, just down the road from the former factory, you'll find two simple graves next to each other: those of Laura and Bernard Ashley.

Above: the Princess of Wales takes a tour of the Laura Ashley empire, 1988.

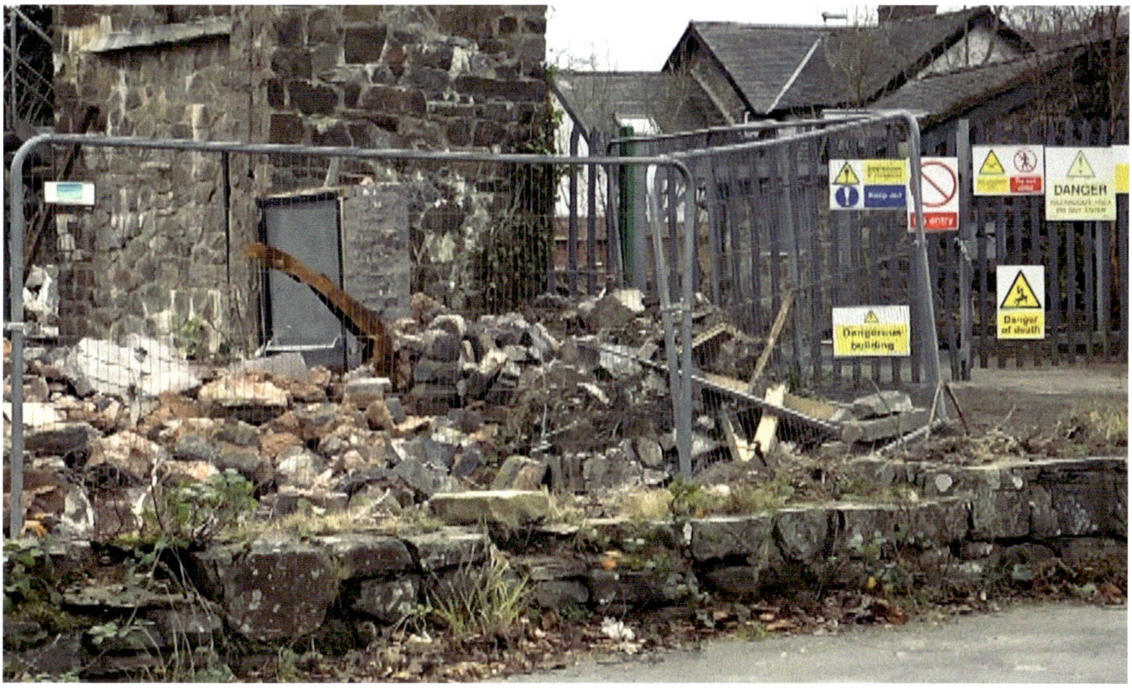

Above: demolition underway at the Carno factory, 2024.

THE FLYING BOATS OF PEMBROKE DOCK

The wartime home of magnificent machines

During the 1940s, daily life in Pembroke Dock was an assault on the senses. The air hung heavy with the deafening roar of aero engines; the old streets vibrated with the voices of men from many nations; the waterways were whipped up by huge metal monsters circling the Cleddau Estuary.

Pembroke Dock had always boasted strong links to the military, and during WW2 that bond went into overdrive. The town became the world's largest base for flying boats.

The RAF had established a station there back in 1930. Just four years earlier, the town's Royal Dockyard which had been a bastion of ship building since 1814, was soberly shut down by the Admiralty. The town's fortunes wavered until the Air Ministry swooped in to take advantage of Pembroke Dock's secret weapon: its sheltered harbour. A new breed of aircraft was evolving: seaplanes that could take off and land on water. They came in different designs of contrasting capabilities, with stirring names like the Short Rangoon, the Short Singapore and the Supermarine Southampton. What these aircraft needed more than anything else was a protected body of water to deploy as a floating runway. The fact that the infrastructure of Pembroke Dock was already configured for seafaring clinched the deal.

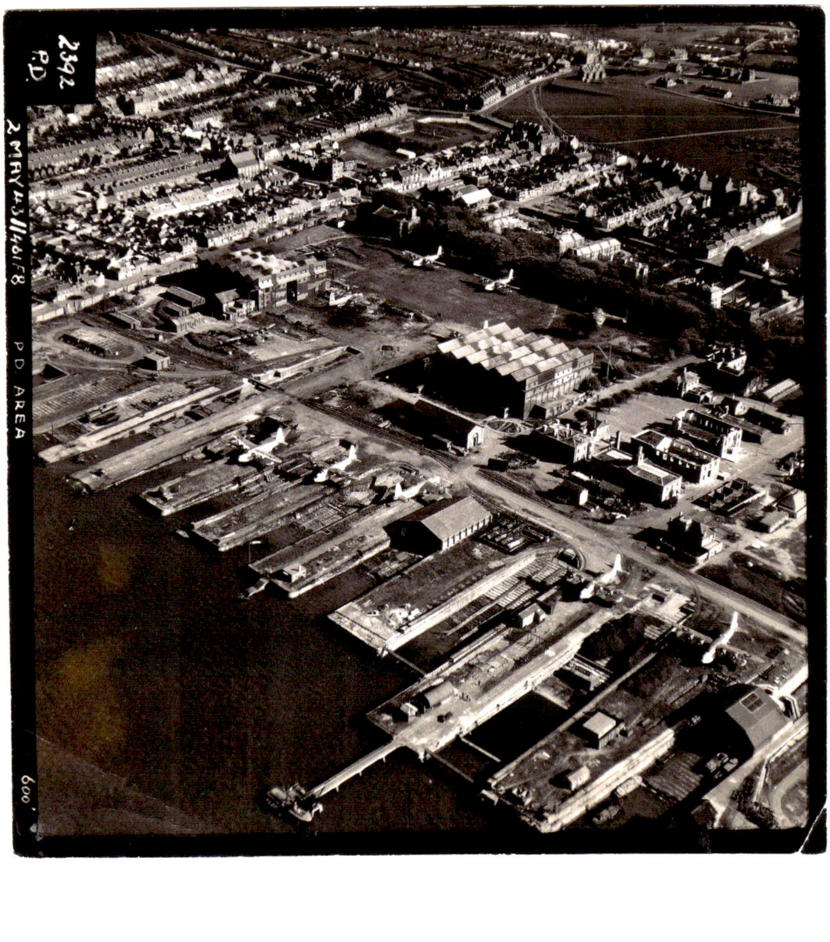

Of all the hybrid aeroplanes that made their home in West Wales, the jewel in the crown was the Short Sunderland. It was an icon of the skies, a testament to the boldness of British engineering. This was the winged equivalent of a battleship, a graceful beast with a range of up to 3,000 miles. It had three tactical functions: long range reconnaissance, the airborne protection of Allied shipping and the detection and destruction of enemy vessels.

Fred Maryon was based at Pembroke Dock with No. 230 Squadron and has vivid memories of flying in a Sunderland:

> "We did long patrols, sometimes for 12 hours at a time. It was a very busy life as part of the aircrew on a Sunderland. You were half airman, half sailor. There were about ten in the crew, two men for each discipline. We had two pilots, two navigators, two flight engineers, two signallers, and two gunners. We had cooking facilities on board – only a Primus stove but at least we could make ourselves a decent meal. The signallers and engineers would normally do the cooking!
>
> "It was very loud. It wasn't like flying a civil airliner today where they have lots of insulation. Taking off was particularly noisy because you could hear the water under the skin of the plane. It sounded like tearing paper. I used to think we were going to lose the bottom of the aircraft! And when you were landing, if it was flat calm or at night-time, it was quite hard for the pilot to judge the height. He would fly at quite a heavy rate of descent so that he hit the water hard and he knew he'd made it. Otherwise you could think you were safely on water but in fact you'd be 10 or 25 feet above it.
>
> "But we did enjoy those missions and we had some great fun. I loved the Sunderlands. They were the best part of my RAF life."

Opposite: The RAF base at Pembroke Dock, 1943.

Below: a Sunderland flying boat touches down.

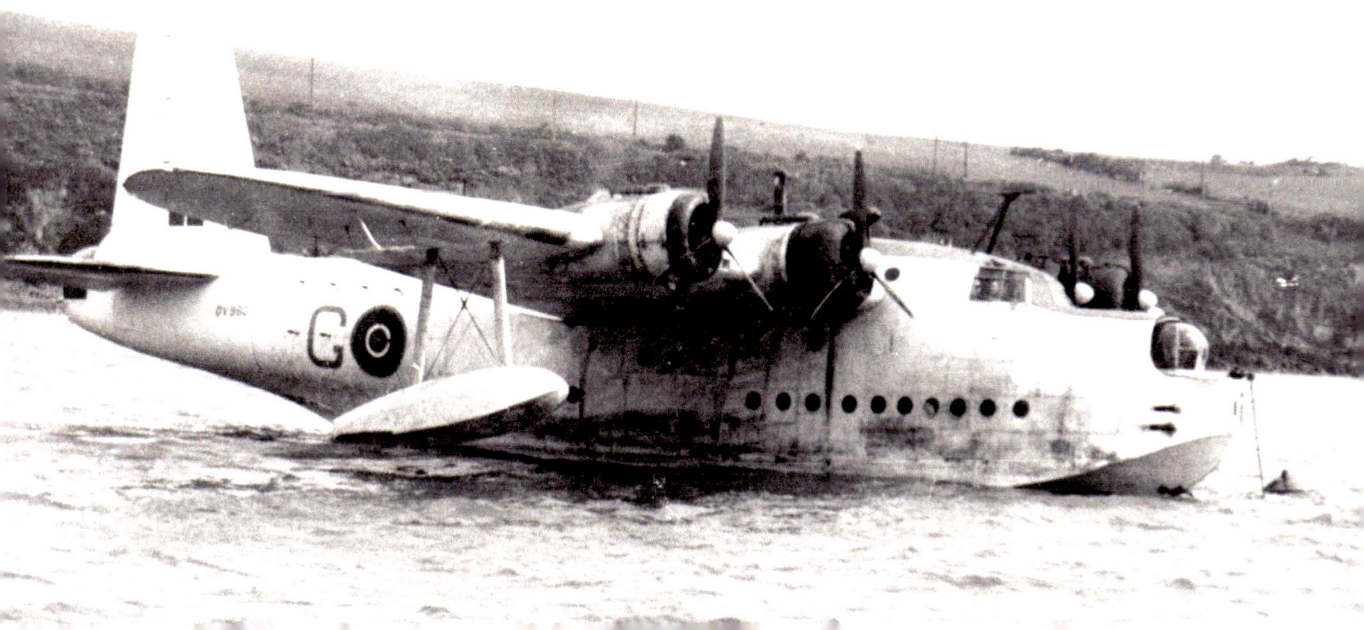

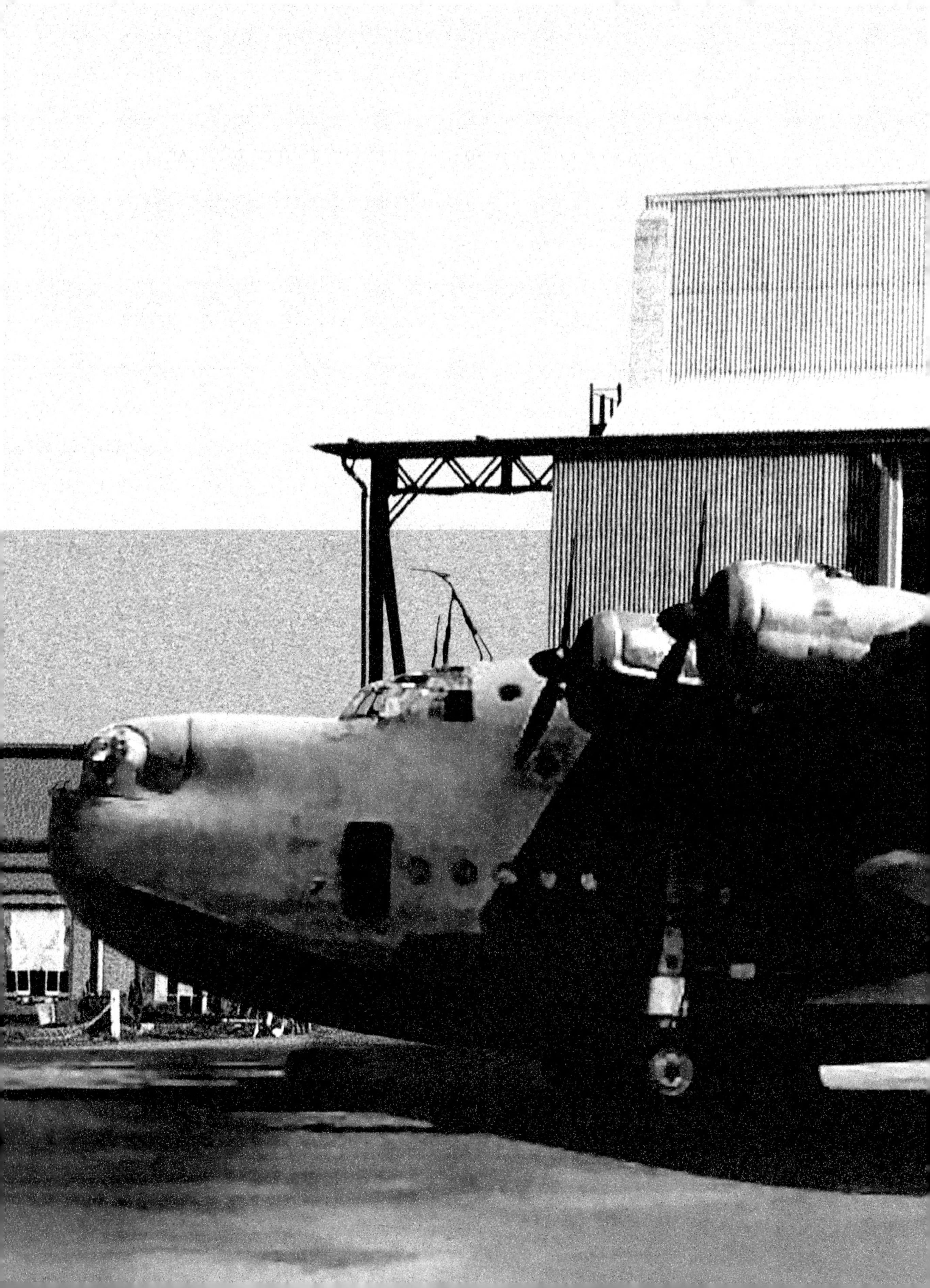

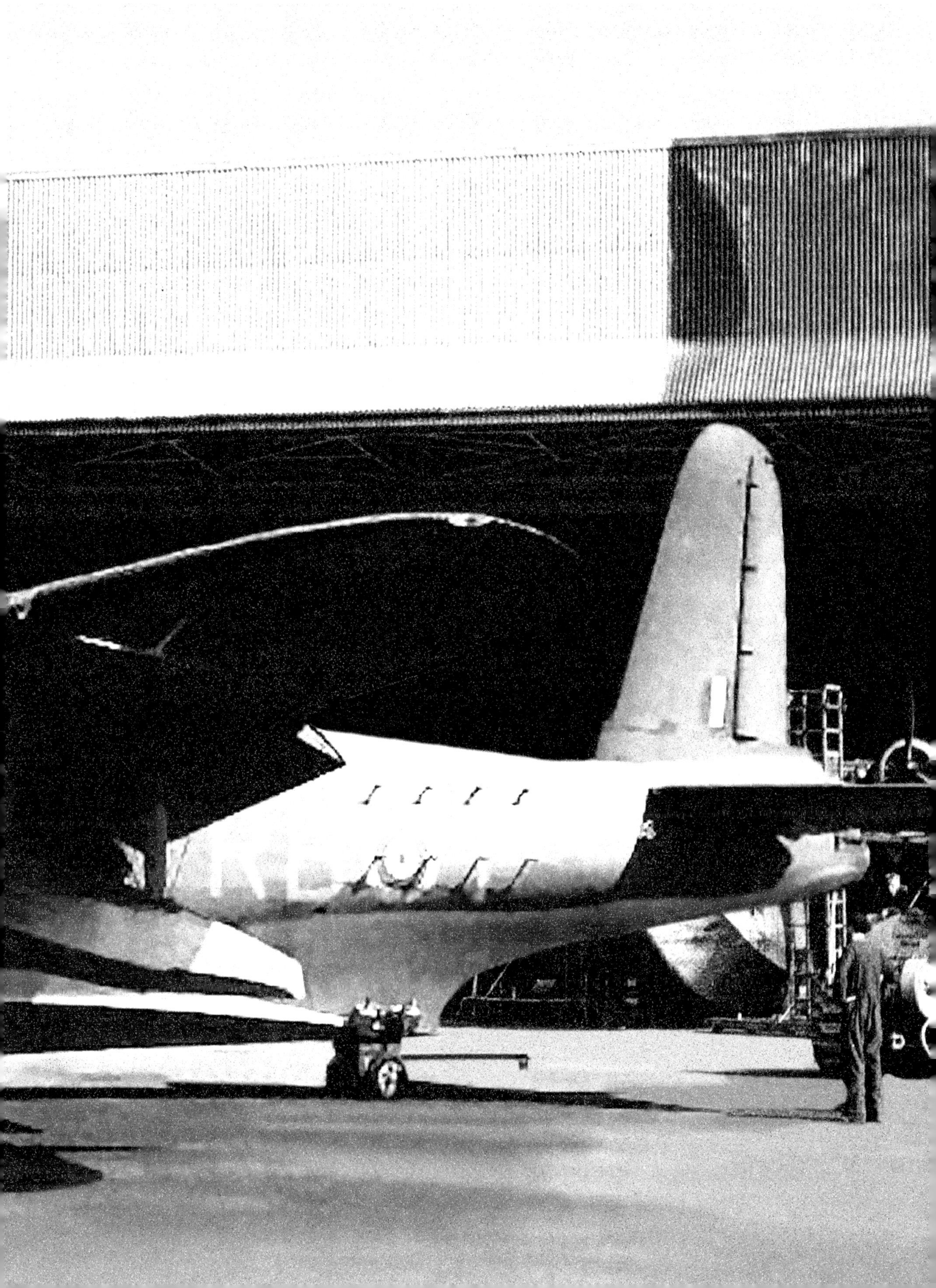

Overleaf: a Sunderland ashore at Pembroke Dock during WW2.

Following the outbreak of war in 1939, the flying boat station at Pembroke Dock swelled with air squadrons from Australia, Canada, the United States and the Netherlands. Almost overnight, the coastal community felt cosmopolitan. Planes pierced the air and slammed into the sea, day after day, night after night. By the Spring of 1943 there were, at one time, 99 flying boats in Pembroke Dock, both on the water and brought ashore on special beaching gear. Most of those were Sunderlands.

Today, two towering reminders of the town's wartime clout still dominate the quaysides. Adjacent to the ferry terminal you'll find a pair of almighty aircraft hangars. These steel Goliaths, now Grade II listed, were constructed to house and repair the fleet of sea planes and they remain the only structures of their kind surviving in Wales and England. They're a symbol of just how strategically significant Pembroke Dock had become in the war effort. John Evans, Patron of the Pembroke Dock Heritage Trust, believes the local flying boat patrols held the key to Britain's security:

> "The town was a hive of maritime aviation at a particularly important time during the Second World War: the Battle of the Atlantic and the fight against the German U-boats. The Sunderlands would fly way out over the ocean to protect our maritime trade. If we hadn't been able to continue that trade, we would never have been able to win the Second World War, it's as simple as that. We needed the munitions, the fuel, the food and the troops coming to us from across the Atlantic. Winston Churchill himself said that everything depended on the outcome of that campaign in the Atlantic. To safeguard those Allied vessels you needed to have protection on the sea but also, crucially, from the air.

A Sunderland operated by the French Navy arrives at Pembroke Dock after the War.

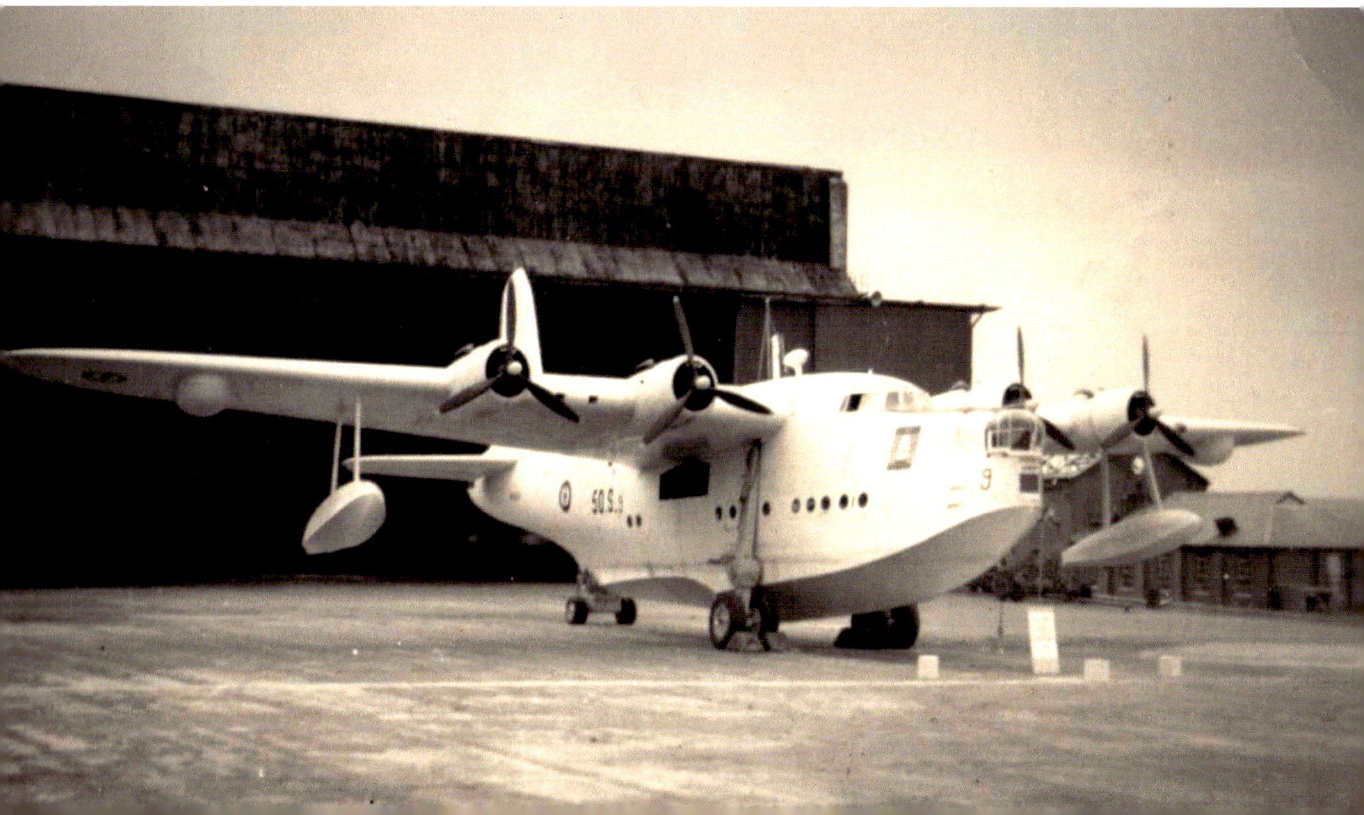

"The Sunderlands were a quantum leap forward in aviation and they played a vital role. The flying boats and Pembroke Dock operated together – each of equal importance to the other. It's a proud chapter in our past and many years on it's still revered and remembered."

When peace arrived in 1945, the RAF retained its operational base in Pembroke Dock. Flying boats still had their uses, and Sunderlands subsequently saw active service during the Berlin Airlift and the Korean War. But the sun was slowly setting on these winged workhorses.

Advances in aeronautical design were moving away from the concept of supersized seaplanes. In 1959, the RAF retired the Sunderlands after 21 years of military service and closed its station at Pembroke Dock. It was a sucker punch for the town. The skies fell silent. The Haven felt eerily serene.

In March 1961, a solitary Sunderland returned to Pembroke Dock as a static tourist attraction sited on the former playing field of the RAF station. Visitors could pay one shilling (6d for children) to access the aeroplane's lower deck. The four-engined colossus proved a huge draw, pulling in tens of thousands of sightseers. But its stay was short-lived. The Sunderland's aged frame didn't appreciate being exposed to the vagaries of the Welsh weather. Reluctantly, the town bade farewell to the plane in 1971 as it was transported to the Royal Air Force Museum in London for preservation, where it remains to this day.

The era of the flying boats in Wales is long gone. But there is one Sunderland left in Pembroke Dock. It's a time capsule and it lies at the bottom of the Milford Haven Waterway.

On the seabed are the remains of *T9044*: an ill-fated Sunderland that sank in the waters off Pembroke Dock during a ferocious storm in November 1940. Miraculously, no lives were lost. For the best part of 25 years, divers have been painstakingly bringing to the surface a vast array of artefacts from the drowned aircraft. Those treasured remnants are conserved at the Pembroke Dock Heritage Centre, based within the former Dockyard chapel. On display you'll find two of the aeroplane's engines, its propellers and even the original front gun turret and Vickers Gas Operated machine gun.

Rik Saldanha is Chairman of the Pembroke Dock Heritage Trust and one of the divers who's been scouring the sea floor:

"The plane lies 20 metres beneath the surface, in a shipping lane. There's a strong current and very poor visibility which makes it an extremely challenging dive. On a bad day I can't even see my instruments. I've been diving for more than 50 years, all over the world, but in the Haven it's like a night dive every time you go down there.

"One of my ambitions is to bring up the four Browning machine guns at the rear of the aircraft. But those guns are down to about a metre in silt. So we're going to have to dig. And one of the problems you have when you start digging is that you can guarantee the visibility is going to go from very poor to totally non-existent."

Recovering anything from the wreckage is a Herculean task. Rik is licensed by the Ministry of Defence to salvage artefacts from the sunken Sunderland for preservation. It's a labour of love but he admits this is no ordinary aircraft. *T9044* is one of a kind:

"What's significant is that it's the most complete Mk1 in existence – the earliest version of the Sunderland. In the world there are only three known whole Sunderland aeroplanes – and they're all Mk5: the final version that was built. The fact that we have an Mk1 in situ is absolutely unique throughout the world."

Overleaf: a Sunderland is hauled up the slipway, circa 1941.

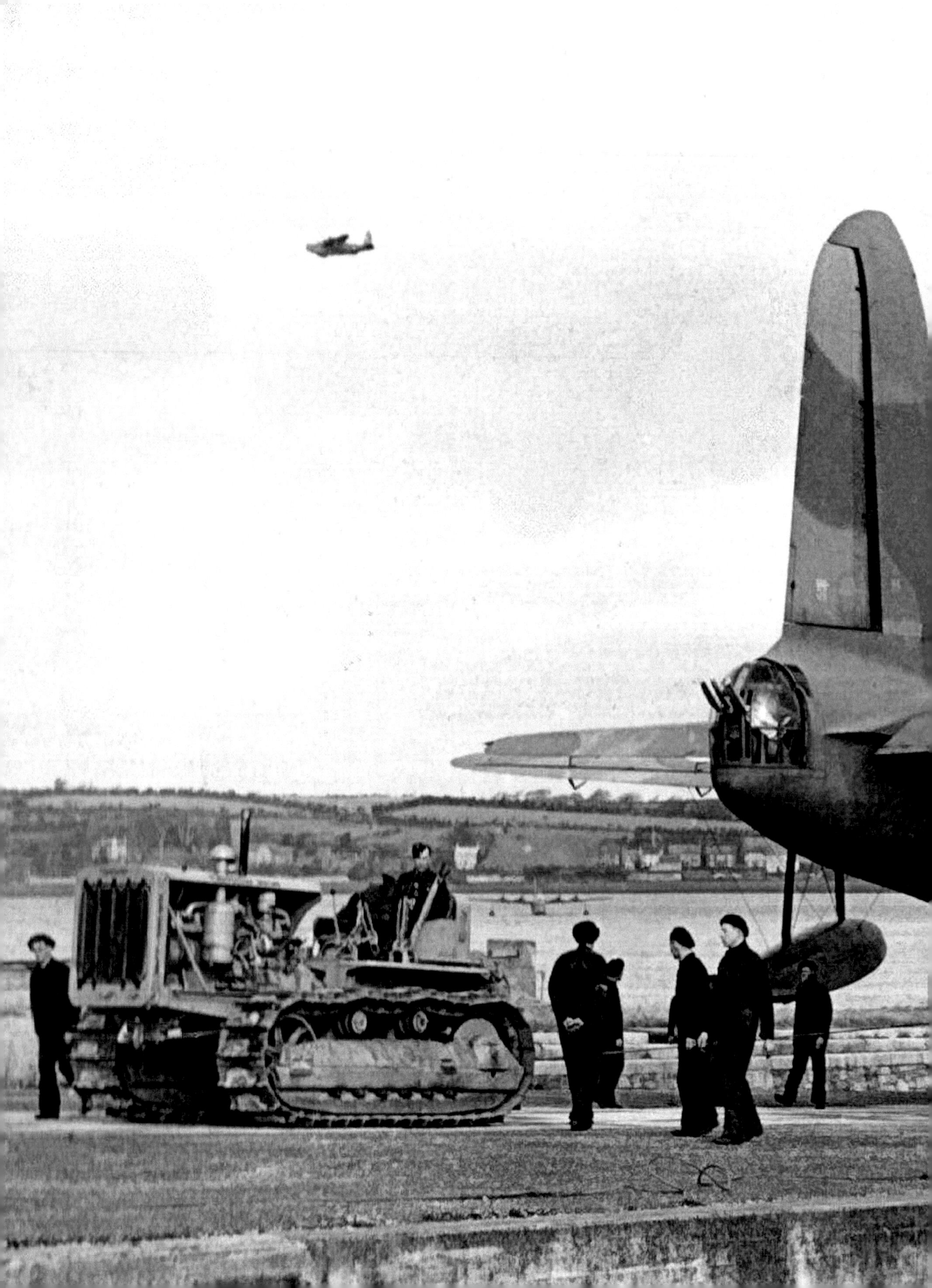

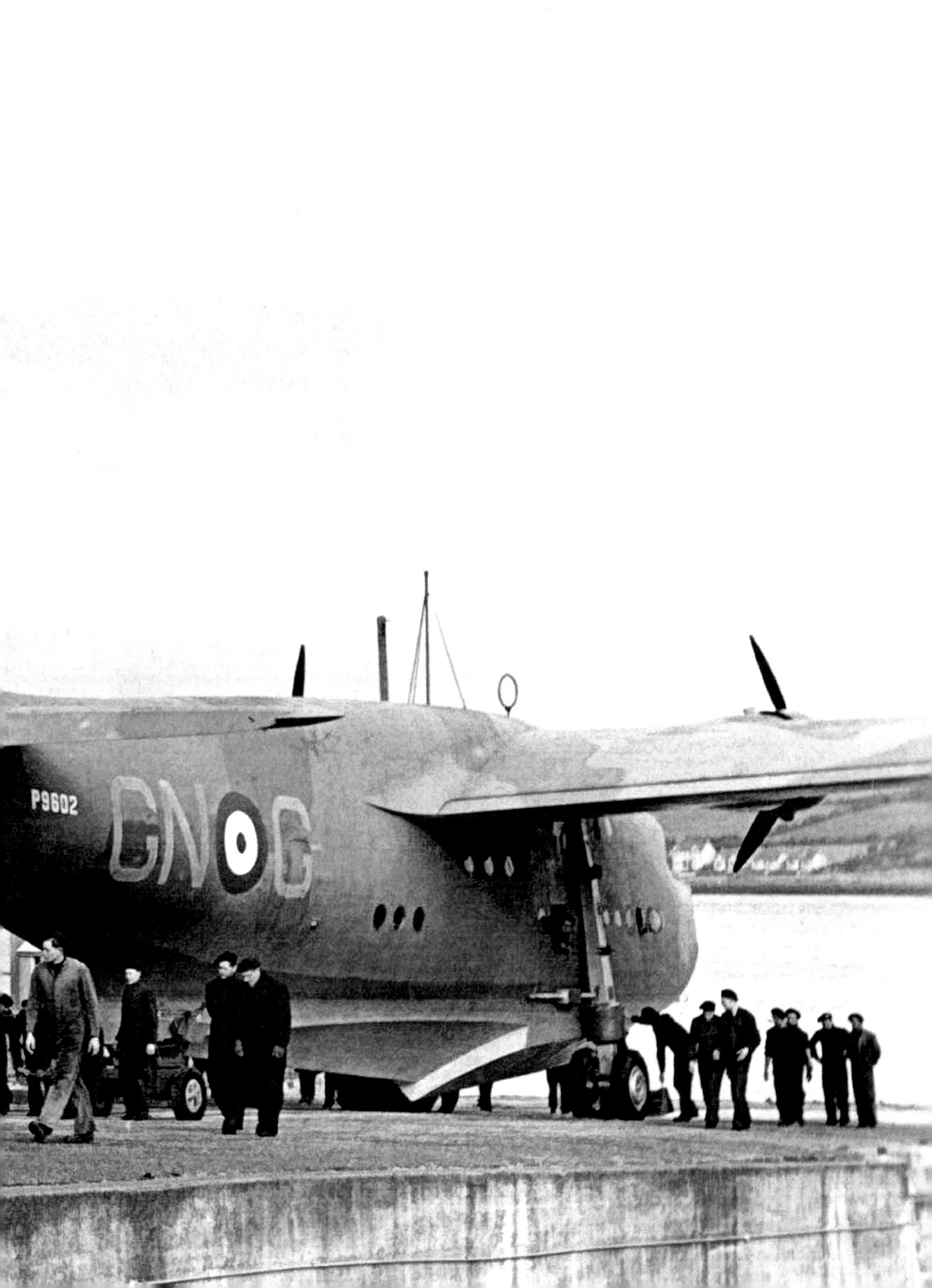
P9602
GN G

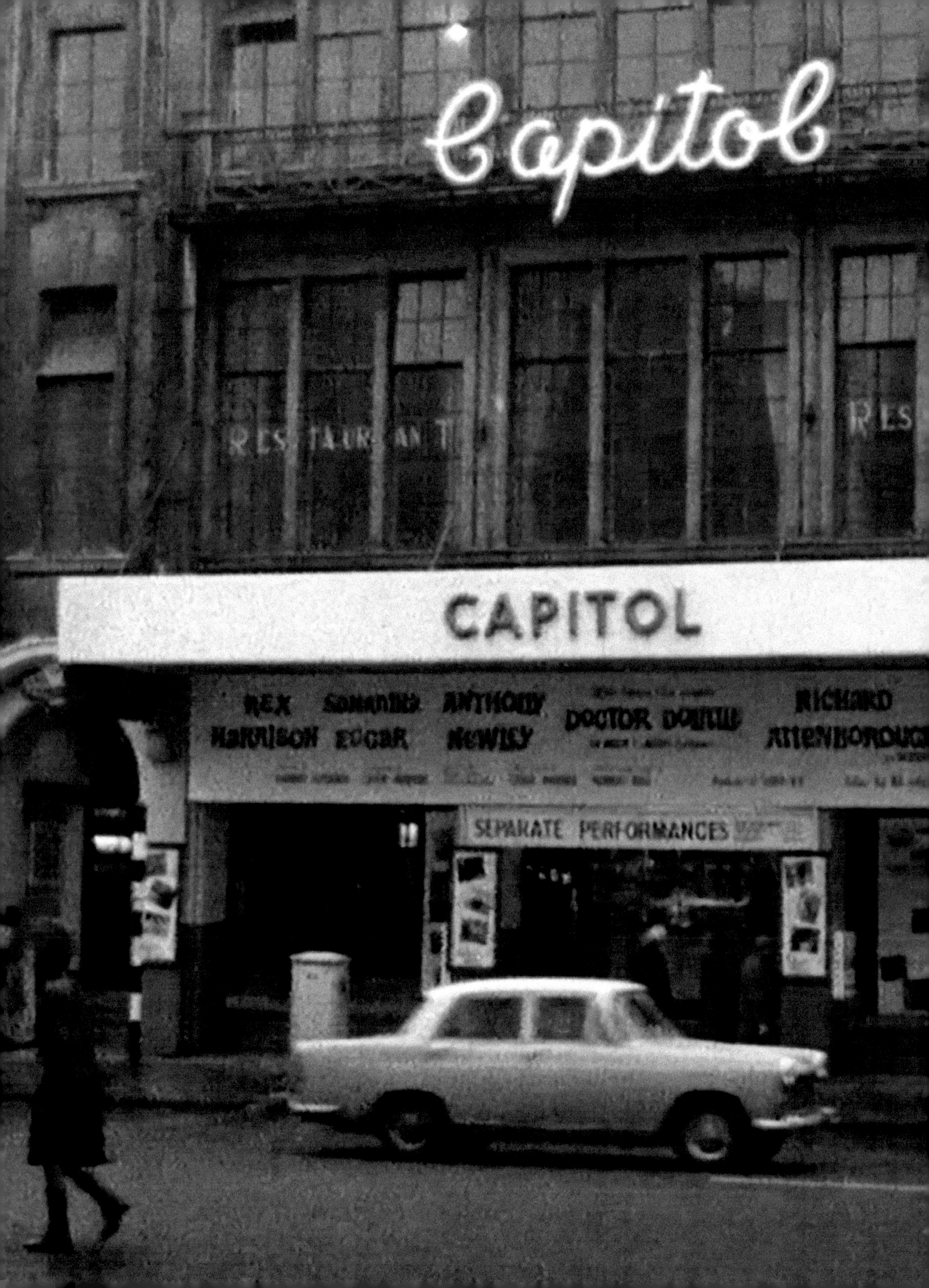
Capitol
RESTAURANT
CAPITOL
REX HARRISON
RICHARD
SEPARATE PERFORMANCES

CAPITOL THEATRE

The pioneering venue that made musical history

In the heart of Cardiff's city centre, on one of its busiest shopping streets, there's a beige brick building with a bittersweet past. At the eastern end of Queen Street you'll find The Capitol Centre, a shiny retail mall that opened its doors in 1990. For Cardiffians of a certain vintage, however, that precise corner of the city once boasted a cherished landmark. It was a paean to music and movies, a sublime salute to popular entertainment. It was the Capitol Theatre.

In December 1921, the Cap (as it was fondly known) began its six-decade reign as Cardiff's grandest cinema. It could seat nearly 3,000 customers in its palatial auditorium, making it the largest purpose-built cinema in Europe at the time. Its working years spanned the evolution of moviemaking, from the silent era and the golden age of talkies to Technicolor epics and the birth of the blockbuster. 'The greatest home for pictures and music in Wales!' screamed the slogan, and it wasn't far off the mark.

Hatted staff in braided uniforms sashayed along the plush red carpets. At showtime, audiences would ascend an elegant staircase surrounded by marble columns, brass handrails and porcelain light fittings. A night at the Capitol meant one thing – prestige. Colin James worked there during the 1960s and it became a home from home:

> "Ever since I was a little boy, I'd always loved the cinema. When I saw an advert for front of house staff at the Capitol I thought, that's it, I'm applying. The day the letter arrived telling me I'd been successful I could have jumped over the moon. It's all I ever wanted.
>
> "It was a wonderful building, so strong and marvellous. We had a huge screen that could show 70mm films. *The Sound of Music* played for a year and eight months! There were four fire engines parked in the side street every night in case there was a fire, because the building was so packed with people. On the one year anniversary of *The Sound of Music* they had a five-tiered cake topped with Julie Andrews and Christopher Plummer made out of icing. The cake was cut up and given to customers at the end of the evening.
>
> "Whenever there was a James Bond film on there would be queues around the block. I thought, 'we're never going to get you all in!' It was brilliant, honestly it was. It was the meeting place for the people of Cardiff and they really were thrilled with it."

The vastness of the Capitol made it a highly versatile venue. When it wasn't screening films, the building hosted a wealth of live music. The roster of stars that performed at the Capitol over the years is simply staggering: Queen, Led Zeppelin, Elton John, Bob Dylan, Ray Charles, The Beach Boys, Chuck Berry, Jimi Hendrix, Bill Haley, Johnny Cash, T.Rex, The Kinks, Roxy Music and countless more. On 8th October 1966, fans were treated to a line-up that typified the calibre of acts making a beeline for the Capitol, as The Rolling Stones, Ike & Tina Turner and The Yardbirds appeared on the same night on the same bill.

The Capitol in the 1960s.

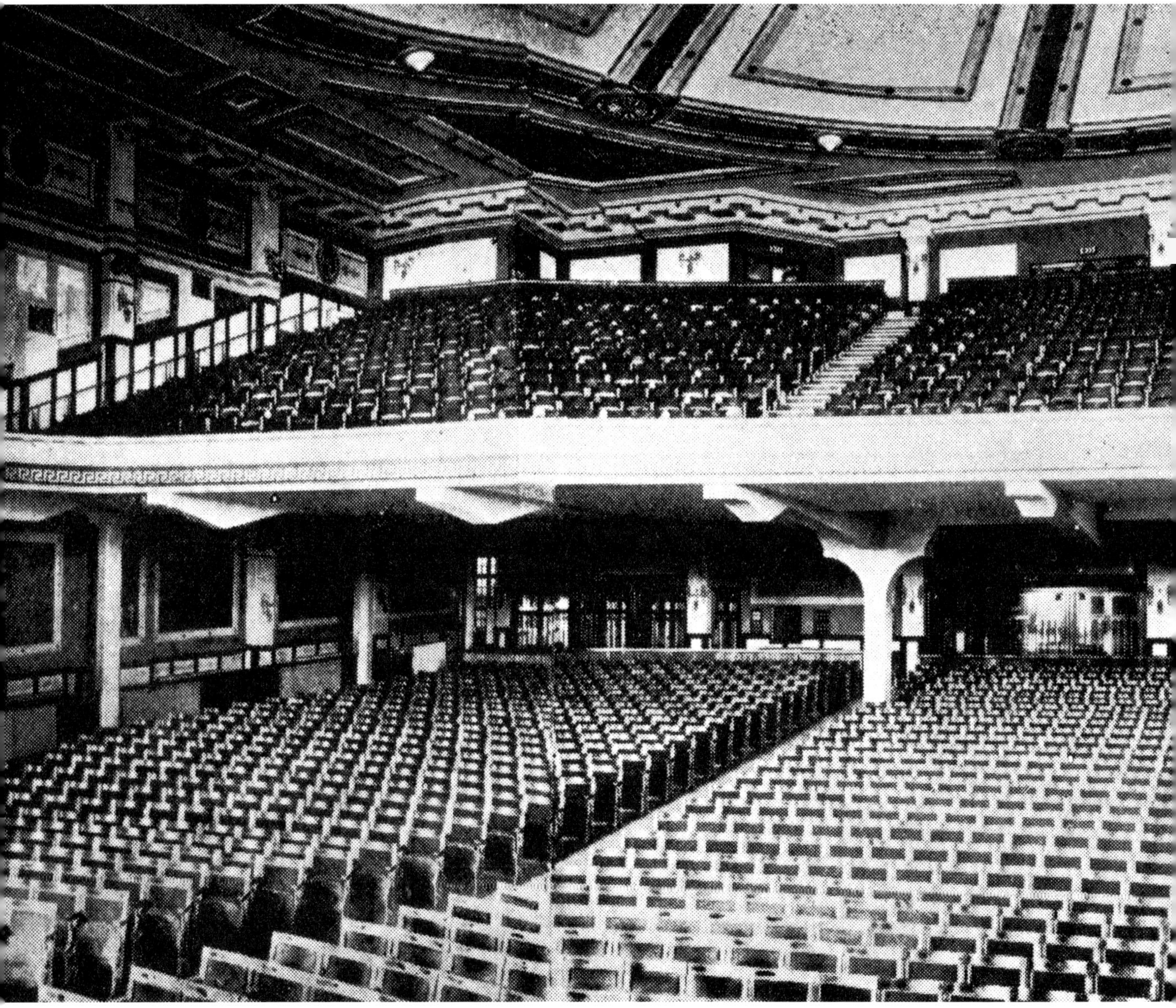

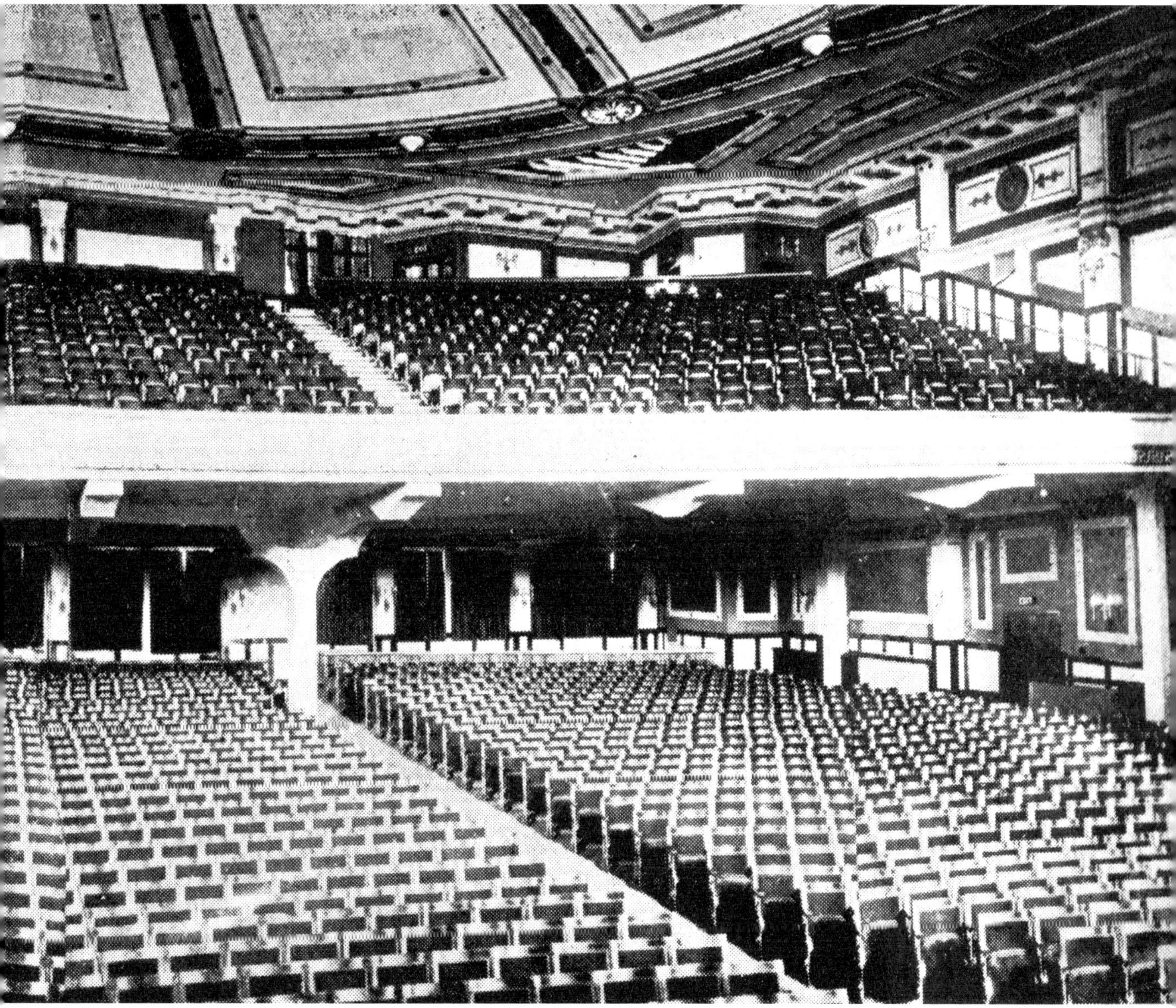

The Capitol's imposing interior. They don't build them like this anymore.

As well as attracting international stars, the theatre was a springboard for local talent too. Musician Bat Godard has gigged all over the world and the fuse was lit by his formative years at the Cap:

"I played in a local rock 'n' roll band in the late 1950s. Back then the Capitol had a teenage show on a Saturday morning, where they'd have live music. Arriving at the building as a youngster you couldn't believe that all these huge stars had appeared there and you were going on to that same stage. I personally never suffered from stage fright but a lot of the youngsters did. They'd go on and they'd freeze. They'd turn their backs to the audience. It was the splendour of it, like you were auditioning for Hollywood on home ground. There wasn't an orchestra pit so the stage felt very close to the audience. It was probably no more than a 20 or 30ft gap between the seats and the stage. But it was such an exciting time, a vibrant time, and it got a lot of young musicians started."

Bat Godard (far left) and his bandmates rock the Cap.

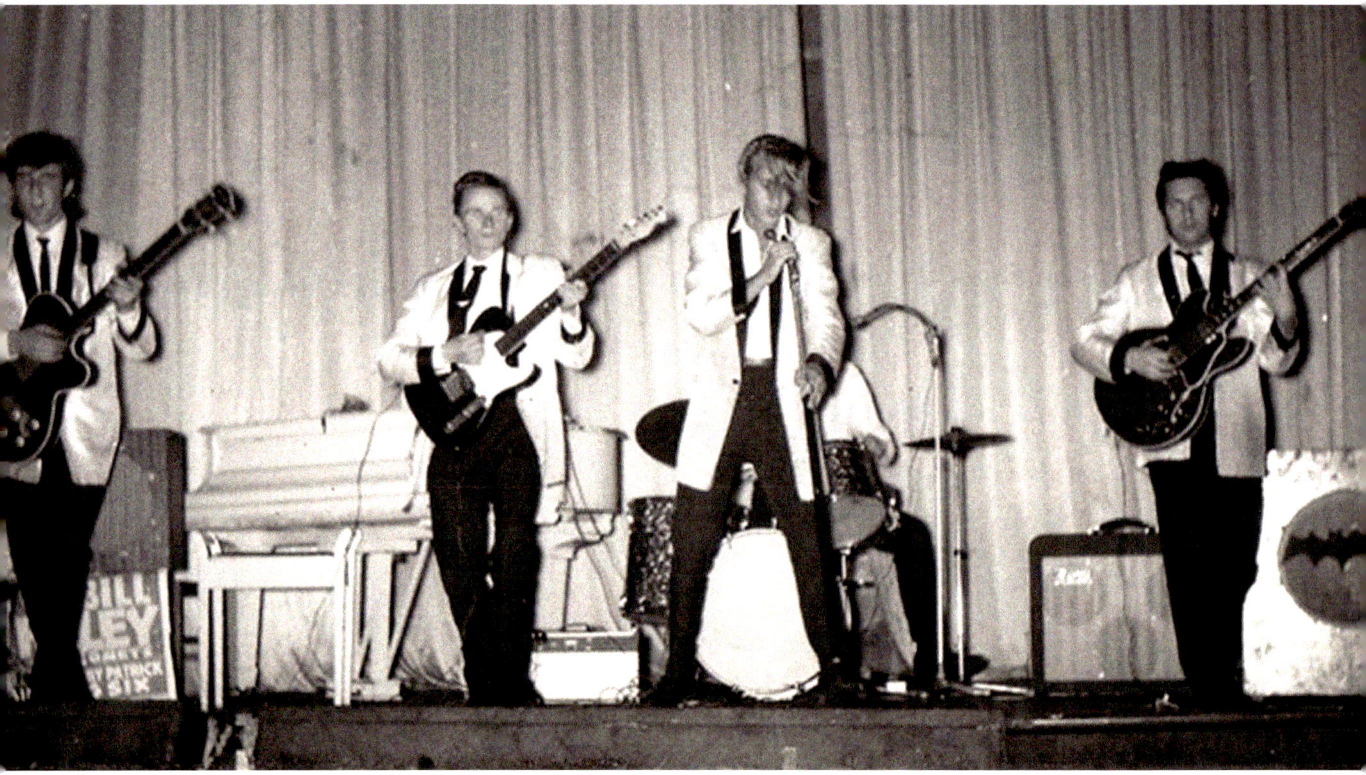

By far, the biggest act to play the Capitol was The Beatles. Their first appearance was on 27 May 1963, sharing the bill with Roy Orbison and Gerry and the Pacemakers. *From Me To You* had just topped the charts and Cardiff was bracing itself for full-on Beatlemania. Philip Davies was at the gig:

"What I remember more than anything is the sheer noise and not from The Beatles. There were girls and women shrieking, screaming, falling on the floor. Elderly commissionaires and St John Ambulance volunteers were carrying off people who had passed out. There was pushing and shoving; the staff couldn't stop people standing up in their seats. Between the screams I can remember hearing bits of *I Saw Her Standing There* and they closed the show with *Twist and Shout*.

"I couldn't believe I was seeing The Beatles. I'd read about them, I'd seen them on television, I'd heard them on the radio. But until I saw them in the flesh I didn't fully appreciate that energy, that swagger. When Paul and George got together around the microphone to do the harmonies the place went absolutely nuts. Amongst the girls there'd be shouts for John, there'd be shouts for Paul. It was absolute mayhem. The place was putty in their hands."

An original ticket from The Beatles' final ever UK tour date: 12th December 1965, at the Capitol.

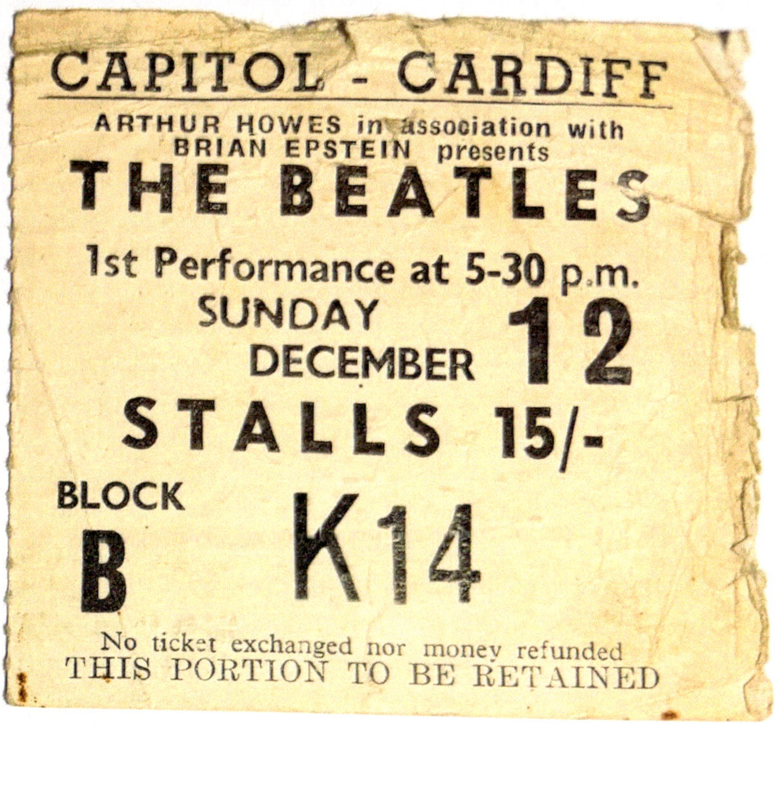

The Beatles returned to the Capitol on two subsequent occasions, on 7 November 1964 and 12th December 1965. They could never have known it at the time, but the fans at that gig in '65 were watching musical history unfold. After the Fab Four left the stage that night, they never again performed on a UK tour. The band fulfilled their overseas commitments in Europe and the US before retreating to the recording studio to make *Revolver* and *Sgt. Pepper's Lonely Hearts Club Band*. They never went on the road again. The final date on the Beatles' final ever tour on native soil was at the Capitol Theatre in Cardiff. How's that for a claim to fame?

While the Swinging Sixties were buzzy times for the Cap, the following decade was an utter disaster. TV had taken hold and cinema-going across Britain was in serious decline. The live music scene was changing too, as audiences demanded bigger and better venues. Without bums on seats, the hulking building was becoming a financial liability. In January 1978, its owners, Rank, decided to cut their losses and close the Capitol. One year later all the fixtures and fittings were auctioned off. Film projectors, cinema seats, pianos, clocks and velvet curtains – everything must go.

For the next few years, the grand old dame stood empty, slowly rotting away. Campaigners feared for its future and organised petitions to try to have the building preserved. At one moment in time there had been serious plans to convert the Capitol into a home for Welsh National Opera, but the scheme floundered due to lack of funding. In the end, Cardiff Council had a fervent rethink and decided that what would be of most benefit to that particular corner of the city was commerce, not entertainment. And so there was no reprieve. In 1983, the Cap was completely demolished. A treasured part of old Cardiff would never be seen again.

Today, many shoppers passing by the Capitol retail centre won't know anything about the distinguished picture palace that once stood within its footprint. The generations to come will never experience that expansive auditorium where music and movies co-existed in such splendour. But memories are a powerful thing. If you ever worked at the Capitol, screamed as your favourite band took to the stage, or simply reclined in those plush velvet seats with a loved one by your side, you'll never forget it.

The shopping centre that replaced the Capitol but retained its name.

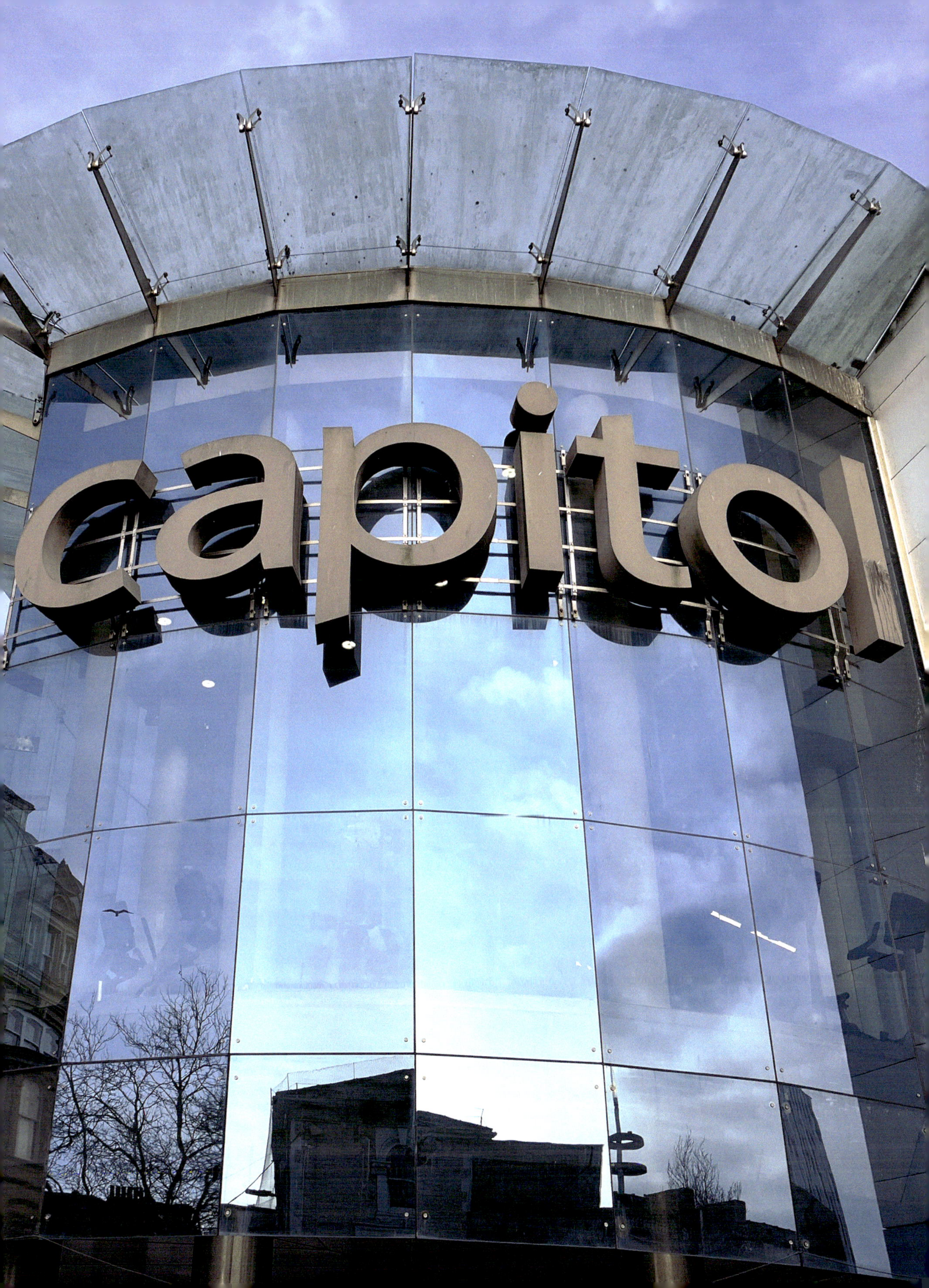
capitol

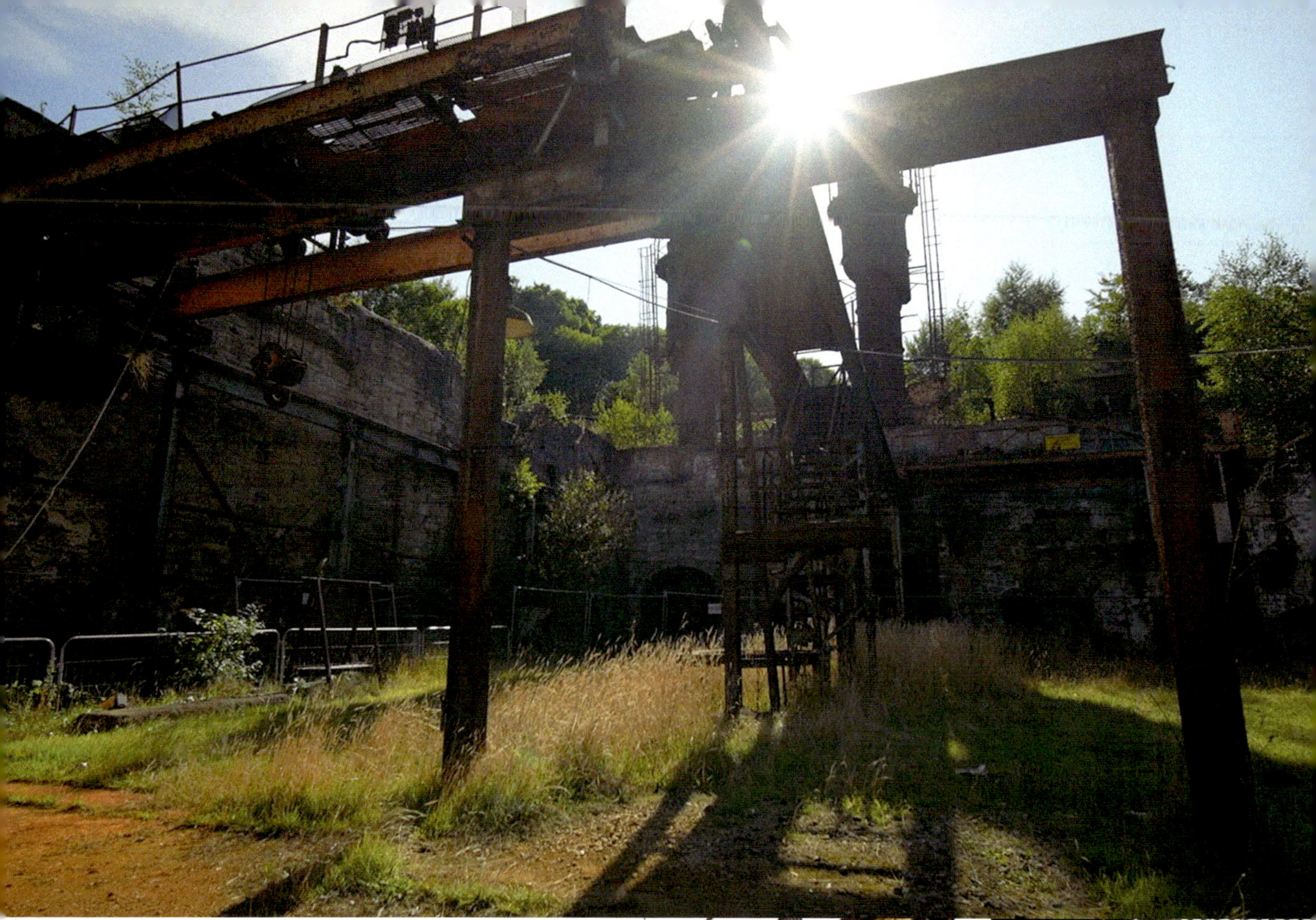

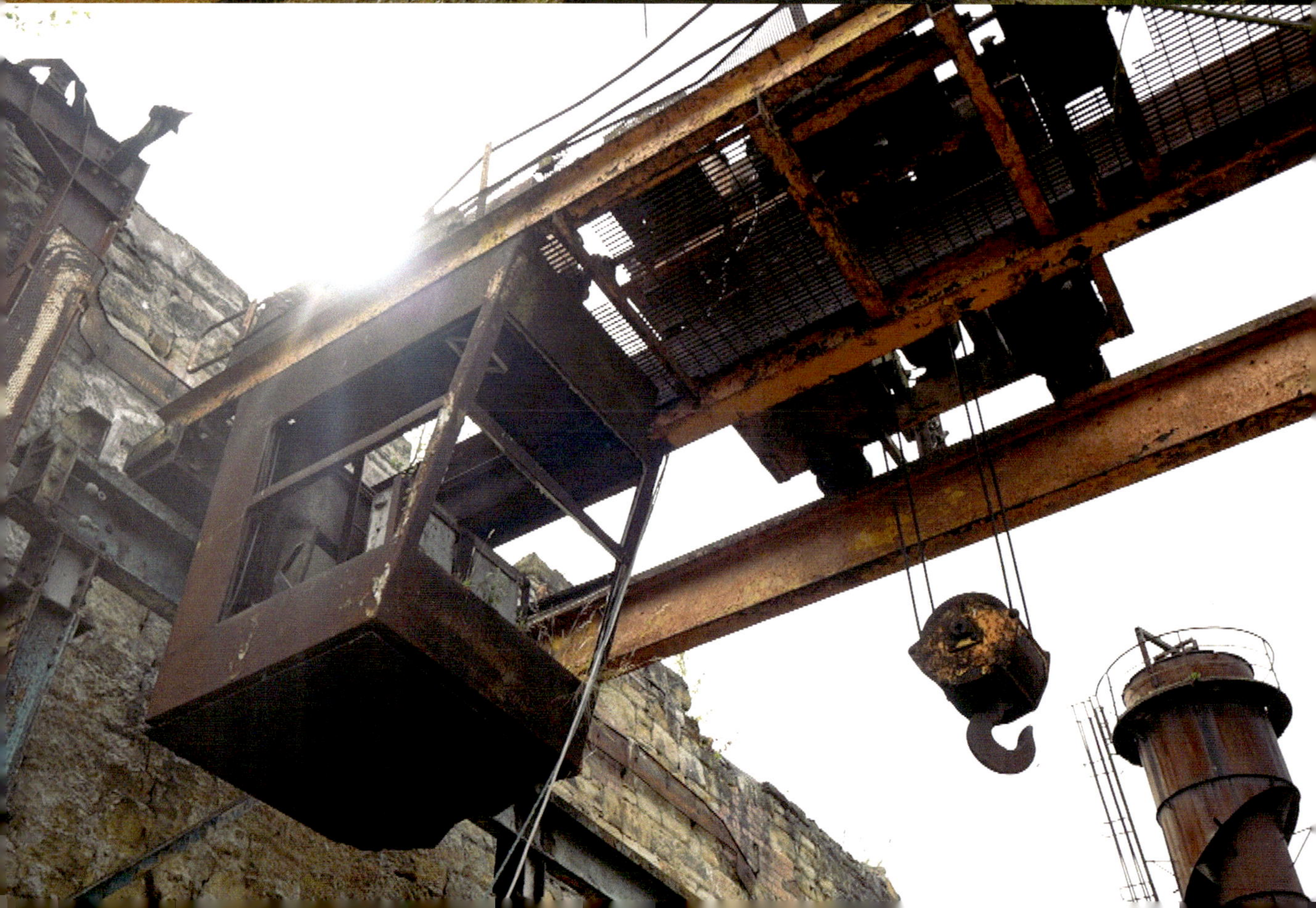

BRYMBO STEELWORKS

The lasting legacy of 'Iron-Mad' Wilkinson

In the hills to the west of Wrexham lie the rusting remains of an extraordinary enterprise. For just shy of 200 years, families worked shoulder to shoulder amid a crucible of smoke, steam and steel. It was a commercial operation first conceived during the adrenaline years of the industrial revolution, accelerating at breathless speed through the ages. It outpaced the reign of Queen Victoria, the Great Depression and the Second World War, surviving the Suez Crisis, weathering the Three-Day-Week and toughing out the Miners' Strike.

Navigating that journey were the men and women of Brymbo, a quiet country village that developed into an economic powerhouse within the blink of an eye. The towering industry on their doorstep would provide them with steady, well-paid work for generations – from the days of George III through to the Gulf War.

Only a fraction of the site still stands, but those fragments are highly significant. The main feature is a huge rectangular stack built of sandstone. This is Old No.1: a distinctive blast furnace dating back to the late 18th century. Surrounding it are the remains of a hulking foundry, comprising a machine shop, a winding house, two vertical furnaces and a network of tracks and railway lines. Close by, wagons, trucks and mangled equipment quietly corrode in the long grass. These abandoned relics are all that's left of an installation that radically reshaped the communities of Clwyd: Brymbo steelworks.

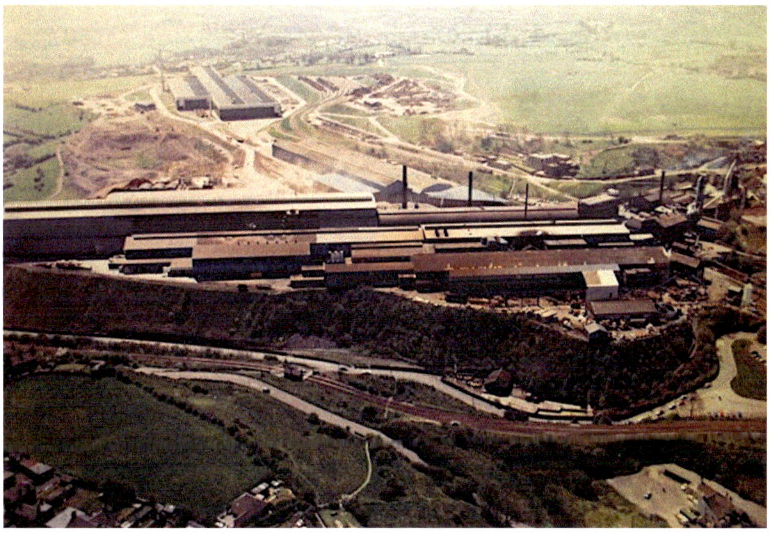

Opposite: the ruins of a thundering industry.

Above: Brymbo steelworks at peak production.

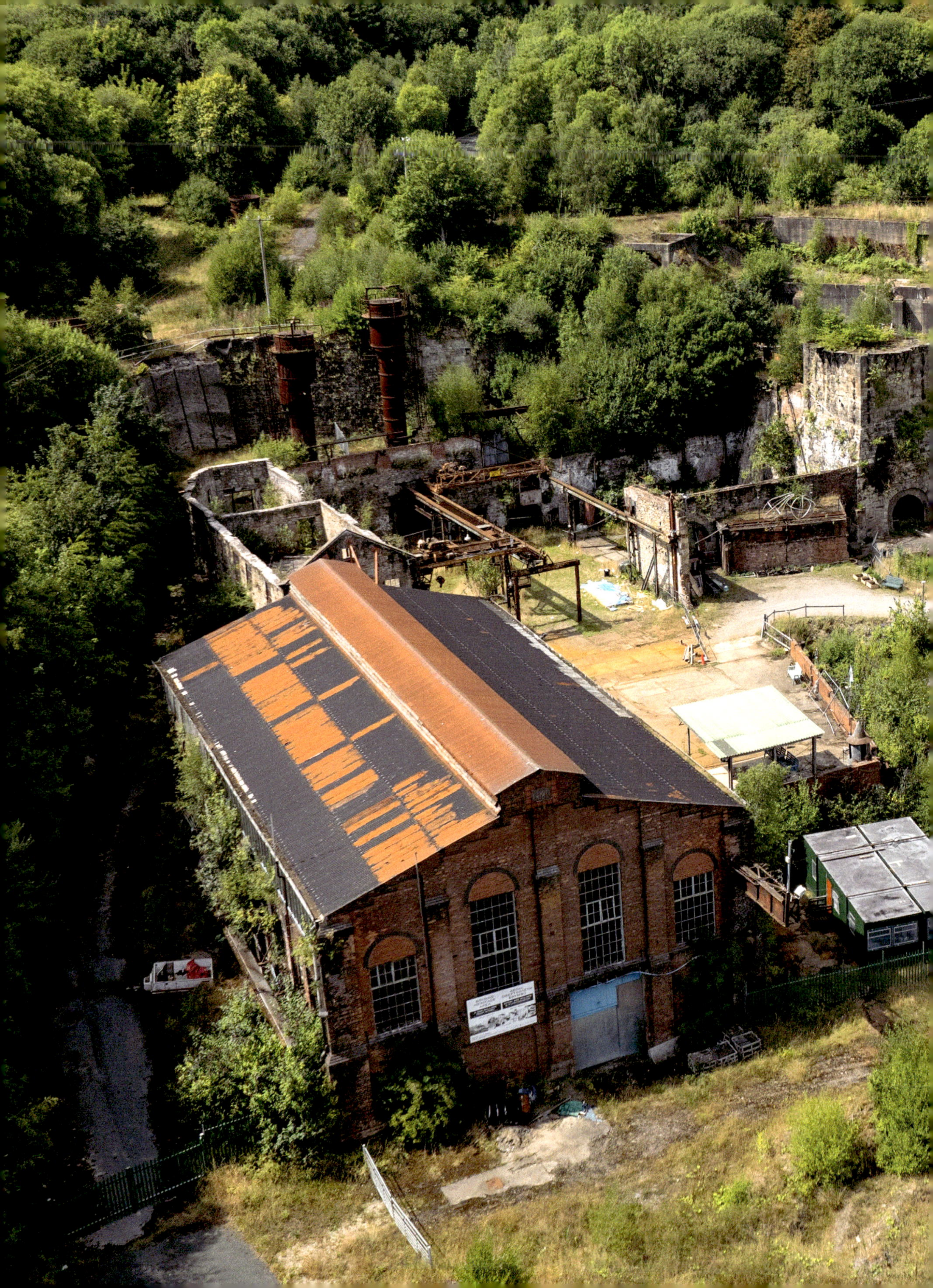

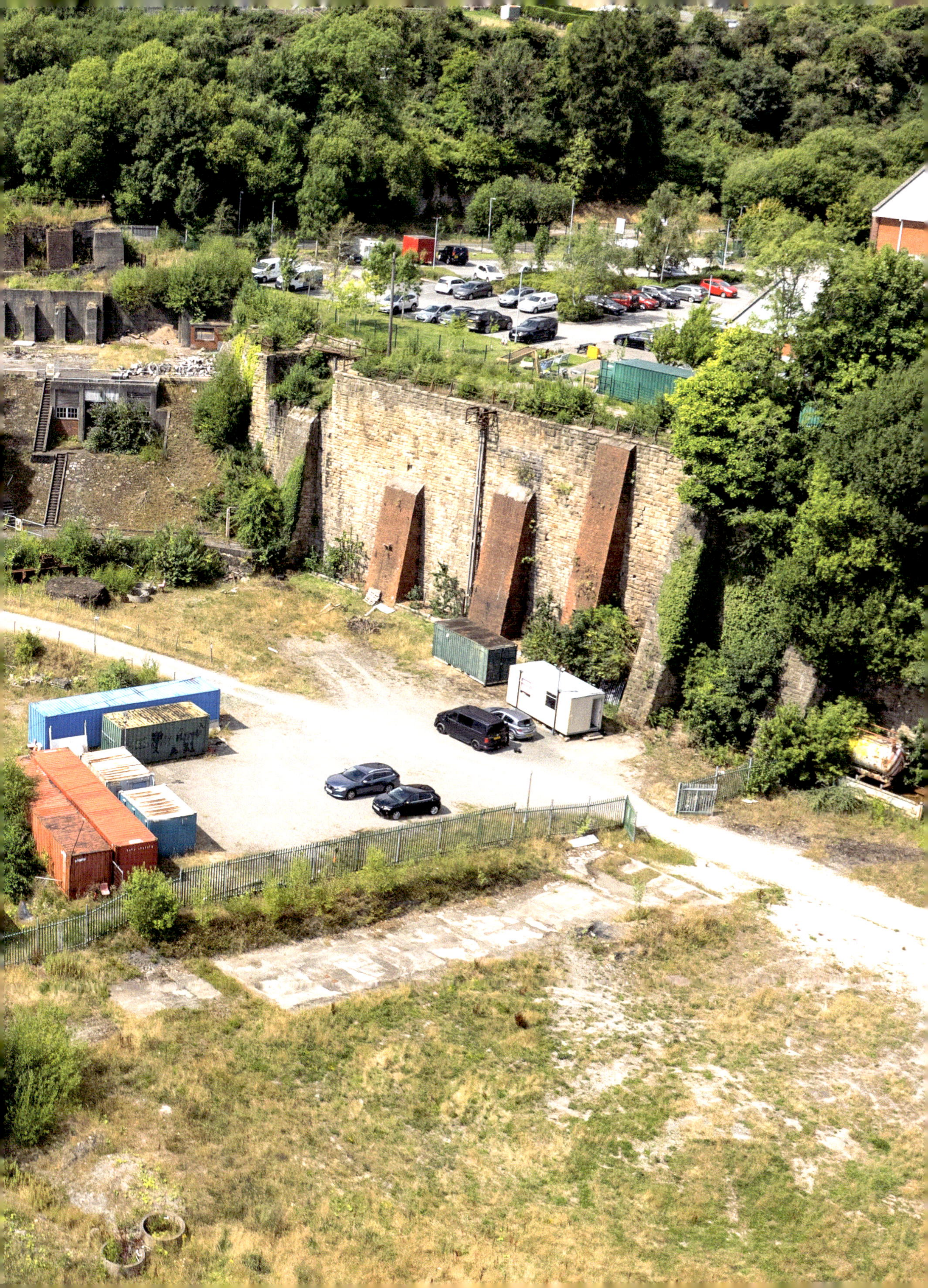

Overleaf: what remains of Brymbo steelworks today (Old No.1 furnace is in the centre of the photograph).

Unfurling over hundreds of acres, this was heavy industry on an inconceivable scale. The work was demanding, dangerous, sometimes deadly. The trade-off was that it was a job you could walk into; and if you proved your worth, that job was yours for life. Colin Davies was just 15 years old when he started at the steelworks, and he was following a family tradition:

"I worked there for 30 years, my dad for 55 years and my grandfather for 56 years. Even my great-grandfather, who originally came to Brymbo in 1872, was a 40-year man. That was typical of the area, to follow your forefathers into industry. What many youngsters had was supper table talk. You'd hear your dad talk about it, your grandfather talk about it, your uncles. You just grew up with it; it was all you knew.

"Entering the steelworks for the first time, you'd be hit by heat, dirt, dust and noise. It was quite a shock to the system. I hadn't been working on the rolling mill long when a big burly fella came up to me, and he quite simply said: 'Don't stand with your back to the mill.' I thought, 'I'm not going to argue with him. He's a bit bigger than me!' His words were wise and that was part of the safety training.

"You see, hot steel coming out of the rolling mill has a mind of its own. If it catches on something, it can buckle. And then there's only one thing to do: run. So from that day on, until the day I finished, I never turned my back on the mill.

"The steelworks were dangerous, but the older hands taught the younger people their safety. And you listened. If you didn't then, one way or another, you'd get hurt. The wisdom of the older workers was wisdom to be listened to."

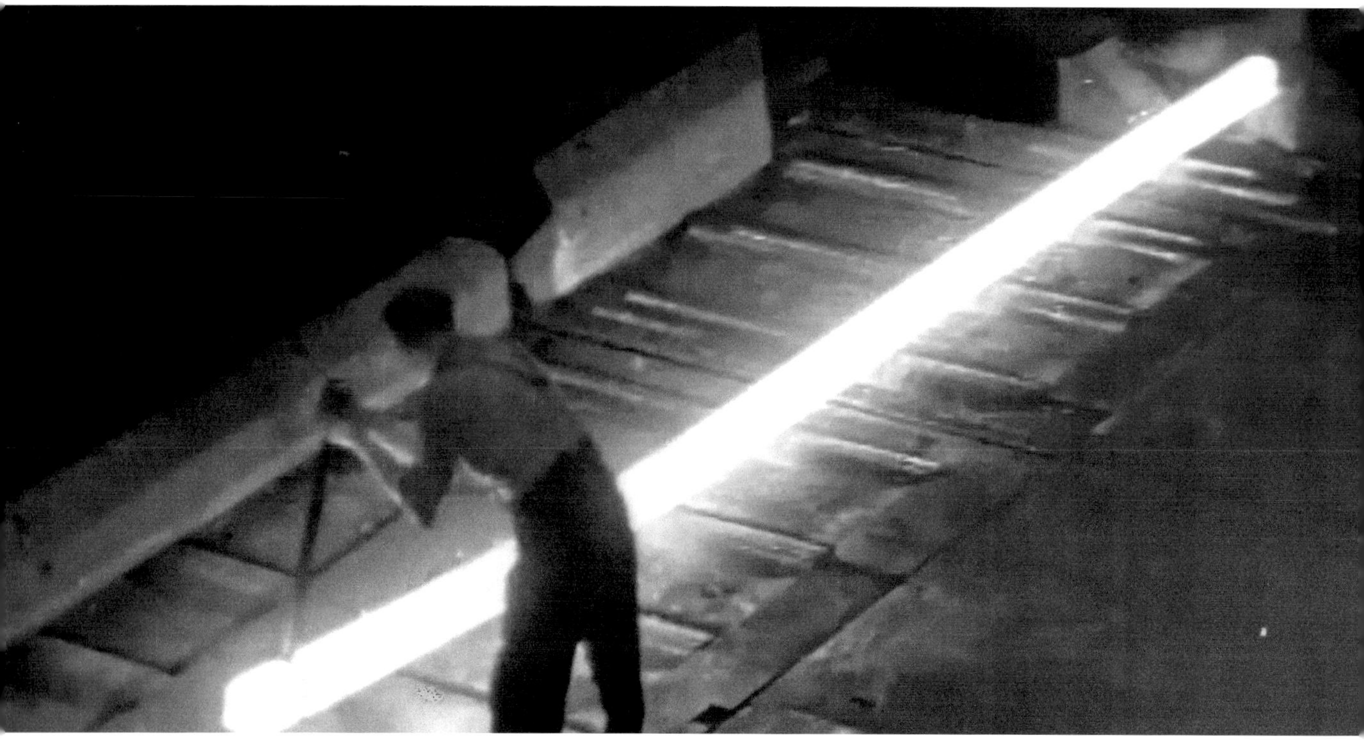

In the 20th century, Brymbo was a key player in the UK steel industry, gaining a reputation for delivering superior, precision-made products that had myriad applications: pit props for collieries, drill bits for oil fields, machine parts for cars and aero engines; the list went on and on. At peak production, more than 2,500 people worked unabating, eight-hour shifts in the inferno.

The steelworks never slept; it was a beast that growled 24/7. The crackling of arc furnaces, fused with the high-frequency squealing of saws grinding through steel, provided the soundtrack to everyday village life. At night, the sky would glow red, as tonnes of slag waste were discharged across the site, emblazing the landscape. It was once said that Brymbo used more energy in one day than the whole of the Wrexham area would expend in a month.

Astoundingly, the business only switched to steel production midway through its lifespan; for the first 89 years it focused exclusively on iron. The venture was the brainchild of an innovative industrialist who had wealth to spare, gumption aplenty and an overriding obsession with metal.

Opposite and below: smelting metal at Brymbo in the 1960s.

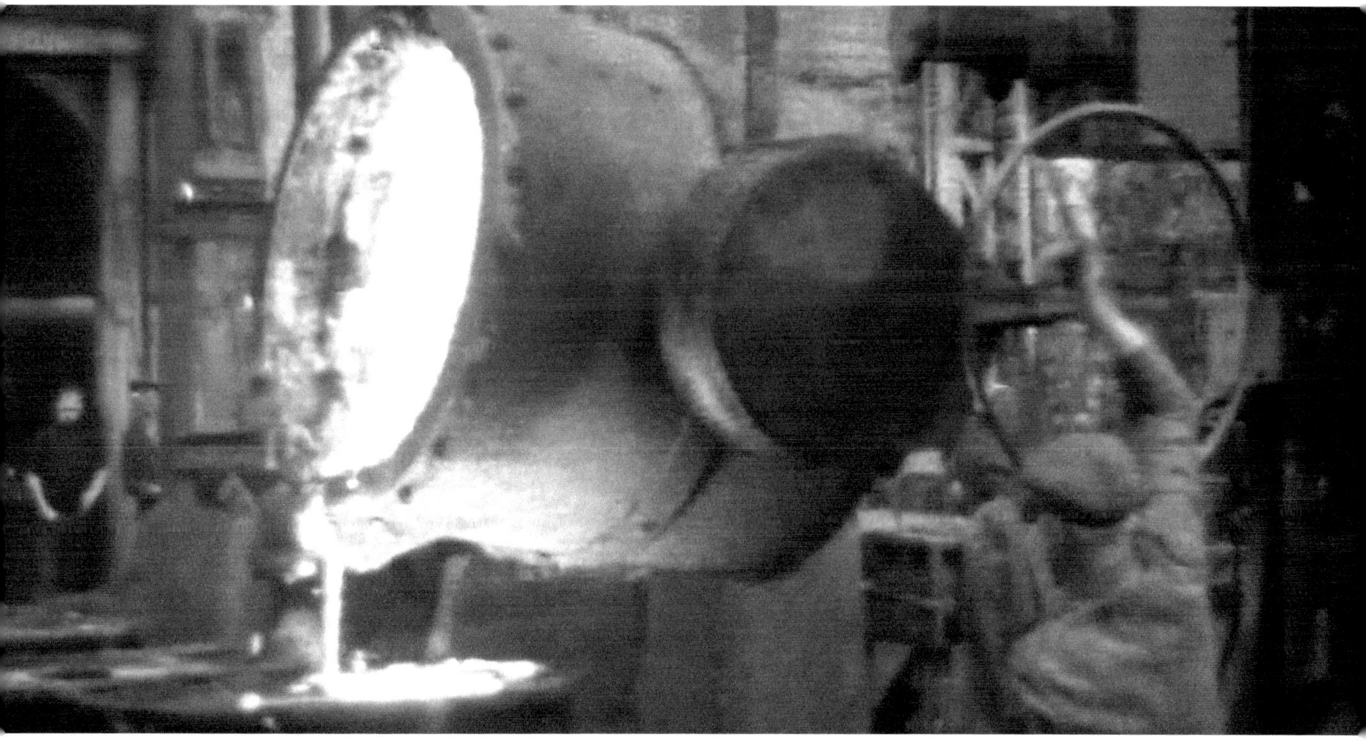

Born in 1728, John Wilkinson spent his working life developing newfangled techniques to incorporate cast iron into every nook and cranny of Georgian Britain – from bridges and barges to cannons and steam engines. Inheriting his father's industrial interests in North Wales, Wilkinson purchased Brymbo Hall and made the mansion and its surrounding estate his home. This was a canny move, as the ground beneath his feet was rich in coal and ironstone deposits; everything you would need, in fact, to establish a fully fledged ironworks, which he duly did in 1796. The first year of operation yielded 884 tonnes of metal, prompting 'Iron-Mad' Wilkinson (as he was nicknamed, not unreasonably) to expand the site even further. When he died in 1808, laid to rest in an iron coffin, he left behind a flourishing foundry for which the residents of Brymbo would forever be grateful.

Steelmaking was so deep-seated in this corner of North Wales that the very thought of it disappearing would once have been laughable. No-one would have believed it. And why would they? Brymbo's industrial lineage stretched back two centuries. Everyone in the village either worked at the steel plant or knew someone who did. The site was simply too big to fail, too important to ever let go. But that's exactly what happened: it was shut down and it was flattened.

The job was dangerous, sometimes deadly, but generations of men found much-needed employment at Brymbo.

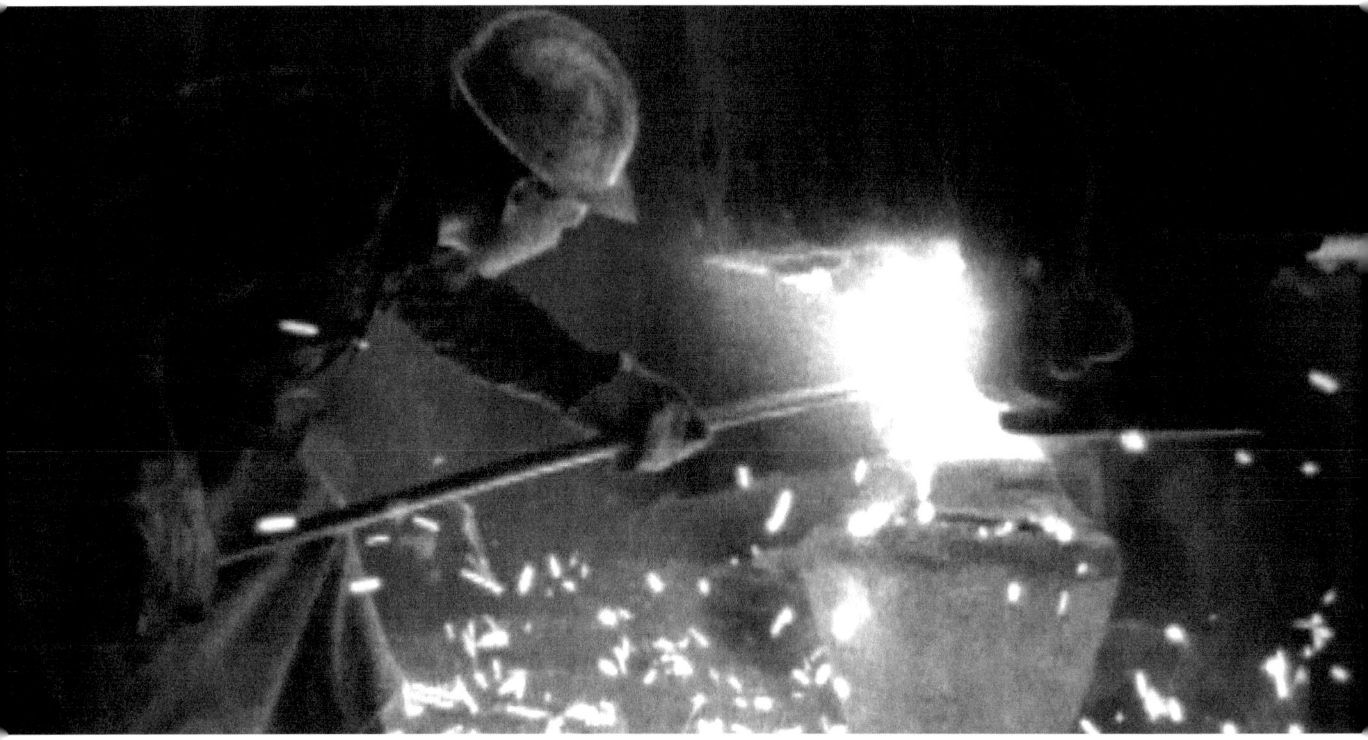

Steelmaking in Britain had been slowly falling apart since the 1970s. Demand for domestic product was waning; increased competition from Europe began to bite. In 1986, Brymbo was taken over by United Engineering Steels, who announced that it would be investing heavily in its operations in Yorkshire, leaving a question mark over the fate of its newest acquisition in Wales. Despite turning in a profit and with a full order book, Brymbo was earmarked for closure. The announcement finally came on 14th May 1990: 1,125 workers would be losing their jobs. The community was shocked to its core.

Avril Smith had worked in the canteen at Brymbo steelworks since the long hot summer of 1976, when she was 17. She had brothers, sisters, uncles and cousins employed at the plant. Her memories of the final shift, on the last ever working day, remain crystal clear:

> "Seeing the elderly men clocking off, with tears in their eyes, was devastating. None of us could quite believe it was really happening. It's sad when you think of what stood there and what it meant to the community. Our children and grandchildren are never going to have the skills that were passed down through the generations. We lost more than work, more than just jobs. We lost the skills of our fathers and grandfathers."

Colin Davies was there too. He was tasked with switching off the main gas valve for the reheating furnace on the primary mill. It was like disconnecting Brymbo's life-support machine:

> "Molten metal went into the ladle, the ladle was carried to the casting pits, and then…silence. The stripper cranes, which would strip ingots out of the ingot moulds, fell silent. It was eerie, it really was.
>
> "I had a reheating furnace, I had the stock to go into the furnace, I had the rolling mill, I had the saws – but I had no men. It was a horrible feeling of: 'That's it, that's the end.' And it was the end. It was terrible."

Following the steelworks' closure, there was a passionate campaign in the village to try, somehow, to preserve the vestiges of Brymbo's industrial heritage. Most of the plant was levelled to the ground, but a scattering of older structures, some dating back to the days of John Wilkinson, were eventually saved and are now protected as scheduled ancient monuments. A huge step forward came in the form of a £10 million investment in the Brymbo Heritage Trust. The money, much of it from the Heritage Lottery Fund, has allowed the community to finally proceed with plans to restore and repurpose the site as a visitor attraction and local resource, amplifying the story of Brymbo's iron and steelmaking lineage. That work is underway at long last.

One startling development in the area, as exciting as it is incongruous, has been the discovery of a 300-million-year-old fossilised forest. It was unearthed completely by chance during clearance work on the site and has since become of immeasurable scientific importance: thousands of fossils and more than 20 large structures resembling tree trunks. They hail from the very earliest days of our planet – the Carboniferous period – long before dinosaurs roamed the earth and when Wales would have sat on the Equator.

It's a find of exceptional consequence and rarity, a unique window on a vanished world. It's perhaps poignant to know that if Brymbo steelworks was still in operation, that forest might never have been found at all.

GILBERN CARS

The boom, bust and rebirth of a motoring dream

In the 1960s and 70s, a small, dedicated workforce achieved something remarkable. On the site of a former colliery, they made automotive history: the only production cars completely designed and manufactured in Wales by a Welsh company. The vehicles even had a red dragon on the bonnet.

That company was Gilbern and it dared to be different. It began life as the brainchild of two motoring enthusiasts who became unlikely business partners in the late 1950s. Giles Smith was a butcher from Church Village, near Pontypridd. Bernard Friese was an engineer and former German POW. They were bound together by a love of cars and a readiness to rip up the rulebook. Both men have since passed away, but Giles' son Jason is justly proud of how their maverick venture became a fully fledged car company:

> "Initially, Bernard tried to discourage my father from making their own vehicle. But my father basically nagged him because he was planning to do it anyway. So eventually they came to the conclusion that they would have a go. In the beginning they did a lot of work in my grandfather's house, which was also a butcher's shop. They had a couple of outbuildings and barns and they converted one of them into a workshop to actually produce the prototype cars. It became a labour of love."

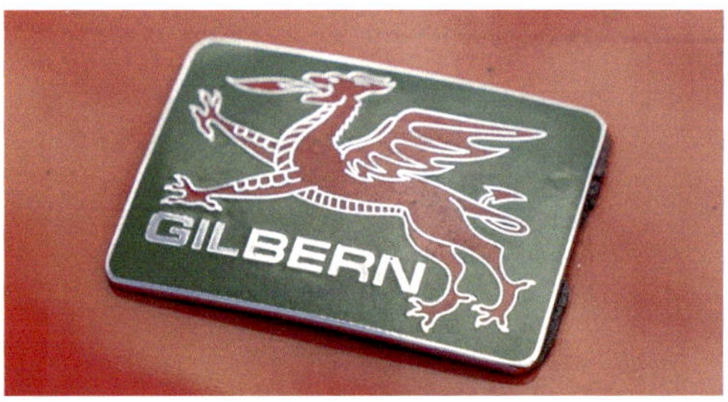

Above: Gilbern's distinctive dragon logo.
Opposite: Bernard Friese and Giles Smith next to their prototype, 1959.

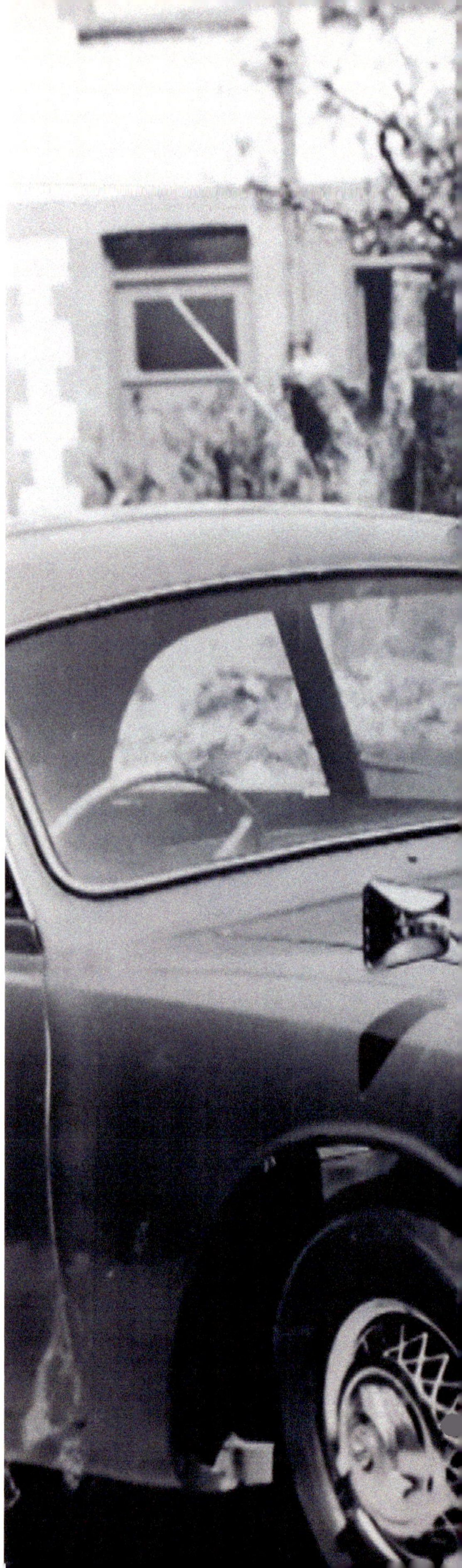

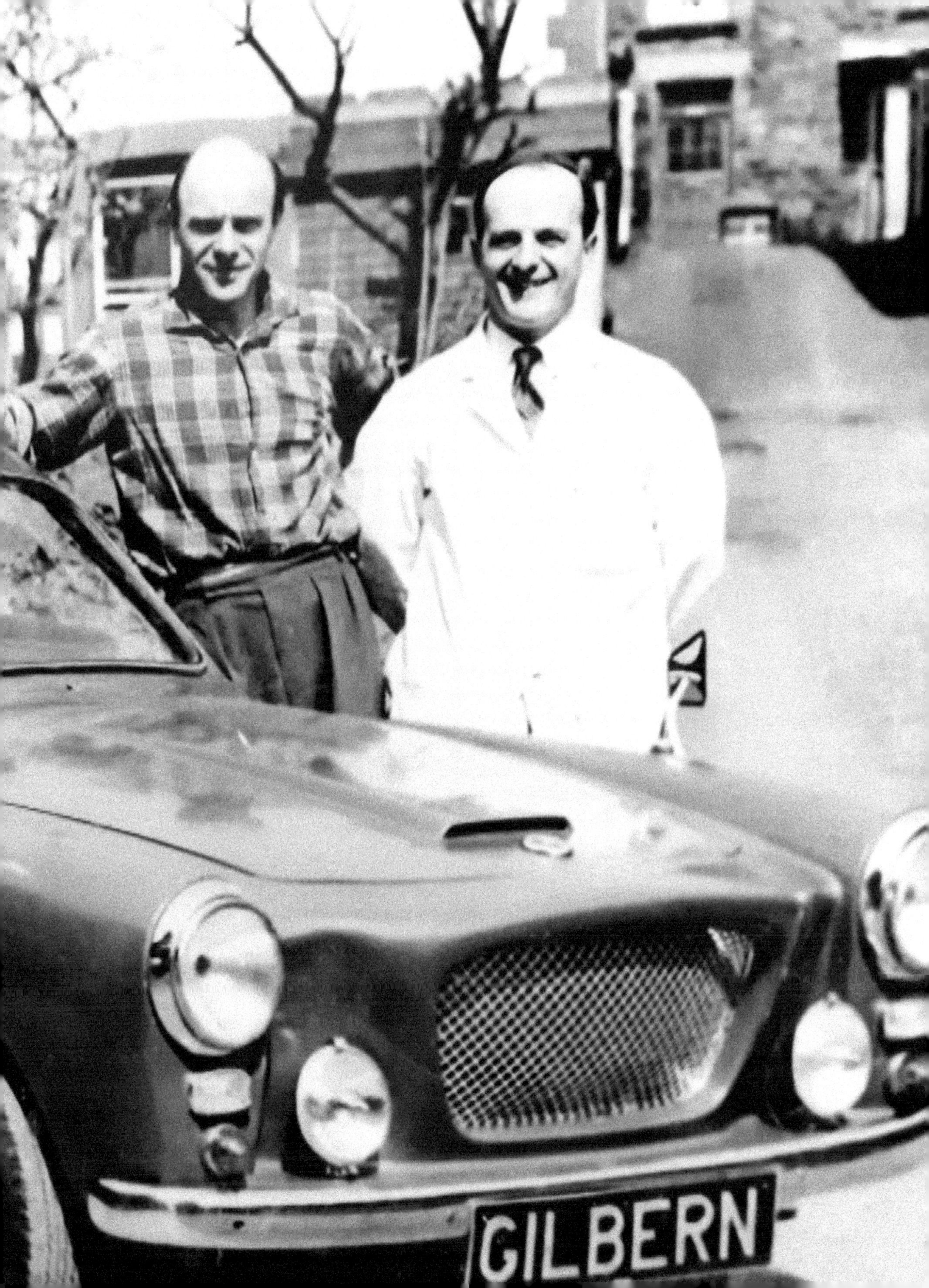
GILBERN

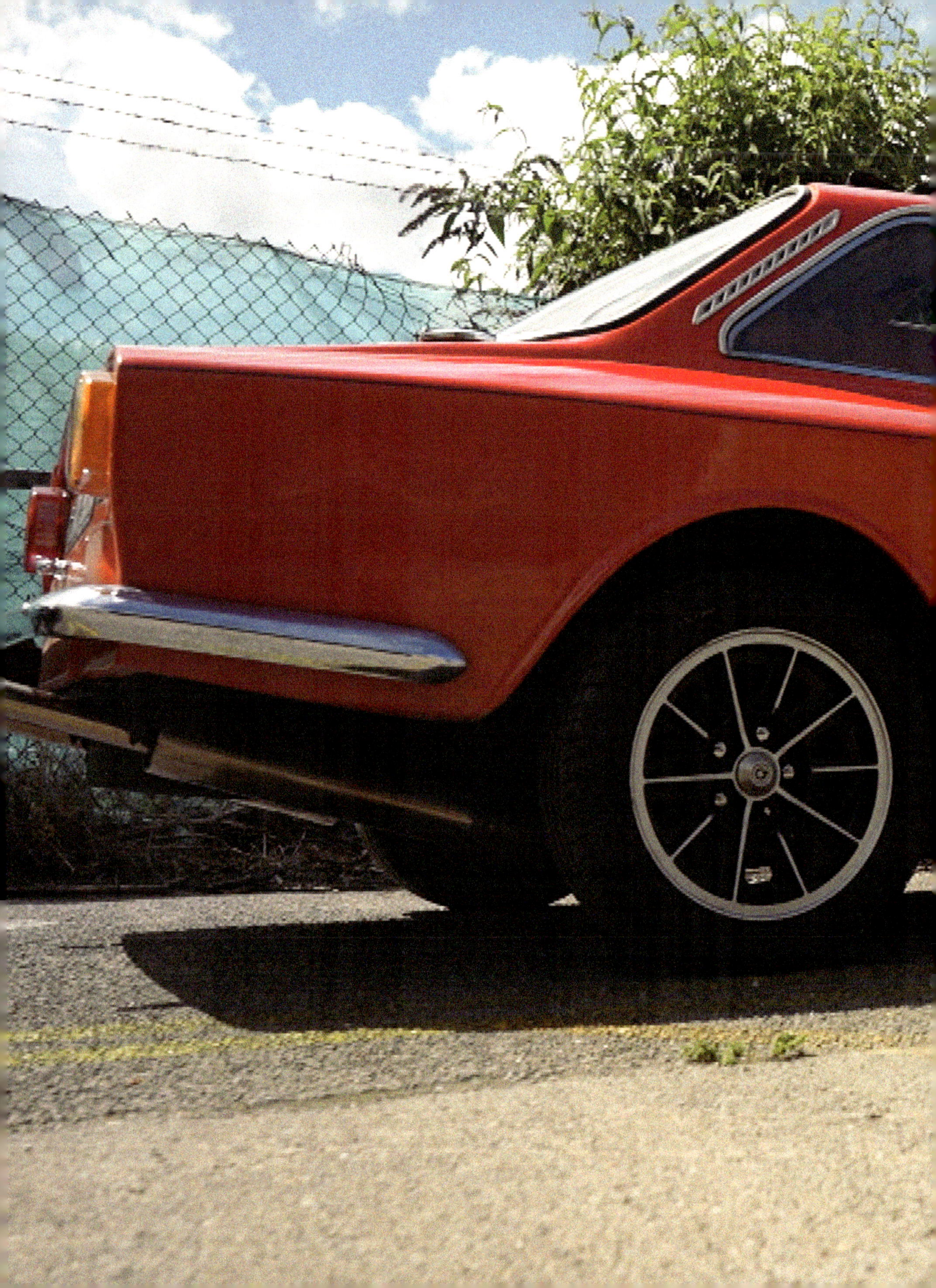

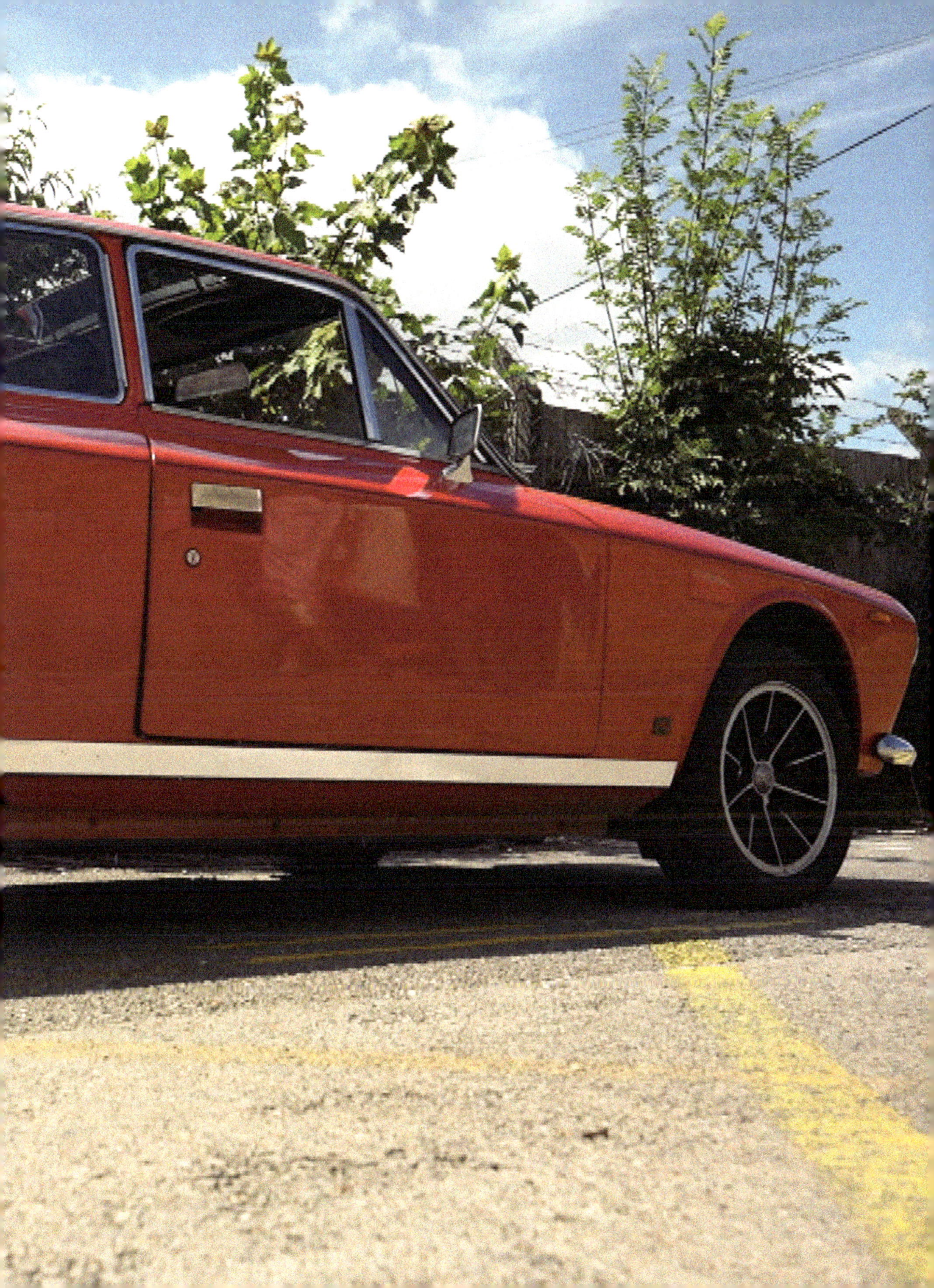

Overleaf: a lovingly restored Gilbern.

Giles and Bernard combined their Christian names to give their embryonic vehicles an identity. With the encouragement of local racing driver Peter Cottrell, who saw potential in their designs, the cars went from prototype to full-on production in 1960. The earliest model was the Gilbern GT (whose sleek aesthetic is a near twin to James Bond's Aston Martin DB5 from *Goldfinger*). Its success paved the way for future Gilberns with rather more quixotic names like the Genie and the Invader. As demand grew, the business moved into a purpose-built factory in Llantwit Fardre in Rhondda Cynon Taf. What had once been the Red Ash colliery was suddenly a centre of home-grown motor manufacturing.

Gilbern's approach to making cars was to gleefully jettison all conventional ways of thinking. For a start, the basic body of the vehicles was made out of fibreglass, an apparently flimsy yet robust form of reinforced plastic. As for mechanised mass production: forget it. Each car was handmade by local workers. Trevor Davies was one of them:

> "I couldn't believe my luck when I walked in there and they said, 'Start tomorrow.' Absolutely brilliant! They used to have an initiation test for new starters. The car boots were all lined with carpet and you'd have to get in to lay the carpet down. Then some clever so-and-so would come up and shut the boot lid on you.
>
> "It was fascinating to be part of that factory, seeing people working with their hands, not machines. There were very few fibreglass cars around back then. And of course Gilbern had started making fibreglass vehicles quite a long time before I even started working there, so the company was very advanced. It was something to be proud of. And I still am proud of having made those cars."

The operation was small-scale compared to the deep-pocketed motoring giants of the day. But, true to form, Gilbern had a trick up its sleeve. You could buy the cars as fully assembled vehicles. But they were also sold in component form. That meant fitting sections like the engine and gearbox yourself, but it made the cars much more affordable as motorists could avoid paying any purchase tax (the precursor to VAT).

All these innovations made Gilbern unique and no two cars were ever the same. Brian and Carol Gent are part of the Gilbern Owners Club and they adore their vintage vehicles. For Carol, they're like a member of the family:

> "The cars all have their own personalities and I think people get very emotionally attached to them. They're so individual and they're all handmade. I think they're absolutely brilliant.
>
> "It's always an adventure to be out in them. Some of the cars we have are probably as old as we are! We take my white Invader out shopping sometimes and there are always people standing around it, always wanting to reminisce. There are also times when you're driving along and other car owners smile and give you the thumbs up. Everybody seems to love them."

For Brian, owning a Gilbern means accepting its brazen eccentricity:

> "If you damaged a door on a GT and you thought, 'I'll go and get another door and fit it', well, it won't necessarily fit. That's because there's an inch and a quarter difference in the various lengths of the doors that are fitted with a Gilbern GT. So they're quirky. Although they were production cars, each one is slightly different and you very rarely find two cars that are identical. It's part of their charm."

A cult classic: the Gilbern GT.

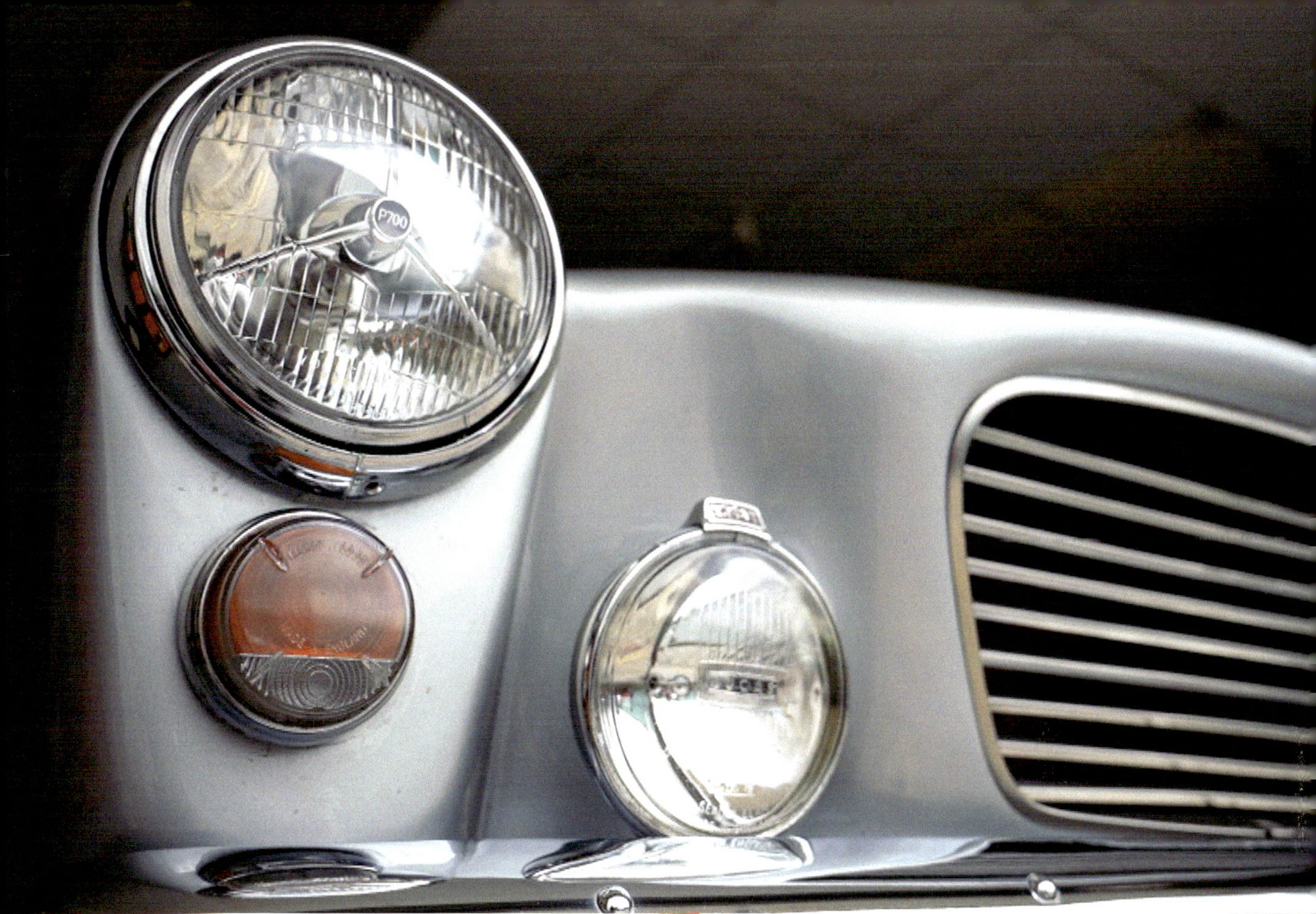
P700

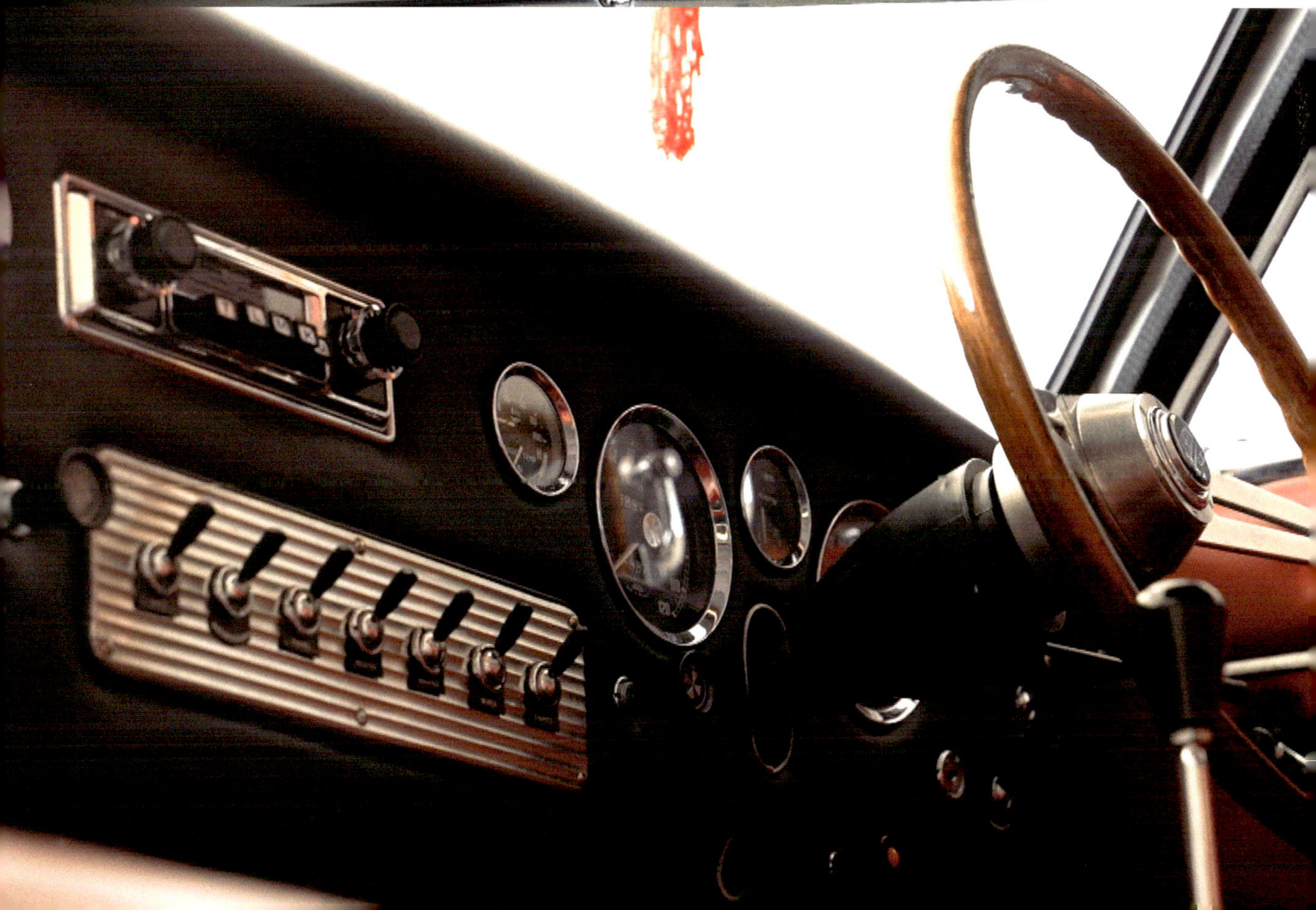

Bernard and Giles, who had kept the company ticking over nicely, decided to sell the business in 1968, feeling it was time to hand over the reins. For the next few years the company passed from owner to owner. In 1972, the new boss Michael Leather announced a bold vision for Gilbern. The cars wouldn't just be made for British customers anymore – the business was branching out. Dutch and German companies were approached. The vision was to see Welsh cars, with their red dragon emblem, speeding along the expressways and autobahns of Europe.

What no-one could have predicted were the economic headwinds that conspired to pummel Gilbern just a few months later. 1973 saw the introduction of VAT, so buying the cars in their cheaper, component form was suddenly no longer an option. Meanwhile the UK economy was being buffeted by the Global Oil Crisis and internal meltdowns like the Three-Day Week. Interest rates soared, inflation began to bite and the price of petrol doubled. For a small motor company from South Wales, it was a perfect storm.

In 1974, Gilbern finally ceased trading. The wheels had come off the motoring dream. A pioneering industry vanished from view.

Half a century on, these Welsh cars are enjoying a remarkable revival. Of the 1,000 Gilberns made during the company's lifetime, more than 600 of them have survived. Every year, Gilbern owners from right across the UK come together at special events to share their passion and show off their cherished motorcars.

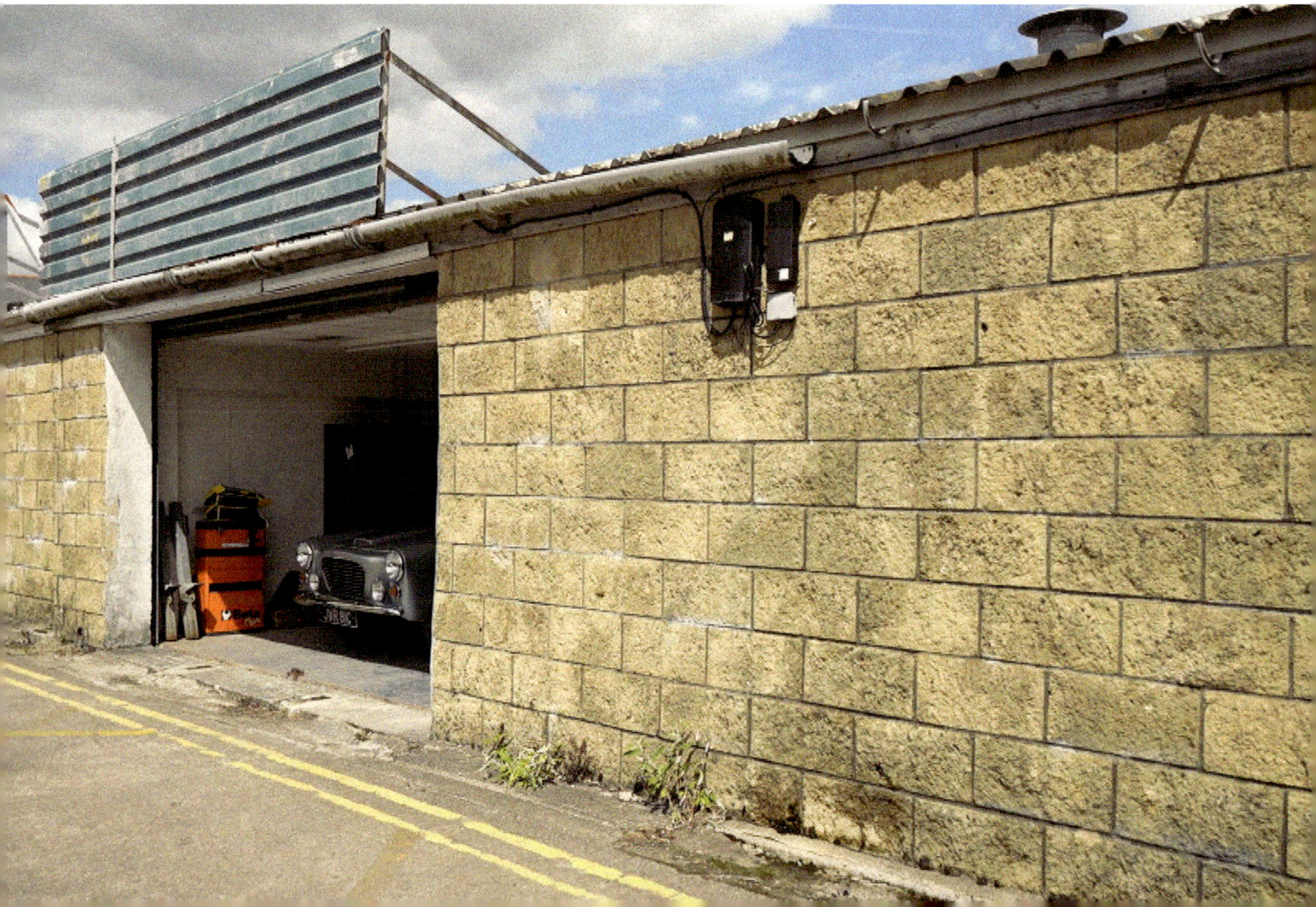

One of those fans is Sion Griffiths, the proud owner of the oldest registered Gilbern that's still on the road:

"In 1974 I was a student and I saw an advert: Gilbern, £50. I bought it and I spent a bit of time doing it up and getting it on the road. I sold it in 1977 and I bought it back in 2010. I don't see it as a car. I see it as a connection to my past.

"I think it's a great pity that Gilbern has died out as a maker of new vehicles. But there's a very strong and very enthusiastic club. So their name lives on."

Each Gilbern car has a story to tell. Cindy Salmon has a special connection with her old GT:

"My dad bought a Gilbern, new, in 1961. My mum was pregnant with me, and she was driven in the car to the hospital. After I was born I was picked up in the car with my mum and all she wanted to do was to be driven the long way home, to look at all the sales in the shop windows!

"My mum used the car to take us to school. It stayed on the road until 1971 when it failed its MOT, and then it just sat in the garden, rotting in the long grass. Dad finally gave us the car, and we've managed to restore it. It holds a special feeling for me because this car has been in our family since new, and it is my grand hope that in the future our girls will be interested in it, to keep it going as well."

Opposite: parts of the old Gilbern factory are still standing.

Below: a fibreglass body is lowered into position.

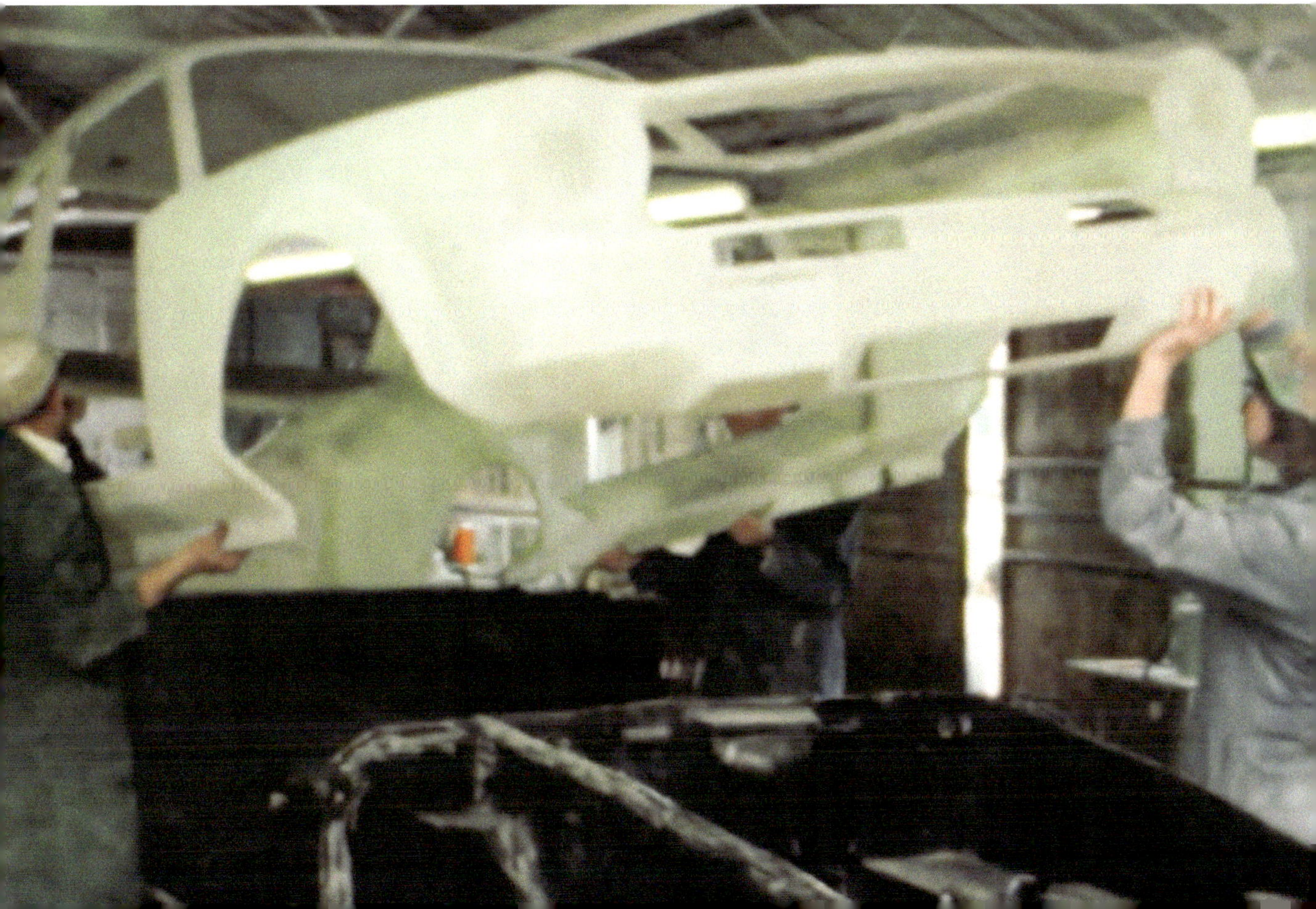

Gilbern is gone but not forgotten. Genies, Invaders and GTs still inspire devotion and delight. A new generation of drivers has fallen in love with these classic Welsh cars. It's a fitting tribute to two men who had no previous experience in the motor industry. Yet, between them, they created a range of vehicles that have stood the test of time. Jason Smith believes his late father would be proud:

> "It's brilliant today that the cars are still here and there's so many of them on the road. The looks are still as good as they used to be. And a lot of people are getting a lot of enjoyment out of them.
>
> "I'm sure Dad would be really happy if he knew that."

A Gilbern on the open road in the early 1970s.

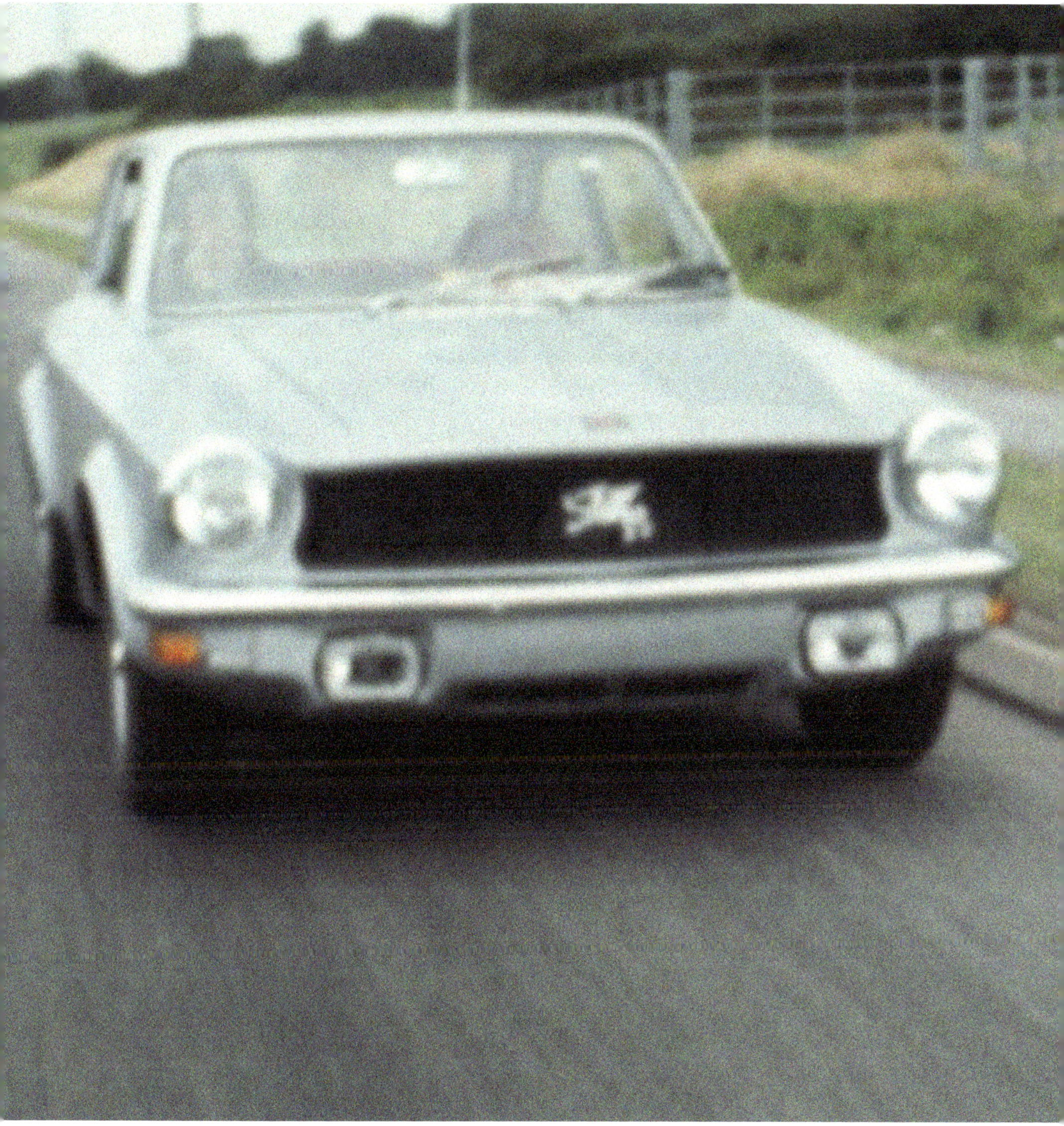

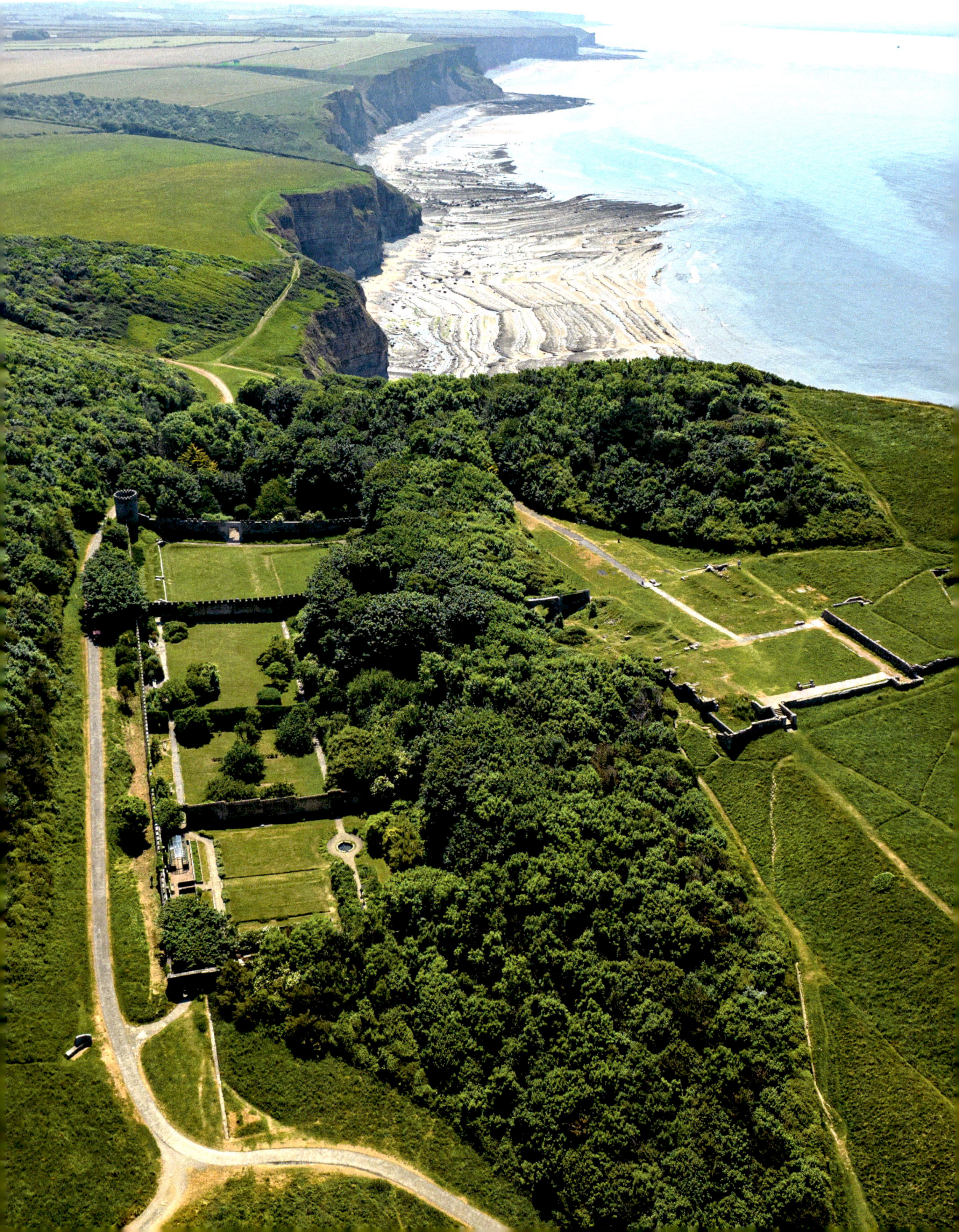

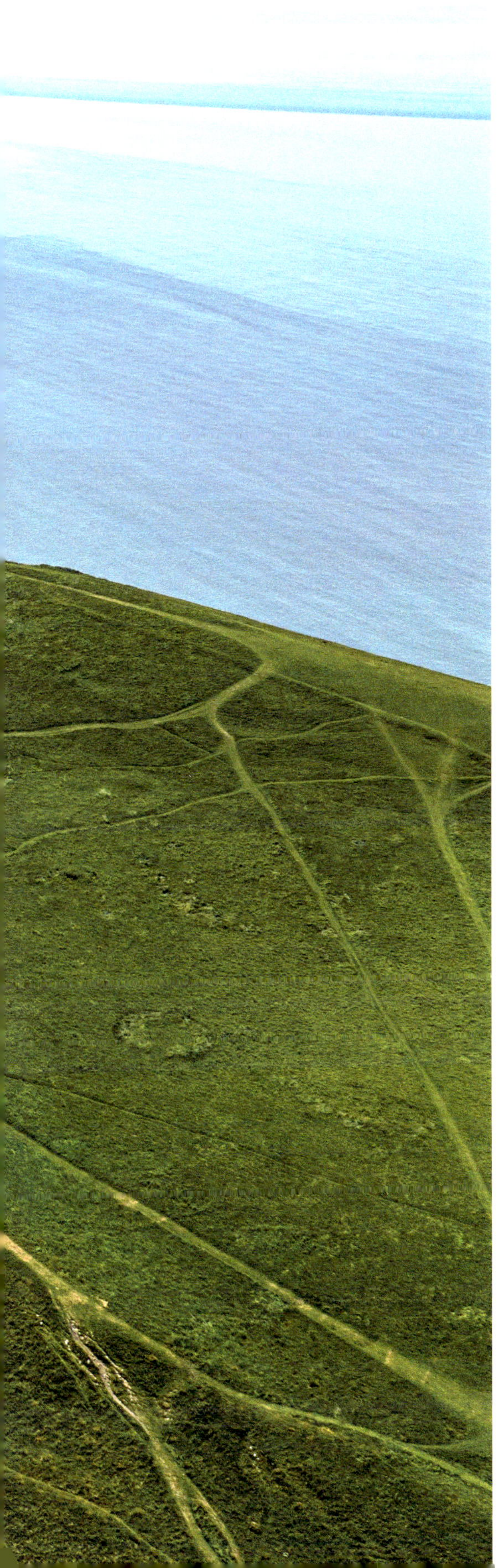

DUNRAVEN CASTLE

A magnificent mansion smashed to smithereens

There was a time when a trip to Southerndown beach in the Vale of Glamorgan would have cost you a sore neck. Swimmers and sunbathers would raise their heads high, *very* high, to admire the grandiose building that rose 200 feet above them. Commanding the clifftop, on the verdant promontory known as Witches Point, stood a structure that was simply impossible to ignore: Dunraven Castle.

As any local will tell you, its name was a complete misnomer. There was no drawbridge, no portcullis, not a hint of a moat. You'd see battlements, to be sure, but these were customisations installed at great expense in the 19th century. In reality, Dunraven Castle was a sumptuous Gothic-styled mansion built by, and for, one of Wales' wealthiest families, the Wyndham-Quins. They had made their money by capitalising on the coalfields north of Bridgend and owned vast tracts of land across South Wales and beyond. Their descendants became the Earls and Ladies of Dunraven, rubbing shoulders with royalty (the ravens we associate with the Tower of London were their gift to Queen Victoria). Unsurprisingly, when the time came to upgrade their waterside rockpile, they were more than happy to splash the cash.

The remains of Dunraven Castle.

Their stately home was constructed on land already steeped in history. It had been the site of an Iron Age hillfort, while later legends tell of Caradoc, the tribal war leader of the Silures, fighting against the Romans from there. Skip forward a few centuries and you'd have found a Norman fort at Dunraven Bay which was subsequently replaced by a resplendent Tudor manor house. In the 1800s, when the property was overhauled by the Wyndham-Quins, the resulting smorgasbord of styles was influenced by a prevailing nostalgia for the past, as historian Graham Loveluck-Edwards explains:

"In the 19th century, the people of Britain fell in love with a very romantic idea of what the medieval world was like. It was fuelled by things like Lady Charlotte Guest's translation of the Mabinogion into English. In Wales you had the Marquis of Bute spending a fortune on making his Cardiff residences look as medieval as possible; another of his properties, Castell Coch, resembled a fairytale princess-castle poking through the trees. It was a very popular style, and some of the best architects in the world who were creating that kind of image were based in Cardiff, because of the Marquis of Bute. So if you wanted to have your manor house look more medieval you couldn't have had a more talented bunch of people on your doorstep to come and do it for you.

"Dunraven Castle was an absolute showpiece and you could see it for miles around. There was an amazing conservatory on the front – an entire wall of glass – filled with palm trees and exotic plants from all over the world. They built a castellated gatehouse, and entrances through the woods. There were huge windows throughout the building that allowed light to flood in and fill the rooms. It had a very grand entrance hall, oak-panelled with suits of armour in the corner and works of art hanging on the walls. So they put an awful lot of thought into making this place look and feel as impressive as it possibly could be."

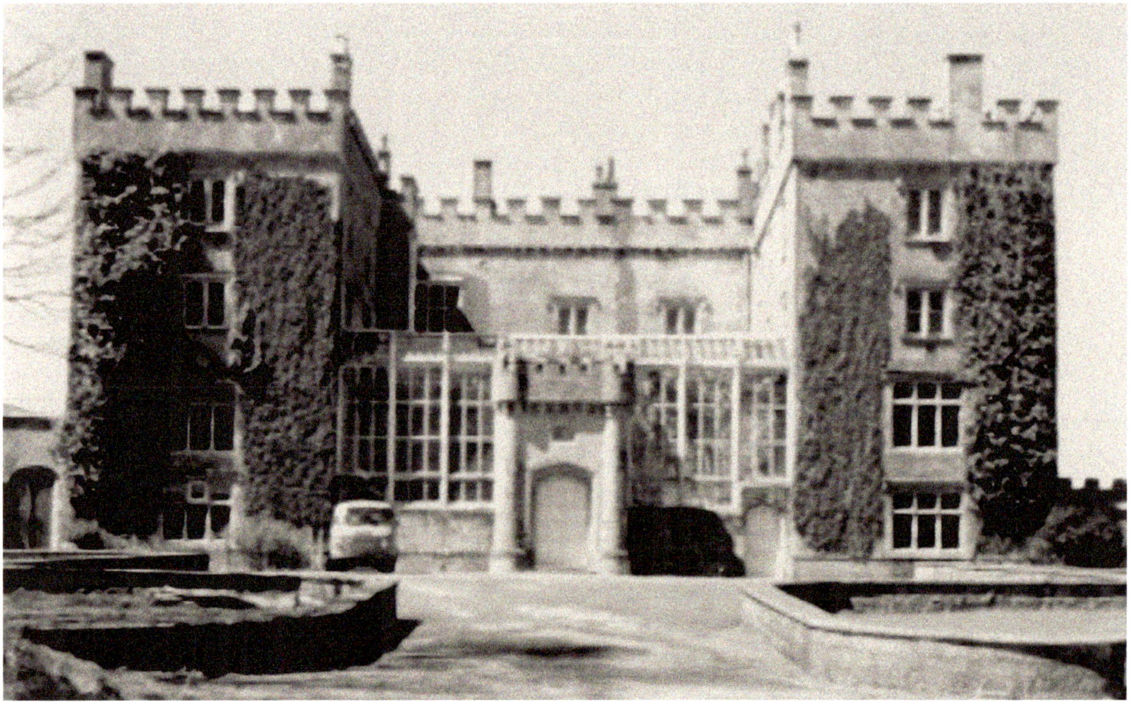

The main entrance to the Castle, complete with conservatory.

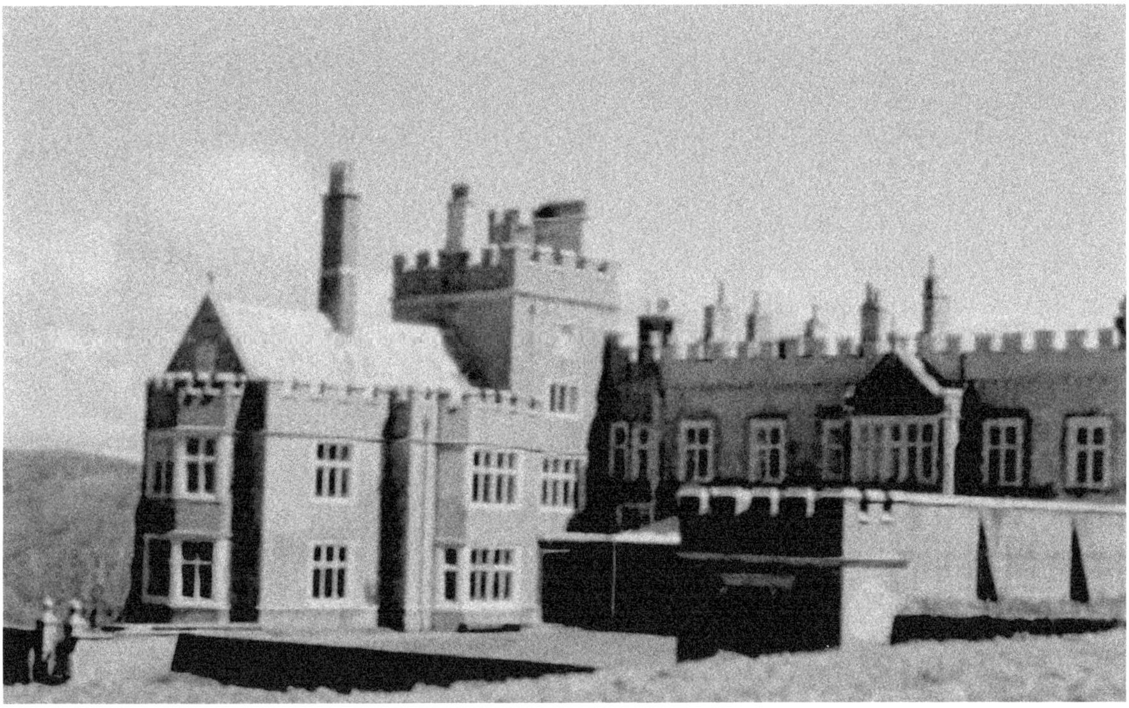

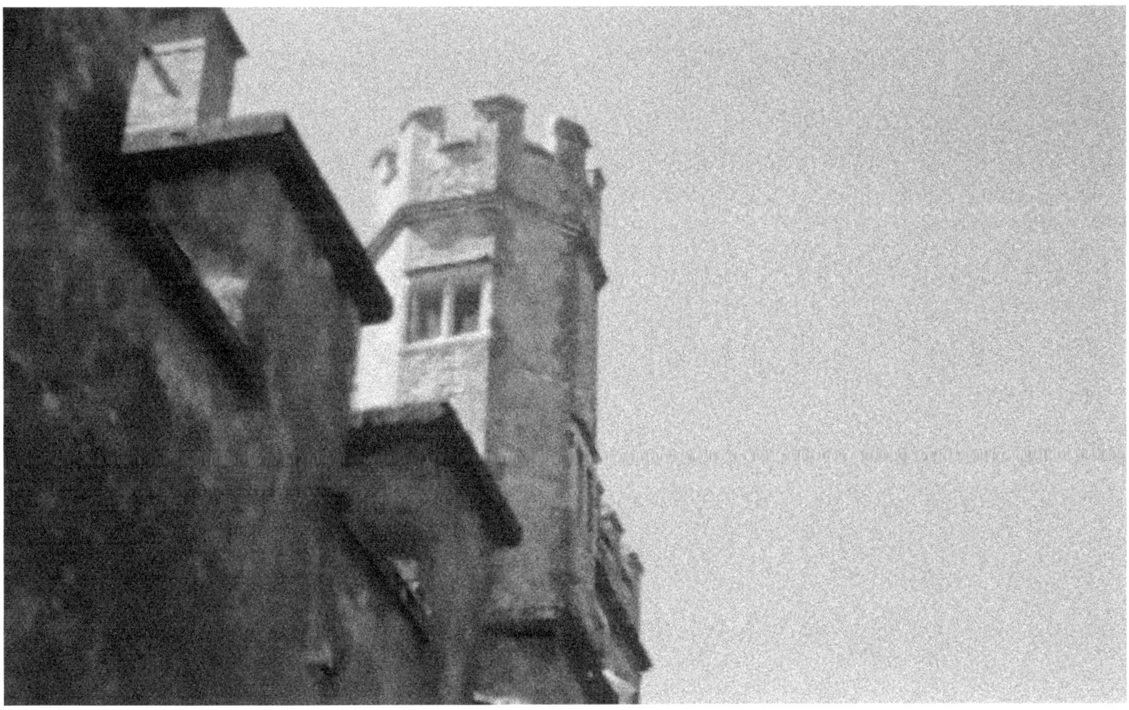

Coastal Gothic: the manor house just a few months before demolition.

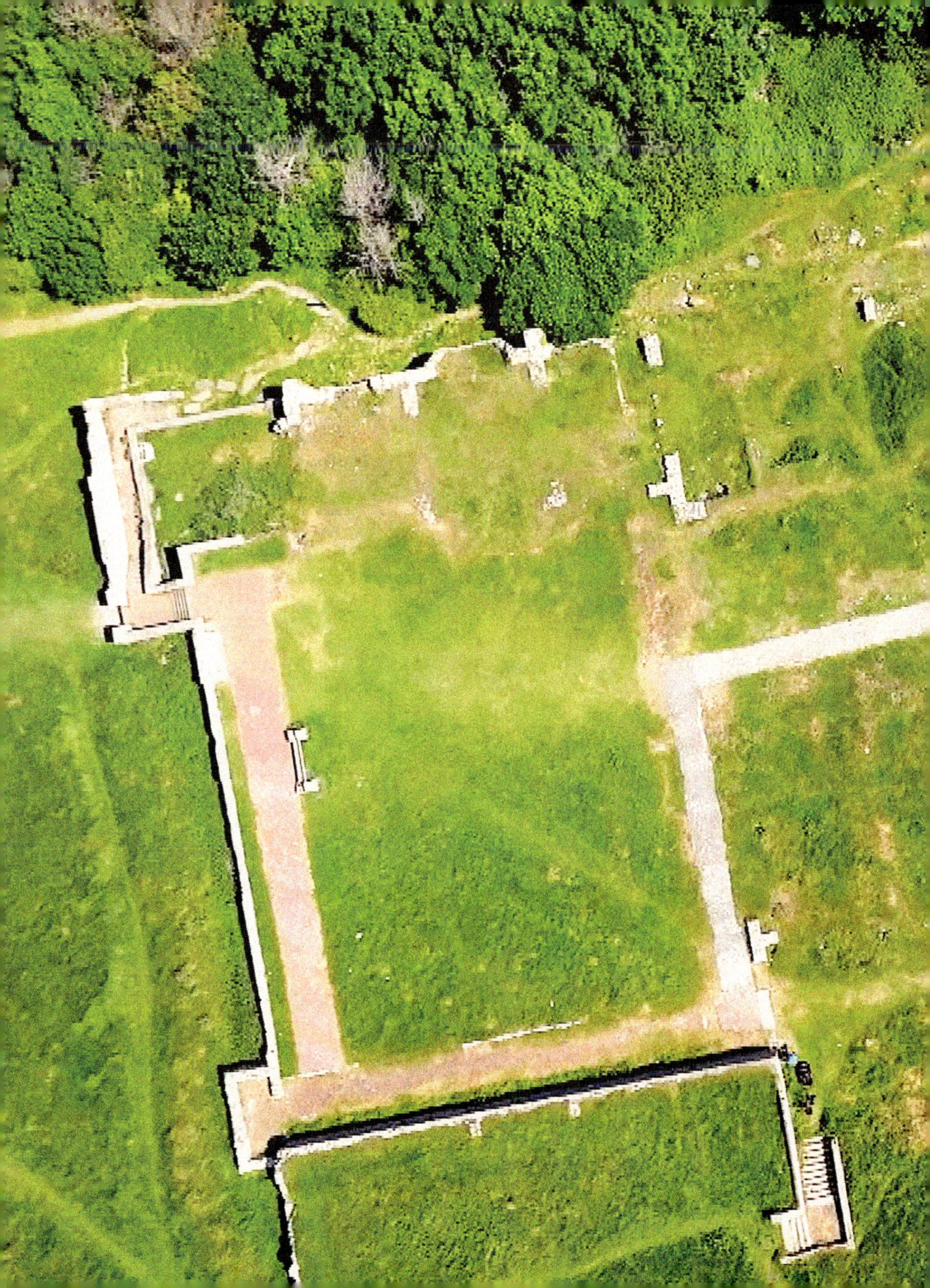

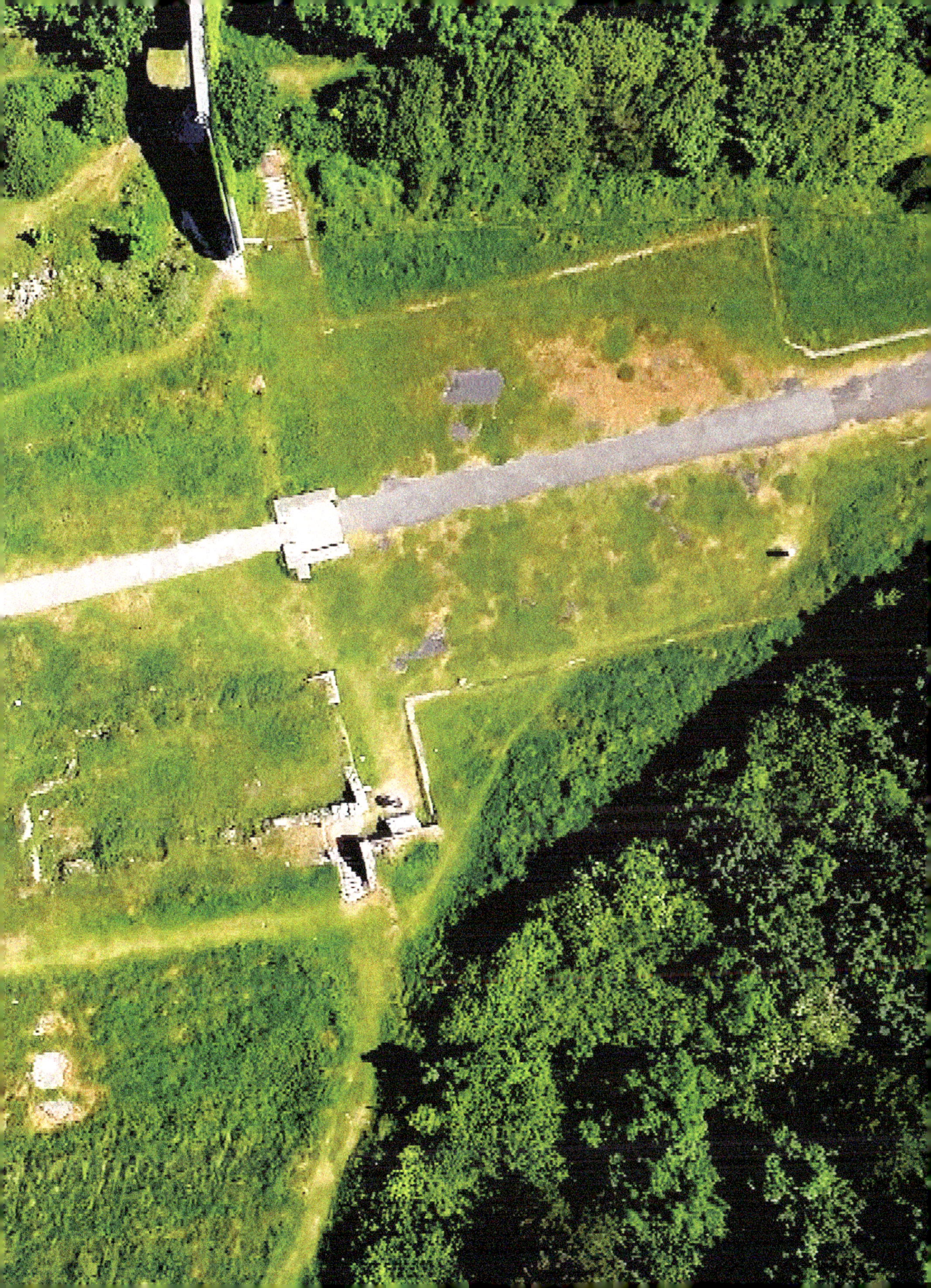

Overleaf: the remains of Dunraven Castle from the air.

For most of its life, Dunraven Castle was the preserve of the aristocracy. Well-heeled guests were entertained in splendour, attended to by a stream of servants from the neighbouring villages (the closest the community would ever get to setting foot inside the crenellated citadel). All of that changed in the 20th century. The Wyndham-Quin family chose to retain the land but vacate the house, their focus shifting to the many other estates they owned, particularly in Ireland.

Suddenly, those imposing doors were opened wide. Dunraven Castle served as a Red Cross hospital during both world wars, with American troops billeted there in the 1940s. By the tail end of the '50s it had been turned into a hotel. Sylvia and Gwennan Rees worked there during the summer months, serving guests and cleaning the myriad rooms. For Sylvia, getting a job at the clifftop mansion was a pinch-yourself moment:

"I was 16 when I started there and I couldn't believe it. As youngsters we'd see Dunraven Castle when we came to Southerndown on a day trip. You'd be looking up at it, thinking it was magical. I never thought I'd ever be working there.

"There was the Lordship's lounge and the Ladyship's lounge, and they had huge bay windows looking down to the coast. One of the master bedrooms even had silk wallpaper. Sometimes we would sneak into the ballroom when there were dances, just to take a look. In the evening, when we finished work, we'd go out for lovely walks in the grounds, where they had a bowling green, a putting green and tennis courts. We'd see deer running through the parkland too. It was just so beautiful."

Gwennan remembers crack-of-dawn starts, offset by glorious pockets of freedom:

"After lunch, until about 6pm, we had time to ourselves when we could do whatever we wanted. On sunny days we'd go down to the beach. In fact we had a *private* path leading down to a *private* beach!

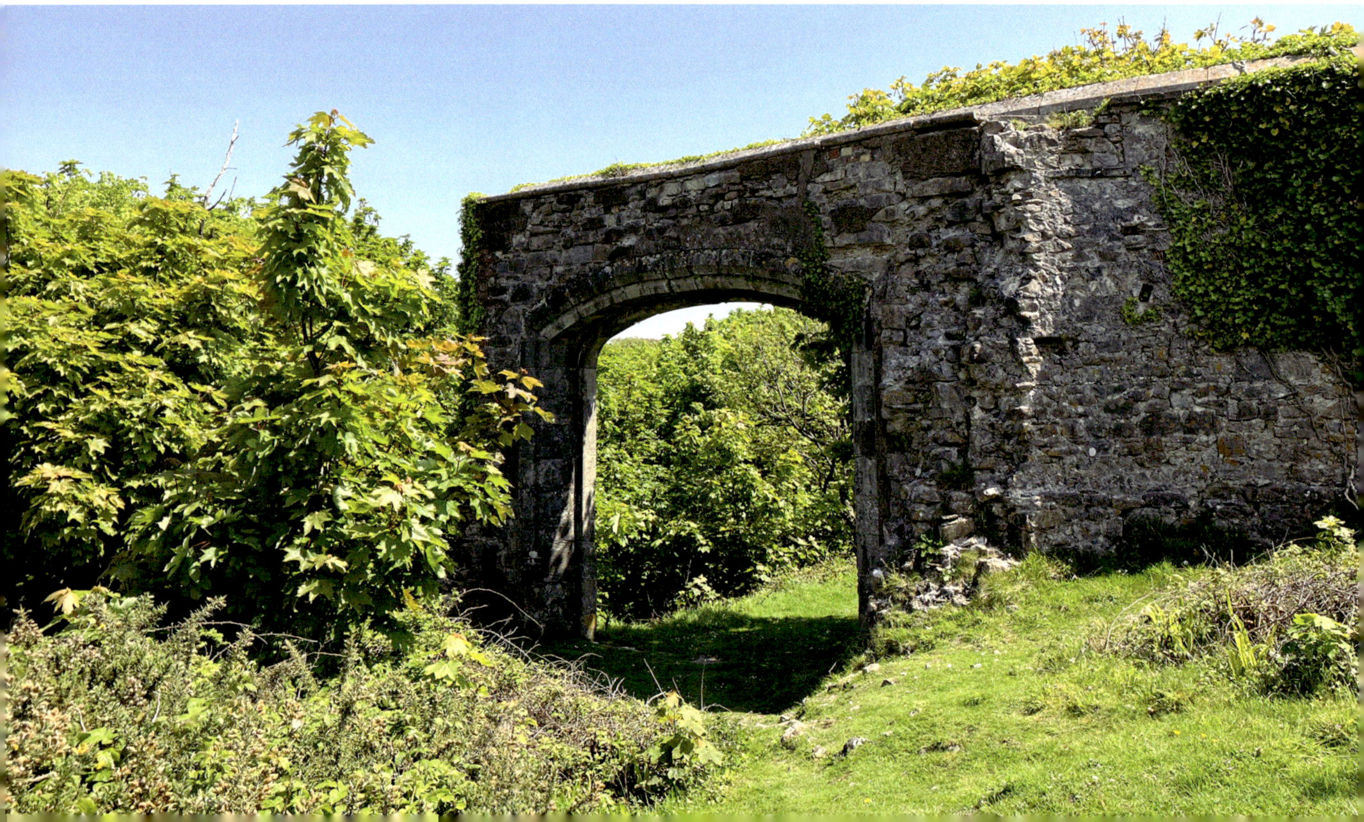

"We did take a lot of pride in our work. We'd have to clean the armoury, polishing all the old weapons. The suit of armour in the corner we named Charlie. We'd greet him every morning. He never answered! There was also a rumour that there was a ghost in the castle. She was supposed to haunt the hallway near our dorm. I never saw her myself, but one of the cleaners absolutely refused to go into that hallway!"

In 1960, the hotel closed and Dunraven Castle was again ripe for reinvention. The Wyndham-Quins decided to sell the property once and for all, inviting developers to suggest a repurposing of both the mansion and its grounds. Plans were submitted for an 800-pitch caravan park, which would have seen the house functioning as a facilities block. Those plans were resolutely rejected by the local council. Dunraven Castle was sold off regardless, and its new custodians wasted little time in getting shot of it.

In June 1962, the contents of the stately home were auctioned off al fresco, like an enormous yard sale. Crowds gathered to place their bids on an endless array of armchairs, cabinets and fireplaces. Even the light fittings and internal doors were up for grabs. Once the property had been stripped completely, the demolition crews swooped in. Dunraven Castle was torn down. The stone was sold for quarrying.

A few features managed to survive the wrecking ball. The walled garden, halfway up the hill and accessed by an arched door, is a charming space that members of the public can freely enjoy. The gabled gatehouse has clung on too; you'll find it next to the main car park at Dunraven Bay. Yet on the clifftop itself, where the Gothic manor house once stood, all you'll find are footings and foundations. You might notice one or two low walls of chipped masonry and a flight of narrow stone steps leading nowhere. But that's it. There's no need for swimmers and sunbathers down on the beach to strain their necks anymore; no need to look up towards the summit of those rocks. There's now nothing to see.

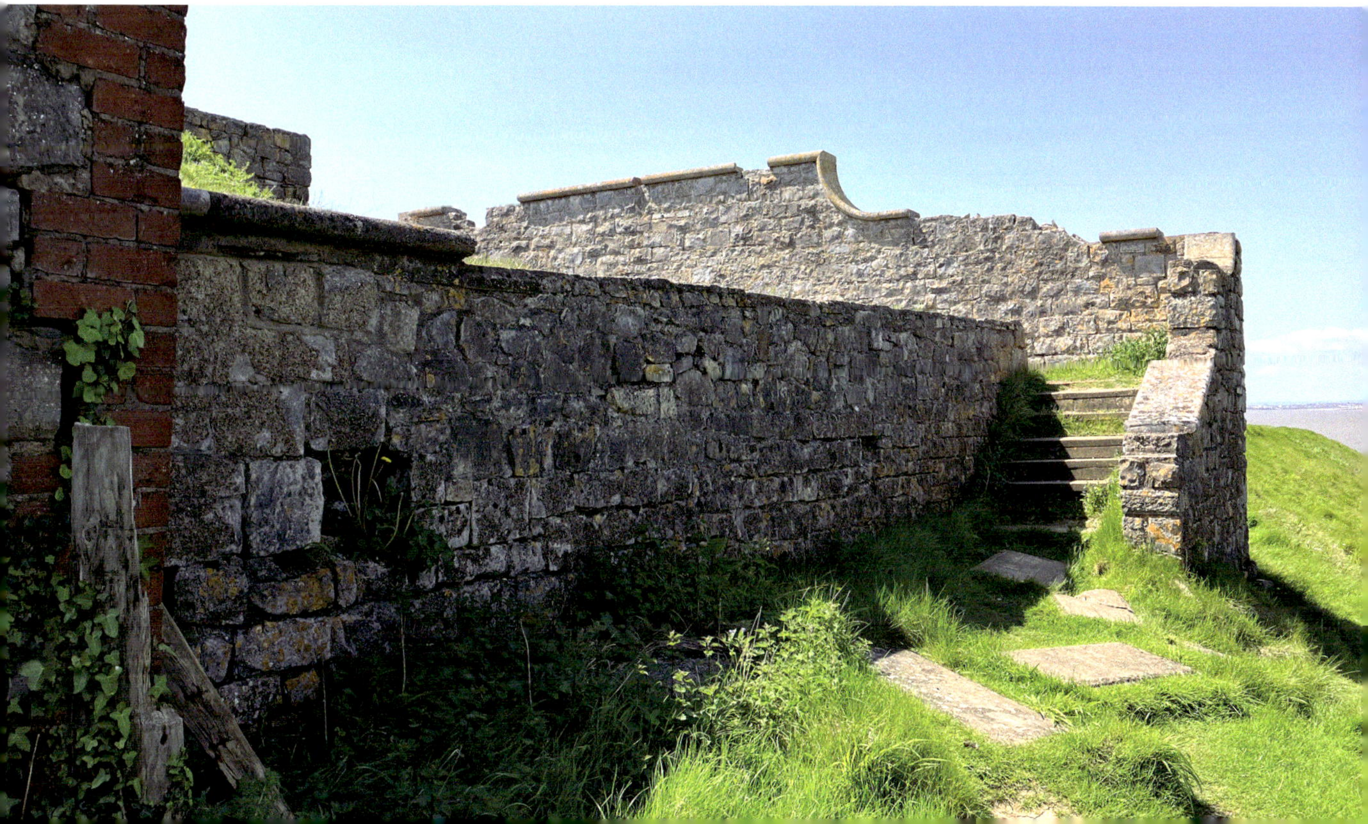

THE TRIANGLE

Merthyr's three-sided cottage community

In the days when Cardiff was little more than a sleepy village, the largest, liveliest and most developed settlement in Wales, by a long shot, was Merthyr Tydfil. It was the beating heart of the Industrial Revolution and could lay claim to having the largest ironworks anywhere in the world. For generations there was a link to that industrial heritage in the lower approaches to the town, at Pentrebach. It's a lost landmark that many people still remember today. And it had a rather distinctive shape.

Built in the 1830s, the Triangle was a huddle of 54 stone cottages arranged in a wedge-shaped formation with a 'village green' in the centre. The homes faced inward, a deliberate design that created a close bond between neighbours.

Residents looked out for, and unavoidably at, each other. The three-sided district was conceived to house ironworkers and their families during a particularly buzzing period in Merthyr's development, when deep-pocketed tycoons went head-to-head in a relentless quest to produce Britain's best quality metal. The Hill family, owners of the town's Plymouth ironworks, knew they would need scores of skilled labourers to pick up the pace. They built brand-new homes to entice prospective employees and the Triangle was born. Merthyr historian Christopher Parry believes the three-way configuration of cottages was light years ahead of its time:

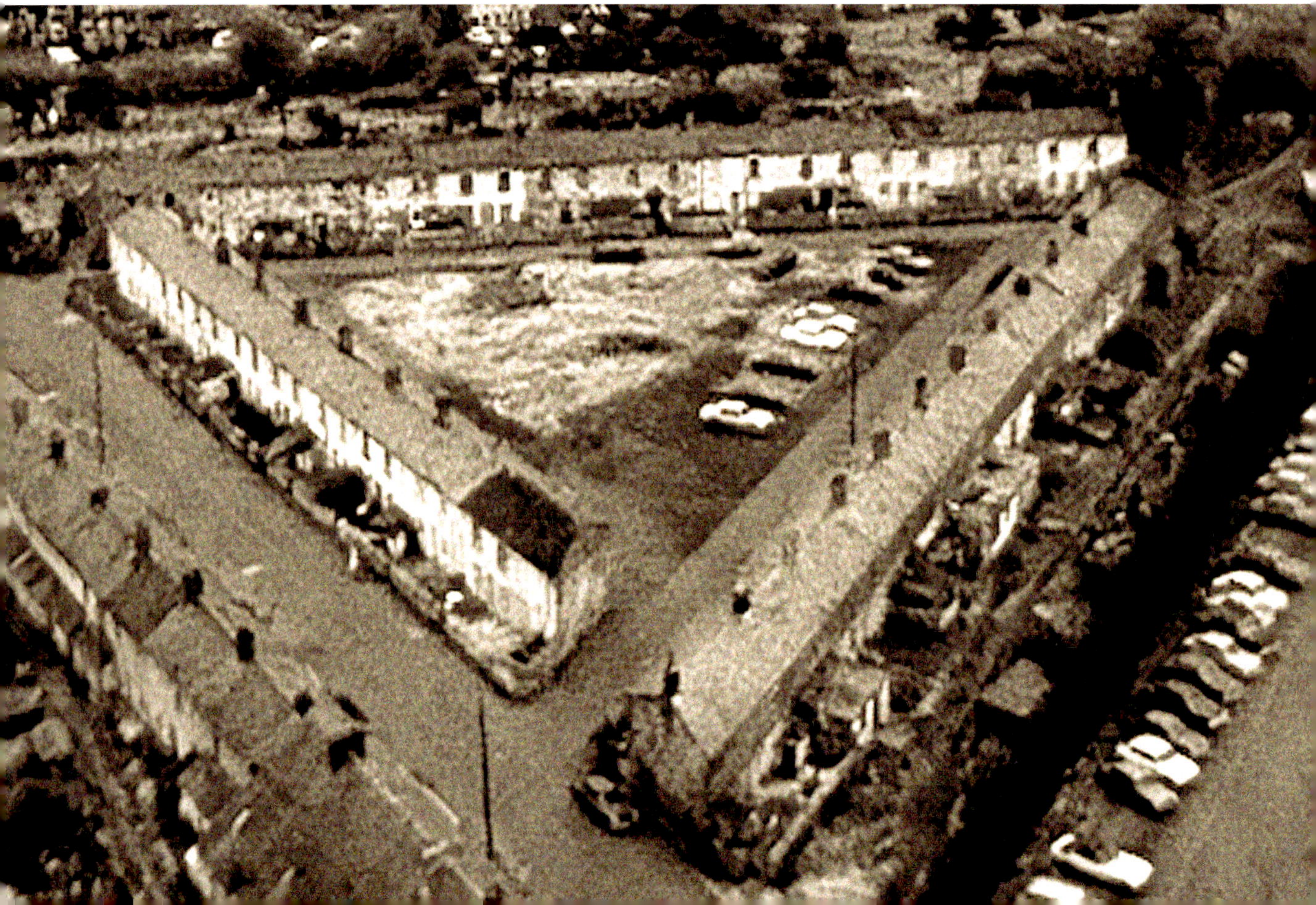

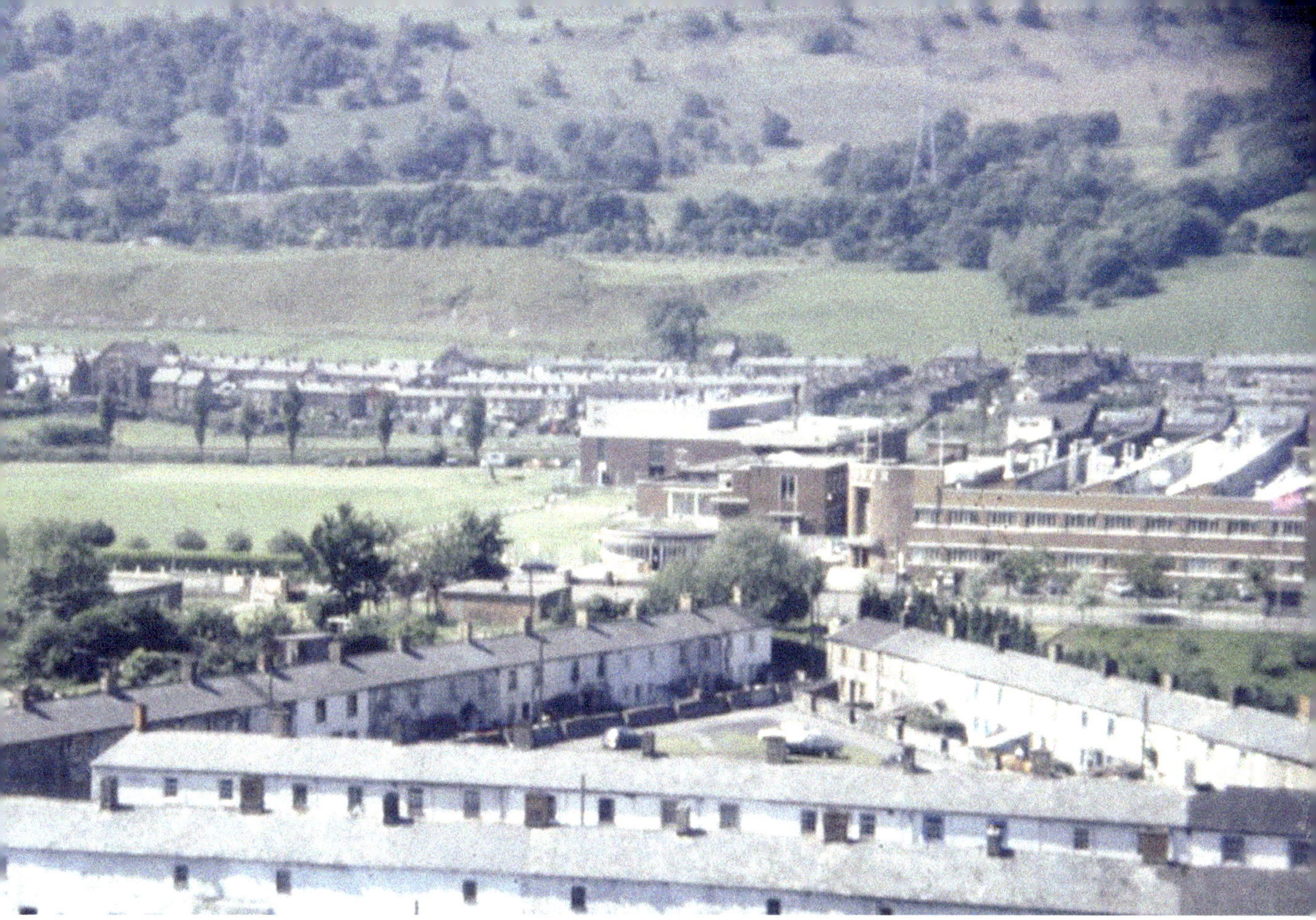

"It was revolutionary. Although the houses didn't have what we would consider mod cons, like piped sewerage and indoor toilets, they did have two very spacious rooms downstairs, two upstairs, a back garden, and a front and back door. You'd be astounded at how many houses in Merthyr didn't have a front and back door that allowed for through ventilation. They also had windows that could be opened, but that wasn't the case at all for houses in Merthyr, especially in that mid 19th century period: some homes only had windows at the front of the property and none behind, while some had apertures that were just decorative and didn't open at all. So all these little additions meant a great deal to how you would live in that space and it really changed your quality of life.

"The Triangle was the top level of what a working-class person could achieve at that time. There was probably a lot of envy from people in other parts of the town because looking at those homes, even though they were situated right next to an ironworks, they must have appeared so pleasant and attractive."

Opposite and above: the Triangle in the 1960s. It was an unmistakable landmark in Merthyr; innovative in its design and completely unique in Wales.

As Merthyr Tydfil expanded, the Triangle retained its distinctive shape and style. By the mid 20th century the iron foundries and furnaces were defunct, replaced by other cradles of industry like the hulking Hoover factory, which stood just across the road from the Triangle. Yet the rows of two-up two-down cottages were untouched by time, a historic corner of the town that had managed to survive the Great Depression, two World Wars and perpetual urban planning. Jackie Sutton and Marion Gossedge both lived in the Triangle and came to depend on the community in which they co-existed. Marion stayed there for 12 years:

"It was wonderful. The neighbours were so kind and helpful. I was in my 20s, not long married and I wasn't the best cook in the world. But the elderly women would help you. If a neighbour had baked a cake they'd bring some round for you. Today, you might not know your neighbours but in The Triangle, you could go to anybody for help. It was a different kind of environment. We were all more or less one family.

"You had an outside toilet at the rear of the house and at the front you'd have a coal cwtch and it would be back-to-back with the one next door to you. There was no indoor bathroom – it was a tin bath in front of the fire. But I loved it, I absolutely loved it. You'll never have that same spirit as you did in the Triangle. I was glad I was born when I was and I could experience it."

Jackie had bought her stone cottage for the princely sum of £50 and raised her baby daughter in the Triangle:

"I could put her in a pram outside the front door in the little yard, in the sunshine, without any worry whatsoever. I knew she'd be 100% safe, and she was. There was one old lady who sold Corona pop from her house. When I was pregnant, I was drinking practically a bottle a day. It's a wonder my daughter wasn't born red! I'd boil her nappies on the cooker and when neighbours saw the washing line of white nappies they would come round and say, with excitement, 'Who's had a baby then?'

In the Triangle we shared washing lines; I would have it one day and the lady opposite would have it the next day. On ash day (when council carts collected the ash from all the coal fires) you couldn't peg your washing out because the men couldn't get down the street to do their job. If you did, your clothes would end up halfway down the road!"

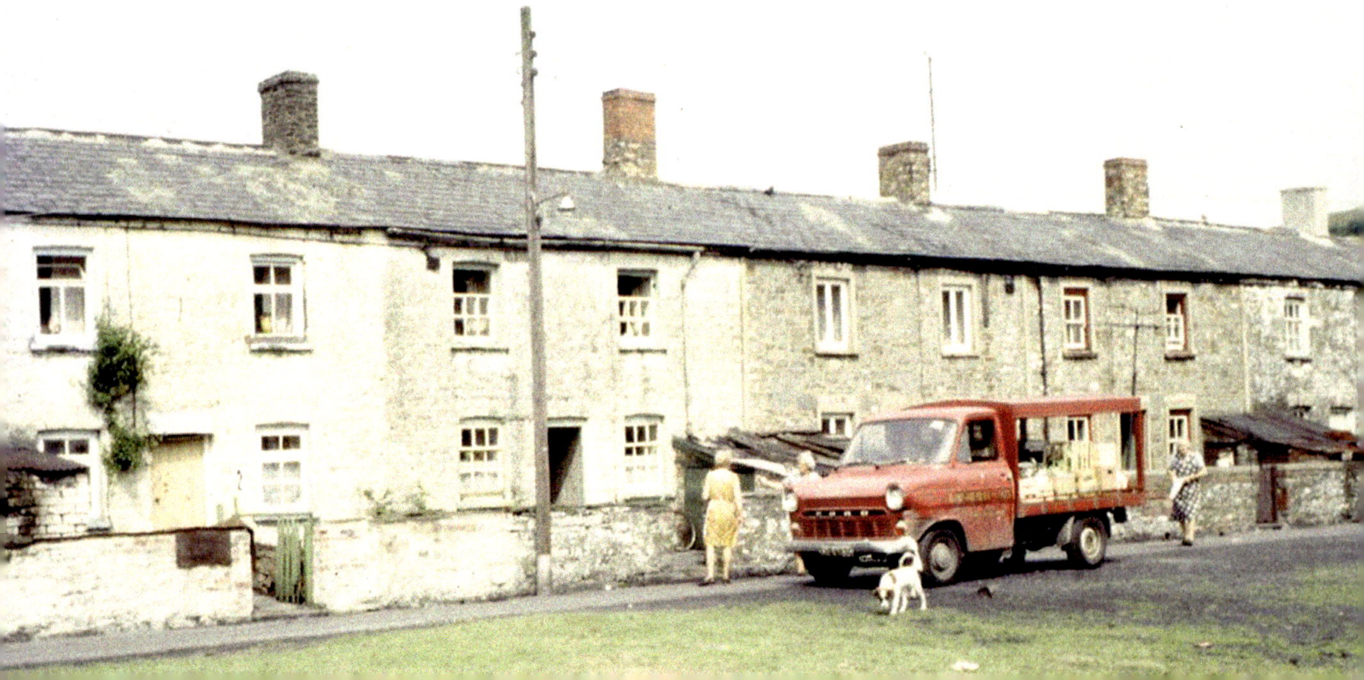

As a native of the Triangle you were part of an exclusive club – a community within a community, housed in one of Wales' most strikingly shaped residential areas. It had been a fixture of Merthyr life for almost 150 years, part of the fabric of the town. But its days were numbered.

In the 1970s Merthyr Borough Council announced its intention to demolish the Triangle entirely. It considered the old buildings as slum dwellings. A new vision was needed: the residents would be moved to more modern accommodation and the land cleared for commercial redevelopment, for the benefit of the town. There was an almighty backlash. Residents, conservationists, civic groups, historians, heritage bodies – even the Welsh Office – all weighed in, asserting with great passion that the buildings should be saved at all costs.

It was a bitter, protracted fight, spanning four years. In 1977, the council finally made its decision: the Triangle would be torn down. In December that year the houses were swept away. Catherine Thomas remembers that time all too well. She lived in the Triangle, with her grandparents:

"They didn't want to move. My grandmother so resented the fact that the reason for knocking down the Triangle was that it was labelled as slum clearance. She absolutely did not believe that she lived and had brought up her children in a slum. That was the worst slur for her.

"They were the very, very last house to move out of the Triangle. It was becoming a ghost village. Houses were empty and boarded up, earmarked for clearance. So it was not a pleasant experience for them. But they were determined to be there until they had to move, until there was no more choice. And that's what happened. The Triangle was wiped out and it was never the same again."

Opposite and below: daily life in the Triangle, featuring the ubiquitous washing lines.

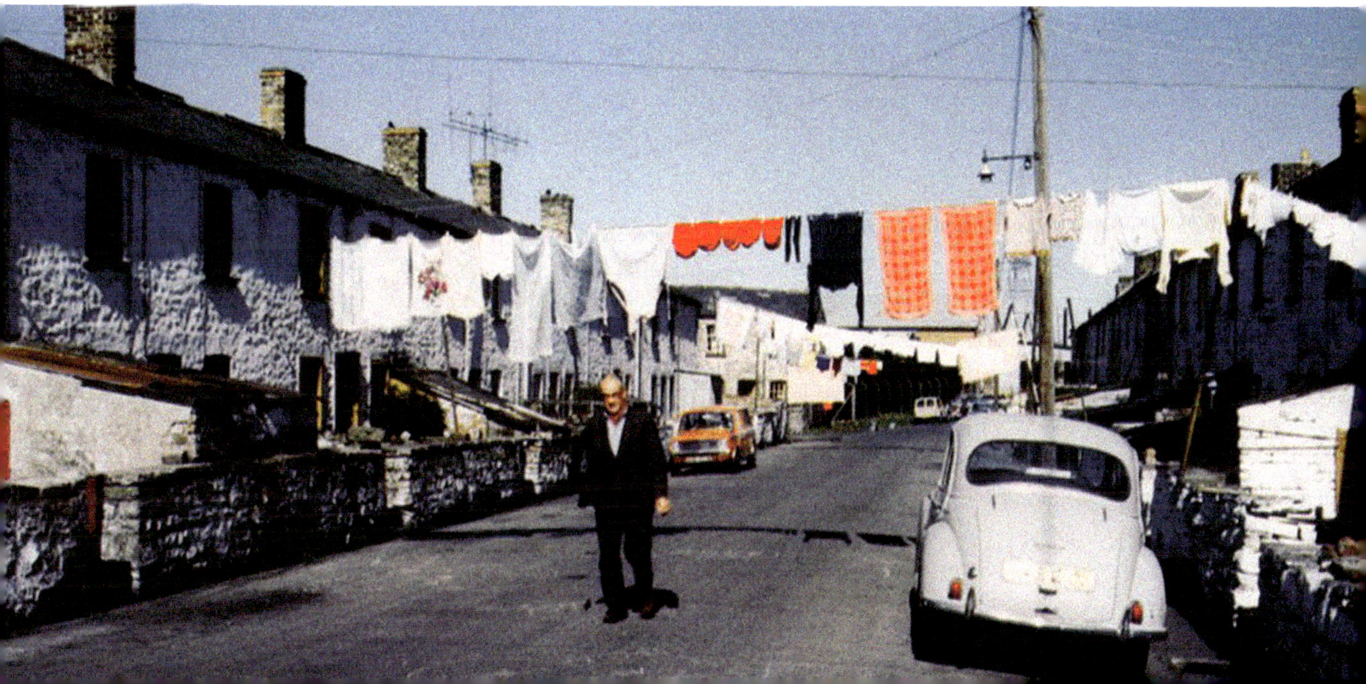

Drive through Merthyr Tydfil today and on the site of that famous three-sided housing estate you'll find a business park. But stay in your car and travel 10 minutes further into town until you arrive at Chapel Row. There you will find a strip of stone cottages built around the same time as the Triangle and similarly constructed as housing for ironworkers.

Chapel Row had also been earmarked for demolition in the 1970s but escaped the wrecking ball. The cottages have been renovated and are still occupied to this day. If the pendulum had swung the other way, could the Triangle have been given a second chance too? Would families still be living on those historic trilateral streets in modern Merthyr? Sadly, we'll never know.

Below: the Triangle's 'village green.'

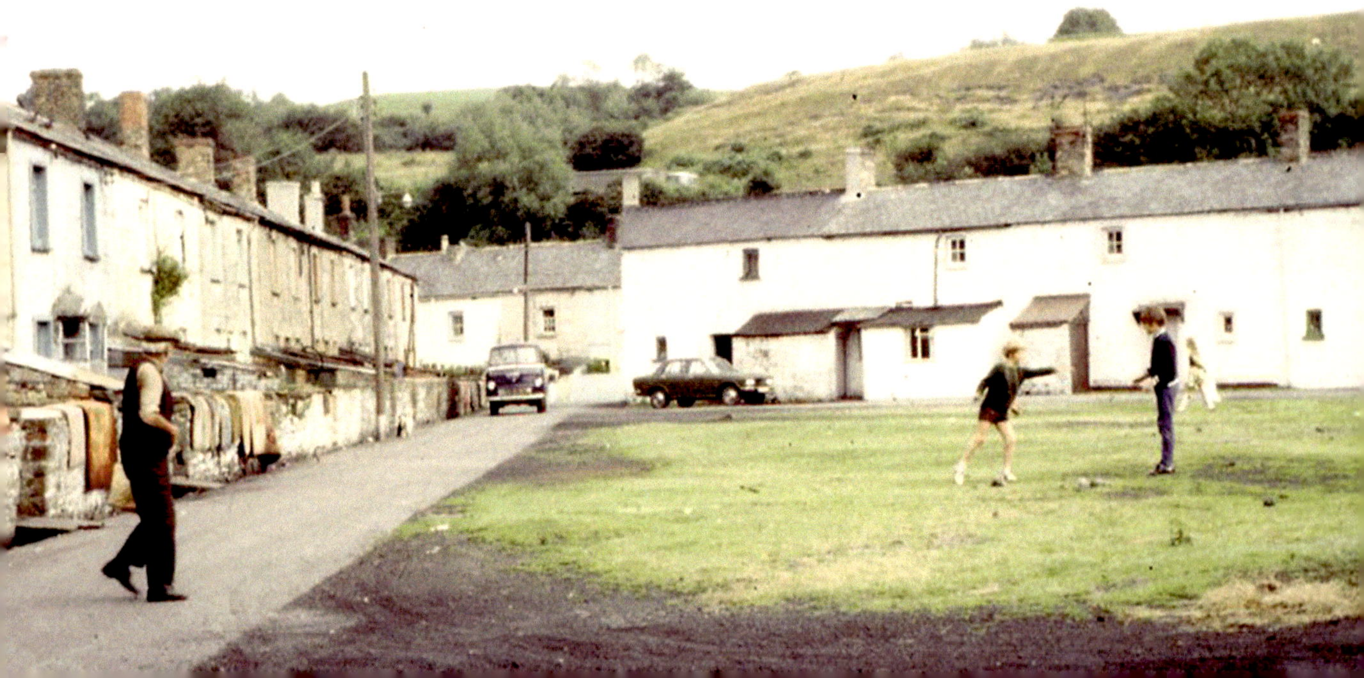

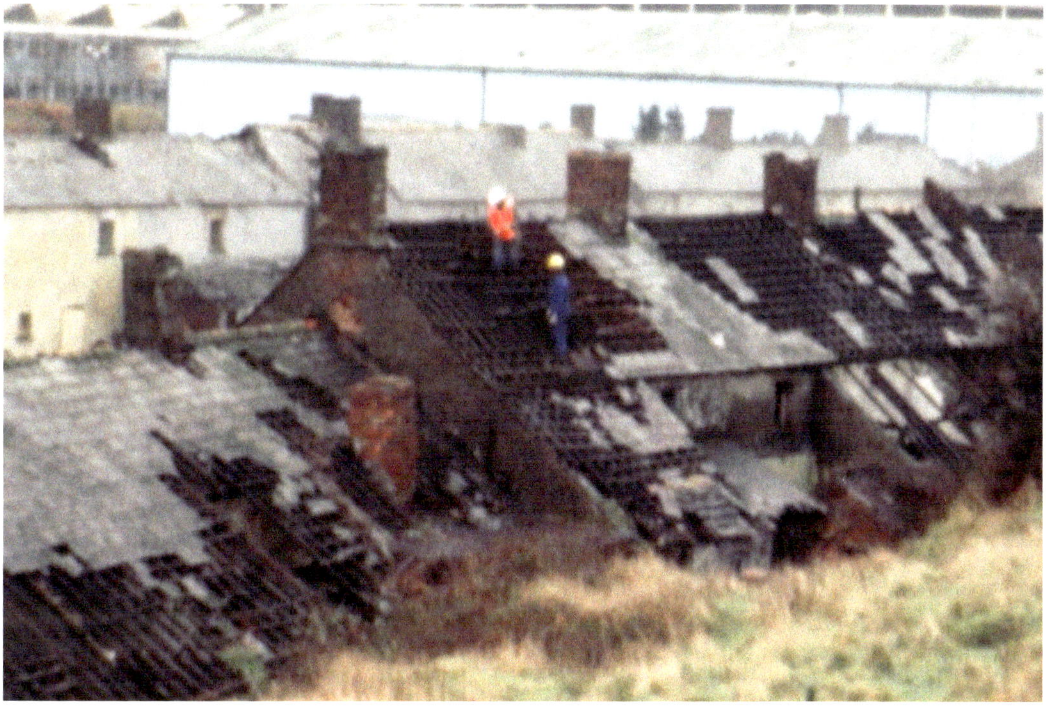

Demolishing the Triangle, December 1977.

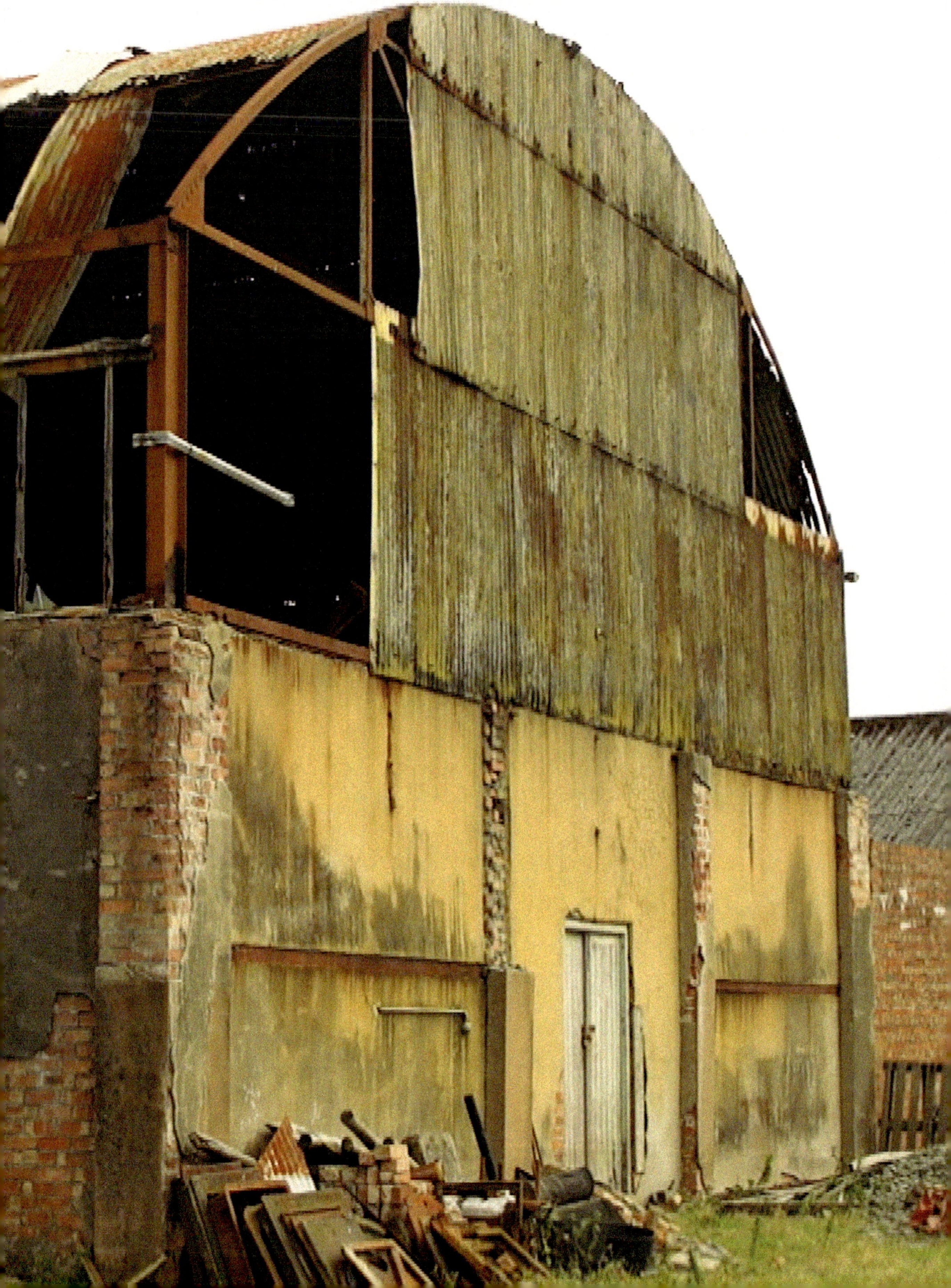

TONFANAU ARMY CAMP

The WW2 base that offered sanctuary in peacetime

On the West Wales coast, where Eryri meets the waters of Cardigan Bay, stand the desolate fragments of an extensive military complex. Two giant metal-framed, semi-cylindrical sheds stand silently in a field, while a nearby smattering of crumbling, roofless structures are regarded with general indifference by the sheep grazing in their shadow. This is all that's left of the former army base at Tonfanau, just up the coast from Tywyn. It was built for war but experienced a remarkable reinvention in the 1970s. In both roles, it served as a shield against the wildness of despots.

Tonfanau camp had been established in 1938 as a priority response to the threat from Nazi Germany. It spanned more than 200 acres and was virtually its own village. There were endless rows of accommodation blocks, a hospital, garages, three dining rooms, two electrical substations and a 1,000-seater theatre-cum-cinema to provide entertainment for the troops. It had its own railway station and was home to some 1,500 men and women from a range of regiments.

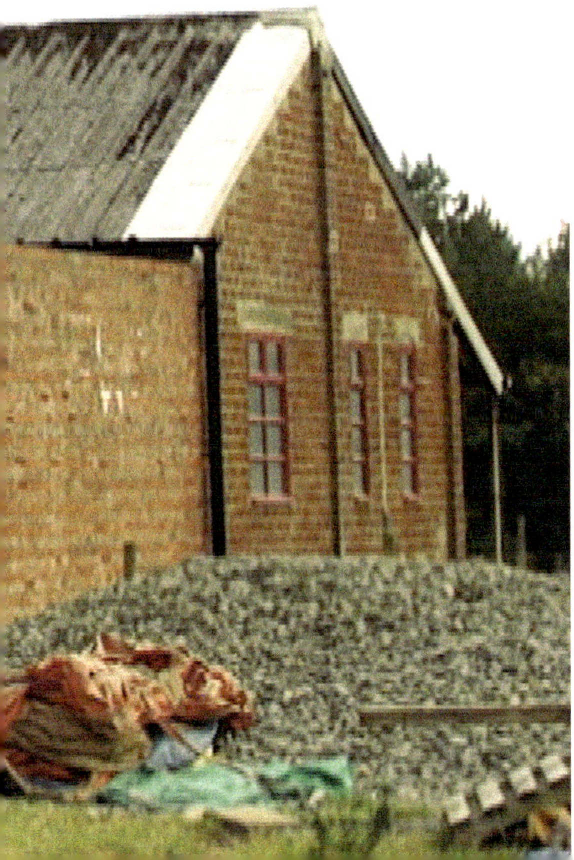

The old army camp stands in silent decay.

The base began life as a training facility for anti-aircraft gunners. Following the fall of France in 1940, the site intensified its operations, ready to pivot at a moment's notice to combat an enemy invasion along the Welsh coast. A chain of heavy-duty guns was positioned at the edge of the sea and there was an open channel of communications between Tonfanau and the neighbouring RAF airbase at Tywyn. The invasion never came but you can still see the footings of the gun emplacements above the beach.

At the end of WW2 – as the Cold War grew hotter – the camp was retained as a key resource for the armed forces. For years, this coastal plain in Gwynedd welcomed waves of young recruits and reservists as they learned the nuts and bolts of weaponry.

In 1965, Tonfanau was finally wound down, having served its purpose at a time of national need. The base stood empty and mute. This could have been where the story ends, a typical tale of a wartime landmark lurching into decline. But the next phase of Tonfanau's life was to prove transformative. And it was triggered by one man's actions in East Africa.

Tonfanau as an active base in the early 1960s.

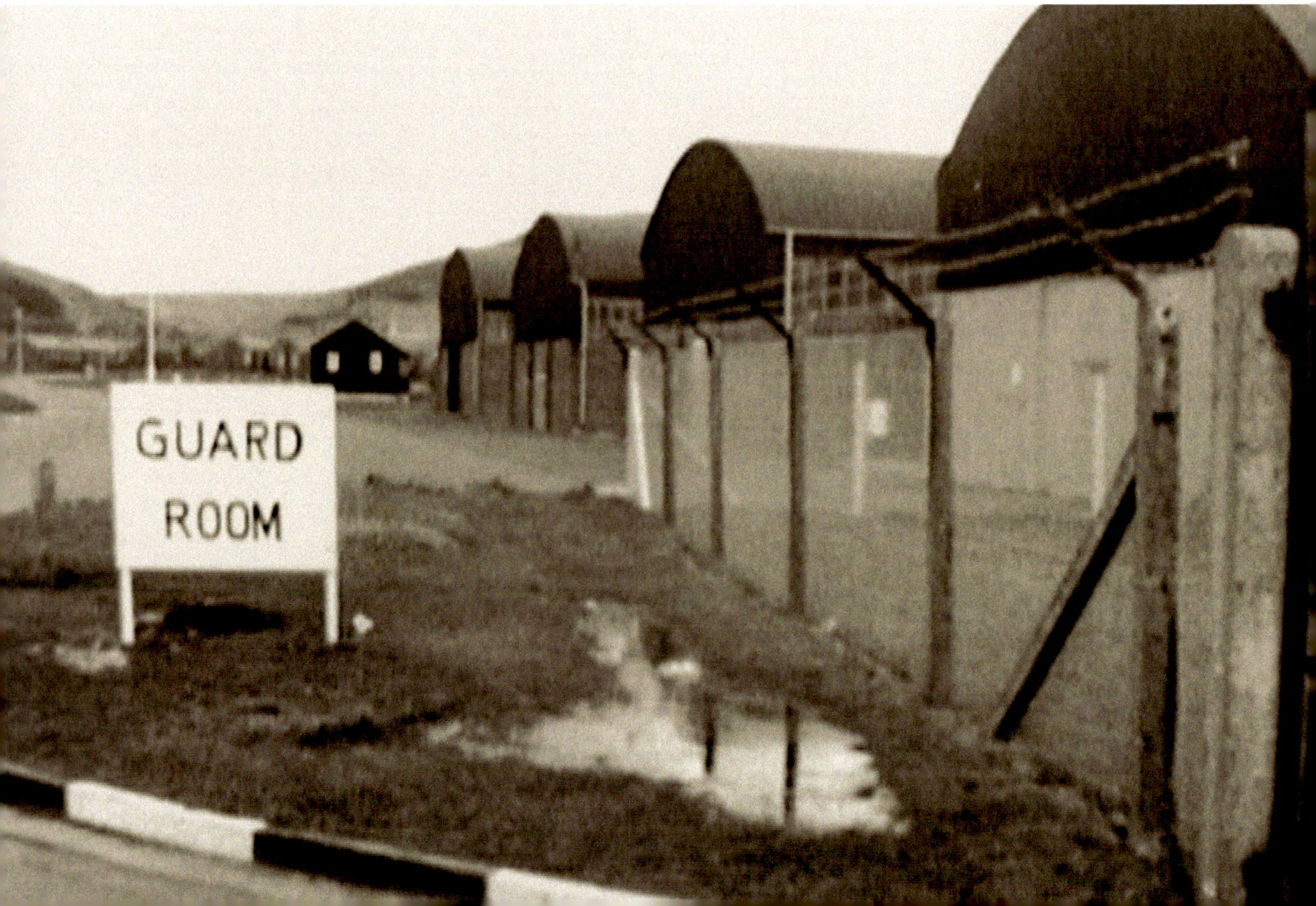

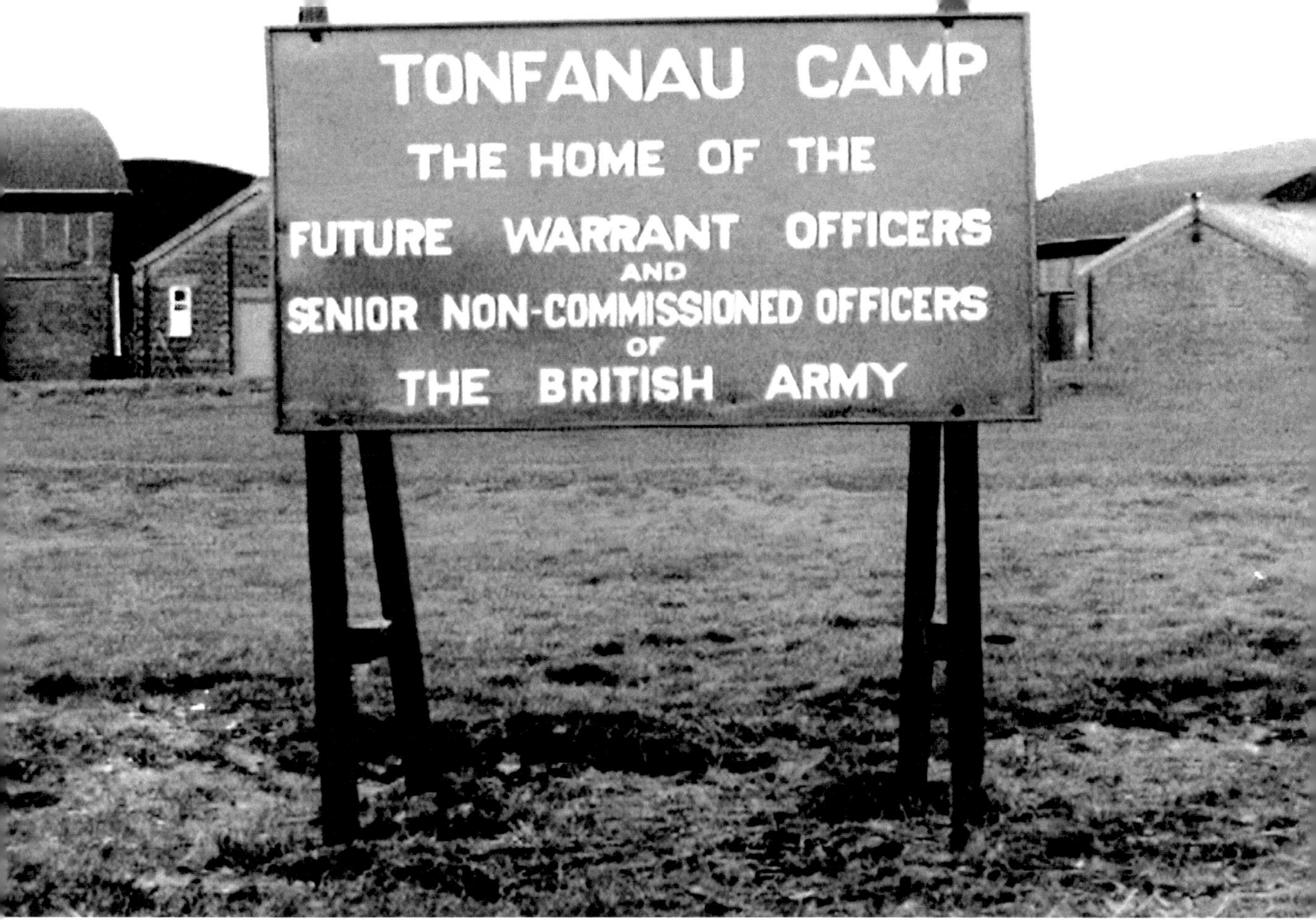

The year was 1972. The brutal President of Uganda, Idi Amin, issued a chilling message. Tens of thousands of Asians, whom he denounced as 'economic bloodsuckers', must leave the country or face his wrath. His announcement shocked the world. Families were given just 90 days to pack up and permanently leave their homeland. They were allowed to take one suitcase, £50 per household – and nothing else. Chandrika Joshi was one of the Ugandan Asians forcibly exiled from their country:

> "We started hearing of people being beaten up, people being killed. There were army checkpoints everywhere, including where we lived. That time was traumatic. I remember we had someone who used to come to the house to help us with domestic work. He was a young man and he was beaten up because the authorities wanted to know where he worked. He knew that if he told them then our family would be harassed. So he said nothing. He didn't come back for a week or so and when he next turned up at the house, he had marks on his back where he'd been beaten. It was a very scary situation.
>
> "We left our home and there was a lot of anxiety trying to get a taxi to take us to Entebbe. There were checkpoints on the way and we were feeling scared every time the army personnel stopped us to check all the bags. We had heard of people being killed. We thought: what's going to happen to us?

After WW2, the camp became a training site for army recruits.

"We made it to the airport. My father was disabled and struggled to walk and while the rest of us were getting onto the plane he was nowhere to be seen. From far away I could see him struggling and I felt this panic: what if he misses the plane and it flies off without him? He managed to get on it and I remember the relief on my father and mother's faces. So the plane took off and we flew into Heathrow airport. From there we were put on a train straight to Tonfanau."

The UK Government had agreed to offer a safe haven for up to 30,000 Ugandan Asians who held British passports. Resettlement camps were set up to provide food, clothing and accommodation for the refugees until more permanent places could be found for them. There were 16 such camps across Britain. Tonfanau flew the flag for Wales. The old army base was quickly repurposed and brought back online. In October 1972, Chandrika and her family arrived at their new makeshift home:

"We were five children, my parents and my aunt. They said we may have to stay in the camp's cinema for a little while. Rows of beds had been laid out there. But in the end they did find us accommodation and we were moved into a little army hut. It had a tiny electric heater. Of course we had come from a warm country so that little heater did nothing, you know! It was so cold. But the camp was run really well. There was schooling for the children, activities and so on. I came from a small town and it was exciting when new people would arrive in the camp and they were from our town too."

Around 1,500 Ugandan Asians made their way to Tonfanau. When they first arrived at the camp's railway station many were tired, traumatised, hungry and cold. They required compassion and care and the nearby communities stepped up. Margretta Young-Jones was one of hundreds of local volunteers who rallied round to help, performing small acts of kindness that made a big difference:

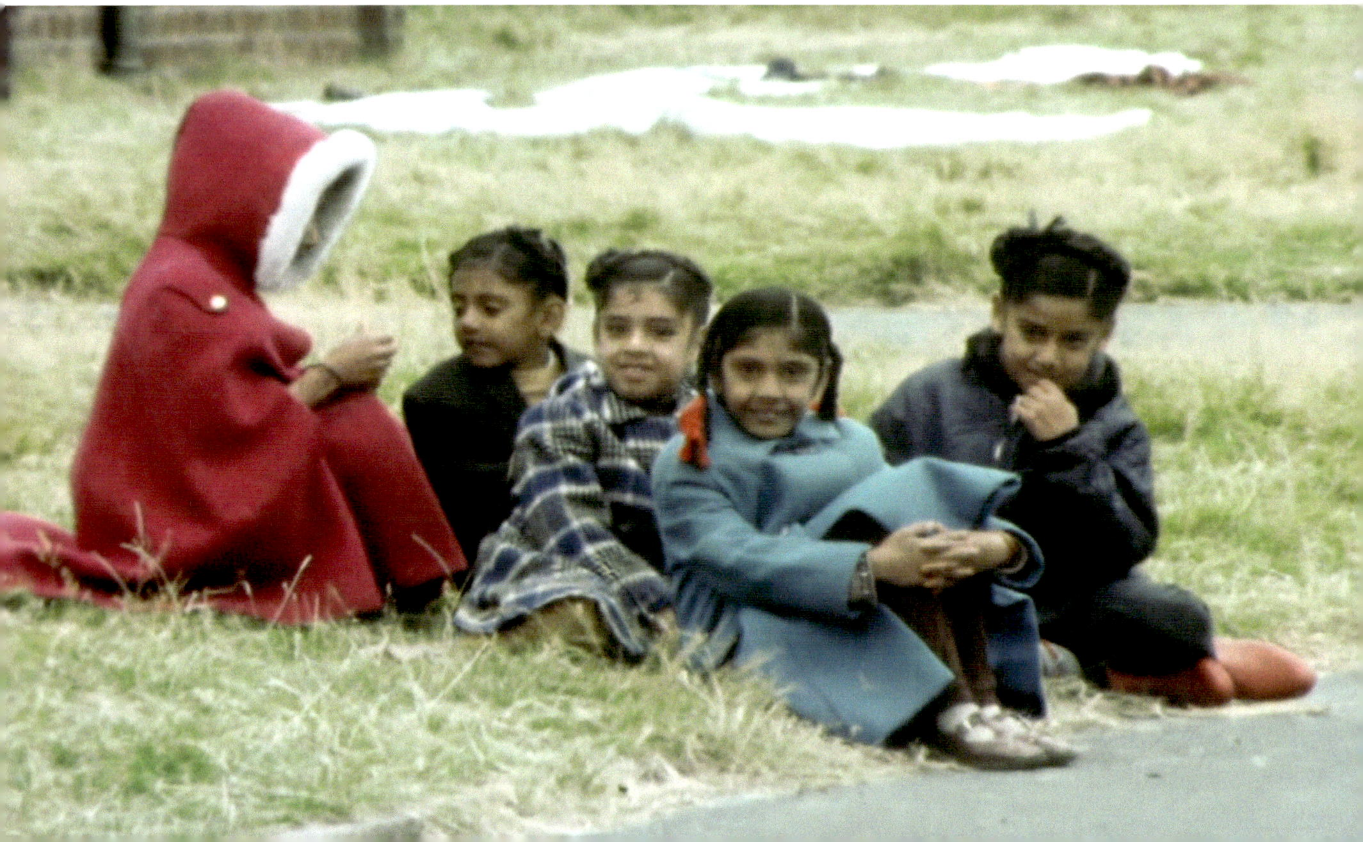

Ugandan Asian families make a new home at Tonfanau.

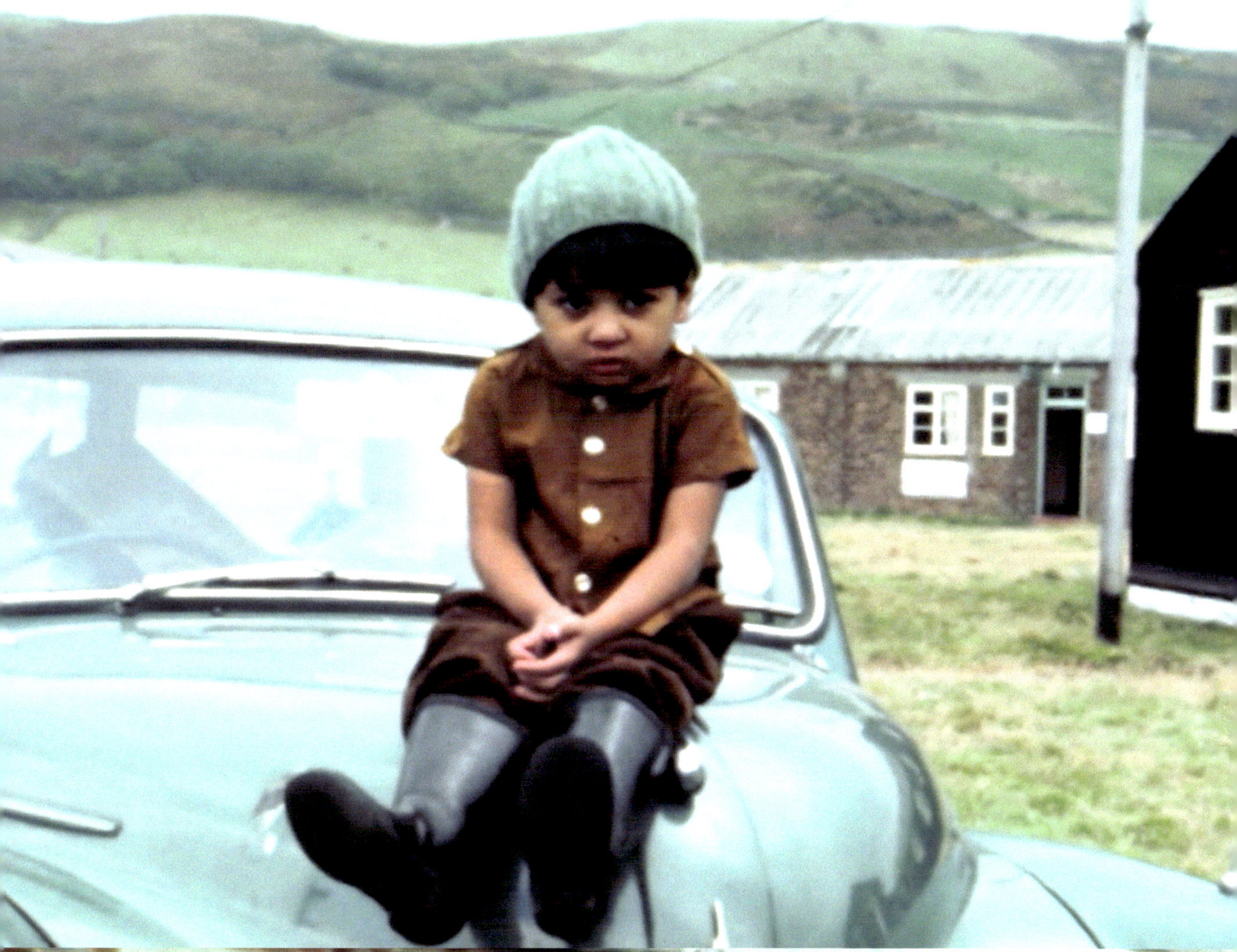

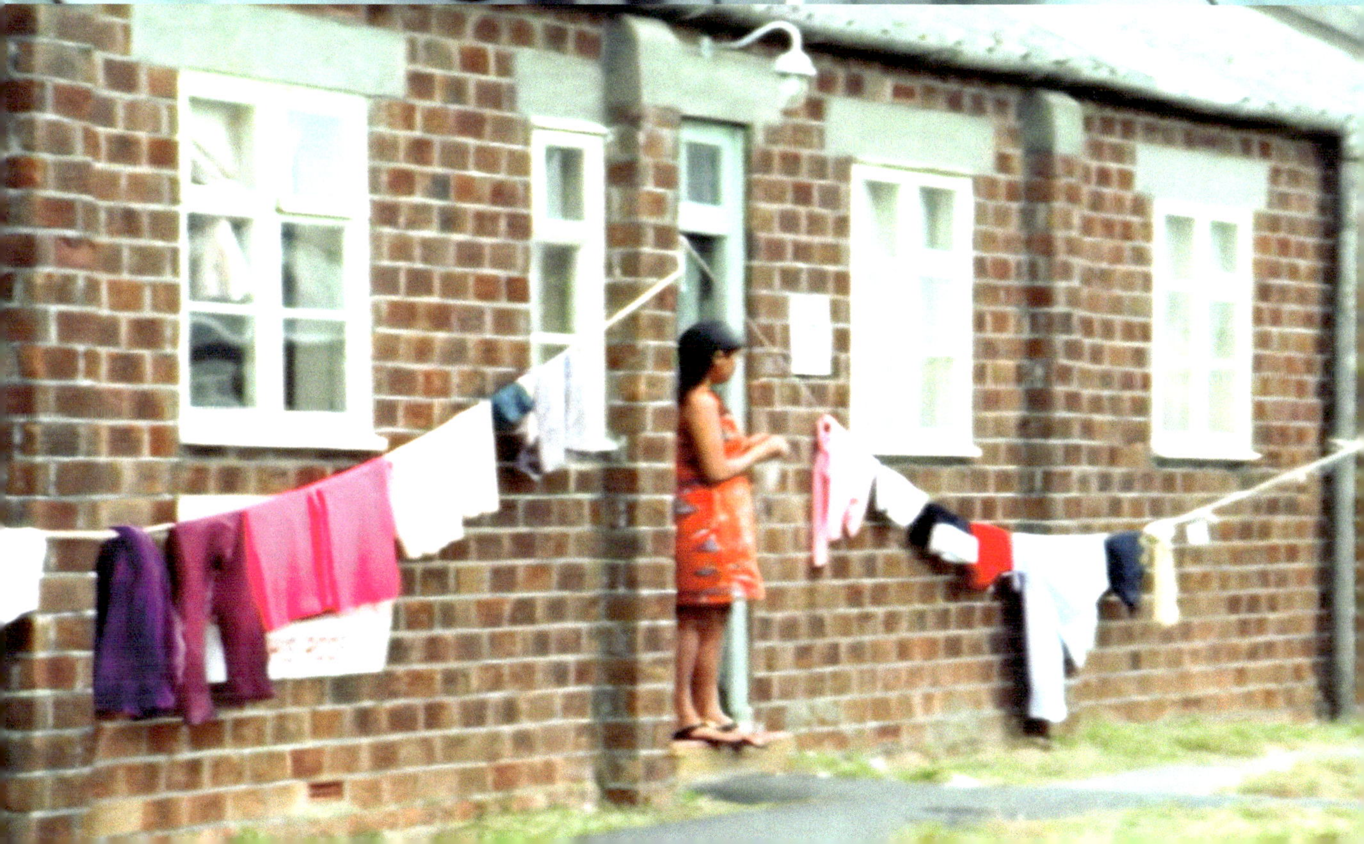

"I went up every night to see them. We were collecting the clothes and the food for them. It was autumn and the women had come in their saris. They wanted jumpers and things like that you see because it was freezing. One of them spoke a little bit of English: a grandma who wanted to make me her daughter because there was nothing else she could give us for being so kind towards them. And that was the greatest honour she could do was to adopt me as her daughter. They were such lovely people."

Gradually, the refugees were offered homes around the UK. One by one they departed the camp to rebuild their lives and put down roots. Chandrika's family eventually settled in the Rhondda Valley.

The army base at Tonfanau suddenly found itself empty once more. This time there would be no reprieve. The entire site was cleared, leaving a handful of ruins as the sum total of this once imposing coastal defence. During the Second World War, Tonfanau had faithfully guarded our shores. In peacetime, it offered hope to families fleeing a ruthless regime; a place of protection where life could begin again.

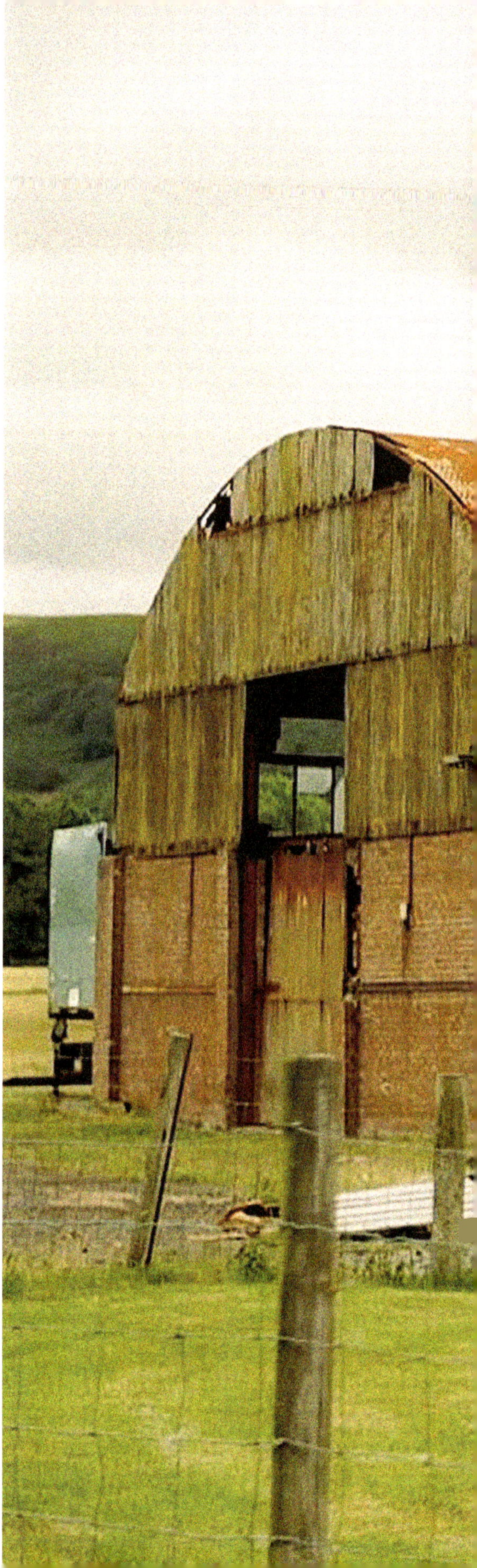

The ruined remains of the base.

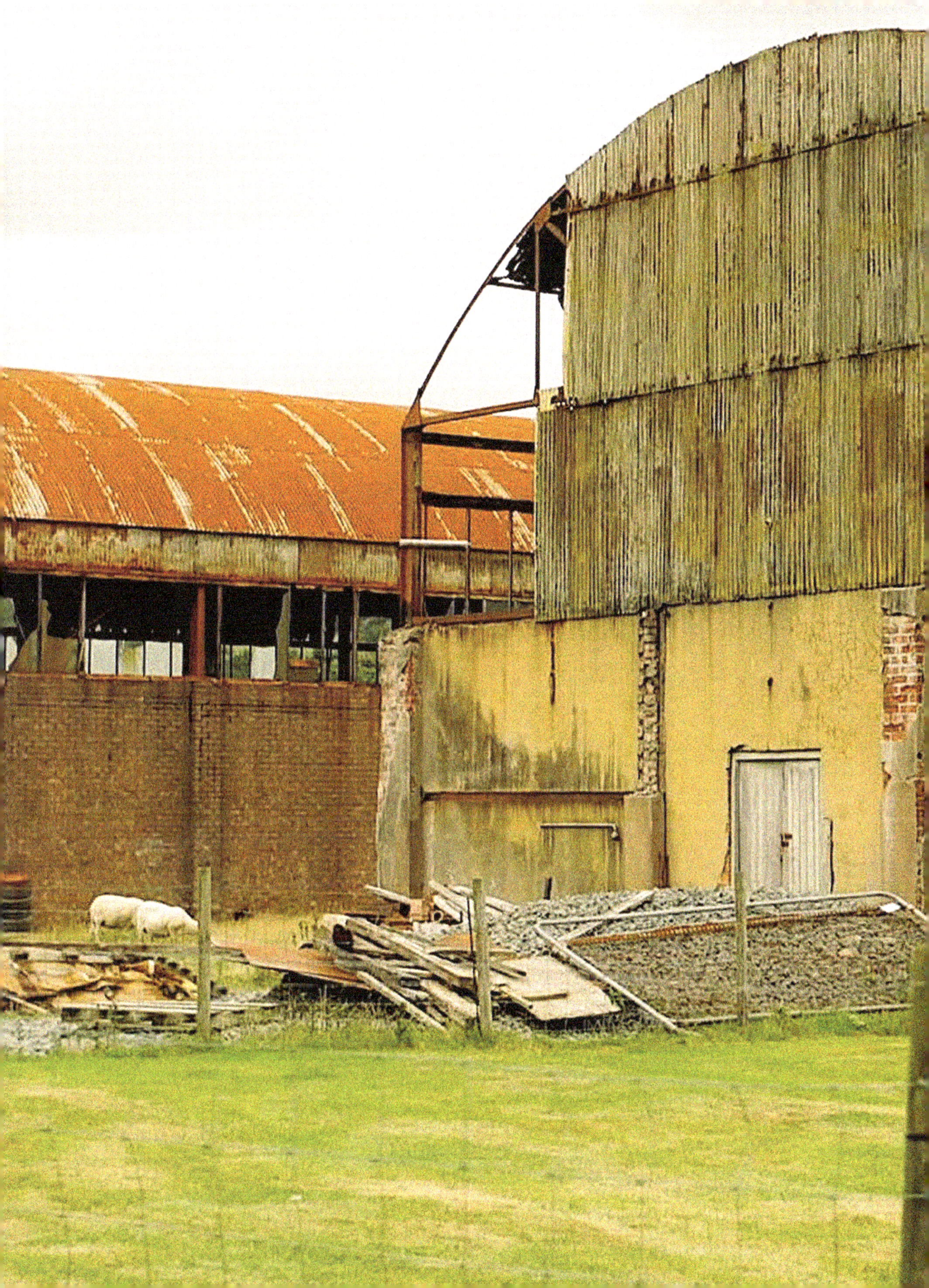

KING'S HALL

Classic art deco on the Ceredigion coast

Amid the sweep of Victorian buildings that grace the seafront of Aberystwyth, it's impossible to miss the cluster of modern, multicoloured apartments that dominate the promenade. They're anomalous, a temporal quirk. The neighbouring buildings echo a far earlier age. Visitors may well wonder: why are those bright, five storey flats such a prominent feature in the town? And what did they replace?

The answer is the King's Hall. Opening its doors in 1934, it was a magnificent multi-purpose venue and a triumph of Art Deco. Its huge, milky-white frame hugged the street, while its distinctive square clock-tower served as a waypost for holidaymakers. Open the glass fronted wooden doors and you'd step into a resplendent hall, complete with balcony, that could sit up to 1,500 people.

Below and opposite: the grace and glamour of the old King's Hall.

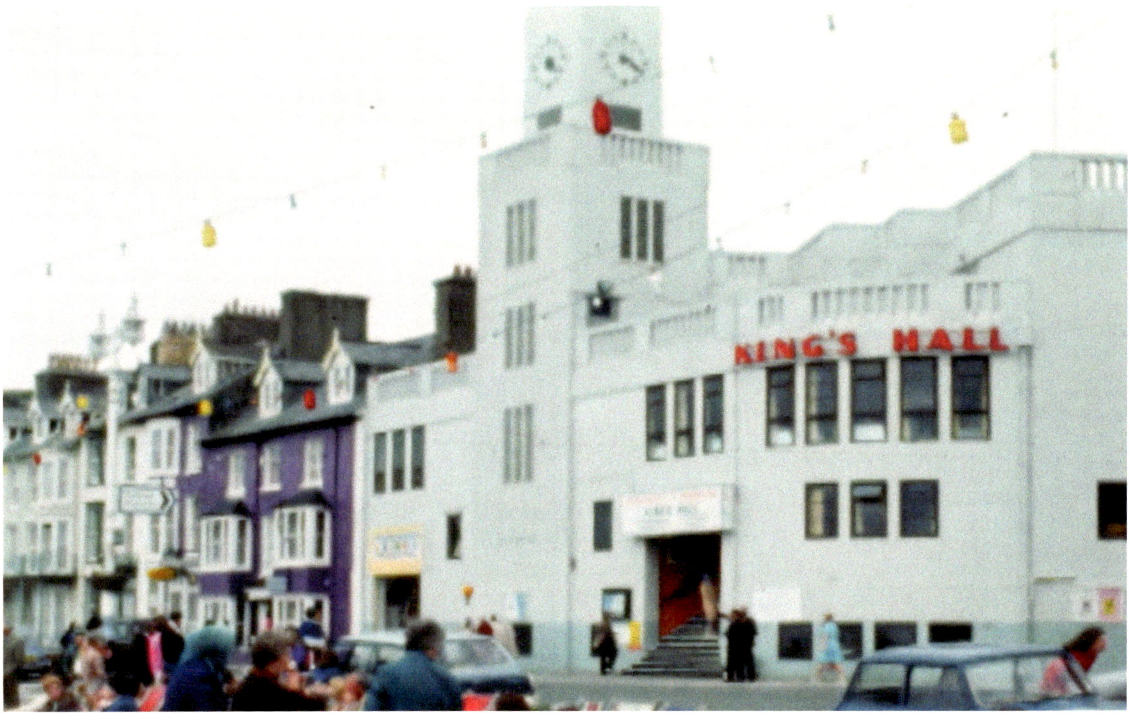

The 1980s were a calamitous decade for Aberystwyth's art deco gem. The University's arts centre was in full swing, taking away some of the events and concerts usually staged at the King's Hall. Attendance was falling and not even a pastel pink facelift seemed to revive the building's fortunes. The death knell was a council inspection indicating that the King's Hall was in a poor structural state and was unsafe. Repair and renovation weren't on the cards: demolition was.

In 1989, the entire building was bulldozed to the ground. The community could only stand and watch as their local landmark became a vast heap of dust and debris. For a structure that had been considered at risk of collapse, it took many weeks to eventually bring down the building. The King's Hall wasn't going without a fight.

Tearing down the King's Hall, 1989.

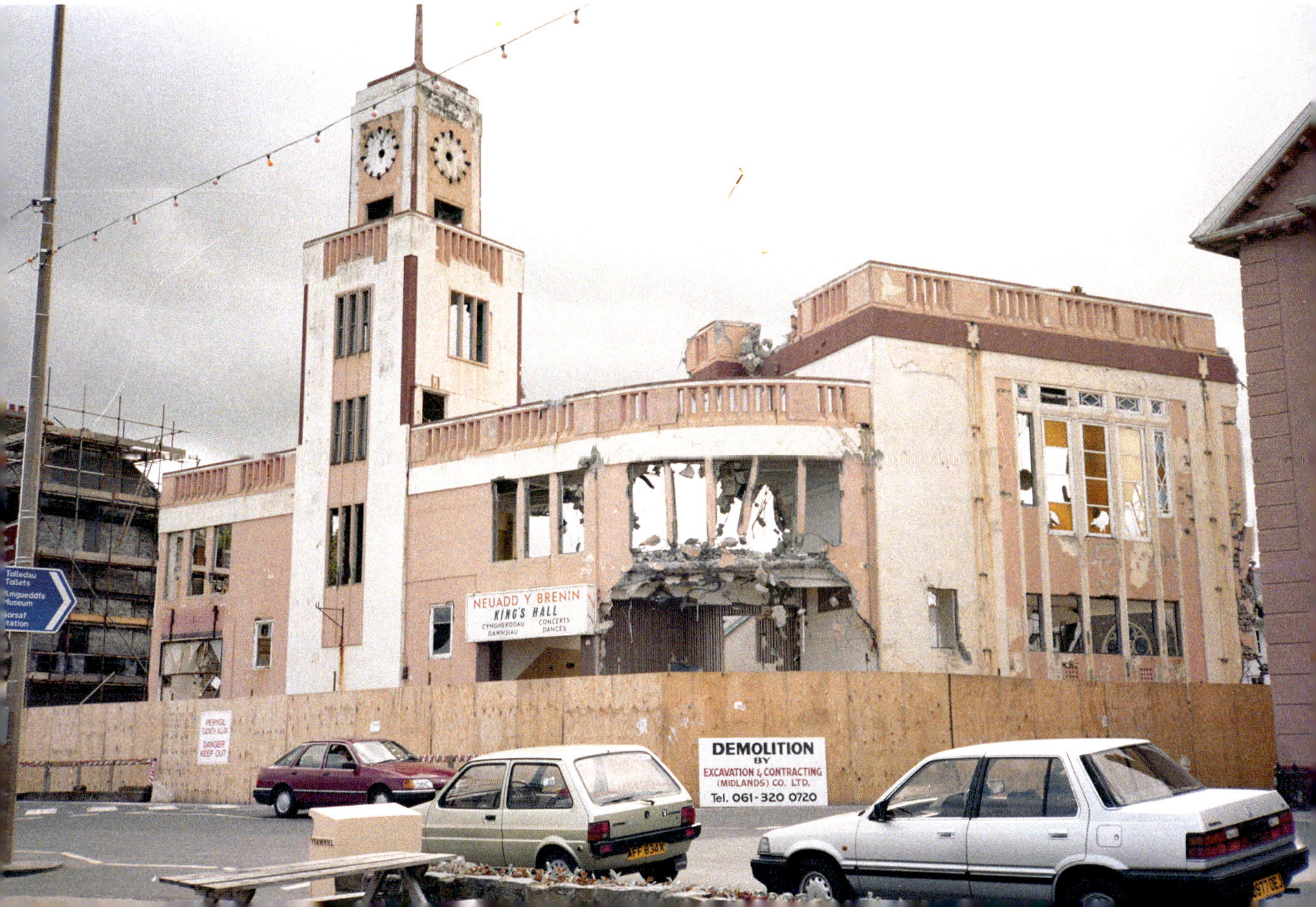

Witnessing the demolition was the late Don Shaw. He'd been the manager of the King's Hall for years; the building was like his second home. As he gazed at its destruction, he put pen to paper and composed a heartfelt lament. The last word on the King's Hall belongs to Don:

Have you ever heard a building cry?
A cry which says, 'Why do I die?'
They smash me with that ball and crane,
Save me and let me live again…

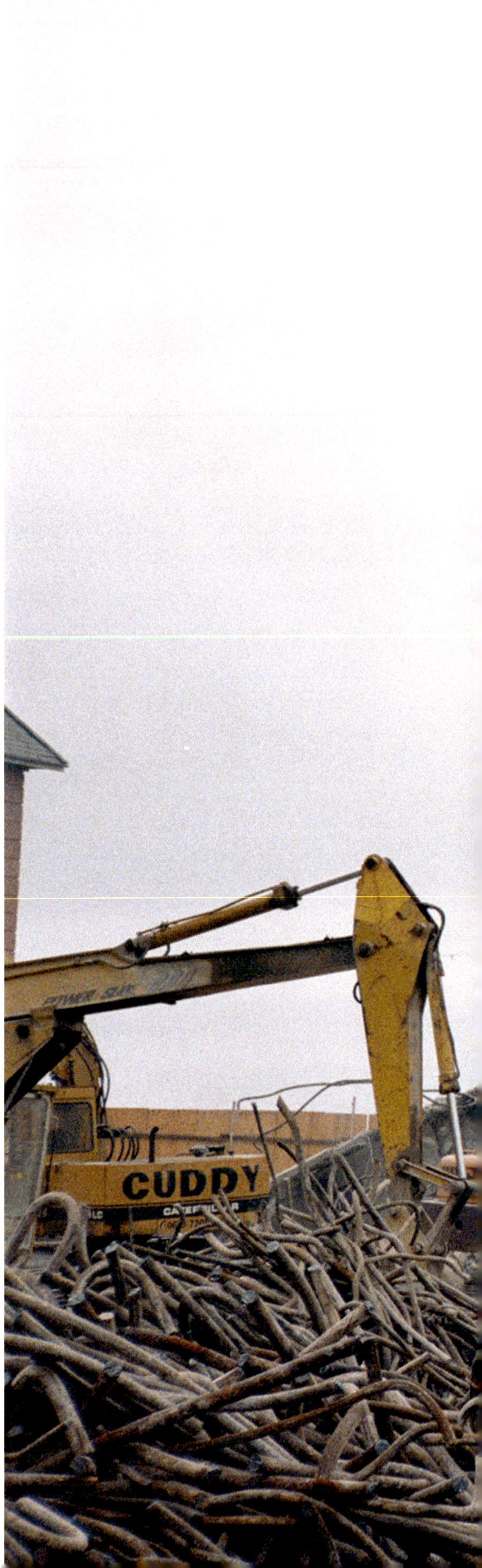

Going...going...gone.
The final stages of demolition.

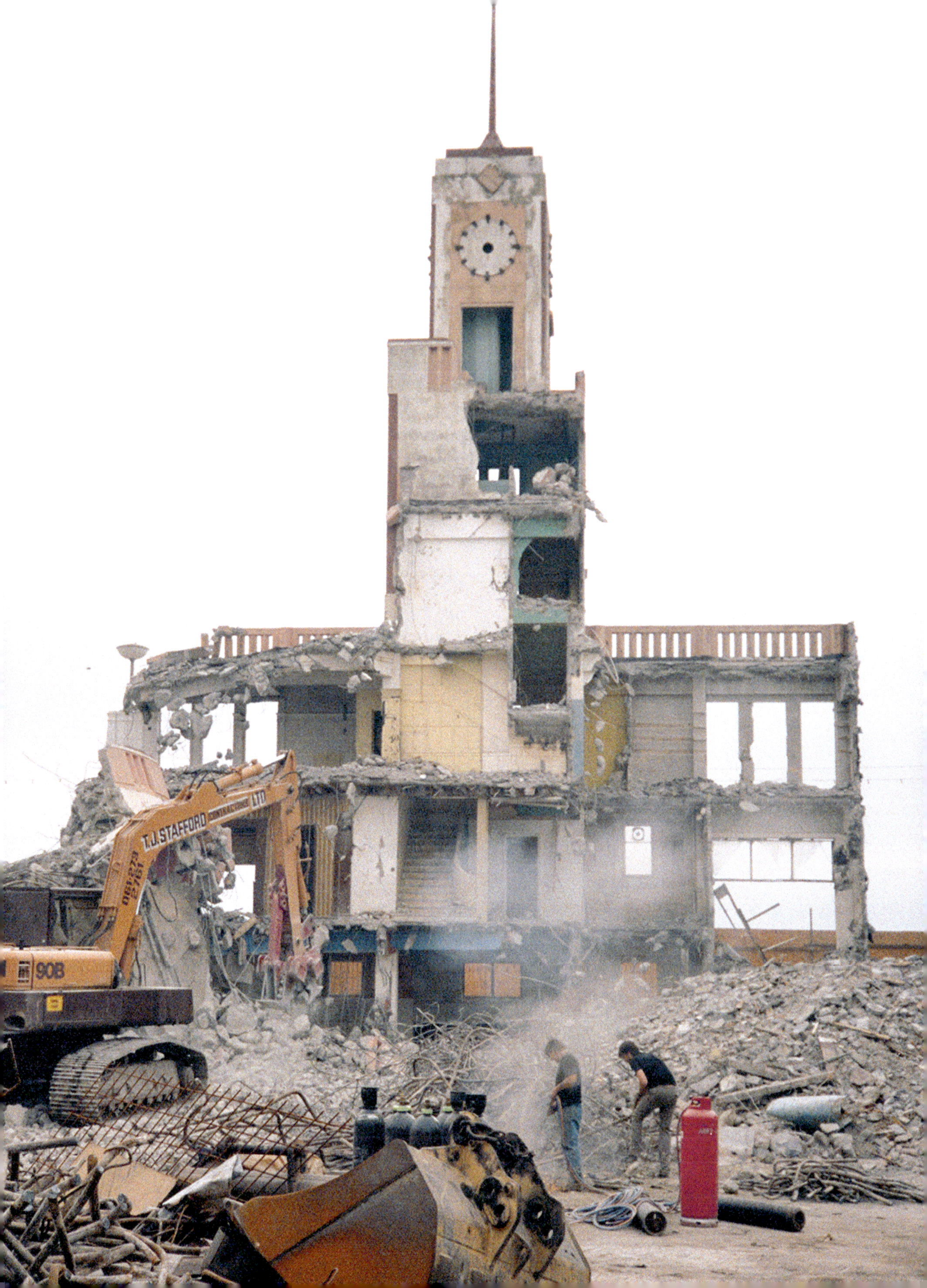
T.J. STAFFORD
LTD
90B

RHYL'S HOVERCOACH

The seaside town that made transport history

In the summer of 1962, the world's media gathered on the golden sands of Rhyl. The holiday town found itself at the heart of a pioneering experiment that would change sea travel forever. It was a world first. An ambitious feat of British engineering. A vision of the future.

All eyes were focused on a gleaming white machine: 54 feet long, 12 tonnes in weight. With its propeller blades and propulsion engines it had the familiar trappings of an aeroplane. Yet it emerged, not from the sky, but from the Irish Sea, moving effortlessly from water onto land before gliding to a halt along the powdery beach. No-one had seen anything quite like it. Part plane, part boat. What on earth was it?

Technically speaking, it was the Vickers-Armstrong VA-3 hovercraft. In the early 1960s, this hybrid technology was still in its infancy and must have been utterly enthralling to spectators on Rhyl's seafront – the equivalent of witnessing an early motor car honk past your horse-drawn carriage. The appearance of the VA-3 in North Wales was no one-off. The coastal town would be seeing a lot more of this curious craft during the summer of '62. Rhyl had been selected as the destination and departure point for a very special trial: the world's first ever passenger hovercraft service.

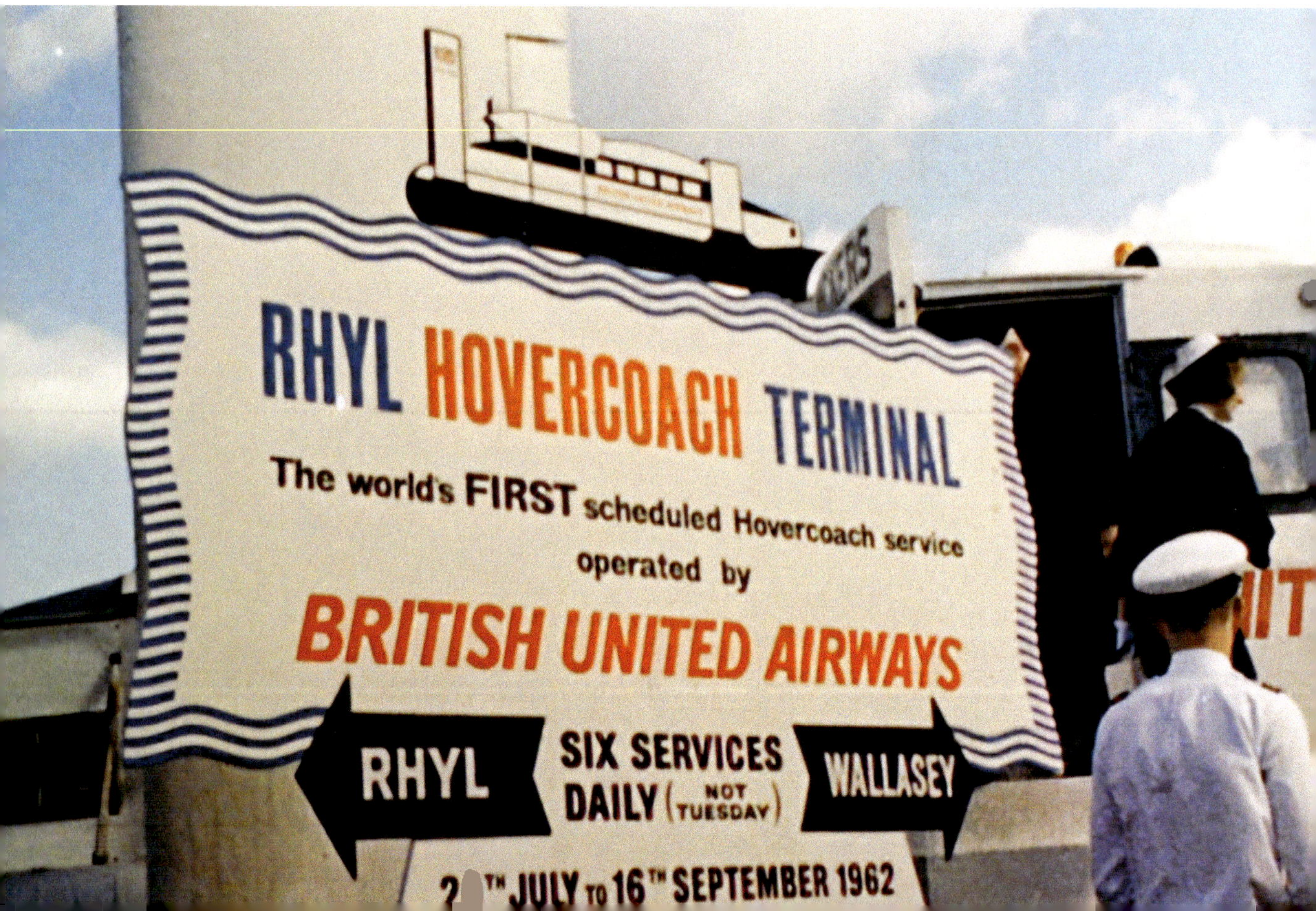

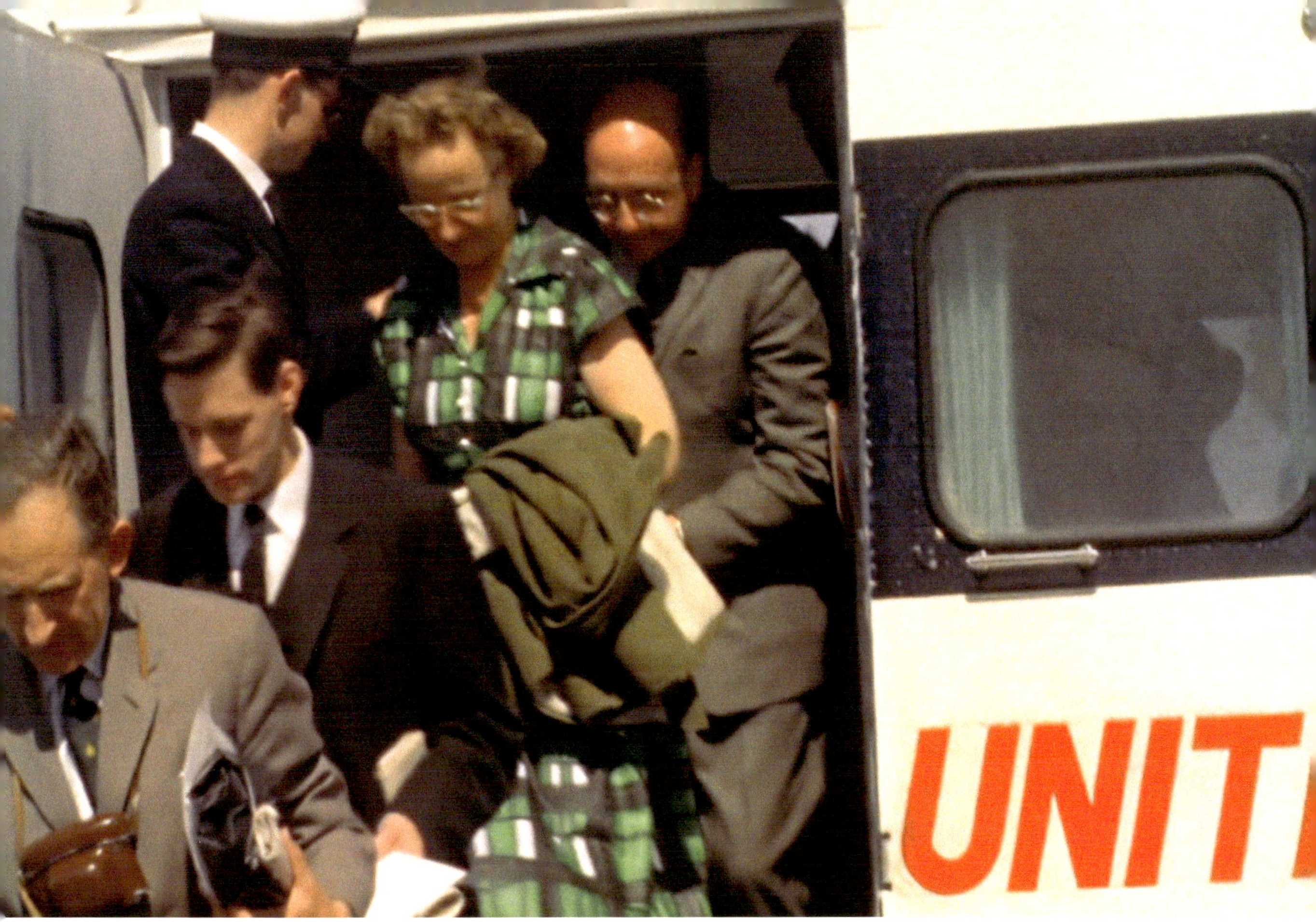

The 15-nautical mile route ran from Rhyl to the shores of Wallasey on the mouth of the River Mersey. There were regular daily crossings for fee-paying passengers (a return ticket would set you back £2) with a travel time of around 25 minutes each way. The Hovercoach, as the service was christened, captured the public imagination at a point in history when the very notion of a sea-skimming amphibious craft seemed like a concept straight out of science fiction. Hovercraft expert Warwick Jacobs believes the VA-3 was, quite simply, light years ahead of its time:

> "Man hadn't even set foot on the moon. The Queen was in the first ten years of her reign. We were still travelling on steam trains. So at the time this really was revolutionary.
>
> "At the very beginning of hovercraft development everyone wanted a piece of the action. Vickers-Armstrong had a mix of technologies: they had the shipbuilding side of the business, they made trains and they had aviation technology – they'd built Spitfires during the War. So they put their minds together and came up with this remarkable machine.
>
> "Their VA-3 was a chance to show that the hovercraft could do a job: carry passengers and make money. The journey from Rhyl to Wallasey would have taken two hours by car, so holiday makers were given the chance to travel by hovercraft instead. It was a great opportunity to test this as a new invention for the very first time."

Opposite and above: passengers at Rhyl take a trip on a newfangled mode of transport – the hovercraft.

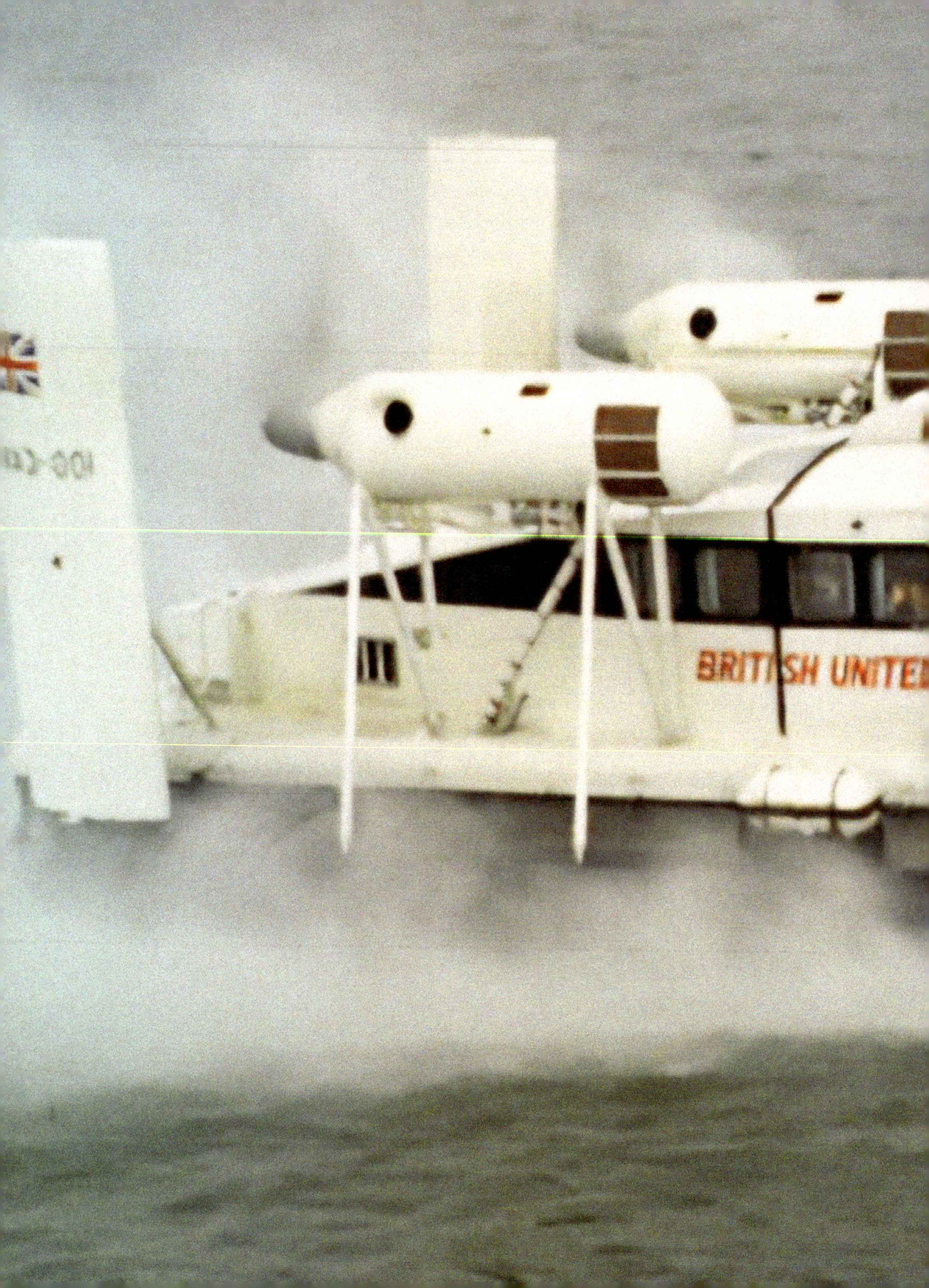
BRITISH UNITED

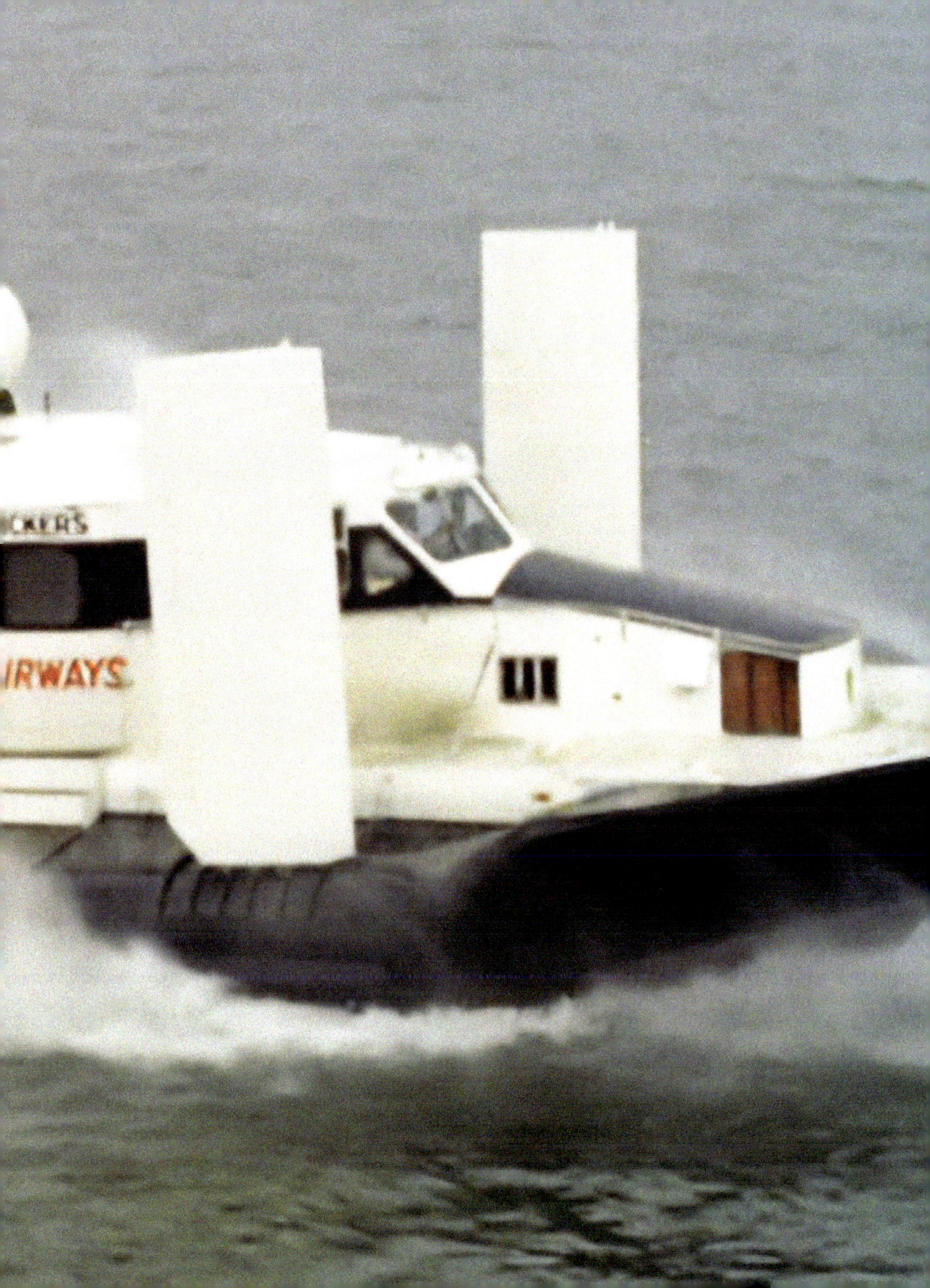

IRWAYS

Between July and September 1962, nearly 4,000 passengers travelled on this trailblazing craft. The promotional pamphlets sold it as a once-in-a-lifetime moment: 'Your chance to make history'. And it was, as long as you didn't mind facing backwards during the journey and you could stomach a sometimes choppy crossing (passenger surveys that summer revealed that 51% found it 'smooth'; 48% 'bumpy').

If you weren't fortunate enough to snap up a ticket, there was always the cost-free option of standing on the beach and watching the Hovercoach in action. A 17-year-old Ken Pemberton did just that:

> "I pestered my parents to bring me to see it. I really couldn't believe what this was. It was so futuristic, like a flying saucer! It was just an amazing thing to see. The noise especially – those aero engines made an almighty roar. And then there was the spectacle of the transition onto the sand and the dust that created. I enjoyed watching the spray getting bigger and bigger when it was on the water: that was fascinating too.
>
> "It was a very big deal. Hundreds of people went down to see it and get dusted! It was something new, something novel, a first in the world. It was unique."

It wasn't all plain sailing for the VA-3. The Welsh weather during the summer of 1962 was particularly unkind, and the craft was often plagued by engine trouble. As a result, the Hovercoach only managed 19 days of operational service – less than half the intended number. The crossings that were successful owed a huge debt to the pioneering pilots, who safely steered the experimental machine across the capricious waters of the Irish Sea. One of those pilots was Captain Raymond Old. His daughter Madeline still speaks tenderly of her late father's role in hovercraft history:

> "He was adventurous, he liked a challenge and he wanted to explore, develop and evolve the hovercraft. He was very excited to be involved in this new development and also felt very privileged to do it.
>
> "I was eight years old during the summer of 1962 and I was aware my father had an unusual job. But he was a very humble person so you'd have to tease it out of him! They were happy times. He was doing something that he loved and I think it's marvellous that we can celebrate these early days. Even now I say, 'My dad was one of the world's first hovercraft pilots!' I'm incredibly proud of him."

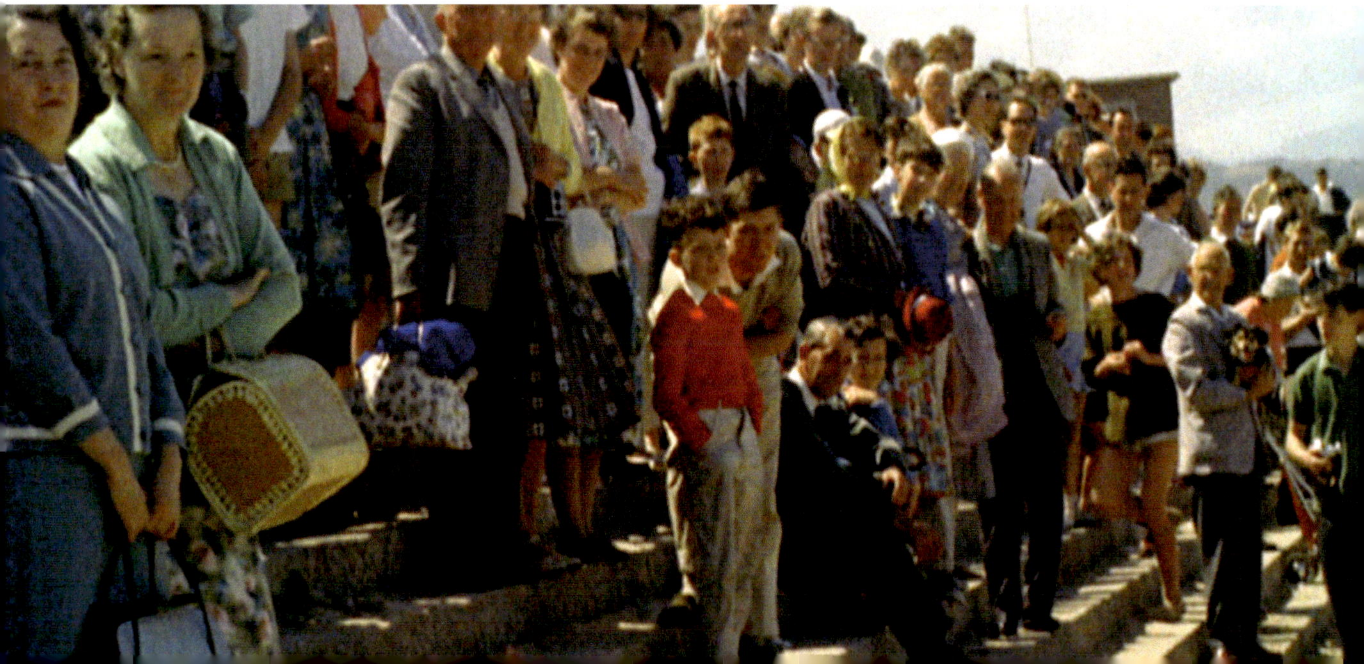

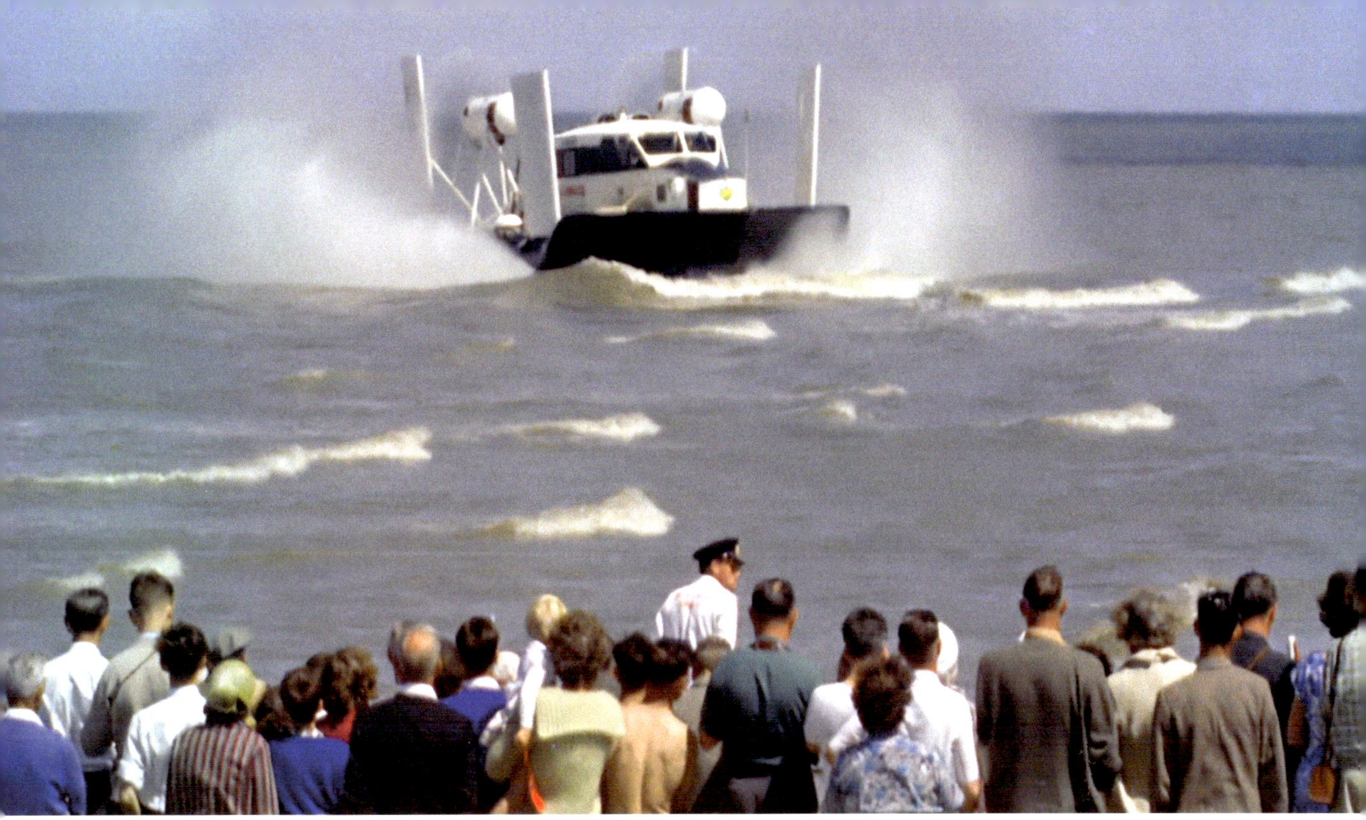

The Rhyl-Wallasey service was scheduled to run until 16 September. Instead it came to an abrupt and rather spectacular halt. Two days earlier the craft had experienced another bout of engine failure and had staggered back to Rhyl for mechanical repairs. An overnight storm and exceptionally high tide whipped up the waves causing the Hovercoach to break free from her moorings. The crew on board was saved, thanks to the volunteers of Rhyl's lifeboat service. The VA-3, however, wasn't so lucky. The wild winds slammed it against the sea wall. The only option was to hoist the damaged craft by crane and transport it by road back to Vickers-Armstrong. The Hovercoach never returned to Rhyl. It was all over. The groundbreaking passenger service had come to an ignominious end.

The VA-3 was eventually repaired and spent the next few years in North America. After a short period when it was used for military testing, it was deemed to have finally reached the end of its usefulness and was deliberately scuppered off the south coast of England in the late 1960s. Its carcass currently resides 70 feet beneath the Solent. One of its huge lift fans, the key component that provided the craft's lifting force, is the only original piece of the VA-3 that has survived and is now lovingly preserved at the Hovercraft Museum in Hampshire.

Back in 1962, the Rhyl-Wallasey crossing made history. The Denbighshire town found itself at the heart of an emerging technology that made headlines around the world and which helped to shape modern sea travel. The Hovercoach isn't remembered quite so much these days. You won't find many references to it in Rhyl and it remains an overlooked chapter in Wales' maritime past. But if you were there during that eventful summer, waiting for that noisy metal machine to approach the beach, you were watching the future glide into view.

Opposite and above: spectators line the beach to catch a glimpse of the VA-3 as it approaches from the sea.

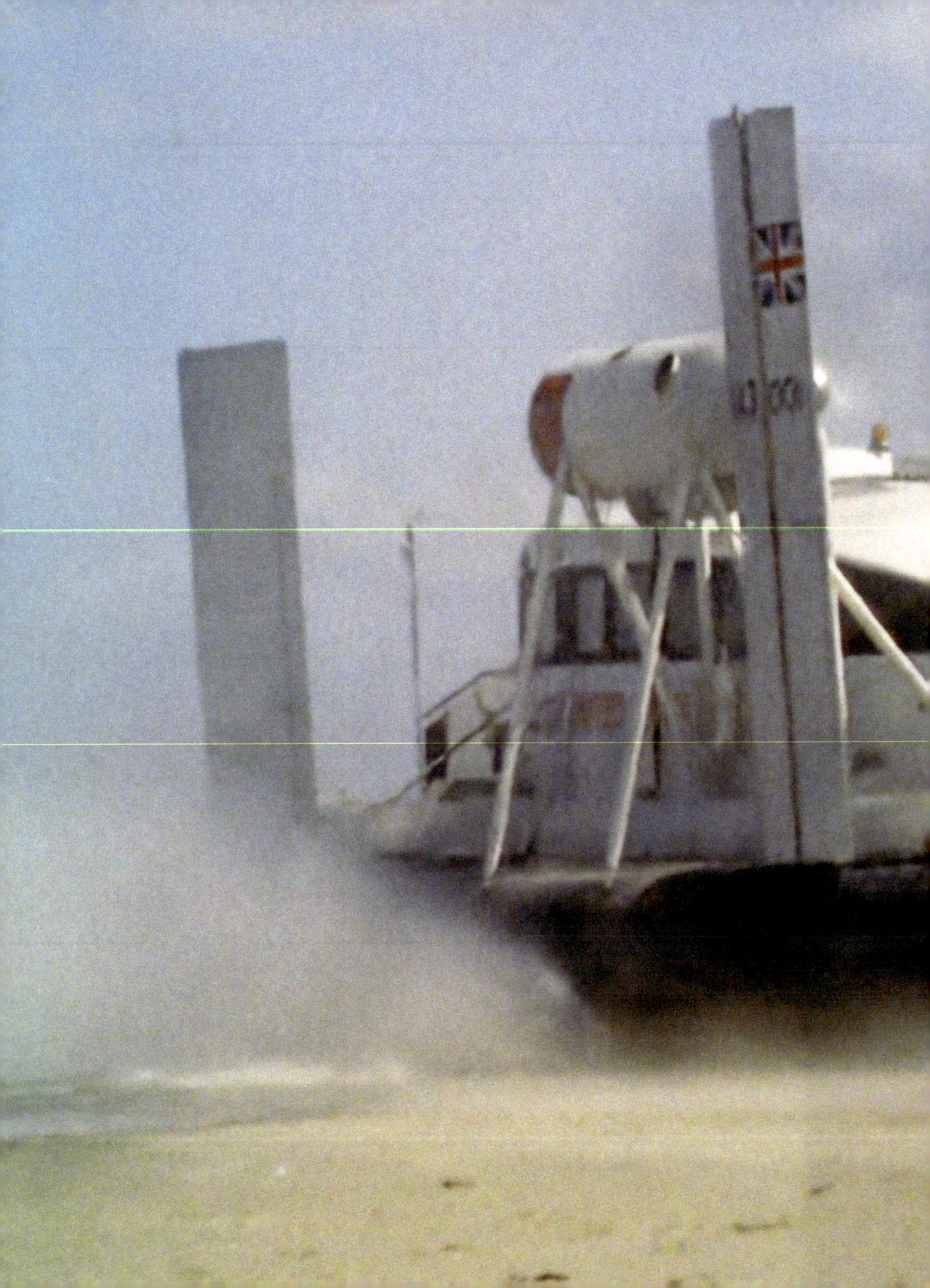

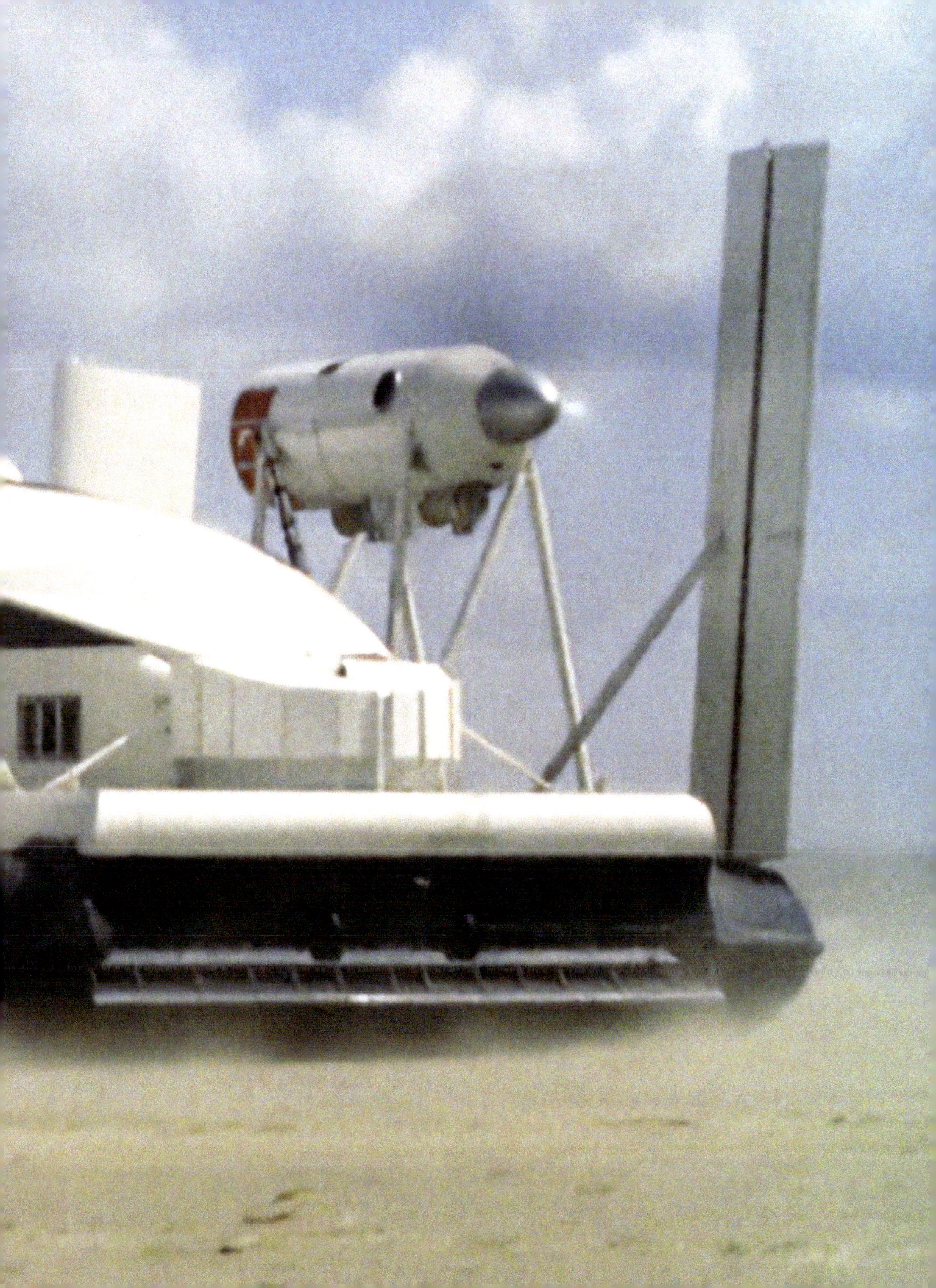

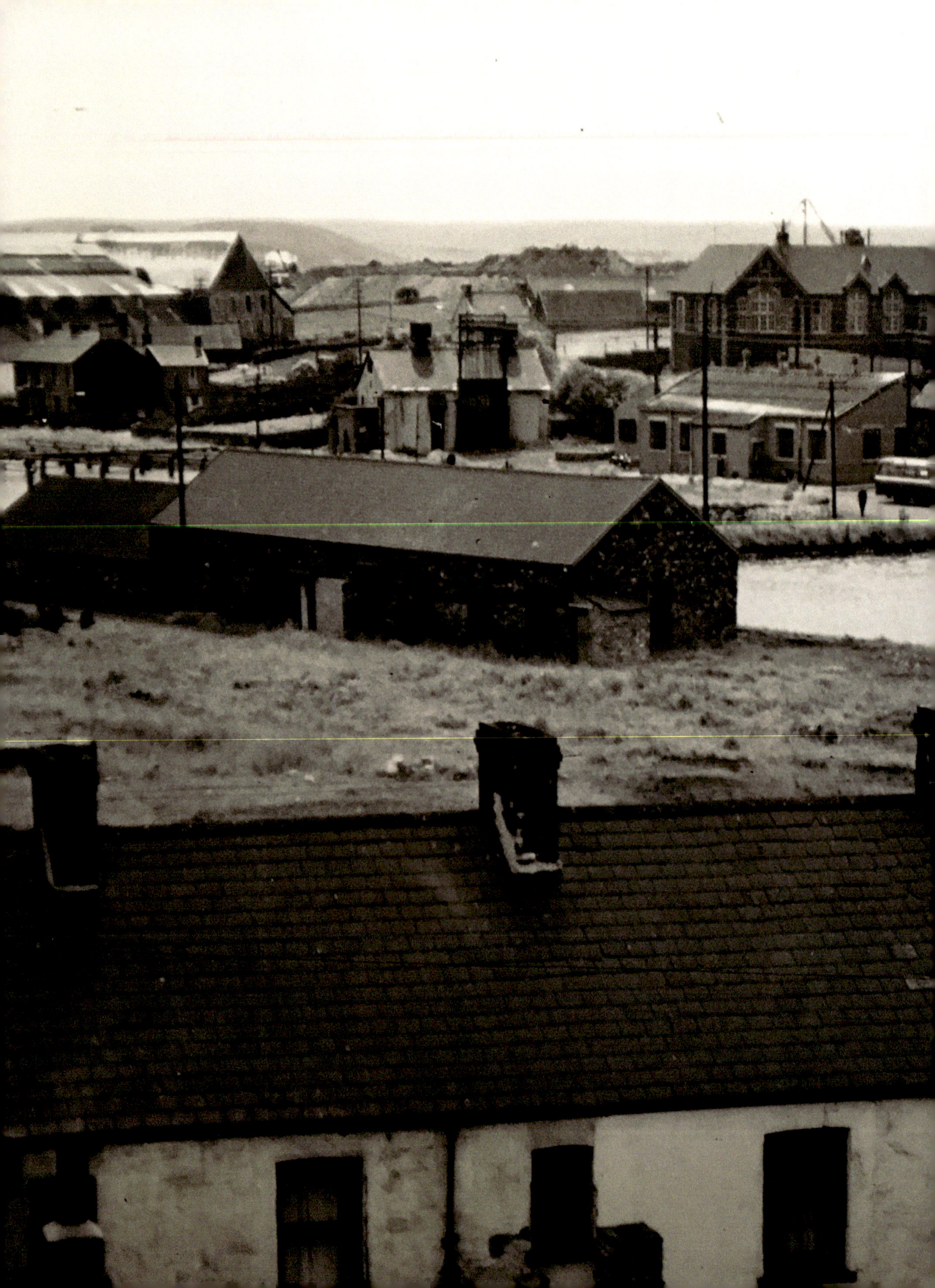

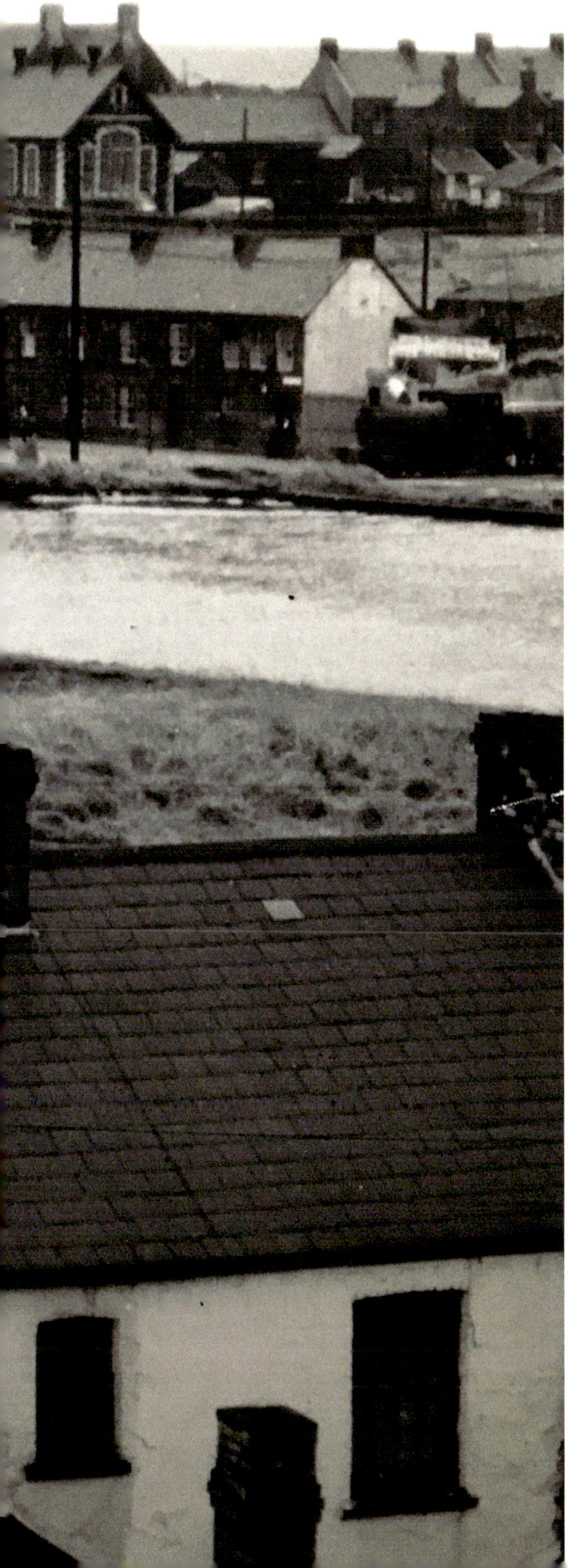

BWLCH-Y-GWYNT & MACHYNYS

The lost villages along the Wales Coast Path

The Machynys Peninsula, south of Llanelli, where the Loughor Estuary meets the land, is a wild, winding stretch of Carmarthenshire's coastline and a popular route for joggers, cyclists and Sunday strollers. But this landscape isn't all that it seems. In the long grass stands a blue heritage plaque that hints at a hidden history: 'Near to this site stood the lost village and community of Bwlch-y-Gwynt circa 1880-1973'. Another sign makes reference to the community of Machynys. There's not a single trace of either of those villages today. So what happened here?

The answer tracks back to the mid 19th century when swathes of South Wales were remoulded from open countryside into hubs of heavy industry. The Machynys Peninsula specialised in steel and tinplate production, becoming a leading exporter to North America. Staff housing was constructed on two neighbouring tracts of land in the shadow of the factory chimneys. Over time, as more streets were built and the population grew, a pair of villages took shape: Bwlch-y-Gwynt and Machynys. Each community had its own identity but lived cheek-by-jowl, leading to a unique bond between residents of both villages. Nevil Williams, who grew up in Machynys, sums it up nicely:

> "We knew each other through and through. People had complete faith and trust in each other. Doors were never locked and if ever you were out and it started to rain, your neighbour would pop over and bring your washing in off the line. It was a very happy community and we were so close-knit."

Houses, churches, shops and factories – Machynys as a thriving community.

Located on the southern tip of the peninsula, both villages were a fair footslog from the nearest conurbation. They found themselves hemmed in by the sea on one side and the belching factories on the other. Yet there was never a sense of isolation. Bwlch-y-Gwynt and Machynys were surprisingly self-sufficient.

Between them they shared shops, a church, a school and two inns. Residents formed rugby and football teams. Although telecommunications were mainly restricted to a public phone box at the end of the street, if it ever rang you could be sure that one of your neighbours would answer it and notify the intended recipient. Very few homes had television sets, and there wasn't a cinema in sight, so the community found novel ways of entertaining itself. Sandra Jenkins, formerly of Bwlch-y-Gwynt, remembers her teenage years:

"Technology for us was a transistor radio. We would go to a corner of the big tinplate works: all the girls would be there. Everyone would take their own transistor radio (for more volume!) and we would dance there until it got dark. In the summer nights your mothers would be calling you and we'd say, 'Yes we'll be there now, we'll be there now.' But then the dads would eventually show up and say 'Now!' and then that's when you knew you had to go!

"We lived behind a shop and inside that shop were chairs and cushions and there was always laughter wafting and flowing from there into our house. People weren't just there to shop, they were there for a chat. And they'd be there for hours!"

Below: residents celebrate the investiture of the Prince of Wales, 1969.

Opposite: life in the shadow of the factory chimneys.

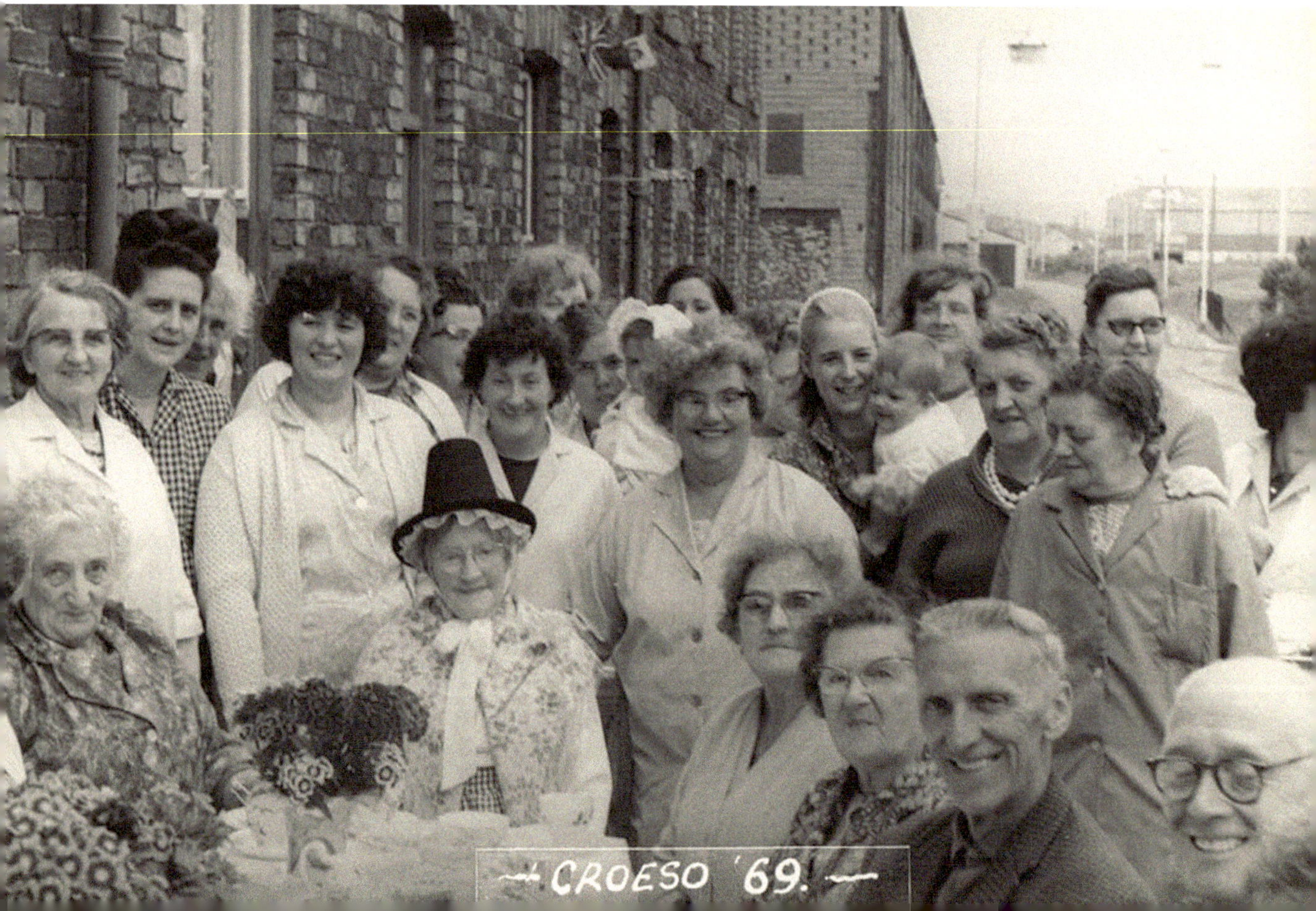

Former villagers Winston Smith and Roger Jones have equally vivid memories of their childhood. Winston remembers the entrepreneurial spirit of the local shopkeeper:

> "They'd sell packets of broken crisps which you could buy for a penny. We were thrilled with it. We didn't mind having broken crisps because most of the time crisps are broken anyway!"

Roger recalls his resourcefulness with fuel supplies:

> "With the steelworks being as close as it was to us, we never went short on coal. We sometimes helped ourselves to it. They were tipping coal everywhere so we'd help them move it! A policeman would come and say 'Don't do that again boys' and we didn't do it. For a week. Or maybe a fortnight!"

Flashbacks like these paint a fascinating picture of the past; of two neighbouring communities that had forged a cohesive way of life, organically. The traditional terraced streets and hyperlocal customs are a snapshot of old Llanelli life. It's remarkable to think that both villages could be so comprehensively wiped out. And yet they were.

That bleak chapter began just after World War Two, when steel production in Britain was in a state of flux. The industry was nationalised in 1951, leading to the consolidation of some plants and the closure of others. The new Trostre tinplate works began to dominate the steelmaking scene in Llanelli and the older works nearest Bwlch-y-Gwynt and Machynys were shut down. Some men managed to transfer to Trostre but many engineers, electricians, mechanics and machinists lost their jobs. It was a body blow for the twin villages.

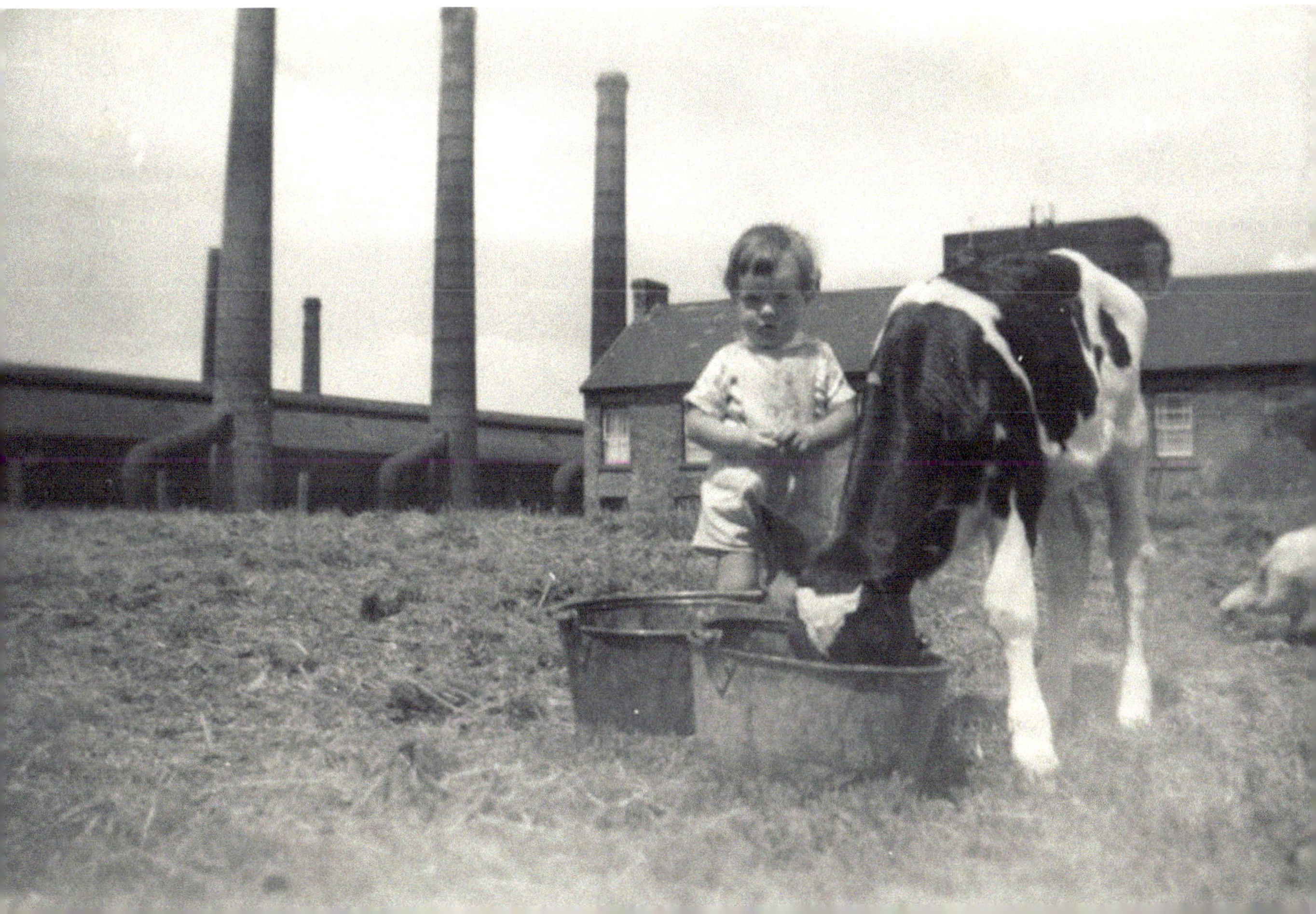

With heavy industry gone, Llanelli Borough Council saw an opportunity to redevelop the Machynys Peninsula. It bought 89 acres of land and the old houses that stood on it – nearly 100 homes. The residents of Bwlch-y-Gwynt and Machynys were informed that their properties were being compulsorily purchased. Between 1966 and 1972 families ruefully moved away, to be rehoused by the council. Sandra Jenkins had outgrown her transistor radio by then. Her final hours in Bwlch-y-Gwynt were spent packing her life into boxes. Six generations of her family had lived in the area and she still remembers the trauma of shutting her front door, knowing she would never again be able to return:

> "I didn't move until 11 o'clock in the night, because I just couldn't leave. It was horrendously sad to go. Everything you've grown up with, you know, you love, swept away.
>
> "In those villages you had extended families and neighbours who had known each other all of their lives. All of a sudden we were scattered over Llanelli. It absolutely broke the hearts of many of the older residents. You were going from something you'd known all your life to somewhere totally alien to you. Those two villages were all they'd ever known. When you're 70, 80, 90 years old, it's so difficult to start over again because suddenly you're amongst strangers.
>
> "When I come down to the area now, I can still see the streets, I remember everybody who lived in every house. Even after all these years, it's still raw."

Below: the Machynys peninsula today.

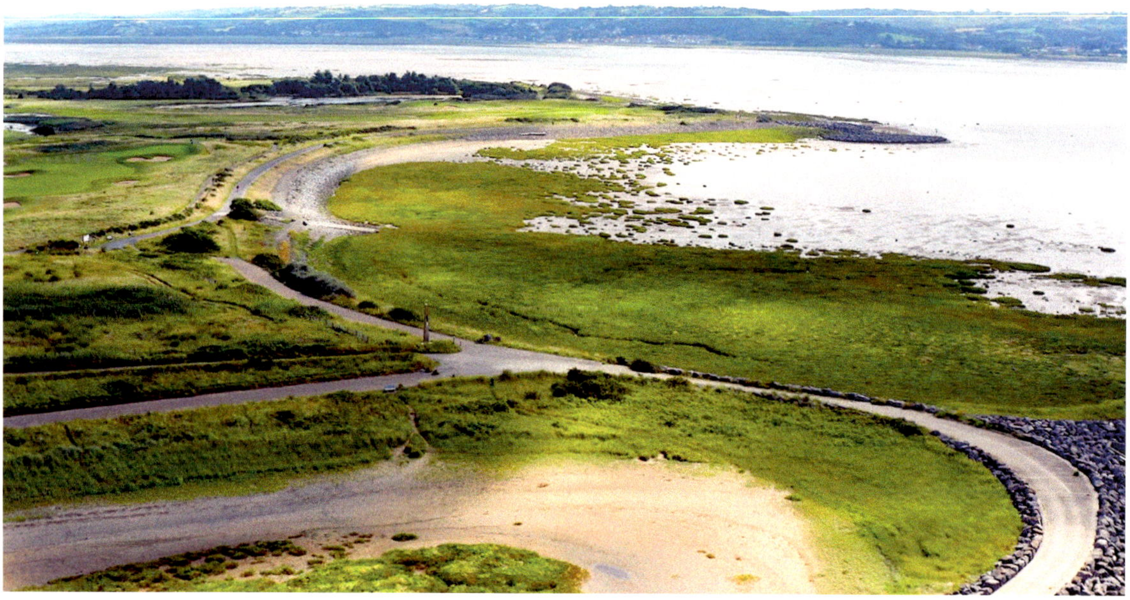

The houses were torn down and the vestiges of industry demolished, in readiness for regeneration. The land stood empty for three decades. Finally, in the 2000s, work got underway. Machynys and Bwlch-y-Gwynt were replaced by a golf course and a cluster of streets lined with upmarket New England-style homes.

In the sunshine, with a gentle sea breeze behind you and birdsong as your soundtrack, the curved route around the Machynys Peninsula ranks as one of the most serene stretches of the Wales Coastal Path. If you ever find yourself walking there, seek out those blue heritage plaques. And when you do, spare a thought for two lost communities that were full of life.

Below: a poignant reminder of bygone Bwlch-y-Gwynt.

Overleaf: Houses and heavy industry, side by side.

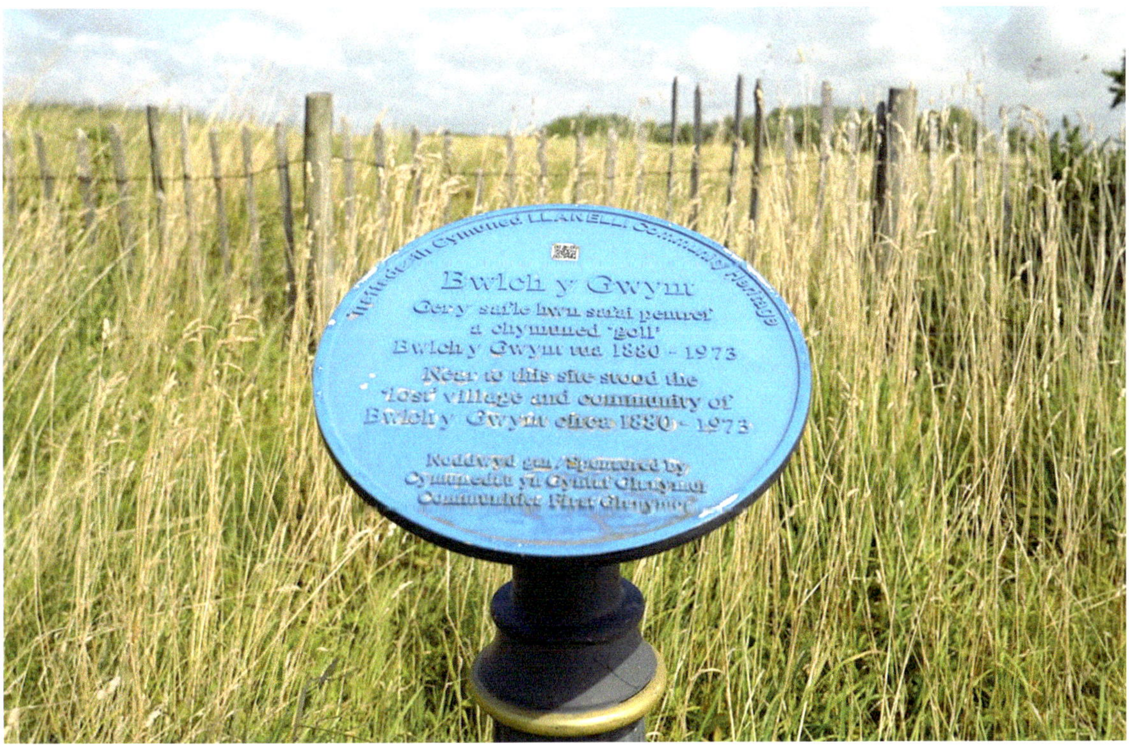

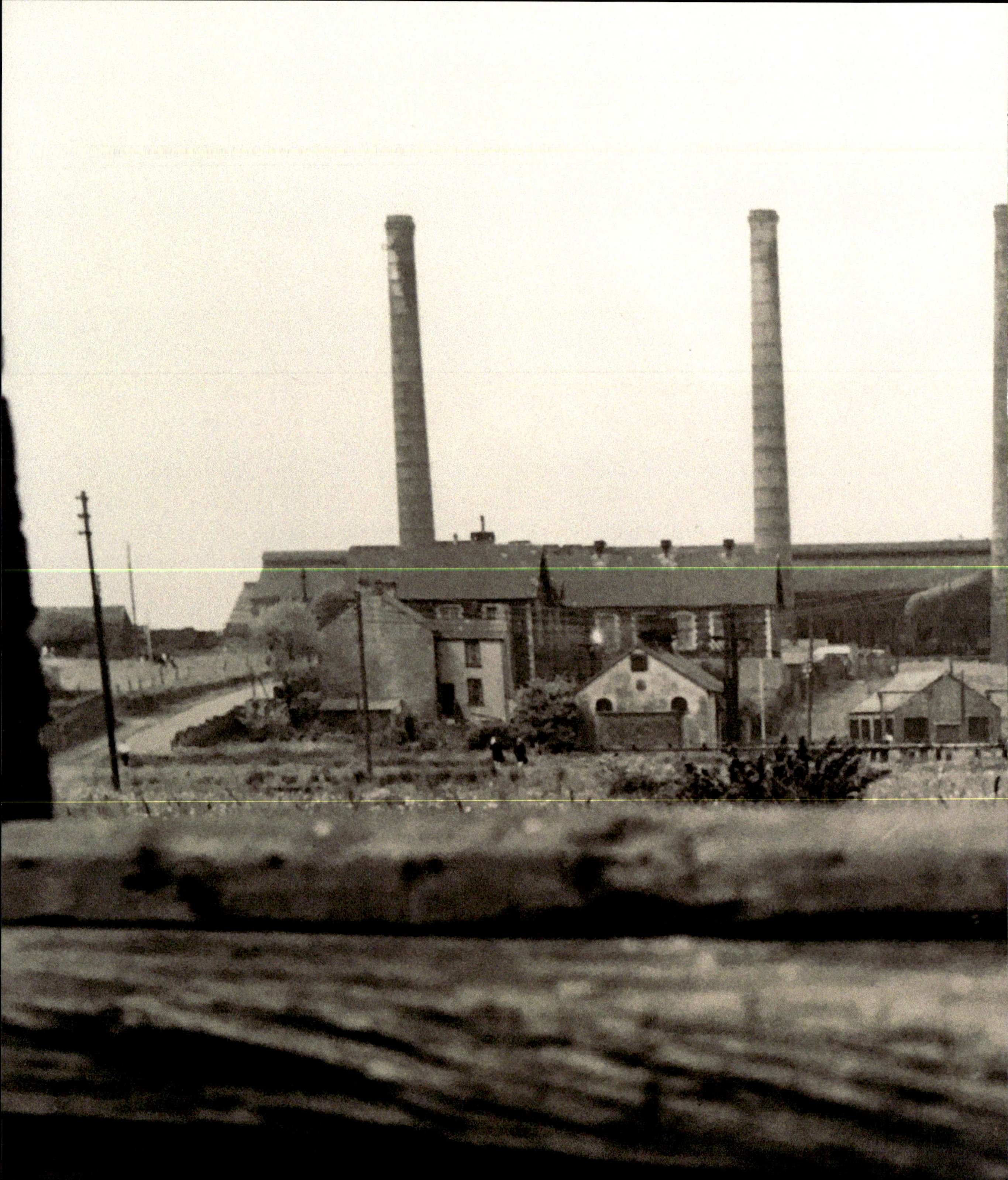

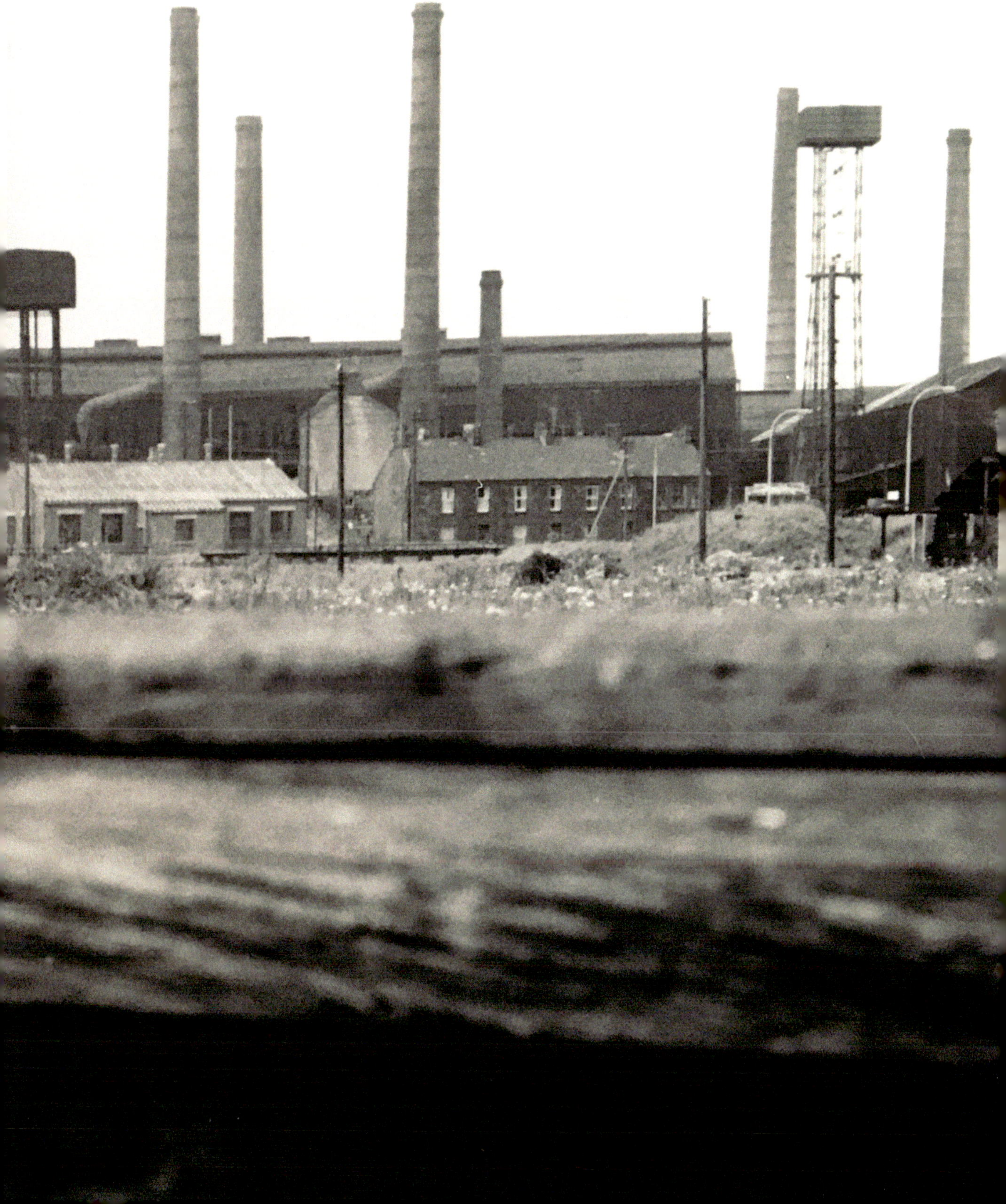

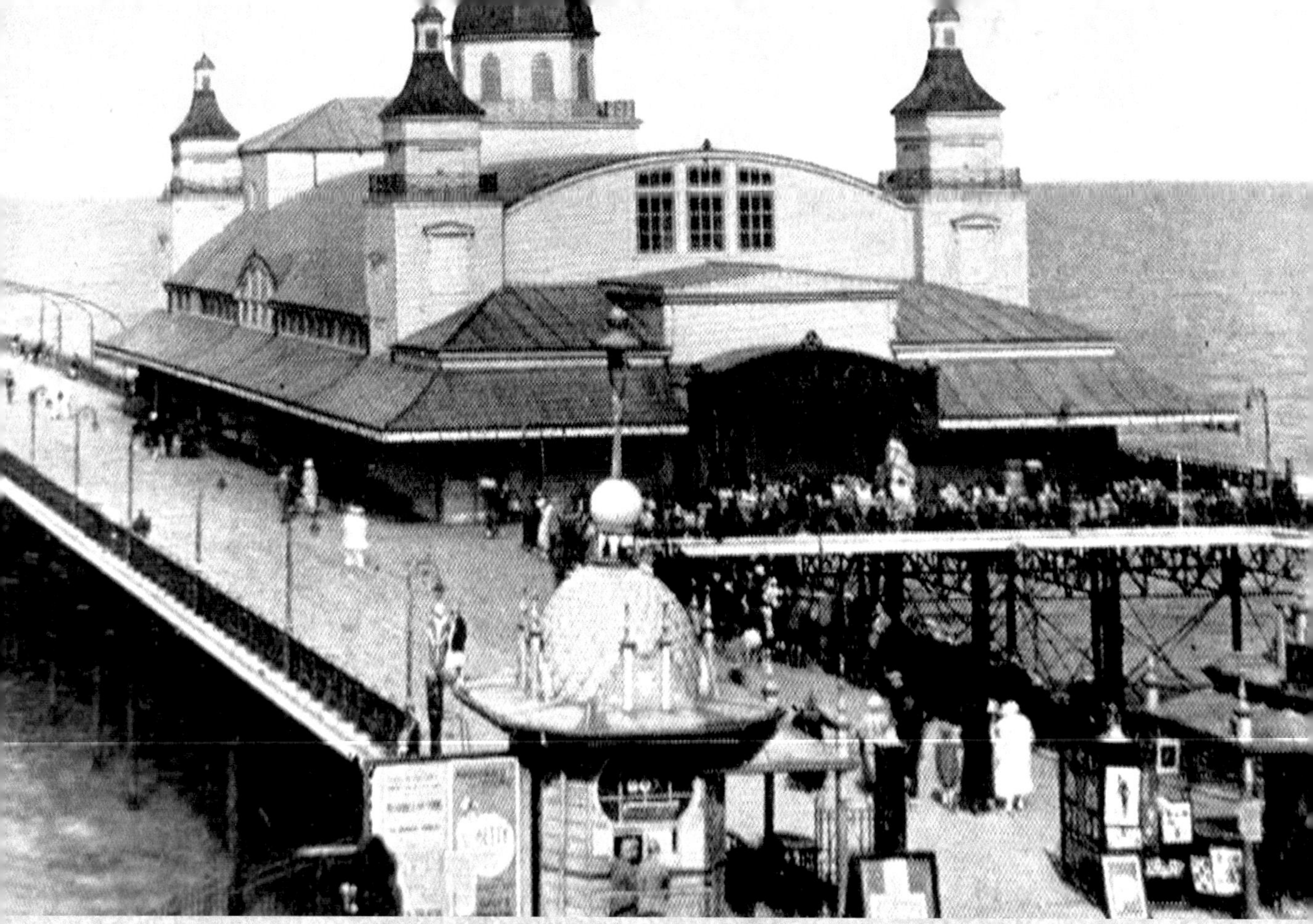

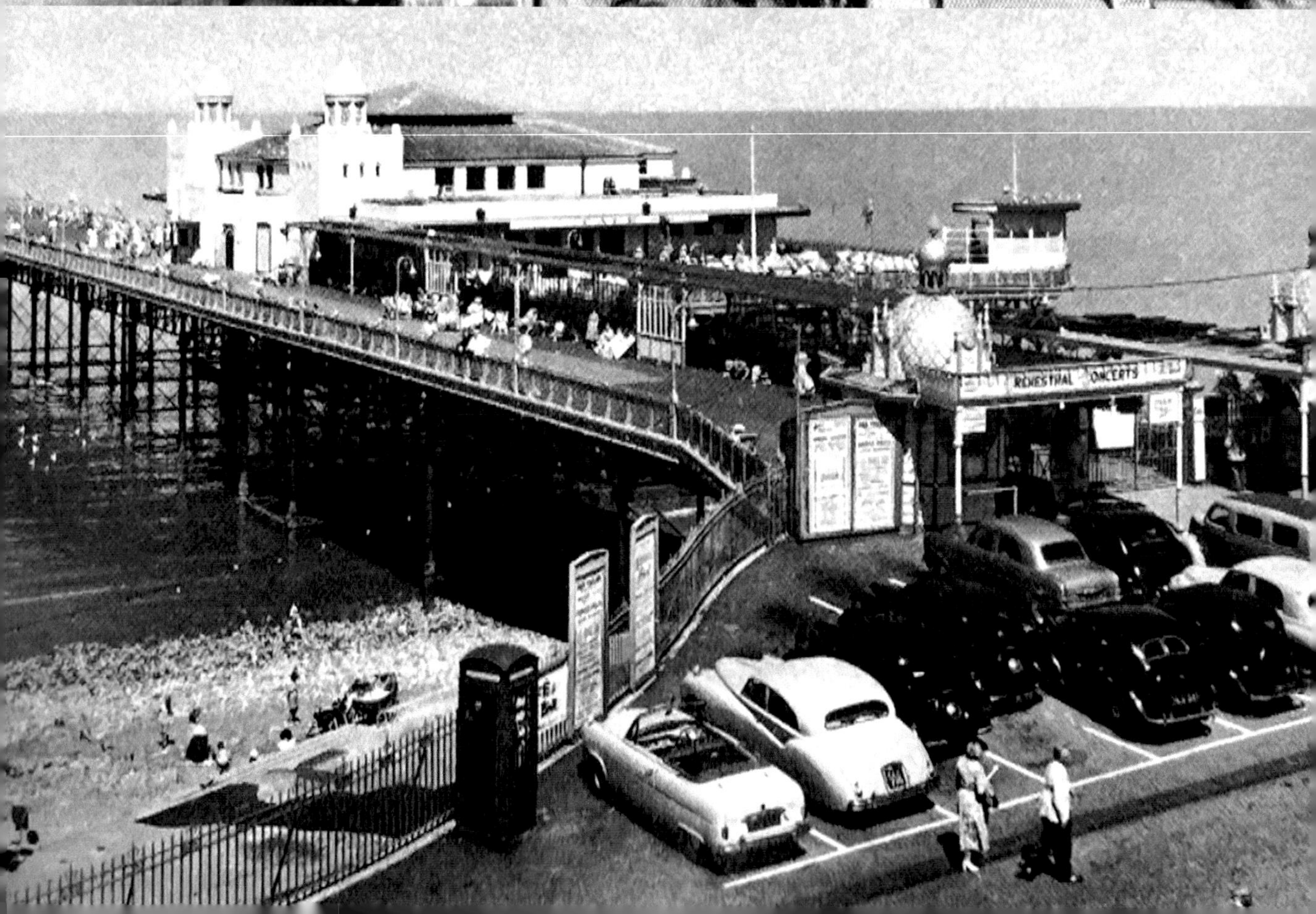

VICTORIA PIER

Ruin and resurrection on the North Wales coast

The Victorians rejoiced in designing the audacious – impossible structures that were big, bold and often bizarre. Three cases in point: the Palm House in Kew Gardens (once the biggest greenhouse in the world), the Royal Albert Hall (a cultural variation on Rome's Colosseum), and the quirky Castell Coch (a fantastical folly where high camp meets the Middle Ages). Those 19th century architects were especially obsessed with pleasure piers. Who else would commit so fervently to the concept of a huge iron structure standing in salt water that leads to nowhere? Still, their slightly madcap vision radically re-shaped the British seaside, turning coastal towns into holiday hotspots. You knew you'd made it if you had a pier along your promenade.

Colwyn Bay wanted in on the action. Work began on 1st June 1899 and exactly one year later crowds converged on the seafront to celebrate the official opening of the Victoria Pier. The focal point was a huge, ornate pavilion that could seat 2,500 people. In a PR triumph, the world-renowned soprano Adelina Patti signed up to be the very first act to perform there. While most piers in Britain had a landing stage at the end, allowing passengers to board ships and pleasure cruisers, this was never the case in Colwyn Bay. The sole function of the pier was to provide entertainment, and it laid it on in style.

Unfortunately, the town's newest landmark had miserable luck. The pavilion was destroyed by a fire in 1922. It was replaced the following year with a sleek, elegant pavilion with a graceful, curved roof. That also burned down. Lessons were clearly learned as the third iteration of the building was made from fire retardant materials.

This 1934 successor managed to stay the distance and it's the pavilion that most people in Colwyn Bay still conjure up in their minds. Richard Coleman has childhood memories that are entwined with the Victoria Pier:

> "When I was five, in about 1960, I started coming to the pier with my parents, usually on a Sunday afternoon. We'd walk to the end of the pier and I'd be totally fascinated by looking through the gaps in the wooden boardwalk at the waves beneath my feet. There also used to be lots of slot machines on the pier and my father would drag me away from there every time I was trying to get near them!
>
> "Colwyn Bay was a very busy place back then, with a lot of holidaymakers. There used to be a band on the pier at least once a week. A hundred deckchairs would be laid out and people would sit listening to the music. When I was older, I was in a band in the North Wales area and we actually played at the pier! To do that was something very special. I was 20, surrounded by guitars, a drum kit and 150 people dancing in front of me and it was absolutely fabulous."

Top: the Victoria Pier's ill-fated second pavilion.

Bottom: its more durable replacement.

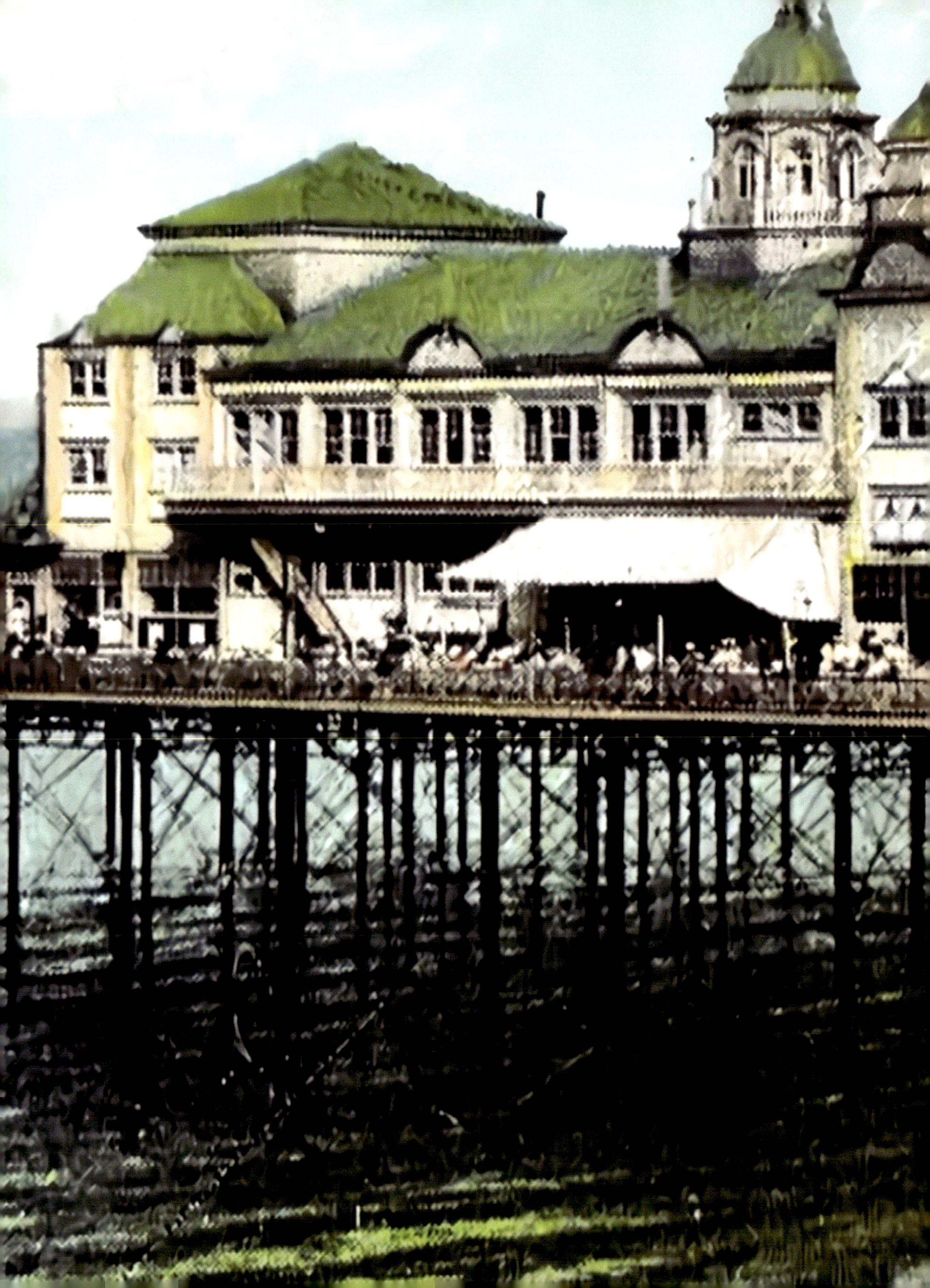

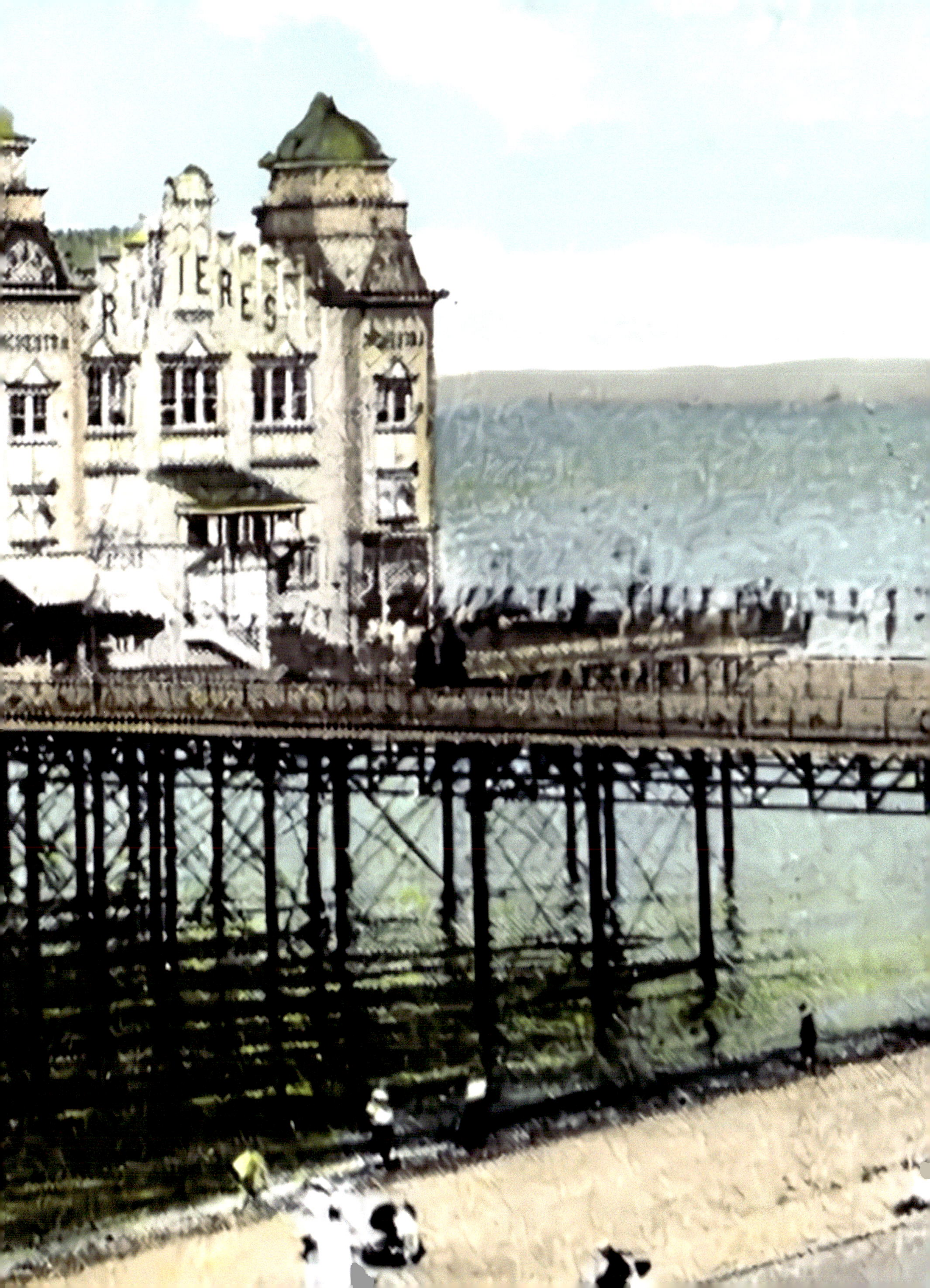
RIVIERES

Overleaf: the Victoria Pier in the early 1900s.

The size of the art deco pavilion made it a prized community resource. It hosted children's art competitions, local produce shows, even five-a-side football. But its bread and butter was always entertainment, especially live music. Some of the big names who played the pier over the years included Gene Vincent, Jeff Beck, The Move, Motorhead, Siouxsie and the Banshees, The Specials and Thin Lizzy. The pavilion's dance floor brought the town together, sparking lifelong connections. One Colwyn Bay family owes their family tree to the pier. It's where Stella Wilson met her husband-to-be John on New Year's Eve 1961:

> "We were jiving. It was the only dance we could do! I remember I was wearing stiletto heels, a blouse and a skirt with hoops underneath – it was great for jiving but embarrassing when you sat down because the skirt ballooned! Roland Mott and his Orchestra were playing and something just clicked with John. We danced the night away. He dropped me home afterwards and he gave me a kiss goodnight."

John was also fashionably dressed that evening:

> "I had an Italian suit on, from Burtons – navy, single breasted. You wouldn't have gone out without a suit and tie in those days. During the evening we got talking to each other and it just took off from there. We've had a very, very happy life together and we've got a lovely family. And I have loved Stella ever since."

The original pavilion could seat 2,500 people. It burnt down in 1922.

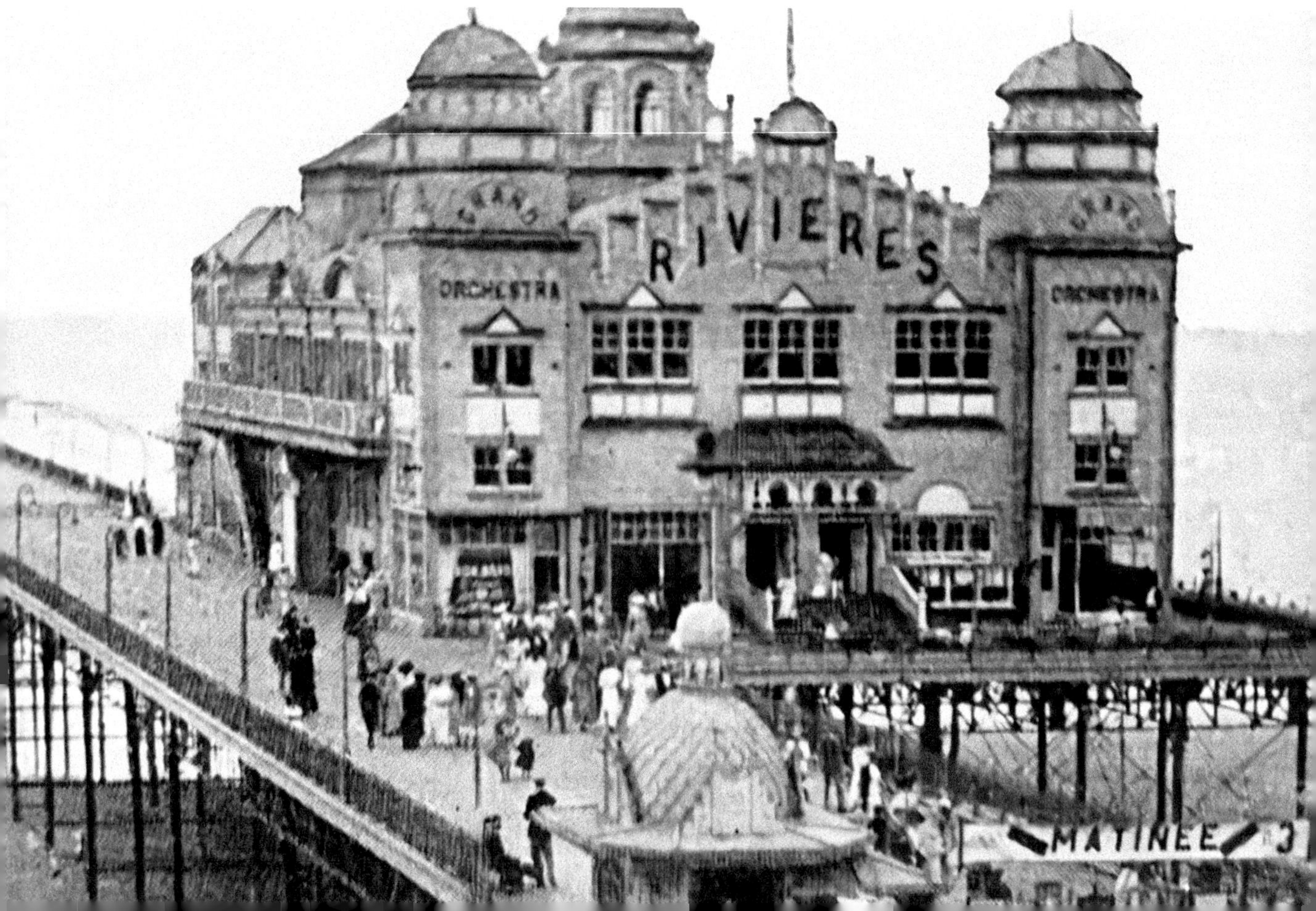

Their daughter Jacqueline went to discos at the pier in the 1980s and that's where she met her future husband, Kevin:

> "We first got together as teenagers. The pier was the centre of our lives back then. I remember New Year's Eve 1984. There was a disco on. Kevin jumped onto the stage and sang Freedom by Wham!"

Now, this is where the family's story becomes really interesting. Kevin's mum and dad had also met on the pier at a New Year's Eve dance in the 1960s, just like Jacqueline's parents. So when Kevin jumped onto that stage in 1984, he set in motion the next chapter of their lives, which he still clearly remembers:

> "There's a line in *Freedom* that says, 'Girl all I want right now is you'. With that line I pointed at Jackie. It was on a packed dance floor but you can't miss those big brown eyes. When we eventually got married, years later, we had champagne drinks on the pier because it had brought us all together. My father had passed away not long before the wedding so it was a good place to come and celebrate, and to raise a glass to him. He would have been smiling down on us and probably thinking: 'Where's *my* drink?'"

Bonds like these made the Victoria Pier so much more than an iron platform stretching out to sea. It was the nerve centre of social life in Colwyn Bay, providing the backdrop to key moments in the town's fortunes and those of its residents. But behind the scenes, the age and enormity of the structure was slowly, inexorably taking its toll.

Jump forward to 2008, and the Victoria Pier was in private ownership. A dispute arose between Conwy County Borough Council and the owner regarding business rates on the pier. It led to eight long years of litigation. As the case trundled through the courts the pier was closed to the public and received limited repair and maintenance. By 2016 the ownership of the Victoria Pier had reverted to Conwy Council and the future of the town's decaying landmark hung in the balance: restoration or demolition?

In quite spectacular fashion, Mother Nature cast the deciding vote. Storms and gale force winds battered the coast in early 2017 and a large part of the seaward end of the pier collapsed. The following year the entire structure was dismantled on safety grounds. It took just a few months for contractors to pull down what Victorian optimism had put up, all those years ago.

Given the pain of the recent past you'd expect to walk along Colwyn Bay's promenade today and see an empty beach. Yet there it is, clear as anything: the Victoria Pier. It's been carefully rebuilt using the salvageable parts of its predecessor. You may have to manage some expectations. It's now a shadow of its former self. The original pier stretched 750ft into the sea – its replacement is almost six times shorter. You won't find a pavilion either, merely a wide wooden boardwalk. But the cast iron stanchions and railings are all original, the lamp posts are exact replicas from its Victorian heyday and the colour scheme of salmon pink and cream mirrors the interior of the original art deco pavilion.

The town's truncated pier may yet yield a further reimagining. The Colwyn Bay Pier Trust is an army of local volunteers, committed to the preservation and restoration of their cherished landmark. They've been working with architects on plans to extend the length of the pier and reinstate a pavilion building. Any finalised design would be shaped by community feedback. The Trust's director, Amy Dyke, believes the Victoria Pier is worth fighting for:

> "Our mission is to see it live again. We're applying for funding and it's all a matter of coming up with the right plan, the right concept. Colwyn Bay without the pier is like Paris without the Eiffel Tower. That's how important it is to us as a community.
>
> "There's a lot of lovely architecture in the town and if you think of that as a family, then the pier is like that really large personality in the family: the flashy one with the impressive suit, the one with all the stories who you like to go and visit slightly more than all your other relatives and the one you have such happy, lovely memories of."

In the early 1900s, Britain had almost 100 pleasure piers along its coastline. Fewer than half that number exists today. There have been major setbacks in Wales: Rhos-on-Sea, Rhyl and Tenby all lost their Victorian-era piers in the second half of the 20th century. The scaled-down version in Colwyn Bay is hardly the queen of the coast that it once was, but it's a welcome resurrection.

Above: Dismantling the pier, 2017.

Below: the new Victoria Pier, rebuilt to a truncated length and incorporating much of the original ironwork from its predecessor.

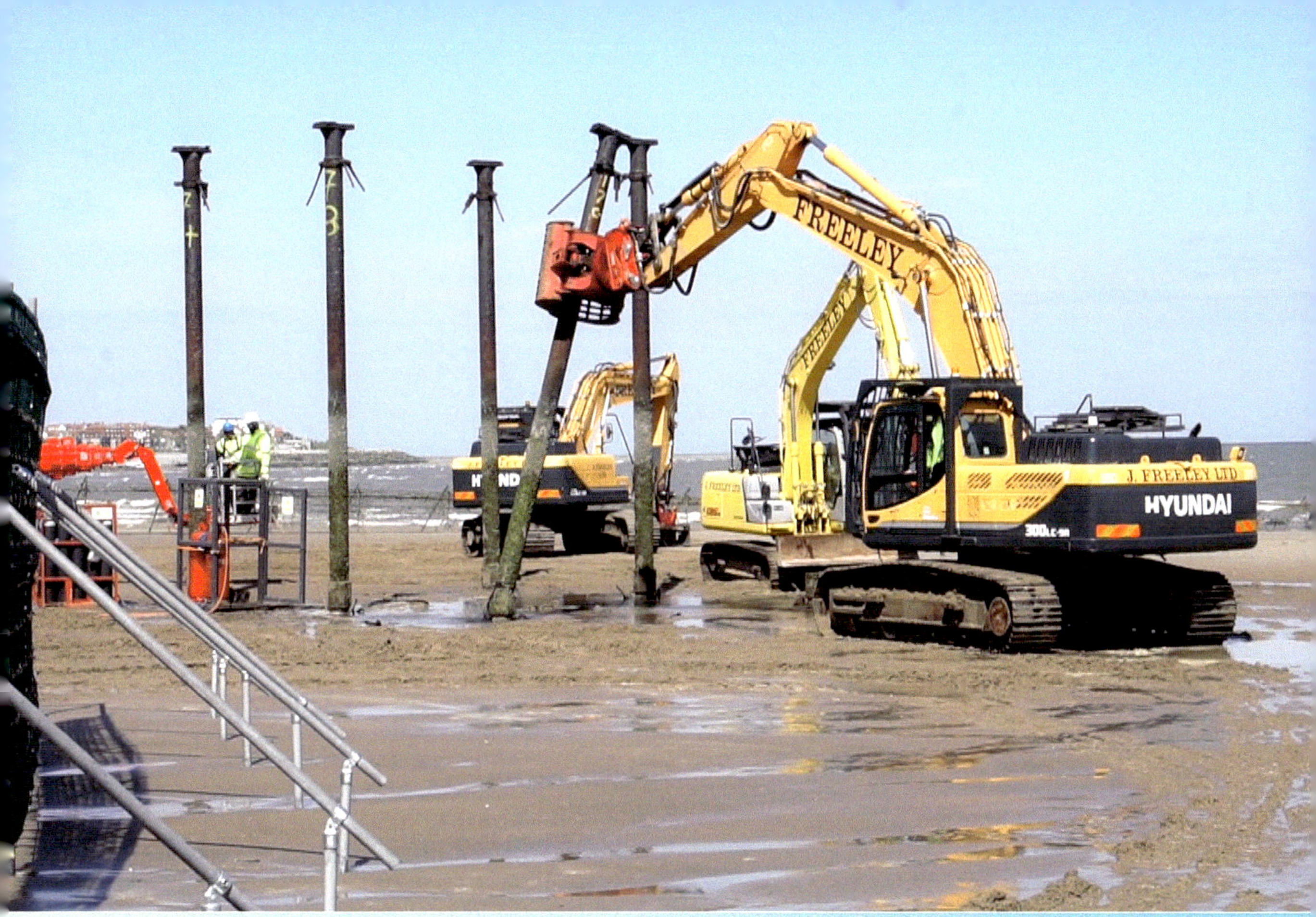
FREELEY
FREELEY
J. FREELEY LTD
HYUNDAI

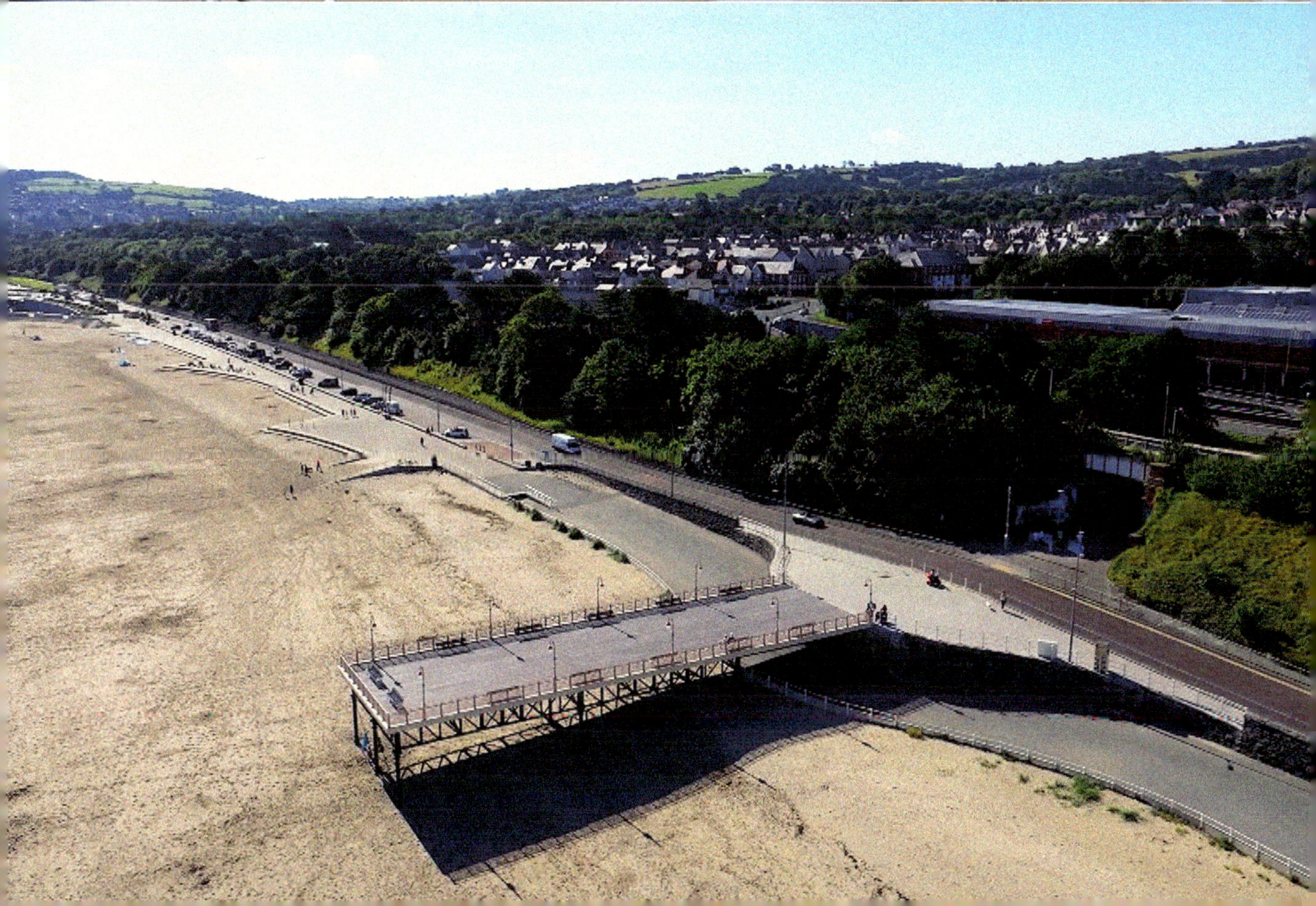

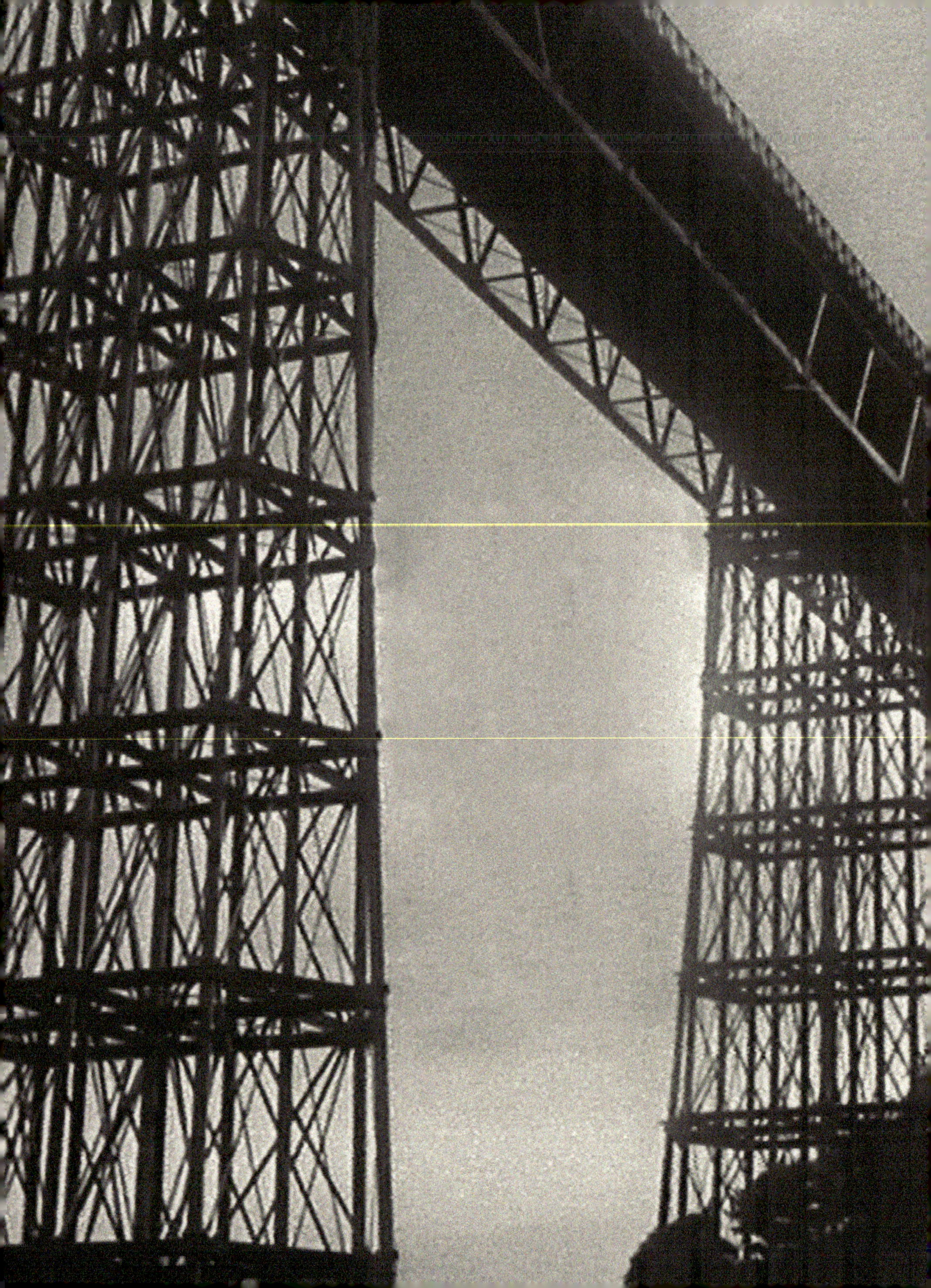

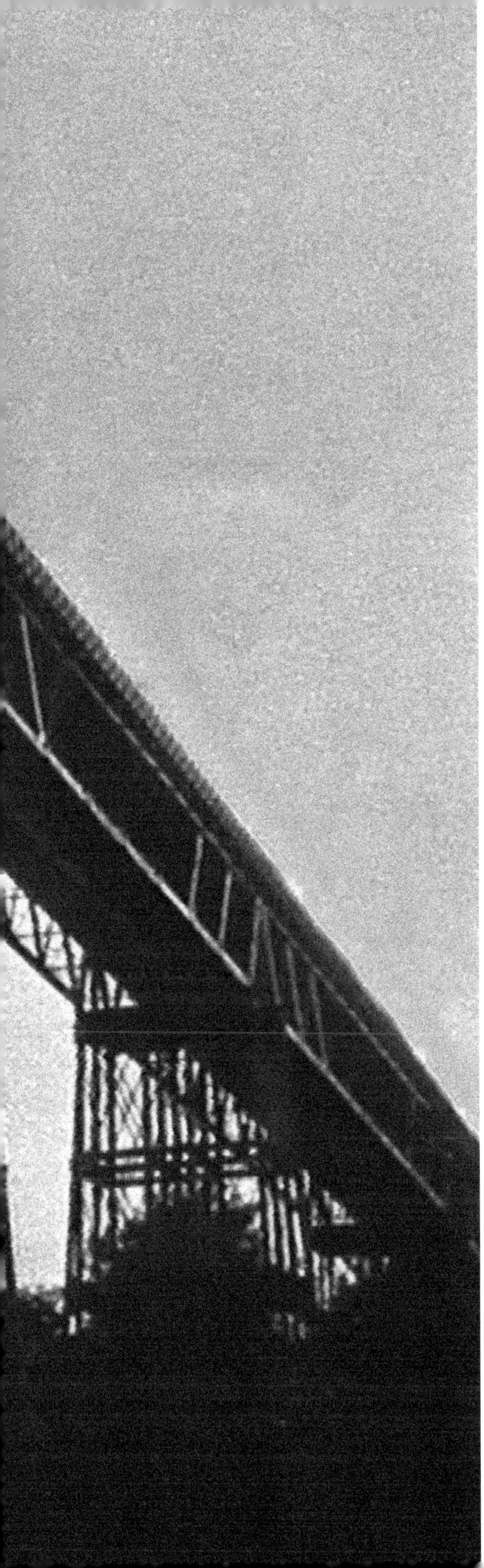

CRUMLIN VIADUCT

The iron giant of the valleys

Of all the landmarks destroyed, dismantled or demolished in Wales during the second half of the 20th century, the most extraordinary loss – in terms of sheer scale – occurred in the county of Caerphilly at the tail end of the 1960s. For generations, a Victorian superstructure had loomed large over the mining communities on the banks of the river Ebbw. It was a sight celebrated throughout the world, widely lauded as a wonder of the industrial age, and it all came crashing down in broad daylight.

Officially opened in 1857, the Crumlin Viaduct was a staggering feat of engineering. A leviathan that spanned deep valleys and steep hills, it connected communities and supercharged local trade. Its dimensions were eye-watering: 1,658 ft long and 208 ft in height. A handbook published in 1862 praised it as a 'stupendous and elegant work of art…a remarkable monument of ingenuity and skill which has attracted many thousands of visitors from all parts of the world to this previously unfrequented locality.' During its lifetime it was the tallest viaduct in Britain and the third highest in the world, surpassed only by the Portage Timber Viaduct in the United States and the Aqueduct of Spoleto in Italy.

Standing tall: the Crumlin Viaduct in the early 1960s.

Unsurprisingly, it was the Victorian obsession with railways that gave birth to the Crumlin Viaduct. Colliery owners were desperate to transport their premium product from the South Wales valleys to the burgeoning docks of Newport and Cardiff. A new East-West rail route opened up between Quaker's Yard and Pontypool, a route that would require coal wagons to cross the expanse of the Ebbw River valley.

A viaduct was on the cards and the contract was awarded to engineering supremo Thomas Kennard. Flush with the gung-ho spirit of the age, he bored and blasted through all topographical hurdles in his path. He also eschewed stone as his construction material of choice and opted instead for iron. The result was a distinctive and thoroughly modern cloud-buster, delicate in appearance yet tough enough to withstand the many tonnes of freight that clattered across its top every day.

Meanwhile, beneath the viaduct's giant girders, the quiet hamlet of Crumlin suddenly found itself in the industrial fast lane. Shops, churches and terraced streets sprang up to accommodate the myriad workers who had made their home there during construction. The community grew even greater when new coal mines were sunk nearby. The bridge became a North Star and residents were thankful for the technological marvel on their doorstep.

The viaduct towered over the community of Crumlin.

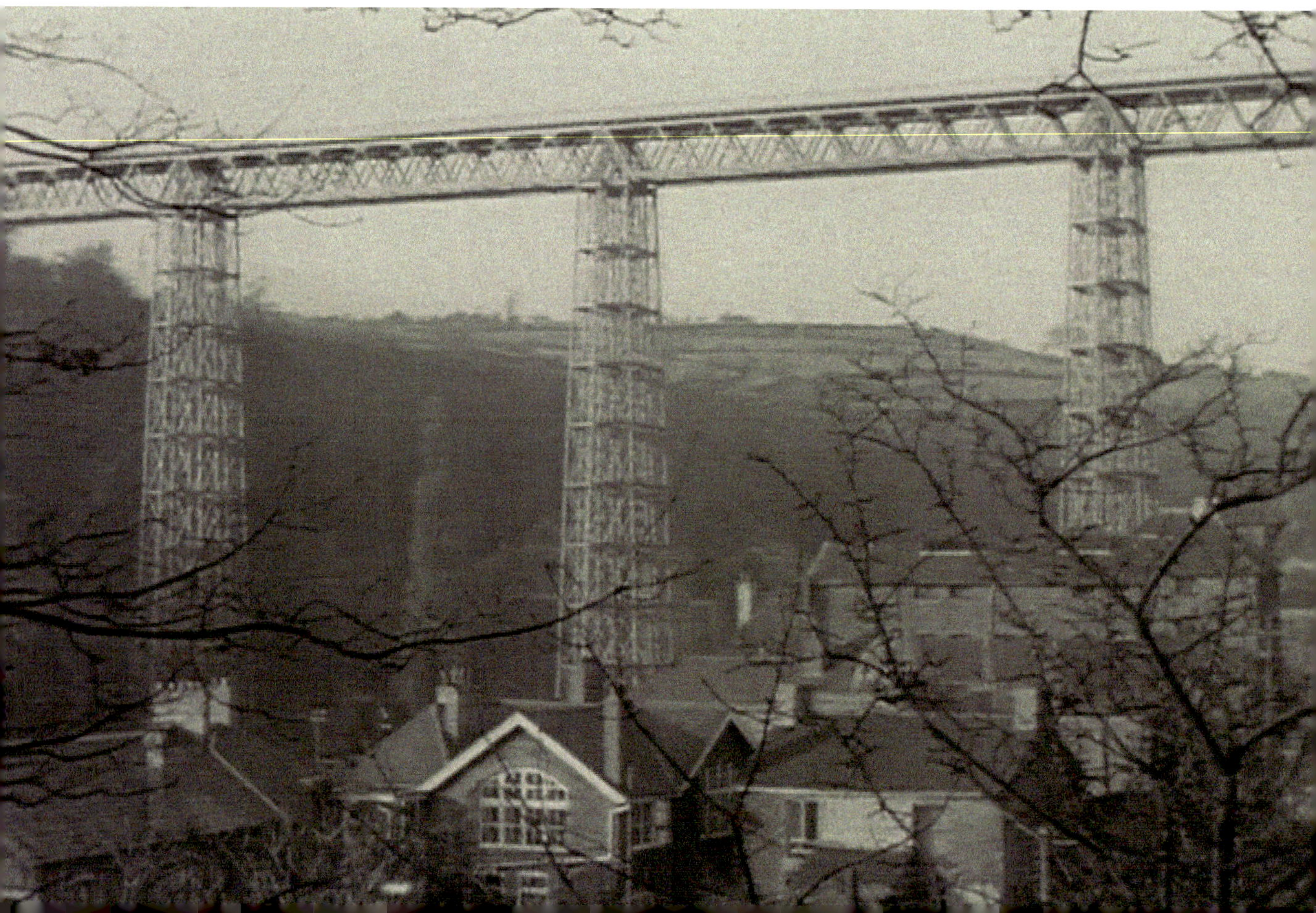

Vera Jenkins and her husband Robert have their very own Crumlin Viaduct in their back garden. It's a metallic mini version, designed by a friend, that takes pride of place next to the flower beds and potted plants. There's even a little train running along the top. For Vera, it's a reminder of the iron spectacle that dominated her childhood:

"When I was younger, we would all go on family walks. At the end we'd sit down with a picnic of bread and jam and we'd put our hands on the viaduct itself and sit and wait for a train to come. That was the thrill of the day, to wait for trains to cross over it. The noise was absolutely incredible. When the train hit the bridge, the sound changed and we'd hold on to the iron of the bridge and you could feel the vibrations of the train going over the tracks. It was our music. And on the walk home we'd pretend we were driving trains over the viaduct. It was one of the things we did on a Sunday as children.

"It was such an iconic bridge and everyone at the time took it for granted. It was there; it was part of our infrastructure. A lot of people felt it was a magnificent piece of engineering, which it was. I thought it was absolutely wonderful. It was big, it was dirty, it was fabulous."

Workmen with a head for heights – 208 ft in the air.

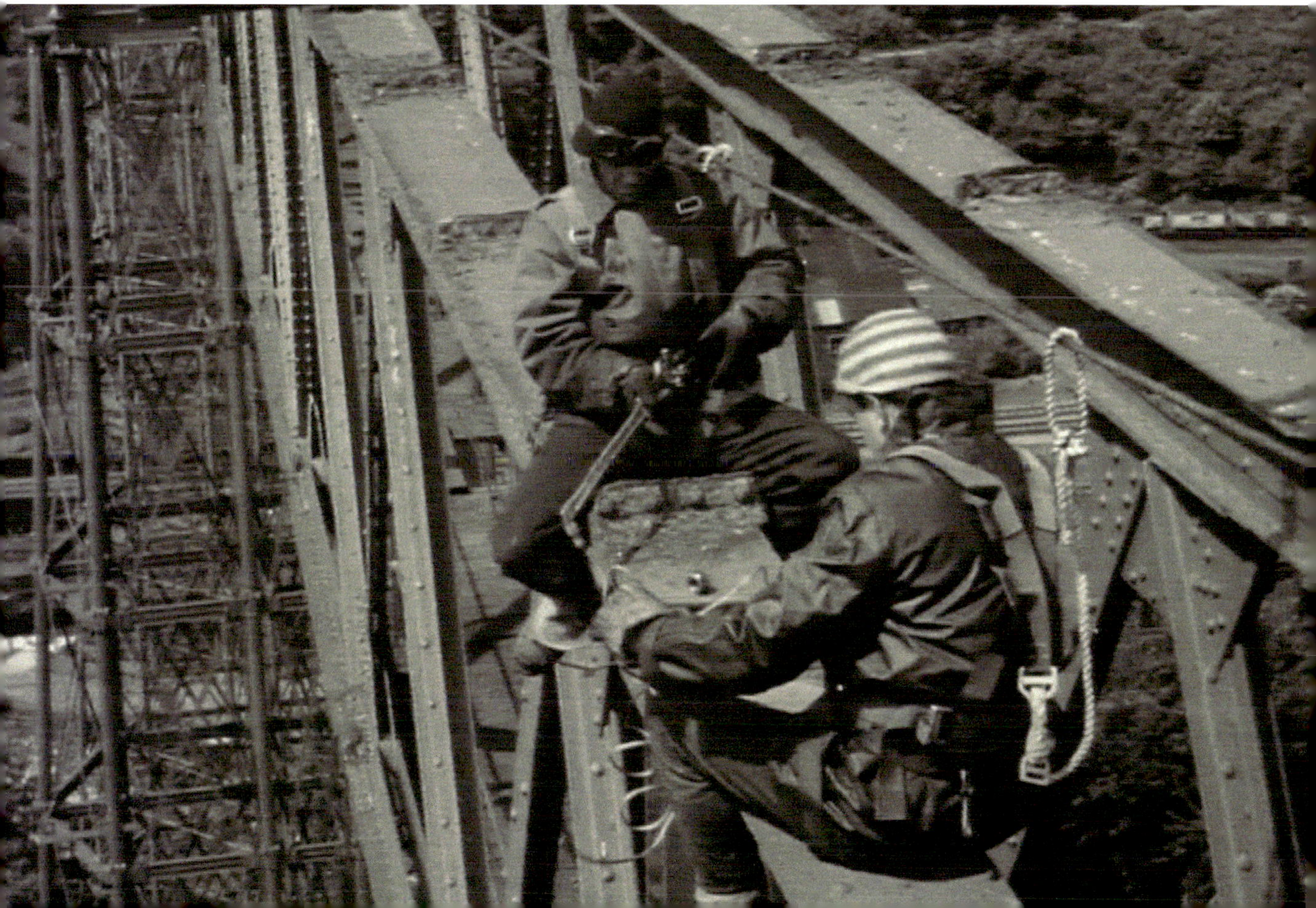

Robert has an even more personal connection with the viaduct:

> "I had a job on the railways as a fireman, stoking the trains with coal. Crossing the bridge was exhilarating but pretty terrifying. You were 200 feet up in the air and it was a long way down! My uncle Tom, love him, used to paint the bridge. It took the biggest part of a year for him to get from one side to the other! That icon was part of our lives. Now it's gone. It's gutting. I miss it, I really do."

Over the years, the majesty of the Crumlin Viaduct made it one of the most sketched, photographed and painted structures in Wales. It even caught the attention of Hollywood. In the mid 1960s, the Oscar winning director Stanley Donen (*Singin' In The Rain, On the Town*) used the bridge for the action-packed finale of his spy thriller, *Arabesque*. The film starred Gregory Peck and Sophia Loren, who rode, ran, clambered and crawled across the viaduct while being shot at from overhead, as the villain's bright red helicopter whizzed through the gaps in the bridge.

Inevitably, the appearance of two Hollywood heavyweights on the streets of Crumlin was the talk of the town. Mike Davies was 13 years old at the time and watched as the cameras rolled:

> "It was a really exciting time. People would come out of their houses and line up to see the filming. They were huge stars. I remember watching as they filmed Sophia Loren running across the bridge and I remember thinking how beautiful that woman was. My uncle was Mayor of Islwyn at the time and he signed Gregory Peck onto the Islwyn Roll of Honour.
>
> "The actors and the crew embraced the community and were all very friendly. And of course the helicopter scene was exciting to watch. To see that helicopter going underneath the bridge was incredible. In a way *Arabesque* has preserved the viaduct forever. When the film came out I watched it and I'll be frank: the viaduct was all that I was looking out for!"

Despite standing proud for more than a century, all that remains of the Crumlin Viaduct today are clues in the landscape. Streets like Kennard Terrace and Upper Viaduct Terrace tell their own story. Venture outside the village and you'll see the masonry abutments, at either end of the valley, that once supported the iron frame of the bridge. Ironically, these silent stone ruins are now Grade II listed – a level of protection that was never afforded to the viaduct during its working years.

Crumlin's world-famous bridge had been determinedly designed as a rail crossing. Its downfall came courtesy of British Railways Chairman Dr Richard Beeching and his almighty shake-up of the rail network. His 1963 report into the state of the industry – forever known as the notorious 'Beeching Axe' – led to the mass closure of stations and rail services up and down the country. Within a year, trains had stopped crossing the Crumlin Viaduct. The entire structure suddenly became redundant.

A vigorous campaign was launched to save it, but British Railways had the bridge in its cross hairs. It argued that the ongoing cost of maintaining the viaduct, which it calculated to be dangerously unsafe, made its future unviable. Demolition teams descended on the Crumlin Viaduct in 1965. Just two years later it was completely gone. And then it hit home: quiescence, an empty skyline, as if a bridge had never stood there at all.

Opposite: Sophia Loren and Gregory Peck film Arabesque in Crumlin.

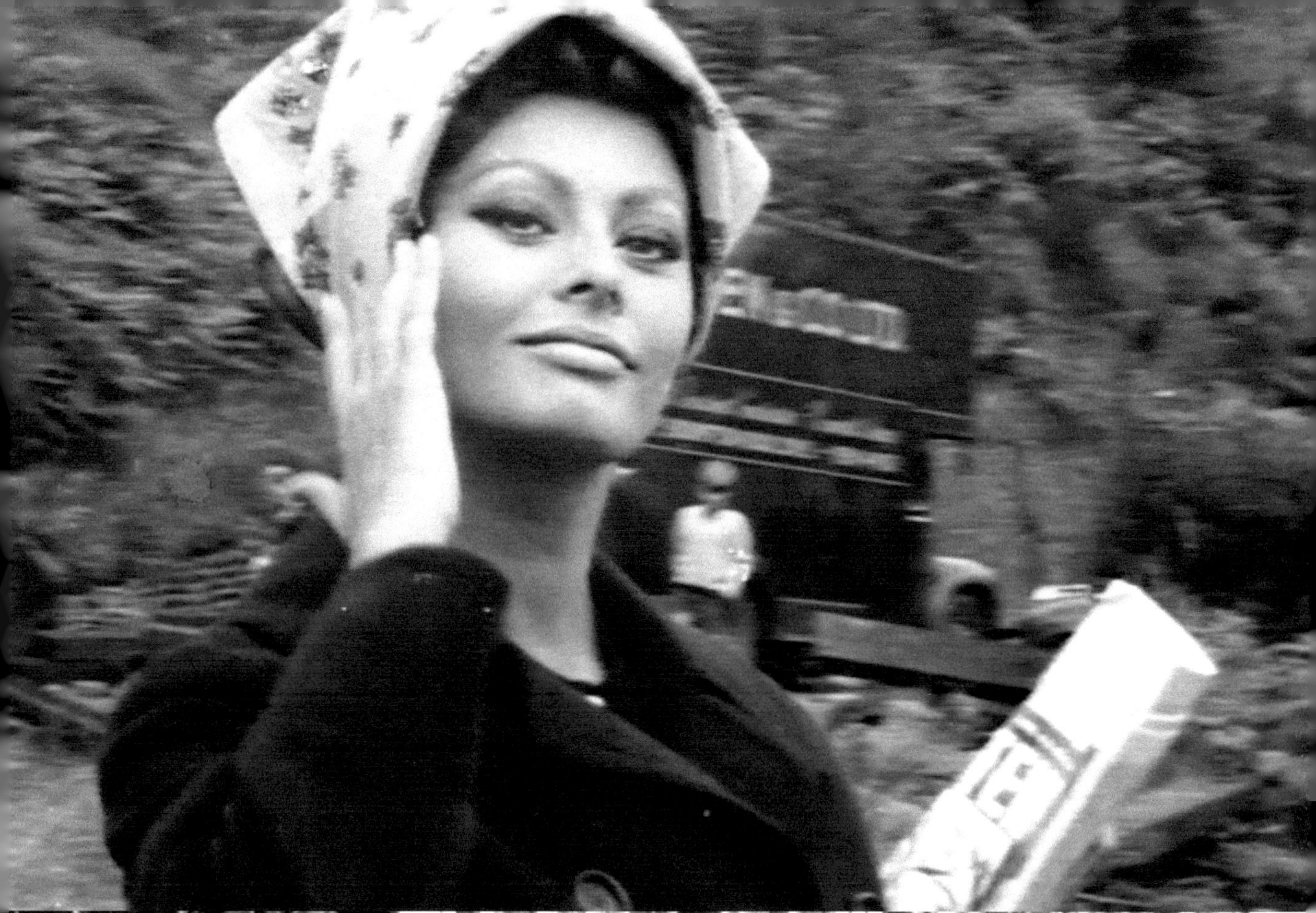

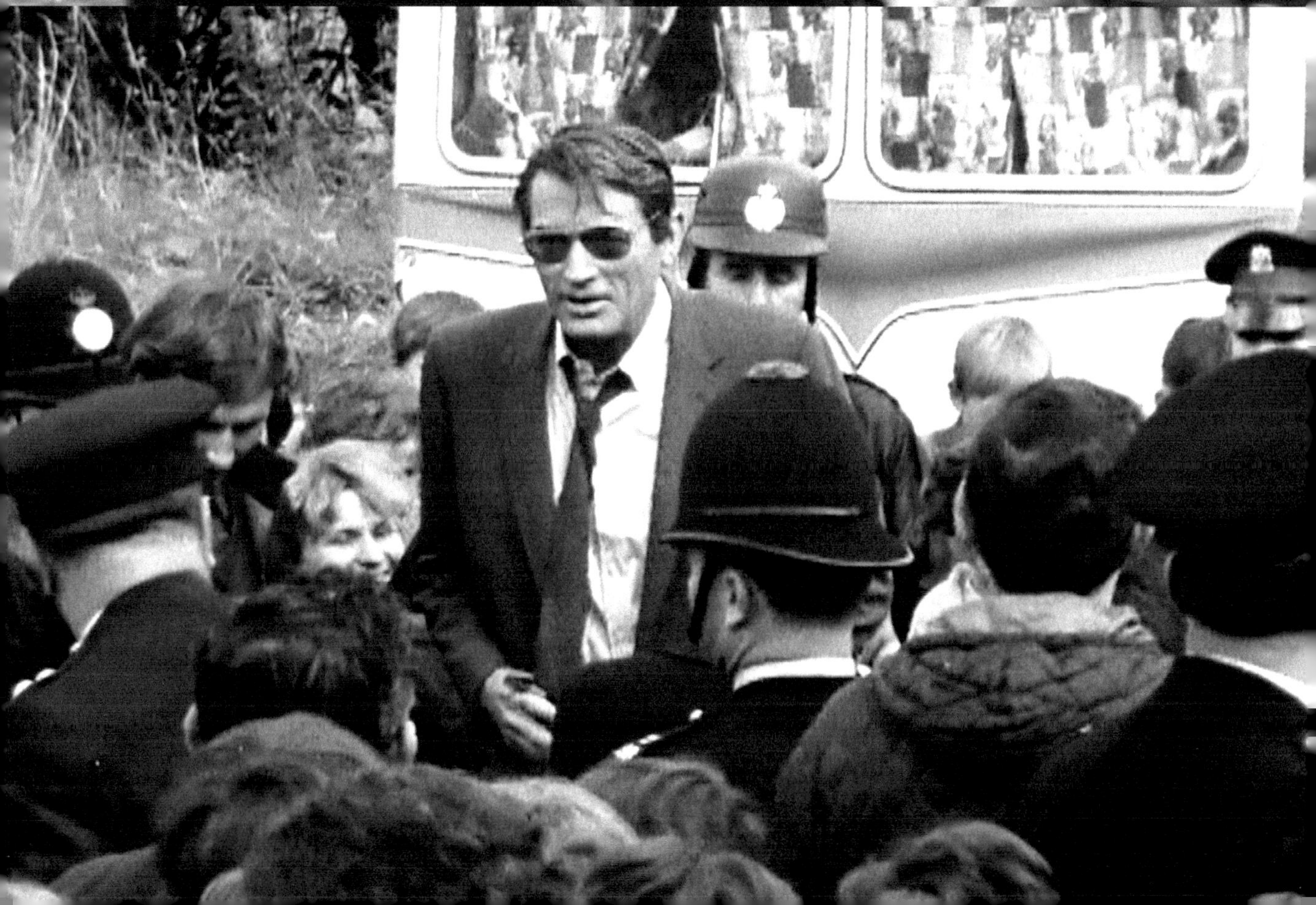

60 years on, parts of Britain's old Victorian rail network – bridges, tracks and tunnels – are enjoying a new lease of life as cycle paths, walking routes and heritage attractions, often reinvigorating the former industrial areas that the railway once served. But it all came too late for the Crumlin Viaduct. Just imagine if that iron giant was still standing today.

Below: the Crumlin Viaduct crashes to the ground.

Opposite: the masonry abutments, taciturn and overgrown, are all that remain today.

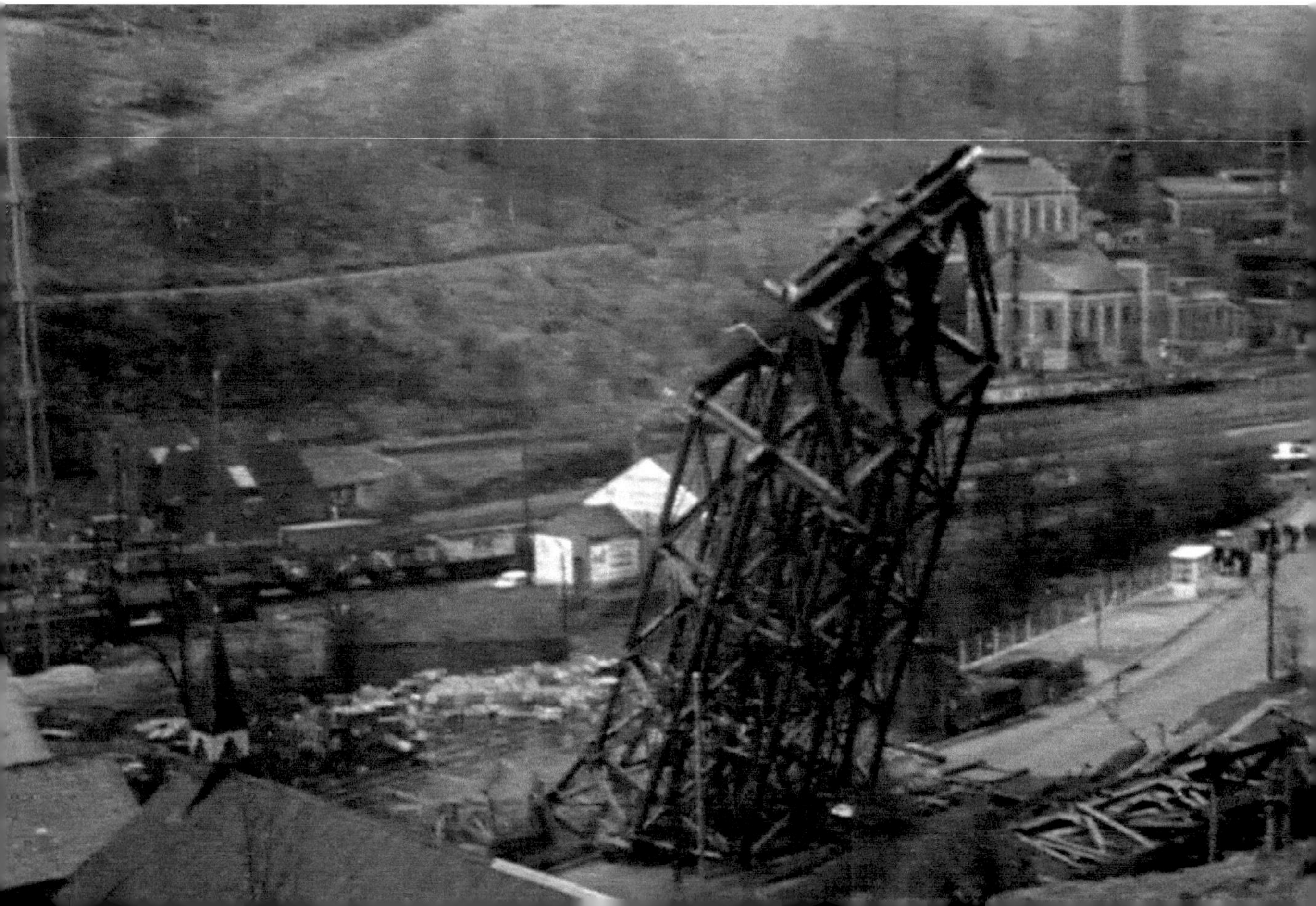

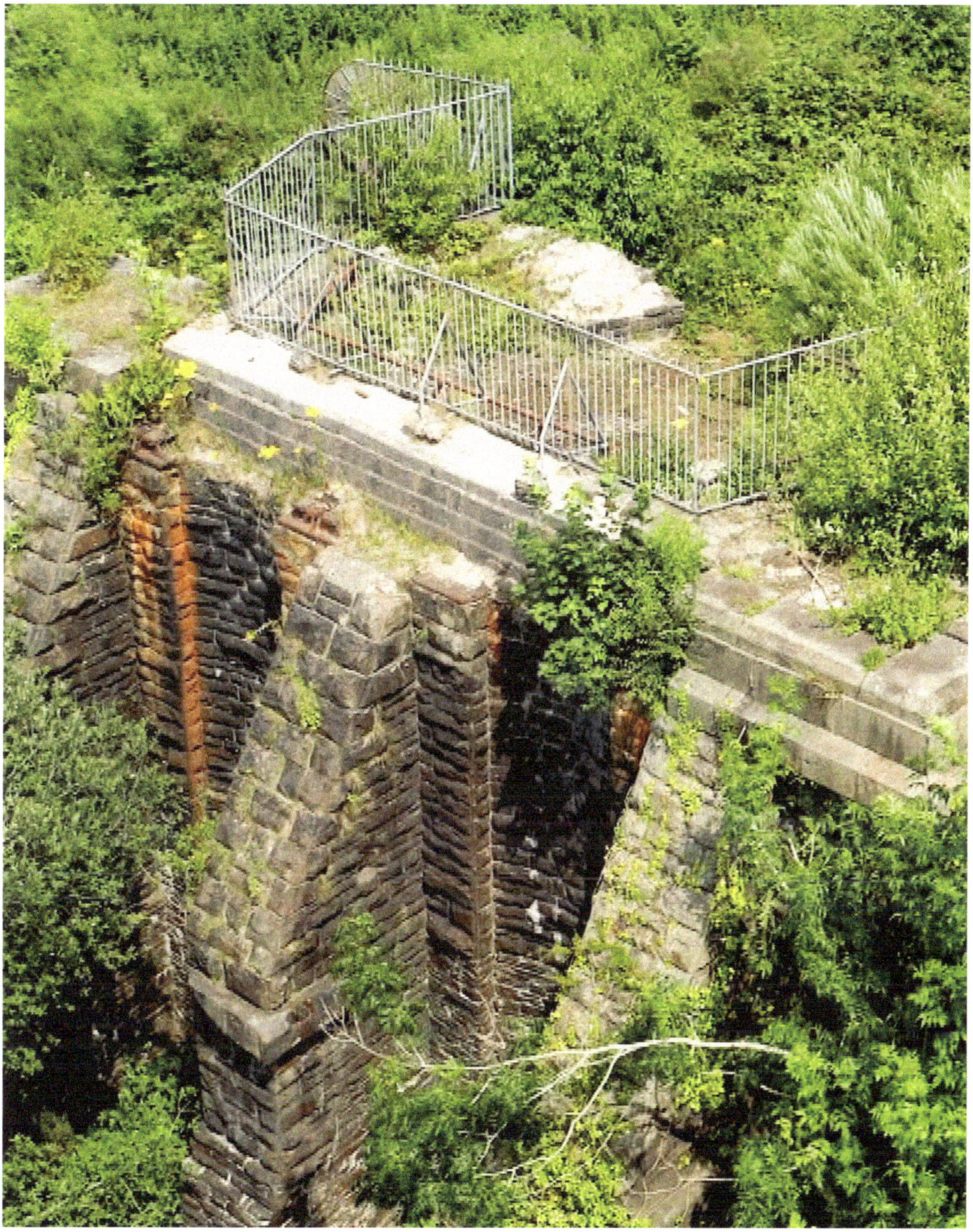

AFTERWORD

by Adeola Dewis

It is in moments like this that I wish I had kept a journal of my filming time on *Vanished Wales*. The long filming days, oftentimes involving different locations, were exciting, exhausting and enriching. In visiting new places and meeting different people, I gained so much insight into Welsh history – through encounters with those who remember their experiences of this past. I recall fondly end-of-shoot journeys, nestled comfortably behind the passenger seat of James, our camera operator, in his high-tech van, the humorous conversation between my co-workers – or listening to the beckoning of Carwyn, our Producer, attempting to persuade me to join in general knowledge quizzes, that helped pass the hours during long drives home.

In those still moments, thoughts of the people who had shared their stories of a time and place no longer visible, come flooding in. These stories, told through laughter and tears, paint vivid pictures invoking the sights, smells, and sounds from their memories of home, of jobs and life. On busy filming days it is far too easy to miss the magnitude of the moment, to miss the honour of being a witness to these precious stories. Like a child sitting wide-eyed and open-mouthed at the feet of an elder, I still find myself mesmerised, curious, enchanted and pained too, by the coming to life of these ghosts of the past.

In moments like this, I value the snapshots, that documented the traces, the landscapes left speckled with glimpses of industry on mountain-sides, of work and wealth. As I shuffle from one location to the next, I imagine the noise, the pink clouds of smoke, the buzz and laughter. Walking on coastlines, or in green fields I acknowledge that, to eyes that have seen the transformation of modernisation, these sites now look like a different place in time altogether. There was and still is, a kind of bewilderment. I use this word to express the sensation of gaps, the space created when only an archive can fully help join the dots between the view in front of you and the words being shared. I feel grateful that the team had captured the car parks, roads and housing estates that now stand aloof on foundations of family homes, schools, pubs and libraries. On those filming days, it is far too easy to miss that the only constant is indeed change – that what we now see, for better or for worse, may not be here tomorrow.

I remember the stories of employees, each unique yet similar – the gentleman who started work, barely fifteen years old, at a loud, imposing local factory – having to grow up too quickly, following in the footsteps of his father, grand-and great-grandfathers who had worked there before. The story of initiation and eventual kinship, of roots and identity. The story of loss when the world that forged him came crumbling down.

I remember the stories of youth, banter, lifelong friendships, gruelling work, excursions, dances and falling in love. Memories retold of tightknit communities that blossomed in the bosom of industry – neighbours whose families knew each other for generations, open front doors, outside toilets, playing in the streets or by countryside rivers. I recall the memories shared of times that were transformed by ideals such as progress and redevelopment.

There are too, those stories that tell of land-marks – cinemas, pavilions, piers and stadiums – that tell of the ways in which structures like these highlighted Wales on the world map and continued to build community spirit and identity. Sometimes these stories reveal that Wales was the first to produce something of a particular type or at a particular scale. At other times, we see nostalgia re-kindled with a proudly made-in-Wales fashion, automobile, sweets or toy brand. Then, there are those stories that reveal the people who have and continue to put concerted efforts into preserving the past – as volunteers, historians and artists. These narratives help us see the roles we can choose to play, in an ever-shifting world.

In moments like this, I feel grateful to have been a part of facilitating the sharing of these stories. The living memories of this history highlight glimpses of how much we have lost. Yet, these glimpses of the past also persuade us to continue documenting, to continue writing, recording, photographing what is in front of us – our environment, the places and people we may take for granted.

The documentation of today becomes the archive of tomorrow. On filming days, I am reminded of just how much the present is enriched by these personal perspectives of the past.

Adeola Dewis filming *Vanished Wales*.

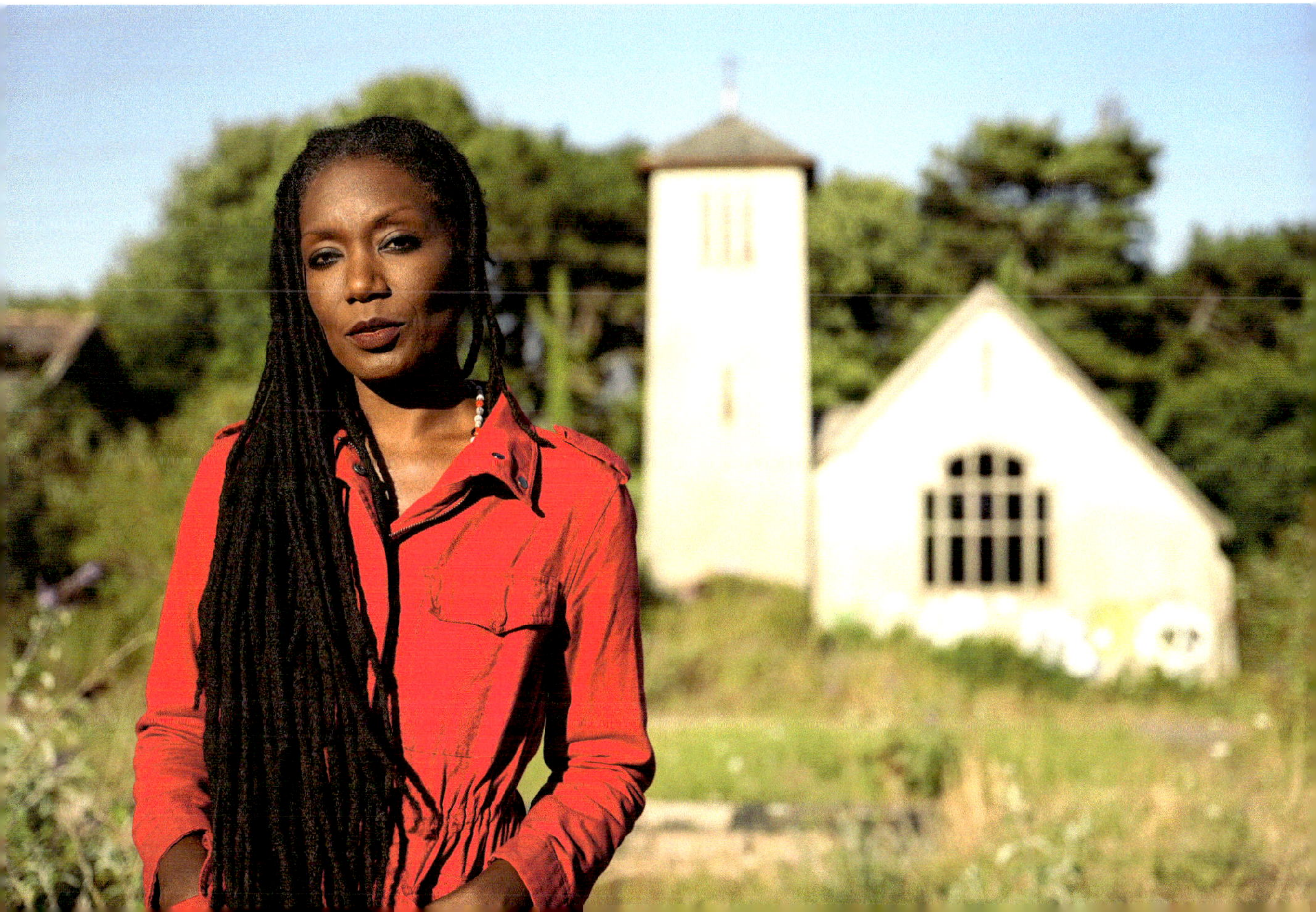

ACKNOWLEDGEMENTS

As both a book and television series, *Vanished Wales* would have not been possible without the selfless contributions of so many members of the public, more than 150 in total, who have shared their memories and personal experiences of their beloved local landmarks. There are too many names to individually list here, but my heartfelt thanks goes to each and every one of them.

Special thanks to my three steadfast companions with whom I have walked in step since the very early days of *Vanished Wales*: Adeola Dewis, James Harries and Owain Meredith.

To my Executive Producers at ITV Cymru Wales, who have championed and protected *Vanished Wales* from concept to completion, and whose sage advice has been a constant blessing: Alun Jones, Branwen Thomas, Zoe Thomas.

There's also a host of talent whom I've been privileged to work alongside on various aspects of *Vanished Wales*. Their skills are formidable: Gareth Axenderrie, Rosie Bell, Caitlin Bryant, Matt Creed, Jess Daly, Aimee Evans, Sofia Lewis, Huw Parry, Annabel Smith, Eugenia Taylor, Steve Thomas and our much missed friend Rob Milburn.

To all the team at Seren Books, thank you for your belief in this project and for your unyielding support. Tracey Rhys, you have the patience of a saint.

Finally, to my wonderful children, Milo, May and Annabelle, and to my dear parents, Christine and Donald, the greatest thanks of all. Your love and encouragement has meant more to me than you'll ever know.

PHOTOGRAPHIC ACKNOWLEDGEMENTS

All images in this book are the copyright of ITV and ITV Archive National Library of Wales, with the exception of the following photographs that have been generously supplied by individuals and organisations with their kind permission:

BRYMBO HERITAGE TRUST (p. 99)

PAUL BUDD (p. 21)

CARDIFF MUSIC HISTORY (p. 95)

COLWYN BAY PIER TRUST (pp. 160, 162, 163, 164)

PAUL DAVIES (p. 65)

GELLIGAER HISTORICAL SOCIETY (pp. 58, 59)

BAT GODDARD (p. 94)

DAVID HOPKINS (pp. 152, 153, 158)

HEFIN & JOY JONES (pp. 79, 81)

IAN MALCOLM (pp. 14, 15, 92, 93)

OLD MERTHYR TYDFIL/ DAVID THOMAS (pp. 125, 126, 127, 128)

ALAN PARFIT (pp. 62, 63)

PEMBROKE DOCK HERITAGE TRUST (pp. 82, 83, 84, 85, 86, 88, 89)

RHYL TOWN COUNCIL (pp. 22, 25)

IAN SANT (pp. 141, 142, 143)

SEVERN PRINCESS PRESERVATION TRUST (p. 49)

JASON SMITH (p. 107)

SWANSEA MUSEUM (pp. 66, 67, 69 – top)

TROEDRHIWFUWCH MEMORIES / CARYS ANN-NEADS (pp. 60, 64)

NEVIL WILLIAMS (pp. 154, 155)

ABOUT THE AUTHOR

Carwyn Jones is a Series Producer, Director and Journalist at ITV Cymru Wales with 25 years of broadcast experience across television, radio and online at ITV and BBC. His *Wonders of the Border* and *Dock of the Bay* television series were both Bafta nominated, and *Vanished Wales* was RTS nominated. Now based in Cardiff, he studied at University of South Wales and gained a Masters at Aberystwyth University.

Adeola Dewis and Carwyn Jones filming on location for *Vanished Wales*.

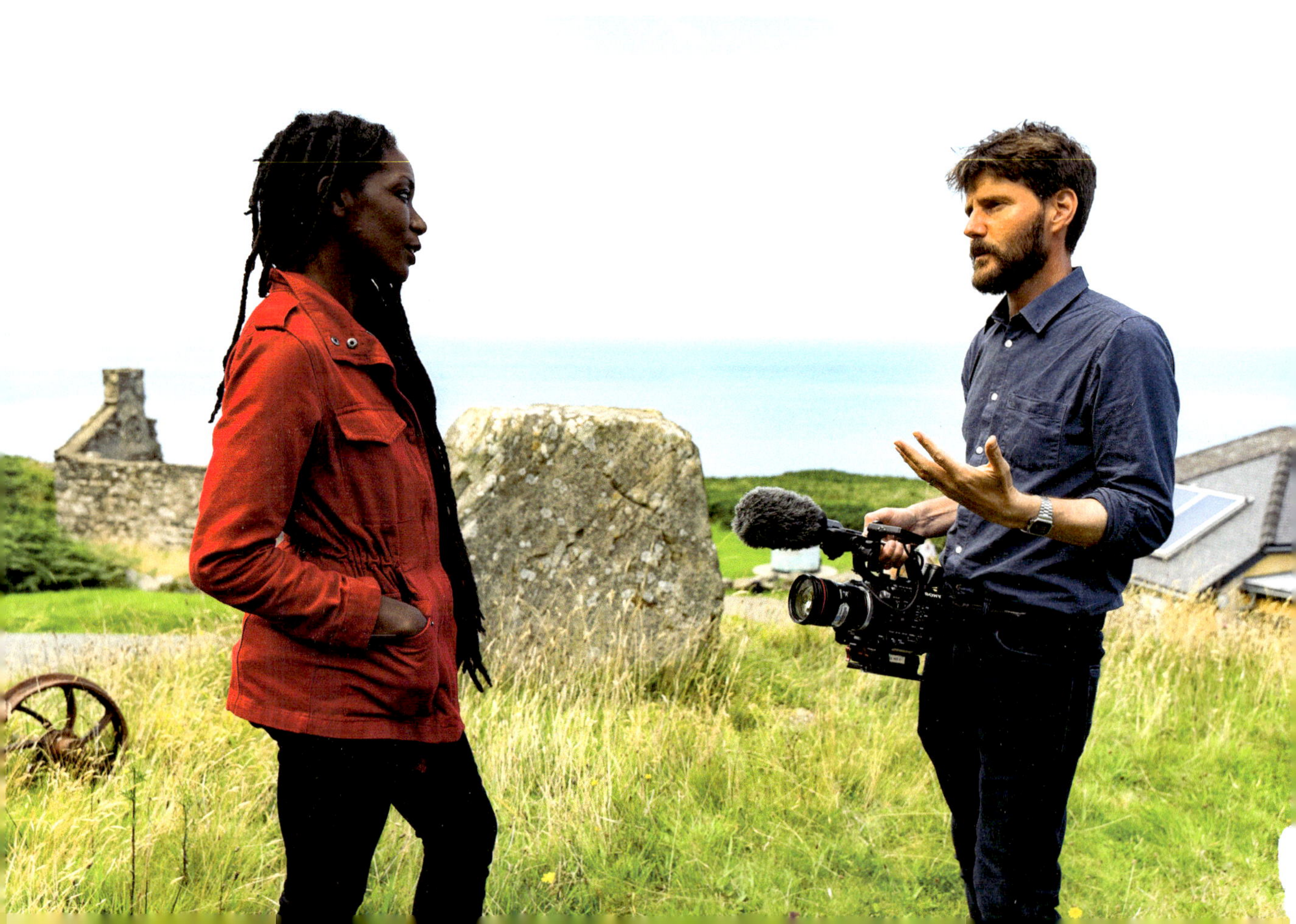